PHILOSOPHY

of

RELIGION

*I*NTRODUCTORY *E*SSAYS

THOMAS JAY OORD, EDITOR

Beacon Hill Press of Kansas City
Kansas City, Missouri

Copyright 2003
by Beacon Hill Press of Kansas City

ISBN 083-411-9951

Printed in the
United States of America

Cover Design: Ted Ferguson

Library of Congress Cataloging-in-Publication Data

Philosophy of religion : introductory essays / Thomas Jay Oord, editor.   p. cm.
    ISBN 0-8341-1995-1 (pbk.)
  1. Religion—Philosophy. I. Oord, Thomas Jay.

  BL51.P535 2003
  210.1—dc21

2003011048

10 9 8 7 6 5 4 3 2 1

To Edwin Crawford and Albert Truesdale

Contents

INTRODUCTION AND ACKNOWLEDGMENTS

"'Come now, let us reason together,' says the LORD," according to Isa. 1:18. Or as the *New Revised Standard Version* translates the same passage, "Come now, let us argue it out." The writer goes on to record the Lord's appeal to rationality and wisdom when presenting Judah with the terms of a covenant. Various Proverbs also praise those who cultivate rationality and wisdom. For example, "[it is] better to get wisdom than gold" (16:16), and the writer bluntly commands, "Get wisdom" (4:5). Numerous biblical authors appeal to reason, and the pages of monotheistic history are filled with examples of those who rely upon reason to a lesser or greater degree.

Christians, Jews, and Muslims are not the only religious peoples, however, who have placed importance upon reason or rationality. Theists in non-Western and less well-known faith traditions have stressed the value of loving God with the mind when considering ultimate reality. Nontheists in religious traditions such as Buddhism also reserve a significant role for reason.

In many ways, the rationalities of philosophy and the traditions of religion are inseparably intertwined. Individuals throughout history, however, have related philosophy to religion—or reason to faith—in a variety of ways. Some have used philosophy as a descriptive tool to analyze the grammar or practices of a particular religious tradition. Others have used it as a comparative tool to note similarities and differences between religious traditions. Sometimes individuals have turned to philosophy as a means to cultivate wisdom for the personal or communal living of fruitful and judicious lives. Philosophy has been used to construct defenses, arguments, or apologies for or against various religious doctrines and theories. This constructive use sometimes involves employing philosophical reasoning as a supplement for what is already affirmed by faith. Sometimes the constructive use of philosophy involves employing philosophy as a basis from which to construct particular religious precepts. Other times, individuals rely upon philosophy to assemble an entire worldview that, among other things, seeks to account adequately for religious experiences. In this book Henry W. Spaulding II addresses many of these issues in his chapter on faith and reason.

This text extends the rich heritage of philosophy and religion interchange. A glance at the contents, however, reveals that this book is unlike others. While most philosophy of religion books are comprised of short, primary readings from selected authors or brief overviews of particular questions, this book offers a lengthy introductory essay for a variety of key issues. This approach provides a stylistically uniform presentation of the ideas while allowing the reader to consider central concepts without having to struggle through historical texts with widely divergent forms and styles. The reading of some primary sources is still important, of course, and for this reason each essay herein concludes with recommendations for further readings on the topic covered.

This text also offers complete essays on topics rarely if ever found in other philosophy of religion texts. For instance, there is no other philosophy of religion text available offering extended discussions of divine love, gender and race issues as they relate to philosophy of religion, divine holiness, religion and aesthetics, and the Trinity all in one book. These novel offerings fill a void while breaking new ground for introductory philosophy of religion texts.

This text also differs from other philosophy of religion books in that most essayists possess strong ties to the Wesleyan-Holiness Christian tradition. All essayists affirm central tenets of John Wesley's thought, including Wesley's great appreciation for the role and power of reason. Perceptive readers will notice the greater and lesser degrees to which the Wesleyan-Holiness tradition affects how authors address particular issues of philosophy of religion.

It takes a community and a history to put together this kind of project. As editor, I acknowledge and express my gratitude to the scholars who carefully and creatively penned the chapters herein. While working on their various chapters, many were keenly aware of philosophers and theologians who have blazed trails, in one way or another, as members of their particular heritage. This book is dedicated to two such trailblazers, Albert Truesdale and Edwin Crawford, for their faithful contributions to the heritage of which many book contributors are members. Among other trailblazers in that heritage who deserve recognition for their instruction in philosophy are Otho Adkins, Earle E. Barrett, Hal Bonner, Tom Boyd, Russel V. DeLong, J. Lauriston DuBois, H. Ray Dunning, Russell Gardner, Delbert Gish, John David Hall, M. Estes Haney, Wes Harmon, Albert Harper, Donald Hoyt, J. Prescott Johnson, J. Williams Jones, Alvin Kauffman, Joseph Mayfield, Darrell Moore, Jack W. Moore, Wilbur Mullen, Ralph Neil, Theda C. Peake, L. C. Philo, Ross Price, Herb Prince, Gerard Reed, Oscar Reed, M. Francis Reeves, Mel-Thomas Rothwell, Henry Smits, S. S. White, Paul Whittemore, and H. Orton Wiley.

The students of Eastern Nazarene College's 2001 philosophy of religion class are also to be thanked for their suggestions pertaining to a rough draft of this book, especially students Christy Gunter, Heather Parke, Elizabeth Strong, and Noel Wilson. Finally, I thank those who have become active in the Wesleyan Philosophical Society, a society that seeks to encourage the use and study of philosophy in Wesleyan faith communities.

—Thomas Jay Oord

SECTION I

ARGUING THE EXISTENCE OF GOD

INTRODUCTION TO SECTION I

Brint Montgomery

━━━━━━━━━━━━━━━━━━━━ ◆ ━━━━━━━━━━━━━━━━━━━━

As a simple empirical generalization, people believe in God by means of faith. But this faith can operate in several different ways. Someone who operated by *brute faith* would do so by a pure act of will with no accompanying evidence. But humans do not typically believe things purely at random or with absolutely no background evidence. Granted, one might flip a coin and decide to believe one of two opposing hypotheses based on how the coin lands (i.e., to live as if the case were settled), but the more important the hypotheses, the less attractive such a brute exercise in willing a position becomes. Therefore, in matters of supreme importance, particularly in religion, people advance their conclusions about God based on some degree of rational reflection.

In this section various approaches to the existence of God are explored. Each approach presents a different type of evidence for rational reflection and thus a different means by which one might come to believe (or not) in God.

First, a person might believe in God because of *religious experience.* Terry Fach addresses two sides to this issue: direct religious experience and the experience of good and evil as it relates to our sense of "ought." In the end he finds that the evidential weight of religious experiences and feelings of moral obligation add force to a cumulative case for God's existence.

Second, a person might believe in God based upon the *causal structure* of the universe. Brint Montgomery takes a historical approach and identifies different versions of the cosmological argument that have been put forth with increasing detail by pivotal thinkers in history. He suspects the final success (or failure) of cosmological arguments hinges on which mathematical models are appropriate for an ultimate description of the physical universe. But he worries that such a description might be impossible finally to achieve.

Third, a person might believe in God based upon the *order* noted within the universe. Although various formulations of the teleological argument do not make probable every property that Christians might believe God would possess, Lincoln Stevens thinks such arguments do "go a long distance toward making it probable" that a divine agent exists as the cause of the design in the universe.

Fourth, a person might believe in God based upon what the very *concept* of "God" must mean to any reasoning being employing that term.

Rob Thompson begins his analysis with Anselm, the originator of the onto-logical argument. Thompson notes that while the ontological argument re-mains today the easiest to deny, it is the most difficult to refute.

Finally, because each of these classic approaches have survived and evolved through various attempts to show them flawed, as a group they constitute a corpus of justification for maintaining a belief in God. Put an-other way, even if no single approach to the existence of God is found to be rationally conclusive, the continuing presence of these approaches as a whole makes a *second-order cumulative case* for a belief in God as being reasonable.

Still, someone might worry that too much evidence points the other way: belief in God is ultimately unjustified. This worry leads to the *atheist or nontheist* position. Tony Baker's chapter investigates various atheisms and denials of God's existence, most of which stem from Fredrick Nietz-sche and his 19th-century contemporaries. Baker suggests that the deci-sive moment in the emergence of arguments against God's existence is the point at which faith-narratives give way to the laboratory-like environment of secular science. When God's status is no different than a supporting mathematical hypothesis, it is then no great leap of faith to offer in place of God a series of algebraic substitutions.

EXPERIENTIAL ARGUMENTS

Terry Fach

◆

This chapter focuses on the role played by human experience in three arguments for the existence of God. The first and most obvious argument is one that appeals directly to so-called *religious experience*. Arguments from religious experience have been the subject of much discussion in recent work in the philosophy of religion, and this argument will be the primary focus in what follows. Second, *the moral argument* proposes that our experience of good and evil, and the sense of "ought" that resonates in the human conscience, supports the truth of God's existence. The third argument is the *cumulative case,* which states that, when all the available evidence is carefully weighed, one can affirm that God's existence is a good explanation for why things are the way we experience them. The evidential weight of religious experiences and feelings of moral obligation add force to a cumulative case for God's existence.

Our aim in what follows is twofold. First, we will uncover the basic structure of these arguments and clarify some of the key concepts they employ. Second, we will evaluate the degree to which the arguments support the rationality of belief in God.

I. THE ARGUMENT FROM RELIGIOUS EXPERIENCE

Surveys of religious experience show that even though many of these experiences are extraordinary, they are also quite widespread. A number of well-documented accounts attest to the impressive variety and influence of such experiences across many traditions (James 1902; Otto 1923; Zaehner 1957; Stace 1960). Moreover, these experiences play a fundamental role in the life of believers by giving them direction and ultimate meaning. This is especially true in Christianity because of its powerful vision of what the Christian life means.

There is a distinction between *knowing a fact* and *knowing a person,* which closely resembles the distinction between knowing or believing certain things *about* God and *knowing God.* Rather, the Christian life is about entering into a relationship with that to which the Christian tradition points, which may be spoken of as God, the risen living Christ, or the Spirit (1994, 17).

Looking at religious experience from a *philosophical* perspective requires us to ask about the *evidential* value of such experience. Evidential value means the role of experience in producing or supporting rational religious beliefs. Many feel that arguments from religious experience present more promising options for justifying belief in God than other arguments. But can appeal to religious experience satisfy the demand for empirical, noncircular evidence for the truth of God's existence?

In order to answer this question, we need to be clear about several issues. We need to clarify, for instance, what kind of experience counts as "religious experience." Is religious experience analogous in any way to normal perceptual experience? In what ways could religious experience be said to make belief in God rational? Can one person's religious experience be evidence for another person's belief in God?

What is "religious experience"?

In order to examine more carefully what we mean by religious experience, consider the following first-person report:

I attended service at a church in Uppsala. . . . During both the Confession of Sin and the Prayer of Thanksgiving that followed Communion, I had a strong consciousness of the Holy Spirit as a person, and an equally strong consciousness of the existence of God, that God was present, that the Holy Spirit was in all those who took part in the service. . . . The only thing of importance was God, and my realization that He looked upon me and let His mercy flood over me, forgiving me for my mistakes and giving me the strength to live a better life (Unger 1976, 114).

This example suggests some basic features of religious experience reports—they are reports of a person's *experiential awareness* of God. This awareness is *direct,* and the awareness is reported to be *of God.*

To narrow our focus, we can begin with the following definition: *a religious experience is one that seems to the subject to be an experience (awareness) of God (either of his God being there, or doing or bringing about something) or some other divine aspect or thing* (cf. Swinburne 1979, 246). There are a number of noteworthy features of this definition and a few terms that need clarification. First, religious experiences must have a certain *structure.* That is, religious experiences must seem to involve an encounter with some external reality that is not to be identified with the subjects themselves. We could say that such experiences have a subject>awareness>object structure to them.

Another feature of religious experience is *the way it seems to the subject.* There are a number of ways that "seems" can be understood. When looking up the railway line, I report that "the tracks seem to converge." This suggests that, in the case in which I am aware of the effect of distance and depth of field on my visual array, what I really mean is "the tracks merely *appear* to converge but actually do not." This is a *comparative* sense of "seems," in which my use of it suggests that these tracks look the way converging lines or objects normally look. A different meaning of "seems" occurs when I report that "my golf ball seems to be sitting on the edge of the rough, though in this light it may or may not be my ball." This is the *epistemic* sense of "seems." We use this when reporting something we are inclined to *believe* (however weakly) as being the way things really are, regardless of how *in fact* they are.

We can use "seems" in an internal sense to describe a religious experience without committing ourselves to the existence of an external object. An experience that seems to its subject to be an experience of God, when described in this internal way, does not presuppose the question of its truth. As such, it gives believers and sceptics alike an uncontroversial starting point from which to examine the argument that a religious experience lends rational support to a particular belief. Consider this example: "It seems to me that God is directing me to change my career plans." It may be true that few who have similar experiences would describe such experiences in this way. Yet such internal descriptions are helpful when the experiential claim is more controversial, as in this example: "It seemed to me that Jesus' face appeared on the side of the oil tanker." Describing religious experience in this internal way does not entail anything about an external object or state of affairs. It only entails one's own experience about the way things appear to be.

Finally, religious experiences tend to be personal, private affairs. Indeed, some take subjectivity to be the defining feature of religious experience. This subjective feature also goes some way to explaining, for instance, why Brian, when attending chapel, can report, "I sense the presence of the Spirit all around." And yet Susan, Brian's equally attentive pewmate, reports no such awareness of Spirit's presence at the exact time Brian senses this presence. Other religious experiences are not private in just *this* way. For instance, a person might witness a delicate flower in bloom on a still May evening and be "filled with a sense of God's creative power," while another person might witness the same sight and merely be "filled with a sense of nature's beauty and mystery."

One way to sort out the apparent diversity of experience is to divide religious experiences into *those that involve the interpretation of public phenomena religiously and those that do not* (Swinburne, 1979, 249-253). In the list below, the first two types of religious experience involve taking public phenomena religiously, while the last three are instances in which the divine is experienced via something private to the subject.

1. Experiences of ordinary, nonreligious objects that seem to be experiences of supernatural, religious objects.

2. Experiences of unusual events or objects, e.g., miracles.
3. Private experiences describable by normal sensory vocabulary.
4. Private experiences *not* describable by normal sensory vocabulary.
5. Awareness or feelings unaccompanied by any sensory experience.

Types 1 and 2 involve experiences of phenomena that are public in the sense that other persons (who are in sensory perceptual conditions similar to those of the subject) would report seeing the same objects or events. But this sort of religious experience is not without some perplexing features. Consider, for example, cases in which both Brian and Susan witness the same publicly observable object or event and yet Susan interprets what she sees to be something quite different than what Brian reports seeing. Both may be having the same visual sensory experience and yet have different perceptual experiences. "What is seen by one man as simply a wet day," notes Richard Swinburne, "is seen by another as God's reminding us of his bounty in constantly providing us with food by means of his watering plants" (1979, 253).

Despite the absence of public phenomena in religious experiences of type 3, the subject has certain private experiences that are describable by the vocabulary normally used for describing normal sensory experience. This kind of religious experience is typically mediated through visions, voices, or dreams. A good example is Peter's trance-like experience, as described in the Acts of the Apostles (10:9-16), in which Peter saw a vision and heard the Lord's voice.

Type 4 religious experience is most often associated with mysticism. So-called mystical experiences vary widely, and they have been divided into two broad groups according to whether there is an *extrovertive* or an *introvertive* element to them. Extrovertive mystical experiences typically involve a transformation of the senses that causes the subject to see "the inner essence of things, an essence that appears to be alive, beautiful, and the same in all things." These mystical experiences provide a sense that "one sees things as they really are" and a feeling that "what is experienced is divine" (Rowe 1978, 66-68). Their distinguishing characteristic, however, is that the subjects who report them cannot describe them using normal sensory vocabulary.

Type 5 religious experiences are characterized by an awareness or feeling unaccompanied by auditory, visual, or any other standard sorts of sensory experience. Such a description could apply to experiences involving a subject's awareness of being intimately close or in the presence of God. Or such a description could apply to God's doing or bringing something about, for instance, a sense of God "lifting the burden of sin" or urging one to pursue a particular vocation. Take, as an example, John Wesley's description of his conversion:

> In the evening I went very unwillingly to a society in Aldersgate Street, where one was reading Luther's preface to the Epistle to the Romans. About a quarter before nine, while he was describing the change which God works in the heart through faith in Christ, I felt my heart strangely warmed. I felt I did trust in Christ, Christ alone for salvation; and an assurance was given me that He had taken away my sins, even mine, and saved me from the law of sin and death.

In what follows, our focus will be on religious experiences that are taken by their subjects to be of an independently existing reality that transcends the subject's awareness. While these five types can help us classify reported experiences, we turn next to another question: Could these religious experiences provide some kind of evidence for religious beliefs? If so, is it enough to make belief in God (or some other supernatural reality) rational?

Experientialism

Scrutinizing the epistemic value of religious experience is a fairly recent project. In the case of Christianity, few people disputed the truth of theism (belief in God) until the 17th century. The arguments of philosophers like David Hume and Immanuel Kant in the 18th century were widely thought to have undermined the very possibility of constructing a rational demonstration of religious belief. By the mid-20th century, it seemed improbable that Christian theism could be shown to be more reasonable than not. And, although many regarded religious experience as having important psychosocial functions, religious experience was mainly viewed as a purely subjective phenomenon. Experiential beliefs of the religious kind were taken to be something akin to an expression of feelings rather than meaningful claims about reality that were either true or false. However, over the past few decades many Christian philosophers have boldly argued that people sometimes do have direct experience of God and thereby acquire justified beliefs about God. More precisely, the experience of God plays a role with respect to beliefs about God that is analogous to the role played by sense experience with respect to beliefs about the physical world. We could label this view "Christian experientialism" and include Richard Swinburne, William Alston, and Alvin Plantinga among its proponents.

Let us first consider some general features of experientialism and then look briefly at a prominent version. First, experientialism claims that there is a generic identity of *structure* between sense perception and religious experience. In the case of direct awareness of God, this perception is direct in the same way as the sense perception of physical objects is direct. By "direct" we mean that an object is perceived immediately, not being mediated through one's perception of some other object. So what establishes religious experience (see 1, 2, and 3 above) as a mode of perception is the feature that something (God) has been *presented* or *given* to the subject's consciousness in the same way as objects in the environment are *presented* to one's consciousness in sense perception.

Second, religious beliefs acquired through religious experience enjoy a high degree of initial credibility or justification. Even though no experience guarantees the existence of its apparent object, beliefs that are formed from such experiences must presumably be justified. My perceptual belief is presumably justified unless there are sufficient reasons to think my belief is false. For example, the flower looks yellow to me; but if I have overwhelmingly strong evidence that these flowers just appear to be yellow when these lights are shining on them, the strong evidence overrides that initial justification. Such a principle seems to apply to all kinds of perceptual beliefs. Or, as Swinburne puts it, "it is a principle of rationality that (in the absence of special considerations) if it seems (epistemically) to a subject that x is present, then probably x is present; what one seems to perceive is probably so" (1979, 254). This "principle of credulity" is the basis for the position that Christian perceptual beliefs are justified and, therefore, rationally acceptable in the absence of defeating reasons. In both the sensory and religious cases, perceptions should be treated as "innocent until proven guilty."

Alvin Plantinga's argument that beliefs about God triggered by religious experiences are "properly basic" qualifies as a version of experientialism (1983). Although not usually considered an argument from religious experience, a rough sketch of his argument will show that it is. Plantinga's general strategy is to show that beliefs formed on the basis of religious experience do not fall victim to evidentialist standards of rationality. According to evidentialist understandings of rationality, it is only rational to hold beliefs for which we have adequate evidence, good reasons, or good arguments. Evidentialism is rooted in the doctrine that to be rational, a belief must be based on other beliefs considered rational, self-evident (e.g., 1+1=2), incorrigible (e.g., "I am in pain"), or evident to the senses (e.g., "I see a tree"). Only these three types of belief qualify as properly basic beliefs. But because belief in God does not qualify as basic according to these criteria, evidentialists reject theism unless a good argument based on rational beliefs can be constructed. Those of the evidentialist persuasion insist that the prospects for such an argument look slim, and Plantinga would not dispute that.

Plantinga argues that classical criteria for properly basic beliefs are flawed (1983, 55-63). There is no need for panic if experiential beliefs about God do not satisfy them. He suggests that new-and-improved criteria for proper basicality would allow for beliefs about God generated by religious experiences. Interestingly, he does not himself offer these new-and-improved criteria. Instead, he suggests that criteria for proper basicality be developed inductively by looking at a broad range of beliefs that one considers uncontroversially basic or foundational. For theists, properly basic beliefs could include beliefs about God.

Before we consider the merits of this suggestion, we need to clarify a further feature of the experientialist position. After all, how should we understand the notion that experiential beliefs (properly basic) are *directly* justified? First, while experiential beliefs are not based on an inference from other beliefs, neither are they arbitrary. What confers positive epistemic status is a set of *conditions or circumstances that provide an adequate justifying ground* for the belief in question. Thus, in saying that belief in God is properly basic, it does not follow that it is *groundless*. In each case in which a perceptual belief is properly taken as basic, there are circumstances or conditions that serve as the *ground* of justification. Among those circumstances or conditions will be an *experience,* e.g., seeing what seems to be a tree. In addition, there are other relevant conditions that must hold, like the absence of distorting perceptual conditions, the normal operation of my sensory organs, the fact that there is a tree in front of me, and so on. Plantinga's point is simply that a belief is properly basic only when certain conditions hold.

Consider how this would work in the case of Christian experience. The conditions and circumstances that call forth beliefs about God include *experiences* of a certain sort, e.g., a sense of God's presence, a sense that God is speaking to one, or seeing certain kinds of natural (public) phenomena. This typically leads to beliefs like

1. God is speaking to me.
2. God has created all this.
3. God disapproves of what I have done.
4. God forgives me.
5. God is to be thanked and praised.

Just as beliefs like "I see a tree" are properly basic in the right circumstances, so, too, beliefs 1 through 5 could be properly basic *in the right circumstances.* Just as the epistemic propriety of my belief that *I see a tree* does not depend upon the availability of an argument or an inference *from* that experience *to* the belief that is formed, so, too, could a religious experience *directly justify* a belief about God.

The experientialist approach to the rationality of religious perceptual beliefs is open to criticism at a number of points. First, it might be objected that religious experience should not be considered a type of perception. But as already noted above, the structure of both sensory and religious experience share in common that something (an ordinary object or God) presents itself to us in a way that enables us to know it in some way. There are certainly important differences between sensory and religious experience. Sensory perception yields a huge volume of richly textured information about the world, while religious experiences tend to reveal God and God's ways in much less detail. It is not clear, however, that this feature necessarily disqualifies religious experience as a kind of perception.

One of the ways we check the accuracy of ordinary perceptual experiences is by appeal to other perceptual experiences. This way is not open, however, in the case of religious experiences. First, many of our perceptual beliefs enjoy the support of multiple sense modalities; for example, what we think we are seeing might be corroborated by smell and touch. This is unavailable for most kinds of religious experiences. Second, there seems to be more cultural and religious interpretation going on in the case of religious experience. This phenomenon also makes it difficult to confirm the consistency and accuracy of such experiences.

Another issue is the criticism that experientialism is too permissive. Theists may include perceptual beliefs about God in their properly basic belief set, but couldn't someone claim their belief that the Great Pumpkin will return on Halloween to be properly basic for them? Plantinga argues that one of the key justifying conditions for perceptual beliefs about God is simply that God exists and has designed us to experience the divine. "God has so created us that we have a tendency or disposition to see his hand in the world about us," contends Plantinga. "More precisely, there is in us a disposition to believe propositions of the sort *this flower was created by God or this vast and intricate universe was created by God* when we contemplate the flower or behold the starry heavens or the vast reaches of the universe" (1983, 80).

The simple explanation for why belief in the Great Pumpkin is irrational is that there is "no Great Pumpkin and no natural tendency to accept beliefs about the Great Pumpkin" (78). This may well explain why many have experienced God and formed basic theistic beliefs of one sort or another. But if we do have this natural tendency that Plantinga describes, then why are there so many who have not experienced God in the explicit ways that we have considered? And what should we make of religious experiences that elicit incompatible religious beliefs (Audi 1986, 165)? Experientialism may not seem too attractive from a Hebraic-Christian point of view if contradictory or alternative (even bizarre) religious perceptual beliefs can equally claim to be rational in this basic sense. This may show that traditional evidential approaches, such as natural theology, have an important role in providing warrant for perceptual belief-forming practices in some traditions and not in others. These are issues that deserve further investigation.

II. THE MORAL ARGUMENT

Some philosophers and theologians have argued that certain features of our *moral* experience provide evidence for the truth of theism. Our encounters with good and evil and the apparently universal sense that we "ought" to do some things point, it is alleged, toward an objective source of that experience. The so-called moral argument for theism has been most famously associated with Immanuel Kant (1724—1804) and C. S. Lewis (1898—1963). After presenting an argument along Lewis' lines and various possible objections, we will briefly consider an updated version of Kant's argument that the hypothesis of theism helps to make sense of our moral experiences.

Can we make good sense of our moral language and behaviour without presupposing some kind of objective moral order or "law?" Consider our experience of temptation to do or say what we know we should not. Bill would like to exaggerate the merits of Tom's work record in his reference letter in order to help him get an important job, but he realizes that such deception would be wrong. Janet would like to buy the new Madonna CD, but she acknowledges that it endorses the very lifestyle she finds destructive and irresponsible. Susan owns shares in a multinational drug company, but she starts to feel deeply disturbed about the company's unwillingness to forego profits in order to help end the AIDS epidemic in central Africa.

What these examples suggest is that the experience of "ought" is pervasive. This sense of obligation points to a standard of behavior that we can judge ourselves against. Notice that this standard or "law" is not simply a description of how things are or how people do sometimes behave. It is a prescription for how people ought to behave, even if they often do not. Although such claims are not strictly descriptive, we feel as if the standards these claims presuppose are real. We *do* believe the sexual exploitation of children to be depraved and inexcusable; we *do* view the atrocities associated with ethnic cleansing as heinous and cruel. In other words, there is, it seems, an objective moral order in the universe that exists independently of what I or anyone else may believe or practice. That a certain kind of action is wrong is a truth we discover, not one we invent.

Today the idea of an objective moral order is doubted by many. A typical objection is that moral beliefs are the product of one's culture. Moral "truth" is a socially constructed reality, contend some, and morality has no basis in objective fact. This view seems to explain why different cultures differ in what they regard as right and wrong. But such a position introduces some truly puzzling results. If cultural relativism is true, how does one explain the many points of similarity in moral beliefs? There is good reason to believe that these similarities far outweigh the dissimilarities. In addition, many alleged differences in moral beliefs are really just differences in *empirical* beliefs. The Inuit of Canada's Far North, for example, once practised euthanasia by abandoning dying elders on an ice floe. Their actions were based on the (empirical) belief that such a practice promoted the best long-term welfare of the community, which is presumably the goal of all communities. What appeared to be moral relativity is simply a different evaluation of the results of their practice.

If there is no objective moral standard, it seems impossible to criticize the moral behaviour and beliefs of others. Some past cultures have endorsed slavery and ritual human sacrifice, but few would condone these practices today. Yet if the complete relativity of moral standards is accepted, what each person thinks is right *is* right. But by this individualistic standard we would have to conclude that the beliefs of Hitler and Stalin are morally equivalent to Martin Luther King Jr.'s and Mother Teresa's.

Another problem with complete moral relativism is that it seems to rule out moral progress. The moment we are critical of some part of culture, we seem to be admitting that there is some kind of higher standard than culture itself. Interestingly, we tend to see this more clearly when scrutinizing cultures other than our own. It seems much easier, for example, to criticize the practice of genital mutilation of young girls in some African cultures. But many are morally blind to the destructive influence of advertising on teenage girls in North American society. If moral relativism is promoted in the name of *tolerance,* this implies some kind of objective moral valuation. It implies that tolerance has higher moral value than intolerance. A radical version of this view appears to suffer from incoherence, because, if relativism is correct, one should be tolerant of those who are intolerant.

One weakness in the moral argument as advanced so far is that it does not decisively locate the objective ground of morality in a transcendent mind or being. The possibility exists that the rightness and wrongness of actions could simply be basic to the cosmos, e.g., causing pain to the innocent is wrong simply as a matter of fact. Or perhaps one could build a system of ethics on a reasonable principle of fairness, or on a principle of rationality, or as a kind of social agreement or contract. However, if theism could be shown to be rational on other grounds, theism would provide a much richer metaphysical account as to why there is an objective moral law in the cosmos. Charles Taliaferro proposes exactly this:

Imagine the argument for broad theism based on religious experience and the cosmological argument has some force, as does the teleological argument, and, as a result, one has some reason to believe there is at least one good, purposive force, responsible for the nature and constitution of the cosmos. Theism would then be a rich theory for it could also account for the facts of morality as well. Its fruitfulness lies in its broad-ranging explanatory power. This form of argument, then, would not use morality or objective values as a solitary fact upon which to build a huge metaphysic. It would instead advance something like the following as a description of what theism can explain: The existence of a contingent, ordered cosmos in which life evolves and there is sentience and consciousness, intelligent activity, morality and objective values, and widespread reports of the experience of a divine reality (Taliaferro 1998, 371).

One might ask, however, whether a nontheistic, naturalistic framework gives a more plausible explanation for the objectivity of the moral order. One prominent nontheistic naturalistic explanation for the pervasive use of moral terms and categories is offered by evolutionary biology, or "sociobiology." After all, it may be possible to explain by evolutionary processes why humans *believe* (mistakenly) there is an objective moral law and also explain why they *feel* the way they do about morality. But such arguments, say their critics, fail to account for the sense that there is more to the moral order than *merely* feelings and beliefs. Beliefs about our moral obligations are different than the obligations themselves, and evolutionary accounts provide no explanation for the existence of the latter. Sociobiology, in nontheistic naturalism, seems to end up explaining morality *away*. It is saying, in effect, that our moral judgments are useful but, ultimately, biologically grounded illusions. This view breaks down in the confrontation with horrific evils like sadistic child abuse, ritual murders, and programs of ethnic cleansing. In practice, despite our theoretical inclinations, we are hard pressed to deny that values lie at the heart of reality.

Let us now return to the earlier suggestion that a theistic framework might explain the existence of an objective moral order better than nontheistic naturalism. Herein lies a version of the moral argument that looks most promising. Kant argues that unless reality is itself committed to morality in some deep way (such that a God exists who can, and will, make happiness balance out with virtue), the moral enterprise would make no sense. In the nontheistic, naturalistic world of social agreement, where ethical action is understood as exclusively acting in my own self-interest, the call to live ethically and the instinct for self-preservation can quickly fall apart. For instance, being ethical and looking out for one's own best interests may not always be compatible. Why would anyone act purely out of respect for what is ethical, especially in cases in which the right thing to do is to sacrifice one's own life? For Kant, we can make sense of moral duty only by supposing that an all-powerful divine being will ensure that virtue and reward will be harmoniously balanced—if not in this life, then in the next. George Mavrodes takes a similar approach in arguing that if a nontheistic, naturalist worldview is accepted, moral obligations will seem strange (1986). The nontheistic naturalist, who sees moral values as emerging from morally neutral evolutionary processes, might reply that if this seems strange, then so be it. This naturalist may simply deny the need to offer a comprehensive account of the cosmos. But if theism is coherent and is more probable than not, it may be the best explanation for the wide range of phenomena we experience, including the experience of a moral "ought."

III. CUMULATIVE CASE ARGUMENT

Even if religious experience and/or moral arguments do not by themselves provide strong support for the rationality of theism, perhaps they can provide some evidence as part of a cumulative case argument for God's existence. The basic idea behind such an argument is that a case for theism can be made by patiently accumulating various pieces of evidence that, when weighed together, tip the scales in favor of belief in God. At one time, this approach was considered suspect—a kind of last-ditch effort to salvage something from a series of inconclusive arguments. As Antony Flew opined, "If one leaky bucket will not hold water, that is no reason to think ten can" (1966, 62). However, recent work in philosophical theology shows cumulative case arguments to be worth serious consideration. It may in fact be possible to arrange the ten leaky buckets inside each other in such a way that the holes do not overlap!

Cumulative case arguments can and do differ with respect to their premises, their structure, and their conclusions (Abraham 1987). This is quite obvious, for instance, when one compares the cumulative case arguments of Richard Swinburne (1979) and Basil Mitchell (1973). While Swinburne focuses on the truth of a single proposition ("God exists"), Mitchell seeks to establish a case for the rationality of belief in traditional Christian theism, understood as what the ordinary educated person understands by Christianity. A more obvious difference concerns how the various subarguments are weighed in terms of their overall evidential value. Swinburne sees his cumulative case as an inductive argument, where the full argument's evidential weight is quantifiable by probability theory (Bayes' theorem) in order to substantiate his claim that "theism is more probable than not" (1979, 291). Mitchell's argument is also broadly inductive in character, but the weighing of evidence purposely involves a radical dependence on personal judgment. By emphasizing personal judgment, Mitchell is acknowledging that any attempt to balance the probabilities and considerations by an explicitly formal argument would be hopelessly inadequate for capturing the effect of these arguments on the mind.

Let's take a closer look at Swinburne's cumulative argument as laid out in his book *The Existence of God*. Swinburne's thesis is simply this: belief in God is an explanatory hypothesis that is more probable than not. It is impossible in the scope of this essay to do justice to the subtlety and rigor of his argument, but a brief summary of the argument's strategy can bring out its key features.

There is a range of phenomena in the world that is puzzling and mysterious. Humans typically develop good explanations or hypotheses to account for it. Presumably, some explanations are more probably true than others. But on what basis could we determine which are more probable? Swinburne proposes the criteria of (1) *prior probability* and (2) *explanatory power*. The former involves an evaluation of the hypothesis in terms of its simplicity, scope, and fit with background knowledge. The explanatory power of a hypothesis is its power to predict the phenomena that we do in fact observe. Although we may not normally think of the belief that God exists as an explanatory hypothesis, there is a strong case for its prior probability. According to Swinburne, the key feature of theism as explanatory hypothesis is its *simplicity*. "Theism postulates a God with capacities that are as great as they logically can be," he argues. "In postulating a person with infinite capacity, the theist is postulating a person with the simplest kind of capacity possible" (1979, 94)

Our experience of the world, however, is of a wide range of remarkable and sometimes puzzling phenomena that seems far from simple. The existence of such phenomena constitutes the premises of the cumulative case argument. In each case, puzzling phenomena are to be expected more if there is a God than if there is not. Swinburne summarizes the data as follows: "The existence of the universe, its conformity to order, the existence of animals and men, men having great opportunities for co-operation in acquiring knowledge and moulding the universe, the pattern of history and the existence of some evidence of miracles, and finally the occurrence of religious experiences, are all such as we have reason to expect if there is a God, and less reason to expect otherwise" (277).

It should be noted that religious experience plays a decisive role in the cumulative case argument Swinburne presents. While religious experience has evidential value in its own right, it can only show that the existence of God is more probable than not if the prior probability of God's existence is very low. The central argument of *The Existence of God* is that the prior probability of theism is not very low (though it is not very high either). Religious experience provides evidence that tips the balance in the cumulative case and makes belief in God more probable than not.

In evaluating the success of cumulative case arguments, one important issue concerns the way in which the evidence is gathered and weighed. In Mitchell's version, the appeal to "personal judgment" to weigh the accumulated evidence as a whole seems to fit the common experience of many Christian believers. But if this kind of judgment involves the capacity to weigh evidence without using some kind of objectively specified rule or standard, what would prevent any manner of nonrational factors (emotions, bias, wishful thinking) from influencing the outcome? Perhaps such informal personal judgment can be refined through training—perhaps the religious community could inculcate appropriate intellectual, moral, and spiritual values. But in weighing the evidence for a whole belief system, one would be appealing to personal judgment to support the very belief system that helped to create it—an obviously circular appeal (Abraham 1985, ch. 9).

Swinburne's version of the argument is much more careful about how evidence is recognized and weighed, but it seems to break down in other ways. First, his account of the reasonableness of belief in God seems out of touch with the kind of religious belief usually associated with Christian devotion. Simply put, most Christians do not think of their belief in God as "more probable than not!" Yet from a broadly religious perspective, such a formal account of theism's explanatory power seems necessary. Another problem concerns the alleged simplicity of the hypothesis of theism (i.e., in positing God as perfectly good, all-knowing and all-powerful). If God is the Creator of all phenomena, then why does God allow evil? In the eyes of many, the horrors of undeserved suffering in the world cry out for explanation, and theism appears vulnerable here.

CONCLUSION

The experiential arguments for the existence of God vary. This essay has addressed arguments derived from religious and moral experience. It also explored briefly a cumulative argument that adopts aspects of religious and moral arguments when suggesting that belief in God's existence is more plausible than belief that He does not exist.

Works Cited and Suggested Reading

Abraham, William. *An Introduction to the Philosophy of Religion.* Englewood Cliffs, N.J.: Prentice-Hall, 1985.

_____. "Cumulative Case Arguments for Christian Theism." In *The Rationality of Religious Belief.* Ed. William J. Abraham and Steven J. Holzer. Oxford: Clarendon, 1987. 17-37.

Alston, William P. "Christian Experience and Christian Belief." In *Faith and Rationality: Reason and Belief in God.* Ed. Alvin Plantinga and Nicholas Wolterstorff. Notre Dame, Ind.: University of Notre Dame Press, 1983. 103-34.

_____. *Perceiving God: The Epistemology of Religious Experience.* Ithaca, N.Y.: Cornell University Press, 1991.

Audi, Robert. "Direct Justification, Evidential Dependence, and Theistic Belief," in *Rationality, Religious Belief, and Moral Commitment: New Essays in the Philosophy of Religion.* Ed. Robert Audi and William J. Wainwright. Ithaca, N.Y.: Cornell University Press, 1986. 139-66.

Broad, C. D. *Religion, Philosophy, and Psychical Research.* London: Routledge & Kegan Paul, 1930.

Flew, Antony. *God and Philosophy.* London: Hutchinson, 1966.

Franks Davis, Caroline. *The Evidential Force of Religious Experience.* Oxford: Clarendon, 1989.

Haught, John F. *What Is God? How to Think About the Divine.* Mahwah, N.J.: Paulist, 1986.

James, William. *The Varieties of Religious Experience.* New York: Modern Library, 1902.

Kant, Immanuel. *Critique of Practical Reason.* Book II, ch. 2. Trans. L. W. Beck. New York: Macmillan, 1993.

Lewis, C. S. *Mere Christianity.* London: Collins, 1952.

Mavrodes, George. "Religion and the Queerness of Morality," in *Rationality, Religious Belief, and Moral Commitment: New Essays in the Philosophy of Religion.* Ed. Robert Audi and William J. Wainwright. Ithaca, N.Y.: Cornell University Press, 1986. 213-26.

Mitchell, Basil. *The Justification of Religious Belief.* London: Macmillan, 1973.

Montefiore, Hugh. *The Probability of God.* London: SCM, 1985.

Plantinga, Alvin. "Reason and Belief in God." In *Faith and Rationality: Reason and Belief in God.* Ed. Alvin Plantinga and Nicholas Wolterstorff. Notre Dame, Ind.: University of Notre Dame Press, 1983. 16-93.

Proudfoot, Wayne. *Religious Experience.* Berkeley, Calif.: University of California Press, 1985.

Rowe, William L. *Philosophy of Religion: An Introduction.* Belmont, Calif.: Wadsworth, 1978.

Runzo, Joseph and Craig Ihara, eds. *Religious Experience and Religious Belief.* New York: University Press of America, 1986.

Swinburne, Richard. *The Coherence of Theism.* Oxford: Clarendon Press, 1977.

_____. *The Existence of God.* New York: Oxford University Press, 1979.

Taliaferro, Charles. *Contemporary Philosophy of Religion.* Malden, Mass.: Blackwell, 1998.

Underhill, Evelyn. *Mysticism.* New York: New American Library, 1955.

Unger, Johannes. On Religious Experience: A Psychological Study. Uppsala, Sweden: Acta Universatalis Upsaliensis, 1976.

Yandell, K. E. *The Epistemology of Religious Experience.* Cambridge: Cambridge University Press, 1993.

COSMOLOGICAL ARGUMENTS

Brint Montgomery

$$\diamond$$

Among the various proofs for God's existence, cosmological arguments attempt to prove the existence of God from empirical facts about the world. These facts might be of a very broad nature, such as the claim that there is a world at all, or they might be developed from more specific elements within the world, such as that there is motion or that there is a chain of causation through time.

Cosmological arguments (*cosmos* [gk. world] + *logos* [gk. word(s)] = words about, or study of, world; hence, argument from the observed world) can be found in the writings of many major philosophers. We begin our examination of them with Plato and then proceed through some of the more well-known philosophers, giving our attention to their formulations of cosmological arguments. Finally, we conclude our investigation by noting where some contemporary formulations of cosmological arguments take their stand.

I. PLATO

In Book X of *Laws,* Plato introduced one of the most important developments in his writing, namely, several of his views on theology. He was convinced that there are certain truths about God that can be rigorously demonstrated, and he was convinced that one's denial of such truths would lead one to live a bad life. Plato believed there to be three heresies that could result in a morally pernicious life. He lists these as the heresy of atheism, the heresy of thinking that the gods are indifferent to human conduct, and the heresy of thinking that the impenitent can escape the judgment of God. We shall concern ourselves with the first heresy, given the subject of our inquiry.

For Plato, atheism is identical with a doctrine that the world and its contents are merely the result of unintelligent motions among its material elements. Contrary to this, Plato argues that all material movement ultimately depends on the motions of soul and that the world is therefore a work of soul (or souls). Plato believes that these souls are good, and that there is only one perfectly good soul at the head of all corporeal reality.

Also in Book X, Plato noted that "nearly all of [those who have fallen into error about the true nature of the gods], my friends, seem to be ignorant of the nature and power of the soul, especially in what relates to her origin: they do not know that she is among the first of things, and before all bodies, and is the chief author of their changes and transpositions." Plato goes on to argue that because "the soul is older than the body, the things which are kindred to the soul must be of necessity prior to those which appertain to the body. . . . Thought and attention and mind and art and law will be prior to that which is hard and soft and heavy and light" (Jowett, 633-34). Plato is concerned with changes and transpositions as dependent upon this mind. Here, then, we must deal with the notion of motion, or perhaps "process." Ultimately, Plato will address and distinguish two types of motion. Some motion is self-originated, while other motion is imparted to entities. One can say, then, that there is spontaneous motion and communicated motion. Given this, Plato wonders,

> When one thing changes another, and that another, will there be any primary changing element? How can a thing that is moved by another ever be the beginning of change? Impossible. But when self-moved changes other, and that again other, and thus thousands upon tens of thousands of bodies are set in motion, must not the beginning of all this motion be the change of the self-moving principle? (Jowett, 636).

Plato considered imparted motion to be ultimately dependent upon self-originated motion. All motion, he thinks, is ultimately due the activity of soul. In all of this, Plato is doing natural theology, arguing for the existence of the divine as demanded by our understanding of the way nature appears to us.

Unlike some of the pre-Socratic philosophers, Plato seems to think that the order and change of nature requires the divine as a foundational causal explanation. Exactly what Plato means by "soul" is not always clear. Sometimes "soul" can mean the self-movement of any object. But in Plato's own words, "soul" is also dubbed "divinity." He notes that the soul "ought by every man be deemed a god. At least by every man who has the least particle of sense" (Jowett, 641).

II. ARISTOTLE

The idea of motion and its origin comes up again in the thought of Plato's disciple, Aristotle. Aristotle had a slightly different worry than Plato. Anything that is moved, as well as being the mover of other things, is intermediate. In light of this, Aristotle believed that there must be something that moves things without itself being moved. Aristotle considered motion to be eternal, and, if motion is eternal, it requires an eternal cause. This cause cannot itself be in motion, so it must be an "unmoved mover." There is certainly no potential for it to be moved; therefore, it must be pure actuality. As pure actuality, it cannot be matter, because matter *can* be moved.

From this, Aristotle concluded that the only activity this unmoved mover would undertake would be the exercise of pure thought.

Aristotle did not straightforwardly call this unmoved mover "God." Plato had thought that everything in motion is moved either by itself or by something else. A soul is the only self-moving thing, so there must be a world soul. But Aristotle was worried that nothing can be essentially self-moving, for to be self-moving is to be active, and to be moved is to be passive. Something could not be both active and passive, that is, not at the same time and in the same respect.

The heavenly bodies presented an interesting dilemma to Aristotle in terms of self-moving entities. Because the heavenly bodies show continuous eternal motion, they must, paradoxically, be considered eternal, material things. But their material is of a stilted nature. They have only one kind of potentiality, namely, that of moving eternally in circles. Yet what triggers this eternal movement? There must be something that provides the motive for these heavenly souls to move as they do. This is, of course, the unmoved mover.

Even if one grants that the unmoved mover is the first principle of eternal, material things, a question arises. Must the unmoved mover be the first cause of *all* movement? Aristotle thought so:

> Evidently there *is* a first principle, and the causes of things are neither an infinite series nor infinitely various in kind. For neither can one thing proceed from another, as from matter, *ad infinitum,* (e.g. flesh from earth, earth from air, air from fire, and so on without stopping), nor can the sources of movement form an endless series (man, for instance, being acted on by air, air by sun, sun by strife, and so on without limit). Similarly, the final causes cannot go on ad infinitum. . . . If there is no first, there is no cause at all (Jones, 230, from Ross, *Metaphysics,* in *Works,* VIII, 1928, 994a1*ff.*).

A first mover is necessary to avoid affirming an infinite series of causes back into eternity. The infinite series is a pivotal issue in the cosmological argument. We will say more about it when we consider Thomas Aquinas. Even later, we will also discuss how the denial of an infinite series can be argued from cosmological positions about the expansion of the universe when we come to consider more contemporary versions of the cosmological argument.

III. THOMAS AQUINAS

The most well-known formulations of the cosmological argument come from Thomas Aquinas. He offers five ways that one might prove God's existence. We will concentrate on the first three of these, because they are directly relevant to the cosmological arguments. Again, the arguments are based on what we can experience through our sensory data and not just on what pure reason can establish. Before a proof can get started, Thomas concerns himself with three objections.

The first objection, and a quite interesting one at that, concerns whether pure reason supercedes the effort necessary for constructing an argument from what we experience. After all, if God's existence is self-evident, there is no need to consider arguments based upon how we observe the world to be (Knight, *ST, Part I, Q2*).

Another objection to why a cosmological argument is even necessary concerns Anselm's ontological argument. This argument is fully covered elsewhere in this book, therefore, we shall not address Thomas's specific criticisms of it. However, we should note in passing that Anselm's argument is a special case of the first objection. Anselm's argument is strictly *a priori,* and if it were deemed successful by Thomas, further empirical proofs would be unnecessary. It would be akin to proving that 2+2=4, and then going out to count sticks in order to give further support to the matter.

A third objection concerns the existence of truth as self-evident. If someone denies the existence of truth, he or she grants that truth does not exist. And if truth does not exist, then the proposition they utter, "Truth does not exist," must be true. This leads to a contradiction, indeed a self-refuting proposition. Once we allow a statement such as "Truth does not exist" to be true, we have already shown that truth must exist. Perhaps on the ground that truth cannot otherwise but exist, we must affirm God's existence as likewise self-evident and undeniable.

As one can see, the notion of "self-evident" plays a very important part in these opening objections to developing a cosmological argument. Thomas answers these by claiming that a thing can be self-evident in either of two ways—on the one hand, self-evident in itself, though not to us; on the other, self-evident in itself and to us. A simple and clear way to explain his distinction is in terms of the *meaning* of the terms we use and our *knowledge* of what these terms imply.

Anyone who utters "A square has four sides" utters a necessary truth. It is evident to anyone who understands the meaning of the word "square." As Thomas notes, "It is self-evident because the predicate is included in the essence of the subject." So in the case of this statement about a square, its meaning is self-evident and known to be so by those who use the word.

However, there are classes of statements whose meanings are self-evident but that are not known to be so by those who utter them. For example, it is necessary that the equation $(x^2+2x+1) / (x + 1)$ simplifies to $x + 1$. But unless one has studied algebra (and remembers it), it is hardly self-evident in the way that "A square has four sides" is self-evident. Therefore, this distinction addresses what Thomas is trying to separate into two notions of self-evidence. God's existence is self-evident inasmuch as it is a necessary truth, but we do not know its self-evidence. Thomas notes that "in a general and confused way" God's existence is implanted in us by nature, but we do not "know absolutely that God exists." Thomas gives an example where we might know that someone is approaching us and not know, in particular, that this someone is, say, Peter. In this case, we would have a general knowledge of someone coming to us but not absolutely know who is coming to us. Because we may not recognize this necessary truth, a cosmological argument becomes a legitimate exercise for proving the existence of God. Having established the possibility of a cosmological argument, Thomas moves on to develop it.

A. The First Way. The first two ways to prove the existence of God, as outlined by Thomas, are somewhat similar in their approach. Thomas begins with a discussion from motion: "The first and more manifest way is the argument from motion. It is certain, and evident to our senses, that in the world some things are in motion." He is using the word "motion" more akin to our use of the word "change." On this view, everything within our purview undergoes change. But Thomas notes that no change is isolated. Whatever is in motion is put in motion by another, for nothing can be in motion except it is in potentiality to that toward which it is in motion; whereas a thing moves inasmuch as it is in act. For any given change that we note, that change must be explained in terms of an earlier explanation.

Thomas explains more fully what Aristotle has already noted. Because change is the reduction of something from potentiality to actuality, it cannot undergo a particular type of change unless it has the potential to enter into the final state in question. Seeds generate plants of their own kind. And Thomas believes that this change is caused by something that is already in the state of actuality. Thomas gives us an example of what he has in mind: "that which is actually hot, as fire, makes wood, which is potentially hot, to be actually hot, and thereby moves and changes it." Something that is not initially hot—wood—is heated by something that is hot—fire. The wood could not be the cause of its own change here, because it would have to be both actually hot, to bring about the change, and potentially hot, to be changed. In Thomas's own words, "it is not possible that the same thing should be at once in actuality and potentiality in the same respect, but only in different respects."

Whatever changes is changed by another. Change No. 1 (C1) has been caused by Change No. 2 (C2), and so on. We can then give a diagram that immediately suggests a question:

. . . □ **C4** □ **C3** □ **C2** □ **C1**

How far does this change go back? Perhaps it is an infinite change with no end. Thomas denies this infinite change,

> This cannot go on to infinity, because then there would be no first mover, and, consequently, no other mover; seeing that subsequent movers move only inasmuch as they are put in motion by the first mover; as the staff moves only because it is put in motion by the hand. Therefore, it is necessary to arrive at a first mover, put in motion by no other.

Here Thomas is not committing himself to the impossibility of an infinite series of finite things. For instance, Thomas would agree that once one starts counting, in principle this process could continue without end. What is actually being argued here is the impossibility of an infinite series of moved movers or, more accurately, intermediate movers. "First" in the quotation above is being used in a hierarchical sense, akin to how the Bishop of Rome used to say his see was "first" among equals. "First" is not used in a linear sense, as when one says one is first in the lunch line. Let us mark this special sense of the word as "first."

We turn now to consider these intermediate movers. If there existed only intermediate movers—that is, one that is moved itself is also moving yet another—there could be no first* mover, which would result in there being no other mover. Just for illustration's sake, let us posit the first mover as C1000. First cause C1000 moves ending cause C1 through the intermediate causes C999-C2. In this context, C999-C2 serve only as intermediaries for the delivery of the final cause. From this perspective it becomes clear that the existence of C999-C2 depends exclusively upon the fact that there exists cause C1000 from which concluding cause C1 proceeds. It is likewise clear that intermediate causes C998-C3 function likewise for C999-C2, and so forth. Thomas, consistent with what Aristotle developed in his *Physics,* equates observable motion with C999-C2, or some such boundary, and from this finds both that such intermediate motions cannot possibly go on to infinity, so as to preclude the possibility of there being a first mover; and, that a first mover necessarily exists.

Naturally, this has drawn criticism. It looks as if Thomas has posited what was to be proved, or at the least posited a metaphysical entity without justification. Thomas wants us to think that unless there were a first mover, there would be no other intermediate members of the series. Because in our own experience we readily note that there are intermediate members, there must be a first mover. An objector might not agree, counterarguing that so long as each individual change has a cause outside itself, there is no need to posit a first mover. Let the infinite series stand on its own! Ultimately the issue pivots on whether one thinks an actual infi-

nite series is possible. Aristotle and Thomas thought not, but other thinkers, such as Leibniz, thought it possible, although, with Leibniz, one needs
to account for some sufficient reason for this infinite series. At the very
least, it does not seem anyone has yet shown an infinite series to be impossible.

B. The Second Way. Thomas's second way to prove that God exists is
an argument from the nature of efficient cause. "Efficient" means "maker"
or "doer;" we might think of a statue where the sculptor would be the efficient cause of the statue. Thomas once again draws on Aristotle's views of
efficient causality. In Aristotle's *Metaphysics,* he had analyzed the notion
of cause into four types, and he argued that an infinite regress of causes
was impossible for any of the four causes. By the efficient cause of something, Aristotle simply meant the thing, circumstances, or event that pre-
cipitates a change in something.

Thomas argues that it is not possible for a thing to be its own efficient cause, "for so it would be prior to itself, which is impossible." Much
like the first way, Thomas will not permit efficient causes to go back to infinity, "because in all efficient causes following in order, the first is the
cause of the intermediate cause, and the intermediate is the cause of the
ultimate cause, whether the intermediate cause be several, or only one."
Just as earlier, when there was an impossibility of an infinite series of
moved movers (or intermediate movers), now Thomas likewise claims the
impossibility of an infinite series of efficient causes:

> To take away the cause is to take away the effect. Therefore, if
> there be no first cause among efficient causes, there will be no ulti-
> mate, nor any intermediate cause. But if in efficient causes it is possi-
> ble to go on to infinity, there will be no first efficient cause, neither
> will there be an ultimate effect, nor any intermediate efficient causes;
> all of which is plainly false. Therefore it is necessary to admit a first
> efficient cause, to which everyone gives the name of God.

Again, we might be tempted to think that Thomas is trying to rule out
the possibility of an infinitely long series of efficient causes and their effects stretching back into the temporal past, with each efficient cause existing prior in time to its effect. This would be closer to what the Kalam
version of the cosmological argument advocates, which we shall identify a
bit later. Instead, Thomas is still espousing a hierarchy of causes where any
subordinate efficient cause (or set of subordinate efficient causes) depends
on the causal activities of a higher member (or set of higher members, as
we noted using C2-C999 notation above). A noted scholar of Aquinas,
Frederick Copleston, explains further:

> We have to imagine, not a lineal or horizontal series, so to
> speak, but a vertical hierarchy, in which a lower member depends

here and now on the present causal activity of the member above it. It is the latter type of series, if prolonged to infinity, which Thomas rejects. And he rejects it on the ground that unless there is a "first" member, [some] cause that does not depend on the causal activity of a higher cause, it is not possible to explain the . . . causal activity of the lowest member. . . . [Thomas's position comes to this:] Suppress the first efficient cause and there is no causal activity here and now. If therefore we find that . . . there are efficient causes in the world there must be a first efficient, and completely non-dependent, cause. The word "first" does not mean first in the temporal order but supreme or first in the ontological order [118-20].

Once more we see that the word "first" is used in a very specific sense by Thomas. He does not mean to rule out an infinitely long temporal series of efficient causes and effects; he allows for this possibility elsewhere (Knight, *ST 1, Part 1, Ques. 46, Art. 2*). Rather, he is ruling out a hierarchy of efficient causal series that proceeds to infinity.

Both the first and the second ways share a denial of an infinite hierarchy, whether of motion or of efficient causes (which may come to the same thing, though not without further argument). Although Thomas can and does allow for some types of infinite series, there is apparently something about infinite hierarchies that precludes their being part of the metaphysical furniture.

Let us take a moment to consider this by taking a coda on our earlier symbolism of intermediate changes. There we gave a diagram of changes causing changes, and we eventually posited a first change of C1000.

C1000 . . . ▢ C4 ▢ C3 ▢ C2 ▢ C1

Our diagram suggests another question when we reconsider sets of intermediate changes. These would be C999-C2, C998-C3, and so forth. (Obviously there have been vastly more than 1,000 successive changes in the universe. We merely post a number to show relationship among intermediate sets.) What happens to the series when we consider the intermediate set C501-C500? That is, what happens between any two sequential, successive changes? Perhaps the total number of successive changes is infinite, even if the total number of hierarchical changes is not. But are there limits, or minimum packets of change? Perhaps there cannot be an infinite hierarchy because there is not an infinite continuum between changes.

John Barrow, writing on the applications and limits of mathematics for completely describing the physical world, addresses this point:

Although we habitually assume that there is a continuum of points of space and time, this is just an assumption that is very convenient for the use of simple mathematics. There is no deep reason to believe that space and time are continuous, rather than discrete, at their most fundamental microscopic level; in fact, there are some theories of quantum gravity that assume that they are not. Quantum theory has introduced discreteness and finiteness in a number of places where once we believed in a continuum of possibilities. Curiously, if we give up this continuity, so that there is not necessarily another point in between any two sufficiently close points you care to choose, the space-time structure becomes vastly more complicated [225-26].

Thomas's denial of an infinite hierarchy seems to turn on whether there is only a finite number of terms needed in an ultimate mathematical description of the physical world. Unless we can determine whether space-time is discrete or continuous, we cannot take a stand on whether Thomas's position on infinite hierarchies is sound. So far, the physical sciences have not (and perhaps cannot) give us a solution to this discrete/continuous issue. Therefore, we are currently (if not perpetually) in a rather uncomfortable position on having to reserve judgment on this matter of infinite hierarchical series. A more optimistic view is that Thomas has specifically identified just that metaphysical premise that believers in God happen to take as an axiom of faith within the cosmological argument.

C. The Third Way. The third way is based on what need not be and what must be, or as Thomas puts it, what is "taken from possibility and necessity." The argument runs as follows: Some of the things we come across can be but need not be, for we find them coming into existence and then subsequently passing away–being and then not being. Now everything cannot be like this, because a thing that *need* not be, once was not. And if *everything* need not be, "then at one time there could have been nothing in existence." But were that to be the case, there would be nothing even now, "because that which does not exist only begins to exist by something already existing." Put differently, something that does not exist can be brought into being only by something that already exists. "Therefore, if at one time nothing was in existence, it would have been impossible for anything to have begun to exist; and therefore even now nothing would be in existence—which is absurd." This contradicts our immediate observation of matters. Not everything, therefore, is the sort of thing that need not be. There has to be something that must be. As Thomas concludes, "Therefore, not all beings are merely possible, but there must exist something the existence of which is necessary."

"Every necessary thing," as Thomas puts it, may or may not owe this necessity to something else. But as was argued in the earlier ways, we must stop somewhere in a series of causes. So it is with the series of necessary things that owe their necessity to other things. "Therefore," Thomas concludes, "we cannot but postulate the existence of some being having of itself its own necessity, and not receiving it from another, but rather causing in others their necessity. This all men speak of as God."

I am following the standard interpretation of Thomas's third way by describing it as two parts. The first part ends with the conclusion that there has to be something that must be, "something the existence of which is necessary." The second part ends with the conclusion that there is something "having of itself its own necessity" that is the cause of other things having their necessity. One can raise objections to both parts. One objection says that it is false that one must stop somewhere in a series of causes. Another objection says that from the premise that everything at some time is not, it is fallacious to conclude that at some time nothing exists. We will eventually address both of these, but let us first consider Thomas's notions of "possible" and "necessary."

"Possible" and "necessary" are here being used in a temporal sense (as opposed to a logical sense that is seen in Anselm's ontological argument). For our analysis, we will regard these terms respectively as "having a proclivity to eventually cease existing" and "having no proclivity to eventually cease existing." This usage seems odd, but it was commonly held among advocates of Aristotelian philosophy. As a point of metaphysics, Aristotle believed that the world had existed from all eternity, and it appears he held that whatever is possible is at sometime, somewhere realized. He also believed that that which is always the case is necessary. On the one hand, Aristotle does not believe that anything can just happen to be always the case. On the other hand, neither will he allow any universal or everlasting truths to be contingent. Whatever is "necessary" is *always* the case; it is everlasting. (We avoid the word "eternal," because this might have connotations of atemporality and transcendence.) Likewise, that which sometimes is and sometimes is not we call "contingent." What is contingent is "possible" in this sense: maybe it is at this moment; maybe it won't be in the next or some later moment.

Let us fashion a skeletal outline of the third way for developing our commentary:

1. There are contingent beings (i.e., "merely possible beings").
2. For every contingent being, there is a time when it does not exist.
3. If everything is contingent, then there is a time when nothing exists.
4. Anything that begins to exist does so only through something that exists.
5. So if there is a time when nothing exists, then nothing would exist now (this follows from 4).
6. But there are things that exist now.

7. So it is not the case that everything is contingent (this follows from 3, 5, and 6 taken together).
8. So there is something that exists necessarily (this follows from 7).
9. Every necessary being has its necessity either because of something else or because of itself.
10. There can be no infinite chain of necessary beings.
11. So there must be something that has its necessity because of itself (this follows from 9 and 10).
12. So God exists (this follows from 11) (Mills, "Aquinas' Third Way").

Premises 1 and 2 merely affirm what we have already covered on contingency. In premise 3 and subconclusion 5, Thomas is likely purporting that given infinite time, which is metaphysically affiliated with the type of infinite regress under consideration in 10, the potentiality of all beings in this regress to cease to exist would *inevitably* come about. That is, there would, given an infinite amount of time, be nothing. And Thomas points out that, if there ever was nothing, there would *still* be nothing. But that obviously is not the case, as our own experience shows in 6. Thomas is drawing on the principle (and commonly affirmed Greek proverb) that nothing comes of nothing, which is to say that no thing could bring itself into existence from nothing. Therefore, an infinite regress fails on this ground.

Premise 3 also presents a difficulty of its own. "If everything is contingent, then there is a time when nothing exists." Thomas thinks it cannot be that everything should have a proclivity to stop existing, for if *everything* did have such a proclivity, then, given an infinite time, it would already have stopped, and nothing would exist now.

In 3, Thomas is apparently moving from the idea that "every contingent being will eventually cease existing" to the idea that "there is some time at which every contingent being eventually ceases existing." This is a malfunction. Ask yourself this question: Is the meaning of the phrase "All the nice girls love a sailor" equivalent to "There is a sailor whom all the nice girls love?" There is clearly a problem with linking these two ideas. Even if we were to grant that every nice girl loves a sailor, we are not entitled to conclude from that premise that there is some (lucky) sailor such that every nice girl loves only him! Or again, from the true premise "Every road leads somewhere" we cannot conclude that "There is somewhere—e.g. Rome—where every road leads." This is a type of "quantifier-shift" fallacy, because such words as "every," "all," "some," and even "a" are the natural language expressions of the universal and particular quantifiers in logical notation. In our sailor/nice girl example, as in Thomas's argument, we have inverted the order of the quantifiers between the premises and improperly derived conclusions. That is, we have shifted the quantifiers.

Finally, the move between 11 and 12 is not without controversy. Without giving further argument, we may simply note how one need not draw a connection between (a) something that is necessary because of itself and (b) a personal entity commonly known as "God." Thomas assumes without warrant that such a necessary being must have all of the attributes of God. However, it is a long way from such a metaphysical placeholder to the God of Abraham, Isaac, and Jacob.

IV. HUME AND KANT

David Hume in his *Dialogues Concerning Natural Religion* (Part IX) argued that if we accept that every effect has a cause, the causal chain must be infinite. One cannot rightly speak of a first cause of an infinite series, as this would be logically contradictory. Why? Because if it truly is first, it would be within time. Hume argues that "in tracing an eternal succession of objects, it seems absurd to inquire for a general cause or first author. How can any thing, that exists from eternity, have a cause, because that relation implies priority in time, and a beginning of existence?" Eternal things, such as God, do not have beginnings. So to tie a first cause to God is plain wrong-headed from the outset. A cosmological argument, at least one that relies on a temporal first cause, cannot prove anything about God.

A cosmological argument that furthermore seeks to find a single cause of all caused things, a first cause of the causal chain, involves a fallacy. As Hume writes, if he were to show you the particular causes of each individual in a collection of 20 particles of matter, "I should think it very unreasonable should you afterwards ask me what was the cause of the whole twenty."

Finally, through the voice of Cleanthes, a character in the *Dialogues,* Hume points out the limitations of what is demonstrable: "Nothing is demonstrable, unless the contrary implies a contradiction. Nothing, that is distinctly conceivable, implies a contradiction. Whatever we conceive as existent, we can also conceive as non-existent. There is no being, therefore, whose non-existence implies a contradiction. Consequently, there is no being, whose existence is demonstrable." Hume is not as much questioning a specific premise of some cosmological argument. Instead, he attacks the type of statements that such an argument needs to make its point. It is improper to claim that "God exists" given how we use the term "exists":

1. No statement is demonstrable unless the contrary of that statement implies a contradiction.

2. If any statement of the form "such and such being exists" is entertained, we can likewise entertain that "such and such being does
not exist."
3. Therefore, no statement "such and such being exists" is such that
its contrary implies a contradiction.
4. Therefore, no statement of the form "such and such being exists"
is demonstrable.
5. "God exists" is a statement of the form "such and such being exists."
6. So "God exists" (and "God does not exist") is a proposition that is
not demonstrable.

This is, in essence, an *a priori* argument against the possibility of cosmological argument succeeding. It is a "second order" argument. As such,
it shares some resemblance to a criticism put forth by another enlightenment philosopher.

Immanuel Kant argued that causation was a term (among others) that
could be meaningfully used only about the time-space world in which reasoning beings operate. One could not affirm metaphysical claims by ex-
tending the notion of causation beyond this world. All cosmological arguments start with what we observe in the world and attempt to deduce that
which we do not (indeed, cannot) know. Our existing logical concepts,
causation being one among these, cannot hope to find out about what
"happened" before the beginning of the universe. To argue in this way
would be an example of reason extended beyond its bounds and thus becoming, at that point, an unreliable instrument for telling us about reality.

V. CONTEMPORARY FORMULATIONS

The most active area of contemporary formulations concerns the
Kalam version of the cosmological argument, where temporal succession
becomes of primary importance for proving God's existence. The Kalam
version was first rigorously developed by Arabic philosophers. (Kalam gets
its meaning from the Arabic word for "speech" or "dispute.") Broadly
speaking, contemporary supporters of the cosmological argument often
look to the "Big Bang" theory of the origin of the universe for support.

By extrapolating backward from the speed at which the universe is
expanding, Big Bang cosmologists date the beginning of the universe to be
somewhere around 15 billion years ago. Of course, like any claim made
in the natural sciences, cosmological physical laws are derived from observation. There are two problems immediately apparent here. First, we go
beyond making scientific claims when we further state that God must
have caused the Big Bang that started everything off. As Hume pointed out
in the 18th century, no one was around to watch God do this (i.e., God is

not a part of the data of observation). Second, we really need not defer to such an *a priori* claim about scientific method. Instead, we may simply note that, because the laws that physics purport currently cover the period only after about 10^{-43} seconds, there are a multitude of conditions that are logically compatible with producing the universe we now have. Unless we can move behind this wall at 10^{-43} seconds, we are not scientifically warranted to make further claims based upon reverse extrapolation from how the universe currently appears.

Bibliography and Texts for Further Study

Aquinas, Thomas. *Summa Theologica,* Part I, Q., 2. London: Eyre & Spottiswoode; New York: Mc-Graw-Hill for Blackfriars, 1964.

Barrow, John D. *Impossibility: The Limits of Science and the Science of Limits.* Oxford: Oxford University Press, 1999.

Craig, William Lane. *The Cosmological Argument from Plato to Leibniz.* London: Macmillan; New York: Barnes and Noble, 1980.

Copleston, Frederick C. *Aquinas.* Baltimore: Penguin Books, 1961.

Gilson, Ettienne. *The Christian Philosophy of St. Thomas.* London: Victor Gollancz, 1957.

Hume, David. *Dialogues Concerning Natural Religion* (1779). Indianapolis: Hackett, 1980.

Jones W. T. *The Classical Mind (The History of Western Philosophy).* New York: HBJ College & School Div, 1969.

Jowett, Benjamin., trans. *The Dialogues of Plato.* New York: Macmillan, 1937.

Kant, Immanuel. *Critique of Pure Reason.* Tr. N. Kemp Smith. London: Macmillan, 1933; New York: St. Martin's, 1969.

Kenny, Anthony. *Five Ways: St. Thomas Aquinas's Proofs of God's Existence.* London: Routledge & Kegan Paul, 1969; Notre Dame, Ind.: University of Notre Dame Press, 1980.

Knight, Kevin., ed. *The Summa Theologica of St. Thomas Aquinas* Second and Revised Edition, 1920 Online Edition, 2000. http://www.newadvent.org/summa/100200.htm

Mills, Andrew P. "Aquinas' Third Way" Thursday 12 October 2000. (Otterbein College) http://www.otterbein.edu/home/fac/ANDPMLLS/Religion/

Rowe, William. *The Cosmological Argument.* Princeton, N.J.: Princeton University Press, 1975.

TELEOLOGICAL ARGUMENTS
Lincoln Stevens

◆

The teleological argument for the existence of God represents one of the most persistent attempts in Western philosophy to ground theistic belief rationally. It is one part of a longstanding tradition in Christian natural theology that supposes that "men and women have a certain degree of knowledge of God . . . [that] exists anterior to the special revelation of God made through Jesus Christ, through the Church, [and] through the Bible" (Barr 1). The teleological argument seeks within this tradition to demonstrate systematically the knowledge of the existence of God by carefully constructed arguments. Its history is the continuing attempt to form and defend such arguments against criticism. This essay engages this history by analyzing a few of the most important versions of the argument and by offering an evaluation of their adequacy.

In general, the teleological argument (*teleos* [gk. purpose or design] + *logos* [gk. word(s)] = words about, or study of, purpose or design; hence, argument about purposiveness or design) seeks to demonstrate the existence of God on the basis of some kind of purpose, order, or design in the universe. This has involved reasoning from considerations of various designs, like those of beauty, consciousness, or life, as observed in the universe. The teleological argument reasons from the empirical patterns, regularities, or purposes that are outwardly observable in the universe.

We can see the teleological argument's empirical nature at work in several of its historical expressions. In *Memorabilia,* reputed to be the first recorded teleological argument and written around 390 B.C., Xenophon reports Socrates' argument that humans "do look very like the handiwork of a wise and loving creator." The argument is based on the particular "signs of forethought" and "contrivance" found in the observed arrangement of the parts of human anatomy that "serve some useful end" (Sections 1.4.4 through 1.4.7). Plato's (428—348 B.C.) teleological argument, as given in the *Laws* (Book X), is not based on the arrangements of human anatomy but on the "beautiful order of the seasons." And Aristotle (384-322 B.C.) in his fragment "On Philosophy" argues from a third kind of order in the cosmos that he calls the "dances of the stars." In each case, the argument draws from some specific dimension of design found in the natural or human world. Out of these arguments, the empirical approach became a standard argument for the existence of God throughout the Christian era until the time of David Hume's and Charles Darwin's apparently devastating criticisms in the 18th and 19th centuries. However, in recent years there has been new appreciation for the argument's empirical insight.

Much of the historical impetus for the teleological argument comes from the Christian tradition. That tradition especially encourages the development of the argument because of its theological emphasis on the participatory role of God in creation. The Christian scriptures, for instance, seem to suggest that a natural knowledge of God can arise on the basis of our understanding of the particular order of God's creation, even though it is not clear that the Bible ever actually uses a teleological argument for the existence of God. The Gen. 1 account of creation shows this through numerous references to God's creative involvement in separating the light, making the stars, creating every living creature, and making humans in God's own image (Gen. 1:1-27). The natural implication of these scriptures is that God causes the particular arrangement of the created world.

Moreover, Christian scripture also suggests that the resulting design reveals something about the God who created it. Ps. 19:1 follows this theme in asserting that the "heavens declare the glory of God; And the firmament shows His handiwork" (NKJV). And in the New Testament the apostle Paul continues to develop this theme when he states in Rom. 1:20, "For since the creation of the world His invisible attributes are clearly seen, being understood by the things that are made, even His eternal power and Godhead, so that they are without excuse" (NKJV). Not only is the creation portrayed as God's handiwork, but that handiwork provides specific knowledge of the characteristics of God—invisible attributes, eternal power, and divine nature. Of course, the Scriptures do not themselves develop the argument in any precise fashion. At most, they only identify nature as a basis of knowing something of God's existence and nature.

The most important early Christian version is the argument from purpose given by Thomas Aquinas (1225-74). In what Thomas calls his "fifth way" of proving God's existence, he writes,

> We see that things that lack knowledge, such as natural bodies, act for an end, and this is evident from their acting always, or nearly always, in the same way, so as to obtain the best result. Hence it is plain that they achieve their end, not fortuitously, but designedly. Now whatever lacks knowledge cannot move towards an end, unless it be directed by some being endowed with knowledge and intelligence; as the arrow is directed by the archer. Therefore, some intelligent being exists by whom all natural things are directed to their end; and this being we call God (27).

In a more simple form the argument asserts

1. All natural bodies, which lack knowledge and intelligence, act for an end.
2. Whatever lacks knowledge and intelligence does not act for an end unless it is directed by some being endowed with knowledge and intelligence.
3. Therefore, some intelligent being exists by whom all natural bodies are directed to their end, and this being is God.

Essentially, this argument is composed of two premises and an inference leading to the conclusion that God exists. Although most modern versions of the teleological argument are inductive in structure, as we will discuss later, Thomas's version is deductive. It is deductive because the conclusion in number 3 is purported to follow necessarily from the truth of the premises in numbers 1 and 2. This, of course, differs from the inductive versions of the argument that only purport to establish the probable truth of the conclusion on the basis of the truth of the premises. The important question in this context, then, is whether the argument is sound in establishing the existence of God. In other words, are the premises true, and does the conclusion necessarily follow from the assumption of their truth? To answer these questions, it is necessary to first clarify the argument.

Premise 1 of the argument is the claim that there is a particular order in the universe associated with what Thomas calls natural bodies. These natural bodies, as Anthony Kenny interprets them, are the "lifeless elements, and perhaps the plants and heavenly bodies" found in the universe (97). The particular kind of order associated with these natural bodies is their teleological structure. This just means, as Aristotle would say, that natural bodies have *telos* (end, aim, or purpose) and that they act for the achievement of that end. According to Thomas, natural bodies do not always achieve their ends when seeking them. Additionally, even though natural bodies seek their ends, they do it without intelligence immanent in the natural bodies themselves.

The first difficulty with the argument is its ambiguity. It is not clear initially whether Thomas asserts in Premise 1 that all natural objects seek the same end or that each natural body seeks its own individual end. Settling this ambiguity is, of course, extremely important. If all natural bodies seek individual ends, and not the same end for all, then the argument will not entail the required conclusion that there exists a single intelligent agent that directs all natural objects to their ends.

Because of this problem, it is better to interpret Premise 1 as asserting that there is one purpose or end that natural bodies seek. The problem with this, however, is that there is no obvious way, given the evidence, to identify the one purpose that all natural objects in the universe seek. Take the following three examples. What does the evidence of, say, the arrangement of leaves, the feet, and the front teeth suggest is the one purpose that they all seek? On the surface, no single purpose is obvious. Rather, what seems obvious is that there are multiple purposes, protecting fruit of trees in the case of the leaves, walking in the case of feet, and biting in the case of front teeth. If no single purpose for all natural bodies can be found, there is also no evidence that establishes the existence of a single intelligent agent that directs the natural objects to their single end or purpose.

This latter interpretation, which is usually the one assigned to Thomas's argument, is instructive for one general problem with teleological arguments. They often lack the needed premise to establish the singularity of purpose that the multiplicity of natural objects seek. Without establishing the singularity of purpose, no single intelligent guide can be inferred either. And because Thomas does not provide such a premise, his argument fails to that extent.

Beyond this problem, another exists. Not only does the argument not establish the singularity of purpose in natural bodies, it also does not adequately show that all objects do in fact seek their ends. As Kenny points out, the most that Thomas's argument establishes is that only some natural bodies seek their ends (103). But what does this do to the conclusion? What it does, assuming the rest of the argument is adequate, is establish that some intelligent agent is required for *some,* but not necessarily all, natural bodies seeking their ends. If this is true, then we may have an argument for the intelligent design of only part of the universe and not for all of it. The intelligent design of only a partial order in the universe will not establish the appropriate theistic conclusion—at least appropriate for traditional theism. The following revised argument will reveal this problem:

1. Some natural bodies, which lack knowledge and intelligence, act for an end.
2. Whatever lacks knowledge and intelligence does not act for an end unless it is directed by some being endowed with knowledge and intelligence.
3. Therefore, some intelligent being exists by whom all natural bodies are directed to their ends; and this being is God.

As it stands, the argument is not valid, because the narrowed scope in 1 does not properly entail the universal claim in 3 that all natural bodies are directed to their ends by some intelligent being. This revised argument from purpose in turn only infers the following more limited conclusion:

3. Therefore, some intelligent being exists by whom some natural bodies are directed to their ends, and this being is God.

This conclusion seems to establish a God, but only a God who exercises a limited role—that of directing a portion of the natural bodies to their ends.

If belief in God is established only so far as it is necessary to bring about the *telos* of a portion of universe, there is some question as to what kind of intelligent agent God is. Does this mean that God is not the intelligent designer of the whole universe? Or does it demand that God is of limited power in that deity is not capable of intelligently directing natural objects to their ends in that portion of the universe in which there are no objects seeking their ends?

In answer to both of these questions it must be said that these suggestions are based on a logical confusion between not establishing something as a matter of fact and the logical impossibility of establishing something. The argument does not establish as a conclusion that God is not a designer of the whole universe nor that God is incapable of intelligently directing all objects in the universe to their ends. What it establishes, if it is valid in its revised form, is only that the evidence *thus far* does not imply that God is the complete intelligent designer of the universe. It does not establish that God cannot be the complete intelligent designer of the universe. So far as the evidence goes, God is not established as such, but God could very well be the complete designer of the universe on the basis of some further consideration or argument. The latter claim is beyond the evidence given, but the evidence does not rule out the claim that God is the complete designer of the universe.

Premise 2 of the argument attempts to give an explanation of the purposeful design of unintelligent natural objects. What it does is identify the cause of unintelligent natural bodies seeking their ends. It asserts that such natural bodies seek their ends only if they are directed to them by an intelligent agent. What can be said about the truth of this claim?

On the surface it seems quite true. Things without intelligence do not act intelligently. Things without order do not produce orderly things. But why does Thomas think that this is a true premise? What rational support does he give it? In terms of careful argument, he does not give much of anything to defend the premise rationally.

Yet he does suggest an argument that he does not develop. It is found in the example of the arrow directed by the archer. What this suggests is the argument from analogy for why the acts-to-ends orderliness of natural bodies does not happen unless it is directed by some being endowed with intelligence. Given the fact that some design in the universe is known to require intelligent agency, such as arrows being directed by archers who are their intelligent causes, it is inferred that they, too, probably require intelligent agency to direct the design of their flight. Although Thomas does not develop this point, his argument does suggest what is only more fully developed later in the modern scientific teleological arguments. This is the argument from analogy, which is given as the explanation of design. But before we turn to that, we must evaluate the deductive validity of the argument.

With regard to the deductive validity of Thomas's argument from purpose, it must be remembered that an argument can have true premises and still not establish the truth of the conclusion. Therefore, even if the argument from purpose could overcome all of the objections identified above, it still might be the case that the conclusion is not deductively valid in relation to its premises. For the sake of evaluating this, let us suppose that the problems with the premises dealt with above are sufficiently solved. Does it then necessarily follow that some intelligent being exists by whom all natural bodies are directed to their end and that this being is God? The direct answer to this is "no."

To show this, the argument needs to be converted a bit. Premise 2 says

Whatever lacks knowledge and intelligence does not act for an end unless it is directed by some being endowed with knowledge and intelligence,

and entails the following additional premise:

Therefore, if natural bodies, which lack knowledge and intelligence, act for an end, then they are directed by some being endowed with knowledge and intelligence.

We can now put both of these into the original argument along with the following symbols representing each key claim:

2. (LI) All natural bodies, which lack knowledge and intelligence, act for an end. (LI = Lacks Intelligence)

Whatever lacks knowledge and intelligence cannot act for an end unless it is directed by some being endowed with knowledge and intelligence.

Therefore, if (LI) all natural bodies, which lack knowledge and intelligence, act for an end, then (SIB) they are directed by some being endowed with knowledge and intelligence. (SIB = Some Intelligent Being)

3. Therefore, (SIB) some intelligent being exists by whom all natural bodies are directed to their end, and (DIB) this being is God. (DIB = Divine Intelligent Being)

Notice that the argument form can be reduced to the following:

1. LI

If LI, then SIB (given Premise 2)

2. Therefore, SIB and DIB.

The argument would clearly be deductively valid if the conclusion were only SIB, that is, without the added claim of DIB. The argument as stated by Thomas, however, has also included DIB in the conclusion.

What DIB consists in is the claim that in addition to the fact that (SIB) some intelligent being exists, a *divine* intelligent being exists. It is DIB that the premises do not validly establish. The only way that the premises would validly establish SIB and DIB is if some intelligent being exists (SIB) logically entails that a divine intelligent being exists (DIB). The problem here is that it is logically possible that there are intelligent beings other than divine beings, and these nondivine beings could be the agents that explain the purposes that exist in natural bodies. Therefore, Thomas's argument from purpose is not deductively valid and does not establish the theistic conclusion of the argument.

Modern teleological arguments attempt to make up for the deficiencies in the argument from purpose. In particular, modern teleological arguments seek to develop an argument from analogy that the argument from purpose only suggests. The most well-known development of the argument was given by William Paley (1743—1805). According to Paley, mechanical design in the universe has a remarkable similarity to machines that are known to have been produced by human intelligent agency. And, because similar effects infer similar causes, a divine intelligent agent must have been the cause of the design of natural objects (*Natural Theology* 9-10, 24, 356). Put simply, the argument says

1. Machines, such as watches, ships, and houses, exhibit various levels of complex design as products of intelligent human agents.
2. The universe resembles a machine or machines that exhibit(s) numerous instances of complex design.
3. Therefore, an intelligent agent probably produced the universe; and this intelligent agent is the divine intelligent agent we call God.

Most evaluations of this argument from analogy find the first premise largely self-evident. Accordingly, there is little doubt that humanly constructed machines are intelligently designed. They are "teleological systems," as William Rowe points out, with their parts adapted to ends by human agency (48). However, this is not the case with the second premise, which stresses the resemblance of machines and natural objects of the universe, and the seemingly problematic inference in premise three to a theistic conclusion.

David Hume (1711-76), the argument's most severe critic, objects to the argument in two ways (*Dialogues* 152-87). He defends what can be called the dissimilarity objection and the inference problem, both of which some find satisfying today. The dissimilarity objection, in general, consists in identifying the difficulties in establishing the analogy stated in the second premise. What it claims is that the supposed resemblance between machines of human artifice and natural objects overlooks an abundant dissimilarity. Watches, ships, and houses clearly show design and purpose, but these objects are designed very differently from those of the universe. Because of this, they are not sufficiently similar to justify an inference to a divine, intelligent cause of the universe (144).

It should be noted, however, that this objection ultimately fails. Dissimilarity by itself does not undermine the evidence of the argument for an intelligent agent. The world may not be much like a clock, a ship, or a house, but clocks, ships, and houses are not much like steam engines, computers, or microwaves either. Yet they are still the products of intelligent human agency. So it seems that the kind of dissimilarity that this objection is pointing to is not very effective in overturning the argument (Wainwright 53). There is extensive comparable design between natural objects and human artifacts to establish the evidence for an intelligent designer. And as long as there is sufficient evidence for relevant comparable design, in spite of the dissimilarity at other levels, the argument's force remains.

Closely related to Hume's objection noted above is a second one—the objection from nontheistic naturalistic explanation. What this objection asserts in general is that if the natural objects of the universe can be explained by a natural rather than an intelligent designer, the similarity is again undermined as evidence for a divine intelligent designer of the universe. For Darwin (1809-82), the most forceful exponent of this objection, the natural explanation of design in the universe is biological evolution. In this view, the origin of species, for instance, rather that being similar to the products of an intelligent designer, can be explained by blind biological mechanisms, including (1) variation in species and (2) natural selection in relation to an environment. Accordingly, the characteristics of the species that have the greatest survival value are retained through multiple generations, and those species that have less survival value are gradually extinguished. The result is that, over time, new species develop to the extent that their individual members are naturally selected to survive in competition with other organisms in their common environment.

As neo-Darwinism developed in the 20th century, the account of variation was ultimately explained in terms of genetics (Gould 103). The neo-Darwinian variation necessary for both interspecies and intraspecies evolution was thereby attributed to genetic mutation and gene copy error. The impact of these developments was the apparent undermining of all basis for intelligent design in the biological world and, with it, the undermining of any teleological argument. Darwin himself was moved in this regard to a complete rejection of the teleological argument. He says,

> The old argument from design in Nature, as given by Paley, which formerly seemed to me so conclusive, fails now that the law of natural selection has been discovered. We can no longer argue

that, for instance, the beautiful hinge of a bivalve shell must have been made by an intelligent being, like the hinge of a door by a man. There seems to be no more design in the variability of organic beings, and in the actions of natural selection, than in the course which the wind blows (Darwin *Life and Letters,* Vol. 1, 314; Gaskin 1984, 71).

Even though, historically and scientifically, evolution had tremendous influence in undermining the teleological argument, a whole new set of questions are raised today as to whether Darwin's evolution hypotheses scientifically and philosophically defeat the argument in the final analysis. Not only is biological evolution plagued with crucial questions, but so is biochemical evolution, astrophysics, and cosmology. All have numerous problems that weaken the force of objections to the teleological argument.

The objection from naturalistic explanation, in its broadest form, is the explanation of the universe in its cosmological dimensions, starting with the early moments of the Big Bang continuing through physical, chemical, biochemical, and biological evolution. This is often thought to be a seamless natural evolution from physics to biology, and it is thought that this fact alone is sufficient to defeat the teleological argument. But this claim is increasingly shown to be inadequate. Even if there were a seamless evolutionary explanation of the cosmos, the argument from design really only shifts the argument and its evidence to other features of intelligent design in the universe (Tennent 85). The recent broad-based development of the anthropic design argument does just this. What it points out is that the whole universe is fine-tuned for life, including human life (Denton 381). Accordingly, even for nontheistic scientists (e.g., Stephen Hawking and Sir Fred Hoyle), there is a very small antecedent probability that life would develop in the universe. Yet a vast number of apparently independent conditions necessary for that life did occur, and this infers that an intelligent agent is the probable cause of those boundary conditions. In simple terms, these arguments assert that if something like the Big Bang beginning of the physical universe were a little bigger or a little smaller, the boundary conditions for life would not exist, and life would not have developed. The anthropic design in the cosmos as a whole avoids the objection from naturalistic explanation at the biological evolutionary level by shifting the argument to the cosmological level.

This anthropic design argument, as successful as it may be, still remains vulnerable to objection. This is the possibility that the natural improbabilities of the universe are not so improbable after all. Richard Swinburne points out that if our universe is viewed as just one universe among a trillion universes in a supercosmos, it might be more probable that one universe, presumably ours, would develop the necessary fine-tuning for life (314). Where it is highly unlikely that under purely natural conditions one out of only one universe would develop the 66 boundary conditions that fine-tune the universe for life, it is much more likely that it would develop in a supercosmos of a trillion universes. This is comparable to the improbability of one firing squad completely missing a prisoner, given only one squad. But given a trillion firing squads, the probability that one squad would completely miss is greatly increased.

Yet there is a good answer to the objection postulating a supercosmos of a trillion universes. We have no good evidence that such a supercosmos exists. The argument that a fine-tuned universe can be naturalistically explained because of the possibility of a trillion universes does not make that naturalistic explanation any more probable. There must be more than the possibility of such a supercosmos of universes. Only if a supercosmos has some probability of existing would the naturalistic account be more probable.

Even if this anthropic design does not work, there are still other recent developments of the teleological argument that show much promise in overturning nontheistic evolutionary explanations of the universe. One such answer to the objection from nontheistic explanation is found at the chemical level. Here, evolution has a seemingly intractable problem of showing how life arose out of inorganic chemistry. The bases for life in the universe are the biomacromolecules, in particular DNA. In order for such complex molecules to naturally evolve, it must be possible for a reaction of inorganic chemicals to produce them in the circumstances of prebiotic earth.

The problem with this, however, is that no experiments, which make realistic assumptions about the prebiotic conditions of earth, have yet established convincing evidence for the natural chemical development of these macromolecules of life (Bradley and Thaxton 175). Beyond the problem with the chemical evolution of life, Michael Behe argues that the irreducible complexity of the cell's biochemical machinery also makes biochemical evolution of that cellular machinery largely impossible. Irreducible complexity, Behe says, is "a single system composed of several well-matched, interacting parts that contribute to the basic function, wherein the removal of any one of the parts causes the system to effectively cease functioning" (39). If the biological system of the cell does not minimally have all the parts to perform the function of the system, the system cannot be selected for survival because its function does not exist. Behe argues that this irreducible complexity exists in the mechanisms of blood clotting, the cilium, and the bacterial flagellum. This irreducible complexity, Behe contends, makes their design impossible on the basis of biochemical evolution alone (chaps. 5—7).

It should be noted that these three responses to nontheism's naturalistic explanation are not just arguments for the insufficiency of evolution-ary explanation. They are abductive arguments for intelligent design. In other words, they are not "god of the gaps" arguments in which an ex-traordinary explanation is given when an ordinary one will suffice (Demb-ski 1999, 238-45). Rather, they seek to establish scientifically the best ex-planation of the apparent design features in the universe, including those of cellular machinery, the biochemistry of life, and the anthropic fine-tun-ing of the universe, as requiring an intelligent cause. Like the earlier ver-sion of the argument given by Paley, this argument asserts that, at impor-tant levels in the design and development of the universe, there is a sufficient probability that the design is intelligently caused. Unlike the ear-lier version, this argument develops a precise formulation of the nature of that intelligent design. According to the earlier version, all that was re-quired for the intelligent design was the presence of a "teleological sys-tem," wherein parts are adapted to some end. But as the present intelligent design theorists point out, mere teleology is not enough for establishing intelligent design (Behe 205-8; Dembski 1999, 122-52). For instance, bio-chemical systems of the cell will likely be intelligently designed while subcellular systems may not be, or at least there may not be strong enough evidence that they are intelligently designed (Behe 205).

What is needed for the argument, these recent intelligent design the-orists suggest, is a sufficient account of the criteria for the detection of in-telligent design in the universe. Only with this in place can the abductive argument for intelligent design be established with regard to specific in-stances of design in nature. William Dembski provides the following "complexity-specificity" criterion:

> Whenever we infer [intelligent] design, we must establish three things: *contingency, complexity,* and *specification.* Contingency en-sures that the object in question is not the result of an automatic and therefore unintelligent process that had no choice in its production. Complexity ensures that the object is not so simple that it can readily be explained by chance. Finally, specification ensures that the object exhibits the type of pattern characteristic of intelligence (1999, 128).

The important function of this "complexity-specification" criterion in Dembski's argument is that it reliably picks out intelligent design. When we use it on examples of known intelligent designs, it identifies them as such. When we use it on examples of known instances of unintelligent regularity, it does not select them as intelligent designs.

Yet, as Dembski points out, it might be argued by counterexample that the complexity-specification criterion of intelligent design does not clearly distinguish intelligent design from chance or coincidence. For ex-ample, it might be objected that the Shoemaker-Levy comet, which crashed into Jupiter exactly 25 years to the day after the Apollo 11 moon landing, satisfies the complexity-specification criterion, yet is only coincidence and not intelligent design (1999, 142-43). This would mean that the criterion is not really reliable in picking out intelligent design. But this objection to the criterion does not ultimately succeed, because it does not pay enough attention to the degree of complexity necessary for an event to consist in intelligent design. Dembski argues that assuming "the comet could have crashed at any time within a period of a year and that it [actually] crashed to the very second precisely twenty-five years after the moon landing, a straightforward probability calculation indicates that the probability of this coincidence is no smaller than 10^{-8}" (143). This probability, though small, is not that small compared to the immense improbabilities for the chance developments of various designs in the universe (143). Therefore, the complexity part of the criterion does have the ability to distinguish between coincidence and the improbabilities of truly intelligently designed events.

Applying the criterion to Behe's account of the irreducible complexity of the bacterial flagellum with its acid-powered rotary engine, a stator, O-rings, bushings, and a driveshaft that uses some 50 proteins, the absence of any one of which will destroy the motor function, Dembski asserts that the complexity-specification criterion picks this out as intelligent design, not coincidence or chance (148). The result of all this is that each positive application of the criterion makes probable not just the overturning of the purely naturalistic explanation of these designs, but gives significant rational weight to the abductive conclusion that intelligent design does occur at important levels in the universe.

One remaining objection to the argument from analogy is the inference problem. It consists in the problem of improperly deriving the conclusion from its premises. In the argument under consideration, this consists in improperly proportioning a cause to its affect (Hume, *Enquiries* 136). Accordingly, a divine intelligent agent is not the proportional cause of the design in the natural objects of the universe. The proportional cause may be an intelligent designer, but it is not a divinely intelligent designer as given in the conclusion.

Can this objection be overcome? It is quite apparent that Paley's argument from analogy does not pay attention to this inferential problem. His argument jumps from intelligent cause to God as a person (356). Accordingly, his argument gives us no good reason to think a divine intelligent cause of the intelligent design in the universe exists rather than a mundane intelligent cause of that design. On the other hand, intelligent design theorists do not make this mistake. They pay careful attention to the fact that intelligent design infers only an intelligent cause of the intelligent design in the universe, not a divine intelligent designer of that design. Behe argues, for instance, that irreducible complexity, in certain designs of biochemistry, warrant the design inference to an intelligent cause without establishing the identity of that designer (196). Dembski is careful to point out that "the ontological status of the intelligent designer does not come up in the argument" (277).

Even if the abductive design argument does not display the inference problem that Paley's argument from analogy does, it does fail to make the theistic conclusion probable. By itself, the analogy argument leaves open the question of whether theism is true, and in doing so it fails as an abductive design argument for the existence of God. What is yet needed is evidence that makes a divine intelligent cause more probable than a mundane intelligent one. Can such evidence be developed? In answer to this, it should be noted that even if no further evidence is adduced, the evidence is compatible with the theistic conclusion. It very well could be that the ontological status of the intelligent cause of the design in the universe is that of divine intelligence. But more than this, it is also true that given the evidence, a divine intelligent cause of the intelligent design in the universe is more probable than a purely naturalistic cause of it, as we have seen above. In that sense, the theistic conclusion is more probable than a naturalistic conclusion. But this still does not abductively establish the theistic conclusion of the argument. Evidence that makes a divine intelligent cause more probable than a mundane intelligent cause is still needed. Can this be done?

In answer to this final question it seems clear that much can be done in this direction. Four important criteria for picking out divine intelligent agency seem relevant here: (1) transcendence, (2) meticulous engagement, (3) singularity, and (4) immensity. What makes a divine intelligent cause of the intelligent design in the universe more probable than a mundane intelligent cause of that design is any evidence that would make probable the claim that the intelligent cause is transcendent of the universe itself.

The intelligent cause would have to be nonnatural, in the sense that this intelligent cause would be more than the sum of the nondivine causes of the universe. The evidence of the complexity-specification criterion has already largely done that, however. Because intelligent design is not reducible to naturalistic regularity, one should say that it is nonnatural and to that extent transcendent. In addition, the intelligent cause would need some degree of meticulous engagement with the design in the universe, not just at its origin but continuously in the universe's development. Here again, if the various evidences for intelligent design found in the fine-tuning of the universe, in the chemical construction of biomacromolecules and in the biochemistry of the cell are reliable, meticulousness in the intelligent design is also established at important points throughout the process. The result is that these distributed expressions of intelligent design in turn make probable an intelligent agency that is meticulously engaged with the intelligent design in the universe. This is so, of course, only if there is also evidence for a singular intelligent design, rather than a plurality of intelligent designs. This is crucial. Here again the perspective of the anthropic design arguments is helpful in showing that the fine-tuning of the universe for life is a singular process. Each part of the process is necessary for the development of physics, chemistry, and biochemistry. The whole process is evidence for a unified, fine-tuned design for life. This being so makes it probable that the transcendent, meticulously engaged, intelligent cause of the intelligent design in the universe is not a committee of mundane intelligent causes but something very much like a singular divine intelligent cause.

Finally, for the intelligent cause of the design in the universe to be established as a divine intelligent cause rather than a mundane intelligent cause, the evidence would have to make probable an inference to a cause of immense size and power. Here again the evidence is not sufficient to suggest that the intelligent cause is infinitely large or infinitely powerful. But the evidence for intelligent design in the universe does show enough immense proportions, relative to the macroimmensity of the fine-tuned universe as a whole and the microcomplexity of chemistry and biology, that it is probable that the intelligent cause is immense in size and power. An intelligent cause capable of designing at both the macro and micro levels presumably would be significant in both size and power. Although these considerations do not make probable every property that a Christian divine intelligent agent or God would possess, they do go a long distance toward making it probable that a divine rather than a mundane intelligent agent exists as the cause of the design in the universe.

Works Consulted

Aquinas, Thomas. *Introduction to Saint Thomas Aquinas.* Ed. Anton C. Pegis. New York: Random House, 1948.

Barr, James. *Biblical Faith and Natural Theology.* Oxford: Clarendon, 1993.

Behe, Michael J. *Darwin's Black Box: The Biochemical Challenge to Evolution.* New York: Free Press, 1996.

Bradley, Walter L., and Charles B. Thaxton. "Information & the Origin of Life." In *The Creation Hypothesis: Scientific Evidence for an Intelligent Designer.* Ed. J. P. Moreland. Downers Grove, Ill.: InterVarsity, 1994.

Davies, Paul. *The Mind of God: The Scientific Basis for a Rational World.* New York: Simon & Schuster, 1992.

Darwin, Charles. *The Life and Letters of Charles Darwin.* 3 volumes. Ed. Francis Darwin. London: John Murray, 1887.

Dembski, William A. *The Design Inference.* Cambridge: Cambridge University Press, 1998.

_____. *Intelligent Design.* Downers Grove, Ill.: InterVarsity Press, 1999.

Denton, Michael J. *Nature's Destiny: How the Laws of Biology Reveal Purpose in the Universe.* New York: Free Press, 1998.

Gaskin, J. C. A. *The Quest for Eternity.* New York: Penguin, 1984.

Gould, Stephen Jay. "Darwinism and the Expansion of Evolutionary Theory." In *Philosophy of Biology.* Ed. Michael Ruse. 100-117. New York: Macmillan, 1989.

Hawking, Stephen W. *A Brief History in Time.* New York: Bantam, 1988.

Hoyle, Sir Fred. *Religion and the Scientists.* London: SCM, 1959.

Hume, David. *Dialogues Concerning Natural Religion.* Ed. Norman Kemp Smith. Indianapolis: Bobbs-Merrill, 1947.

_____. *Enquiries Concerning the Human Understanding and Concerning the Principles of Morals.* New York: Oxford University Press, 1955.

Kenny, Anthony. *The Five Ways: St. Thomas Aquinas' Proofs of God's Existence.* London: Routledge & Kegan Paul, 1969.

McPherson, Thomas. *The Argument from Design.* New York: Macmillan, 1972.

Paley, William. *Natural Theology.* New York: American Tract Society, n.d.

Plato. *The Collected Dialogues of Plato Including the Letters.* Ed. Edith Hamilton and Huntington Cairns. Bollingen Series LXXI. Princeton, N.J.: Princeton University Press, 1961.

Rowe, William. *Philosophy of Religion: An Introduction,* rev. ed. Belmont, Calif.: Wadsworth, 1993.

Swinburne, Richard. *The Existence of God,* rev. ed. New York: Oxford University Press, 1992.

Tennent, F. R. *Philosophical Theology.* Vol. 2, *The World, the Soul, and God.* London: Cambridge University Press, 1968.

Wainwright, William J. *Philosophy of Religion.* Belmont, Calif.: Wadsworth, 1988.

Xenophon. *Memorabilia.* Ed. Gregory Crane. The Perseus Digital Library. Available from http://www.perseus.tufts.edu/cgi-bin/ptext?lookup=Xen.+Mem.+1.4.1 Accessed 10 January 2001.

ONTOLOGICAL ARGUMENTS

Robert J. Thompson

◆

"Fools say in their hearts, 'There is no God'" (Ps. 14:1, RSV). On this Psalm, Anselm (1033—1109), the 11th-century Archbishop of Canterbury, meditated and developed the most subtle and intriguing, yet puzzling and vexing, of the traditional arguments for the existence of God—the ontological argument. The ontological argument (*ontos* [gk. being] + *logos* [gk. word(s)] = words about, or study of, being; hence, argument from being) was not so named by Anselm. The argument received its name from great German philosopher Immanuel Kant (1724—1804), who observed that the argument inferred the existence of God *"a priori,* from concepts" alone (1965, 500 [A591/B619]). There is no unanimity among scholars that what Anselm penned consists of an argument *per se,* as opposed to a prayer or spiritual meditation, although Anselm represents it as an argument in subsequent discussion (1962, 153), and there are clear patterns of reasoning in the relevant passages.

In any case, Anselm is held to be the originator of this particular kind of theistic argument. Therefore, we begin our study of the ontological argument by looking at Anselm's most famous version along with a critique of that version offered by one of his contemporaries, the monk Gaunilo. Furthermore, because Anselm is not the only one in the history of thought to offer an argument from being for the existence of God, we follow our treatment of his first proof with a section dealing with subsequent versions that René Descartes, Benedict de Spinoza, and Gottfried Wilhelm Leibniz offer. Coupled with these arguments are various critiques, including what is perhaps the most devastating critique by Immanuel Kant, that have been offered against the argument. Finally, we take a look at contemporary versions of the argument, especially those that claim to find in Anselm a second form of the argument—one that does not suffer from the flaws of the first and more famous version.

I. ANSELM'S ARGUMENT: ANSELM, GAUNILO, AND THE FOOL

Anselm argues in *Proslogium,* chapter 2, that in order to deny the existence of God, the fool must first understand the idea of God. This idea, according to Anselm, is none other than the idea of a being than which none greater can be conceived. And further, because the fool understands his or her idea of a being as one than which none greater can be conceived, it must exist in his or her understanding. In order to deny the existence of God, the idea of a being than which none greater can be conceived must first exist in the understanding of the fool. From this, Anselm reasons in this way:

> Assuredly that, than which nothing greater can be conceived, cannot exist in the understanding alone. For, suppose it exists in the understanding alone: then it can be conceived to exist in reality; which is greater.
>
> Therefore, if that, than which nothing greater can be conceived, exists in the understanding alone, the very being, than which nothing greater can be conceived, is one, than which a greater can be conceived. But obviously this is impossible. Hence, there is no doubt that there exists a being, than which nothing greater can be conceived, and it exists both in the understanding and in reality (1962, 8).

Anselm is here making use of a common argument form: namely, that of *reductio ad absurdum*. He is assuming for the sake of argument that the idea of God—a being than which none greater can be conceived—exists in the understanding alone as a *mere* idea. From this assumption, Anselm proves a contradiction that, according to the rules of formal logic, necessitates the denial of his assumption. The being than which none greater can be conceived cannot exist as an idea alone and must also exist in reality. For ease of reference, I will formalize Anselm's argument as follows:

1. A person can have the idea of a being than which none greater can be conceived.
2. Now, suppose this being exists only as an idea in the mind.
3. Existence in reality is greater than mere existence in the mind.
4. Therefore, we can conceive of a being that is greater than a being than which none greater can be conceived—that is, a being that also exists in reality.
5. But this is absurd, for there can be no being that is greater than that being than which none greater can be conceived.
6. Therefore, the being than which none greater can be conceived must exist in reality as well as in the mind. This being is God.

The argument appears valid, so it only remains to determine whether or not the argument is sound—that is, whether or not the premises are all true and so justify the conclusion that God exists in reality as well as an idea in the mind. If Anselm's argument ultimately holds, he has proven the existence of God by reflecting solely on the idea of God.

As one might expect, not everyone agrees that Anselm's argument holds up under scrutiny. Even so, although there seems to be something suspicious about an argument that begins with a mere idea of a thing and then ends with the existence of that thing in reality (especially when the thing in question is God), it is notoriously difficult to discern precisely where the flaw lies in Anselm's argument. Many have tried to find this flaw, including one of Anselm's contemporaries, Gaunilo, the monk from Marmoutier.

Little is known of Gaunilo, or Gaunilon, apart from his disagreement with Anselm. He was a Christian—that much is clear—so he did not resent Anselm's conclusion. Instead, Gaunilo found fault with Anselm's way of arguing for his conclusion. Taking his cue from the same Psalm that served as Anselm's springboard, Gaunilo wrote *On Behalf of the Fool,* in which he offered several criticisms against the sufficiency of Anselm's argument to prove God's existence. We will look at two of the more important criticisms here.

Because Anselm's argument appears valid, an obvious method of critique is to question one or more of the argument's premises. This is precisely what Gaunilo does when he denies the truth of Anselm's first premise. As far as Anselm is concerned, the first premise merely represents the state of affairs necessitated by the fool's denial of God's existence. To make sense of the fool's denial of God's existence, i.e., in order for the denial to be *meaningful,* one must assume that the fool can conceive of God. Without the possibility of such a conception, the term "God" would be devoid of any meaningful content and, therefore, the fool's statement would be nonsense. Gaunilo, however, argues that one cannot conceive of a being than which none greater can be conceived, because one cannot conceive of God (1962, 148-49).

On the face of it, Gaunilo's claim seems counterintuitive. If Gaunilo is correct, every utterance that makes use of the term "God" ends up being nonsensical. Common experience seems to indicate that one can meaningfully talk about God. Nevertheless, Gaunilo argues that there is no justification for such an intuition. The being in question, God, is unlike any other being in reality. Moreover, Anselm must allow that the fool has had no direct experience of God, lest the question be begged. Now, the fool can surely conceive of possible humans, because the fool has experienced real humans. The fool extrapolates from experience of real humans that possible humans will likely have two legs, two arms, be minimally reasonable, and so on. In fact, the fool can even conceive of certain nonexistent entities, like unicorns. Such conceptions are possible if the fool has experienced things like horses and horns. In such cases, the fool may simply join those experiences and their correspondent notions together to compose the conception of a unicorn. With God, however, the fool has no such experience, whether of God directly or out of which to compose a conception of God indirectly. Therefore, the fool has nothing on which to base his or her conceiving; i.e., the content of the fool's conceiving is vacuous. Hence, Anselm's first premise is faulty, because it assumes that the fool *can* conceive of a being than which none greater can be conceived, when the fool cannot. Because the fool cannot entertain a conception of God, the first premise is false, and Anselm's argument fails.

In his response to Gaunilo's critique, Anselm admits that a *complete* conception of God is impossible. But he denies that a complete conception is necessary for his argument. According to Anselm, while one can never have a complete understanding of God, one does (or can) know enough about God to know that deity is that being than which none greater can be conceived. Indeed, this is one of the more obvious qualities contained in the notion of God. Should the fool deny that God exists, he or she needs merely to reflect on the notion of God (incomplete though it is) to know that God is that being than which none greater can be conceived and so must exist in reality as well as in the mind. Furthermore, Anselm reasons, if Gaunilo is correct that the conception of God is impossible, his argument is literally nonsense and lacks any force. If, however, Gaunilo's argument is meaningful, it still lacks force. On Gaunilo's own account, after all, his argument must fail if it is to have meaning. In other words, Gaunilo's critique is incoherent (1962, 153-56).

Gaunilo's second criticism is more troubling. Rather than attacking any particular premise, he contends that the argument can be used to prove the existence of all sorts of fanciful things, e.g., a perfect island or, as a student once offered, a perfect date. Gaunilo writes,

> It is said that somewhere in the ocean is an island, which . . . is called the lost island. And they say that this island has an inestimable wealth of all manner of riches and delicacies in greater abundance than is told of the Islands of the Blest.
>
> Now if some one should tell me that there is such an island, I should easily understand his words, in which there is no difficulty. But suppose that he went on to say, as if by a logical inference: "You can no longer doubt that this island which is more excellent than all lands exists somewhere. . . . For if it does not exist, any land which really exists will be more excellent than it; and so the island already understood by you to be more excellent will not be more excellent" (1962, 150-51).

Now, if the same form of argument can be used to prove the existence of things that are known not to exist, Gaunilo wonders who he "ought to regard as the greater fool: [himself], supposing that [he] should allow this proof; or [his dialogue partner], if he should suppose that he had established with any certainty the existence of [the] island" (1962, 151). The answer is obvious. The conclusion of Gaunilo's counterexample, namely, that a nonexistent island exists, is absurd and indicates that one should not rely on the form of argument that Anselm employs. Gaunilo is urging that the argument is invalid after all.

At first glance, Anselm's response may appear to be picky. He points out that Gaunilo has not argued in parallel when he argues for the existence of the greatest island. Gaunilo's counterexample concerns what is *in fact* the greatest island, while Anselm's argument concerns that being than which none greater can be *conceived*. The difference between fact and conceivability, however, is actually quite important and will be discussed in some detail later. So because Gaunilo's argument is not exactly parallel, his counterexample fails to undermine Anselm's argument.

But suppose one were to fix Gaunilo's example. What if one were to change the island in the argument from that which is in fact the greatest island to the greatest conceivable island? Would it work then? Not obviously. For the sorts of things that make islands great or greater, e.g., number of coconuts, number of Tahitian dancers, amount and consistency of sand, and so on do not admit of a maximal limit, unlike the characteristics of God. That is, no matter how many of these sorts of things one can imagine on the greatest conceivable island, one can always imagine one or two more. It would seem that the notion of a greatest conceivable island is incoherent—Gaunilo's attempt at a counterexample fails, and Anselm's argument emerges unscathed (Plantinga 1974a, 90-91).

Although the criticisms leveled by Gaunilo against Anselm fall short of refuting the ontological argument decisively, many have continued to feel squeamish concerning the nature of an argument that moves from an idea of a being in the mind of a fool to the existence of that being in reality. This is especially the case when the being turns out to be God. Thinking about God should not mean that God exists any more than thinking about Tinkerbell means that fairies exist. At least that is how the intuition seems to go. Even so, as Gaunilo found, it is notoriously difficult to find the fatal flaw in Anselm's proof. Moreover, many subsequent scholars have purported to find a second, and different, ontological argument offered by Anselm in *Proslogium,* Chapter 3. But prior to looking at what contemporary philosophers have said about Anselm's second argument, we must first examine how other figures in the history of philosophy have used versions of the ontological argument to prove the existence of God and how subsequent critics have challenged them and, by association, Anselm.

II. ARGUMENTS MULTIPLY, REALIZED, AND CRITICIZED: DESCARTES, SPINOZA, LEIBNIZ, AND KANT

Although the ontological argument originated with Anselm, he is not the only philosopher to argue for God's existence using an *a priori* conceptual framework. René Descartes (1596—1650), a French philosopher widely considered to be the father of modern philosophy, offered two arguments for God's existence in his most famous work, *Meditations on First Philosophy.*

The argument we need to examine is found in the *Fifth Meditation.* He argues for the existence of God based on the idea that God is the supremely perfect being. After establishing the truth of clear and distinct perception, he notes,

> The idea of God, or a supremely perfect being, is one that I find within me just as surely as the idea of any shape or number. And my understanding that it belongs to his nature that he always exists is no less clear and distinct than is the case when I prove of any shape or number that some property belongs to its nature (CSM II 1993, 45).

Descartes is explicitly making the point that existence is an essential property of God. An essential property is a property, or characteristic, that some object or kind of object must have in order to be that object or kind of object. For example, an essential property of a triangle is its three sides. A triangle cannot exist, either conceptually or actually, without possessing the property of exactly three sides. Descartes is claiming that, after sufficiently scrutinizing the notion of deity, one will recognize that the property of existence is essential to God.

Descartes immediately notes a potential problem with his claim that existence is essential to God. This is a problem based on the scholastic distinction between essence and existence (CSM II 1993, 46). It had become commonplace in philosophy to distinguish between the essence, or nature, of a thing and whether or not that thing existed. For example, the essence of a unicorn couples equine properties with that of a horn. In fact, given careful consideration, one could come up with the list of all and only the essential properties of a unicorn, thus accounting for its essence, even though unicorns do not exist. The question of its essence is independent of the question of its existence.

With respect to God, and only with respect to God, however, the neat and tidy scholastic distinction between essence and existence fails. The distinction fails precisely because God is the supremely perfect being. Descartes argues in the following way: because God is the supremely perfect being and, therefore, must possess all manner of perfections, and inasmuch as existence is a perfection, because to exist is more perfect than not to exist, God must exist. In other words, because God is the supremely perfect being and existence is a perfection, existence turns out to be one of God's essential properties. The central feature of Descartes' argument is now clear: God *cannot not* exist, because existence is a part of God's essence. In the case of God, essence entails existence (CSM II 1993, 46).

Descartes considers a possible objection to his line of reasoning. Some might initially find it puzzling, Descartes concedes, that an idea in the mind of the meditator entails the existence of God. Some might think it odd that the meditator's thought necessarily imposes the existence of some entity in reality. Descartes responds to this possible objection by arguing that such a construal of the situation is misleading. The thought of the meditator makes no such imposition on reality. Rather, the meditator, who carefully conceives of the nature of the supremely perfect being, cannot help but recognize that this being exists because of the necessity imposed by reality itself. "From the fact that I cannot think of God except as existing," argues Descartes, "it follows that existence is inseparable from God, and hence that he really exists. It is not that my thought makes it so, or imposes any necessity on any thing; on the contrary, it is the necessity of the thing itself, namely the existence of God, which determines my thinking in this respect" (CSM II 1993, 46). Descartes can think of triangles and unicorns without either existing, but he can no more think of God as not existing, so long as he clearly and distinctly perceives the matter, any more than he can conceive of a mountain without a valley. Just as the essence of a mountain entails a valley, the essence of God, that supremely perfect being, entails every manner of perfection, including existence.

Descartes' argument soon found many detractors. When he wrote the *Meditations,* he had his close confidant and correspondent, Friar Marin Mersenne (1588—1648), solicit a total of seven sets of objections. These objections were written by some of the leading thinkers of his day, including Mersenne himself. Descartes followed each with a set of replies. Several of these sets of objections relay concern regarding Descartes' arguments for God's existence, including his ontological argument. One particularly important series of objections, against both the *Third Meditation* and *Fifth Meditation* arguments, was put forward by Johannes Caterus. Caterus, drawing on Thomas Aquinas' critique of Anselm's proof, argues that Descartes has not proved that God actually exists. Rather, Descartes has only proved that the *concept* of God entails the *concept* of existence. Caterus summarizes his response to Descartes as follows:

> Even if it is granted that a supremely perfect being carries the implication of existence in virtue of its very title, it still does not follow that the existence in question is anything actual in the real world; all that follows is that the concept of existence is inseparably linked to the concept of a supreme being. So you cannot infer that the existence of God is anything actual unless you suppose that the supreme being actually exists; for then it will actually contain all perfections, including the perfection of real existence (CSM II 1993, 72).

To first suppose that the supreme being actually exists in order to infer that this being actually possesses the "perfection of real existence" is to beg the question of existence. This is precisely what Caterus is accusing

Descartes of doing. Far from proving the existence of God, Descartes has either proved an unhelpful tautology (a necessary, but trivial, truth), namely, from the actual existence of God one can infer that God exists, or he has begged the question by assuming the truth of the very claim he hopes to prove.

Descartes was undaunted by Caterus' challenge. He does admit, however, of two possible problems with his account. First, he recognizes that the scholastic distinction between essence and existence is ingrained in the thinking of the period, which makes it difficult to gain awareness of the inseparability of existence from God's essence. Second, he recognizes the epistemic insecurity that results from a concern that the essence that one considers be true and immutable rather than a fiction of one's own creation (CSM II 1993, 83). Of course, the latter of these concerns does not ultimately prove problematic for Descartes' argument, because he has admitted that his argument will work only on the assumption that one has a clear and distinct apprehension of God's nature. Because this apprehension is clear and distinct, one's understanding of God's nature must reflect God's real nature. Nevertheless, Descartes does offer further argument in response to these concerns. His response to the first is of special importance here.

In response to the first worry, Descartes holds that one must distinguish between possible and necessary existence. *Possibility* and *necessity* are what logicians call modal concepts, because they are parasitic on the way things could have been and not on the way things actually are, at least not in every case. An example will help. I am currently sitting at my desk. From my desk I can look out over a park behind my house that is covered with a thin layer of snow, because yesterday the temperature never got over 28 degrees Fahrenheit, and the day before that, it snowed most of the day. However, the weather forecast yesterday called for a temperature in the upper 30s to lower 40s. If that temperature had obtained instead of the temperature that actually did, the park outside my house would no longer be covered with snow. This situation can be rendered in explicit modal terms. While it is actually the case that the park outside my house is covered with snow, it is possibly the case that the snow melted and is no longer covering the park. I can look outside my window and see immediately that it is false, that there is no snow covering the park. Even so, it is true that it is possible that there is no snow covering the park, because possibility *does not* entail actuality. We can imagine a situation in which there is now no snow covering the park. In fact, we can imagine quite a few such situations.

Now, actuality *does* entail possibility. It is obvious that the current state of affairs (a snow-covered park) is also a possible state of affairs. So a distinction must be made between what is possible and actual and what is merely possible. What is possible and actual, i.e., the snow-covered park, is termed a *contingent* truth or state of affairs. What is merely possible, i.e., the park with no snow, is simply *possibly* true or a *possible* state of affairs. It is true to say of the current state of affairs that it is also a possible state of affairs. But such a claim is incomplete, because the current state of affairs is also actual and, hence, a contingent state of affairs. The modal notion of necessity can be understood in terms of possibility. If some claim is necessarily true or some state of affairs is necessary, that claim *must* be the case or that state of affairs cannot possibly not be actual or contingent. For example, it is necessarily true that a triangle is a three-sided geometrical figure. It is not possible that a triangle not have three sides. It is necessarily false, however, that a square has only three sides, which means that such is not a possible truth or state of affairs.

Descartes argues that possible existence is contained in any essence that is clearly and distinctly perceived, including the essence of nonexistent things like unicorns and Santa Claus. To say that one clearly and distinctly perceives such an essence does not mean that the thing in question contingently exists—it may merely be possible. In the case of God, however, the modal claim is quite different.

> Possible existence is contained in the concept or idea of everything that we clearly and distinctly understand; but in no case is necessary existence so contained, except in the case of the idea of God. . . . For our understanding does not show us that it is necessary for actual existence to be conjoined with their [ideas of things other than God] other properties. But from the fact that we understand that actual existence is necessarily and always conjoined with the other attributes of God, it certainly does follow that God exists (CSM II 1993, 83).

Descartes appears to be reasoning in the following manner: when one clearly and distinctly perceives the nature of God, he or she recognizes that necessary existence is contained in God's nature. Therefore, God must exist and so certainly contingently exists. However, a confusion arises later in his response when he writes,

> First, possible existence, at the very least, belongs to [the supremely perfect being]. . . . Next, when we attend to the immense power of this being, we shall be unable to think of its existence as possible without also recognizing that it can exist by its own power; and we shall infer from this that this being does really exist and has existed from eternity, because it is quite evident by the natural light that what can exist by its own power always exists (CSM II, 85).

Here an ambiguity is evident in Descartes' reasoning. Descartes' first claim is clear enough. Just as any idea that is clearly and distinctly understood entails possible existence, so, too, does the notion of a supremely perfect being, or God. The ambiguity arises when one attempts to figure out what Descartes means when he says that the supremely perfect being "can exist by its own power" and so "always exists."

The obvious response, based on this passage, is that the being in question "has existed from eternity" or has eternal existence. But eternal existence—the kind of existence that an object has if it must exist at all times previous, present, and future—is quite different from necessary existence. Descartes appears to be guilty of a confusion, or equivocation, between eternal existence and necessary existence in his response to Caterus. If he has only shown that eternal existence is a part of the essence of God, Caterus's objection holds. And it does appear that an object's ability to "exist by its own power" entails, at most, eternal existence. But Descartes needs necessary existence in order for his argument to work, so it looks as though the argument fails.

There were other objections to Descartes' argument, but Caterus's looms large among them. Even so, such objections did not forestall others from attempting their own versions of the ontological proof. At least two other modern thinkers made substantive contributions to this line of argument for God's existence and are worthy of brief mention. Benedict de Spinoza (1632-77) and Gottfried Wilhelm Leibniz (1646—1716) both took up the issue, although from different perspectives. Spinoza argued for the existence of God based on the concept of God as that which consists of infinite attribution and infinite essentiality (1994, 85). Because God is absolutely infinite, argues Spinoza, God also possesses "an absolutely infinite power of existence"; hence, God must exist (1994, 91-93). Leibniz, on the other hand, was of the view that both Anselm and Descartes got the argument right, assuming that the being than which none greater can be conceived, or the supremely perfect being, is itself conceivable. A demonstration of the conceivability of God is all that is further called for, and this is precisely what Leibniz purports to prove in *The New Essays Concerning Human Understanding*.

While many, like Gaunilo and Caterus, have found the ontological argument less than convincing, perhaps the greatest objection to the argument is offered by the philosopher who gave the argument its present name, Immanuel Kant. In his most famous work, *The Critique of Pure Reason*, Kant argues that existence is not a real property (or "predicate") and, as such, cannot add to the greatness or perfections of God. Kant thinks that adherents of ontological arguments are guilty of confusing logical with real or determining predicates,

> Anything we please can be made to serve as a logical predicate. . . . But a determining predicate is a predicate that is added to

the concept of the subject and enlarges it. Consequently, it must not be already contained in the concept.

"Being" is obviously not a real predicate; that is, it is not a concept of something that could be added to the concept of a thing. It is merely the positing of a thing, or of certain determinations, as existing in themselves (1965, 504 [A598/B626]).

To say that a thing exists is not the same as saying that a thing has some property, like, say, the property of being red. Rather, to say that a thing exists is to say that that thing, with all its properties, is instantiated or made actual in the world. There is, Kant would argue, no qualitative difference between a $100 bill that is real in concept only and a $100 bill that sits in one's wallet. Now, obviously one would treat them differently and one would prefer the existing bill in his or her wallet to the one that is real in concept only. Nevertheless, one is considering qualitatively identical concepts when considering the actual bill or the merely possible bill. Nothing is added to the content of one's thought—so long as the content of one's thought is only the concept of the $100 bill—when it is said of the bill that it exists in reality. According to Kant, the concept of God does not change whether God is possible or actual. In other words, there is no change in our concept of God by saying that God exists. Therefore, existence can neither be said to make God greater nor add to God's perfections.

This particular critique is prefigured in the objections offered by Pierre Gassendi to Descartes' *Fifth Meditation* argument, and Kant takes it to be a decisive blow to proponents of the ontological proof. But now suppose, for the sake of argument, that existence *does* add to the concept of a thing. Kant argues that such a supposition is not even open to the defender of the ontological proof to begin with, because such a move would render the argument incapable of proving the existence of a supremely perfect being. "By whatever and by however many predicates we may think a thing—even if we completely determine it," says Kant, "we do not make the least addition to the thing when we further declare that this thing *is*. Otherwise, it would not be exactly the same thing that exists, but something more than we had thought in the concept; and we could not, therefore, say that the exact object of my concept exists" (1965, 505 [A600/B628]). Either existence does not add to the concept of a supremely perfect being or it does add to the concept of a supremely perfect being. If it does not add to the concept, there is no motivation to the notion that a supremely perfect being requires its possession. If it does add to the concept, the argument cannot be used to prove the existence of one's exact concept, and so it cannot be used to prove the existence of God.

Kant's objection follows, at least in part, from his particular metaphysical outlook. For instance, Kant claims that "in dealing with objects of pure thought, we have no means whatsoever of knowing their existence, because it would have to be known in a completely *a priori* manner" (1965, 506 [A601/B629]). No form of argument for God's existence, conceived as an *a priori* enterprise alone, will be successful given this understanding of reality. According to Kant, every argument for God's existence must be conceived as an a priori enterprise. Such are Kant's convictions, in any event, and his critique still proves problematic for ontological arguments that rely on the assumption that existence is a property.

III. ANSELM'S ARGUMENT REDUX: CONTEMPORARY FORMULATIONS

If Kant's critique finds its mark, it likely serves to discredit both Descartes' *Fifth Meditation* argument and Anselm's argument found in *Proslogium,* chapter 2, because both rely on the idea that existence is a perfection or property. Even though it may be admitted that Kant's critique is successful, however, one need not close the book on the ontological argument just yet. One need not because contemporary proponents of the argument have found a second version in Anselm's writings. Although there is no evidence that Anselm took himself to be offering more than one argument, one can find a second, and different, argument in *Proslogium,* chapter 3.

Anselm argues that the being than which none greater can be conceived cannot be conceived not to exist and so exists necessarily:

> And it assuredly exists so truly, that it cannot be conceived not to exist. For it is possible to conceive of a being that cannot be conceived not to exist; and this is greater than one that can be conceived not to exist. Hence, if that, than which nothing greater can be conceived, can be conceived not to exist, it is not that, than which nothing greater can be conceived. But this is an irreconcilable contradiction. There is, then, so truly a being than which nothing greater can be conceived to exist, that it cannot even be conceived not to exist; and this being thou art, O Lord, our God (1962, 8-9).

In this argument Anselm is continuing his supposition that God is that being than which none greater can be conceived. To this he adds the notion that it is possible to conceive of a being whose nonexistence is impossible. And this being is greater than a being whose nonexistence can be conceived, the conception of whose nonexistence is possible. From this, Anselm reasons that if that being than which none greater can be conceived can be conceived not to exist, there is a being greater than the being than which none greater can be conceived. Hence, the being than which none greater can be conceived cannot be conceived not to exist— i.e., is a necessary being—and this being is God.

At base, Anselm has denied the possibility of God as a contingent being. If it is not possible that God is a contingent being, there are only two options left: either God is a necessary being, i.e., God's existence is necessary, or God is an impossible being, i.e., the very idea of God is inconceivable. As was mentioned earlier, Gaunilo denied that one can conceive of the being than which none greater can be conceived, and it is now clear why such a denial is so important. Anselm, not surprisingly, disagrees that Gaunilo can deny the conceivability of such a being: "I call on your faith and conscience to attest that this is most false" (1962, 154). And, as was also noted earlier, Anselm does seem to be on firm footing. In other words, it does seem that one can conceive of a being than which none greater can be conceived, or, at least, that such a notion is not self-contradictory. If such a conception is possible *and* if God cannot be a contingent being, God is a necessary being and so necessarily exists.

Charles Hartshorne (1897—2000) and Norman Malcolm (1911-), among others, have argued that God cannot be a contingent being. Agreeing with Gaunilo, Kant, and others that existence is not a predicate or perfection, Malcolm argues that necessary existence, the perfection attributed to God in Anselm's second argument, does not succumb to the Kantian critique. Therefore, the argument that God's existence is necessary can be validly assigned as a predicate or perfection, and thereby increase the greatness, of that being than which none greater can be conceived (1968, 224-25). After providing an exposition and expansion on Anselm's proof, Malcolm gives a summary argument that I will paraphrase, following Alvin Plantinga at one point (1965, 161), as follows:

1. Either God exists or God does not exist.
2. If God exists, God's existence is necessary.
3. If God does not exist, God's existence is impossible.
4. Either God's existence is necessary or God's existence is impossible.
5. If God's existence is impossible, the concept of God is self-contradictory.
6. The concept of God is not self-contradictory.
7. Hence, it is not the case that God's existence is impossible.
8. Therefore, God's existence is necessary (1968, 227).

Malcolm's reconstruction of Anselm's second proof elicited a firestorm of response. One such respondent is Alvin Plantinga (1932-), himself an able-bodied proponent of the ontological argument, who charges that Malcolm's arguments for premises 2 and 3 are invalid, so those premises are unjustified, and his argument fails. Briefly stated, Plantinga notes that Malcolm needs both premises 2 and 3 in order to generate premise 4. However, Malcolm proves neither 2 nor 3. According to Plantinga, Malcolm argues from the statement *necessarily God never has and never will come into existence* and the antecedent of premise 3, *God does not exist,* to the consequent of premise 3, *God's existence is not possible.* However, all that follows from the statement and antecedent is that God never will exist. In other words, the only conditional statement that Malcolm can validly deduce is the following: (3') *necessarily if there is a time at which God does not exist, there is no subsequent time at which God does exist.* But 3' cannot do the logical work of 3 in Malcolm's argument, so the argument fails. The reason Malcolm cannot rework his argument in light of 3' is that 3'· leaves open the possibility of God's existence being contingent, but this is precisely what 2 and 3 deny (Plantinga, 1965).

While Plantinga's critique is devastating for Malcolm's argument, there are other reasons to think that Malcolm's reconstruction of Anselm's second proof fares no better than Anselm's first proof. For example, one might deny premise 6 and argue with Gaunilo that the concept of God is self-contradictory, or inconceivable. Indeed, as was mentioned earlier, German philosopher Gottfried Wilhelm Leibniz held that the conceivability of God, i.e., the logical consistency of the concept of God, was the great unjustified assumption of both Descartes' and Anselm's arguments.

Far from being an antagonist with respect to the ontological argument in general, Alvin Plantinga has offered his own version in *The Nature of Necessity,*

1. It is possible that the property of possessing unsurpassable greatness is exemplified.
2. Necessarily a thing possesses unsurpassable greatness if and only if it possesses maximal excellence in every possible state of affairs.
3. Necessarily whatever possesses maximal excellence is omnipotent, omniscient, and morally perfect.
4. The property that possesses unsurpassable greatness is exemplified in every possible state of affairs (1974b, 216).

While Plantinga's argument is valid, there is some question as to whether or not it is sound. The troubling premise is 1: that the exemplification of unsurpassable greatness is possible. Of course, Plantinga and every other theist will consider the premise true. But it is not obviously, or self-evidently, true. Indeed, one can deny it without pain of contradiction. For this reason, Plantinga concedes that the argument does not prove its conclusion, though it does make belief in God reasonable (1974a, 112). So although not the knockdown argument proving the existence of God that it was meant to be, the ontological argument, as Anselm first stated it and with certain contemporary modifications, does make belief in the existence of God a rational position.

CONCLUSION

Anselm's ontological argument for the existence of God stands as one of the most impressive monuments to human reason and philosophic speculation found throughout the history of Western philosophy. And yet it was penned by a philosopher who was first a person of the Church: a philosopher who sought faith before seeking understanding. Beginning with the mere idea of a being than which none greater can be conceived, Anselm sought to establish the existence of that being in reality as well.

There is something undeniably suspicious about moving from mere existence in the mind to existence in reality. Even so, of all the theistic "proofs," the ontological argument has stood the test of time and the criticism of its opponents. And it remains today the easiest to deny but the most difficult to refute. While it may well be that the ontological argument ultimately fails to successfully prove the existence of God, the various attempts by Anselm, Descartes, Malcolm, Plantinga, and others do provide some manner of justification for religious belief. Their thought serves to make the theistic position a reasonable one.

Sources and Recommendations

Alston, William. "The Ontological Argument Revisited." In *Descartes: A Collection of Critical Essays*. Ed. Willis Doney. London: Macmillan, 1967.

Descartes, René. *Meditations on First Philosophy and Objections and Replies.* In *The Philosophical Writings of Descartes.* Vol. 2. Ed. and tran. Cottingham, Stoothoff, and Murdoch. Cambridge, England: Cambridge University Press, 1984.

Hartshorne, Charles. *The Logic of Perfection.* LaSalle, Ill.: Open Court Publishing Co., 1962.

_____ and William Reese. *Philosophers Speak of God.* Chicago: University of Chicago Press, 1953. Chicago: Midway Reprint, 1976.

Hume, David. *Dialogues Concerning Natural Religion.* Indianapolis: Hackett, 1980.

_____. *A Treatise of Human Nature.* Ed. Selby-Bigge. New York: Oxford University Press, 1978.

Kant, Immanuel. *Critique of Pure Reason.* Tran. N. Kemp Smith. London: Macmillan, 1929. New York, N.Y.: St. Martin's, 1965.

Malcolm, Norman. *Anselm's Ontological Arguments.* In *Philosophy of Religion: A Book of Readings.* 2d ed. Ed. Abernethy and Langford. New York: Macmillan, 1968.

Plantinga, Alvin. "Alston on the Ontological Argument." In *Descartes: A Collection of Critical Essays.* Ed. Willis Doney. London: Macmillan, 1967.

Spinoza, Benedict de. *Ethics.* In *A Spinoza Reader: The Ethics and Other Works.* Ed. and trans. Edwin Curley. Princeton, N.J.: Princeton University Press, 1994.

SECTION I, PART V
ATHEISTIC AND NONTHEISTIC ARGUMENTS
Anthony Baker

═══════════════════ ◆ ═══════════════════

Friedrich Nietzsche's *The Gay Science* (1882) contains a parable of a madman who runs out into the streets at dawn with a lantern crying out, "I seek God! I seek God!" His ravings get a lively response from the crowd in the streets, who in between fits of laughter, ask him, "Is God lost?" They continue their teasing: "Has God gone on a voyage? Or is He afraid and hiding?" When the madman can no longer ignore their jabs, he jumps into the middle of the crowd and cries, "Whither is God?" When they are silent, he answers his own question for them:

> I shall tell you. We have killed him—you and I. All of us are his murderers. But how have we done this: How were we able to drink up the sea? Who gave us the sponge to wipe away the entire horizon? What did we do when we unchained this earth from its sun? Whither is it moving now? Whither are we moving now? Away from all suns? Are we not plunging continually? Backward, sideward, forward, in all directions? Is there any up or down left? Are we not straying as through an infinite nothing? Do we not feel the breath of empty space? Has it not become colder? Is not night and more night coming on all the while? God is dead. God remains dead. And we have killed him. What was holiest and most powerful of all that the world has yet owned has bled to death under our knives. Who will wipe this blood off us? (1974, 181).

What are we to make of this tirade? How could a people kill the one responsible for chaining the earth to the sun? How could they "wipe away" the one who established the horizons and gave meaning to all of life? This requiem for God that Nietzsche puts on the lips of a madman is perhaps more a historical observation than an atheistic manifesto. It has come about, he seems to say, that the being whom previous generations named "God" has become obsolete—expendable—in our time. We have done away with God. In effect, we have murdered this God.

The present chapter will investigate various atheisms and denials of God's existence, most of which come from 19th-century contemporaries of Nietzsche. But before investigating their arguments, we must first explicate Nietzsche's parable: How is it possible that where there once was a

God, now God is no longer needed? In other words, what *turn of events* allows us to argue against the existence of God?

I. THE TURN TO (A)THEISM

A preliminary response to this question is simple: arguments *against* the existence of God follow closely the birth of arguments *for* God's existence. As odd as it may seem to us today, it was not always assumed that a thinker abstracted from any theological prejudices could reason his or her way to a verification of a divine being. In fact, in the Middle Ages, philosophical reflections on God were either explicitly or implicitly conditioned by the particular faith community in which they were composed, whether Muslim, Jewish, or Christian. This is the case, for example, with Anselm's "ontological proof," which is written in the form of a prayer to the triune God of Christianity (11th century), as well as Thomas Aquinas's "natural theology," which comes in the midst of "instructions to beginning Christians" (13th century). Both are clear examples of exercises for those who already believe in the God whom they go on to prove exists. "God" in such reflections is not an abstract and universal force whose existence is somehow in question. God is a character in a drama who is named according to His actions in the sacred texts (Qu'ran, Tanach, New Testament) and "proved" according to the way He presents himself in the stories.

At the close of the Middle Ages, however, and especially in the 16th and 17th centuries, major shifts took place in the intellectual climate in the West. On the heels of the scientific revolution, writings began appearing in which the dramatic character whose name is God is replaced by a personality-less *idea* of a divine being. This was accomplished mostly (though not entirely) in the works of Christian philosophers and scientists, which described the universal laws of the natural world as the way in which an omnipotent being keeps the world functioning.

Isaac Newton, for example, who first hypothesized that the tendency of things to fall to the earth is a calculable force present throughout the entire physical world, understood the universe to be a kind of organ by which God watches over creation. Newton explained his work in astrophysics by saying, "If there be an universal life and all space be the sensorium of a thinking being who by immediate presence perceives all things in it . . . the laws of motion arising from life or will may be of universal extent" (quoted in Brooke 1991, 139). Like the medievals Newton's theory begins with a suspended faith-hypothesis: *if* there is an omnipresent being, then X should be the case. Quite new in relation to the medievals, however, is his characterization of this being. This is not a loving God who interacts with and even shows preferences for certain groups of people; Newton's God is primarily a "thinking being" who "perceives all things." The word "God" in such a system names a kind of pulsating brain or unblinking eye. This God, who runs the world by means of advanced calculus, will be precisely as discernible as the world is calculable. God is to be known no longer in the prayers of Anselm but in the equations of anyone capable of doing the math.

These early modern centuries, with their divorce of religious philosophy from faith traditions, mark the beginning of a recognizable *theism*. With the collapse of the name of God into the laws of the natural world, we are moving neither in the world of sacred stories nor in the midst of communities who believe that a transcendent being orders the world. Rather, many modern scholars assumed that a secular reason outside any such community can discover universal laws and conclude that a divine being of some sore enforces them. If the stories and dramatics of Allah, Yahweh, and Jesus Christ were understood to be the means by which a believing community joins with God "as to one unknown" (as Aquinas said), the mechanical and calculable universe of modern science became the site in which the intellectual elite could grasp and comprehend a God wholly immanent within that universe.

It was not long until scientists and philosophers began to ask why, if the universal laws in the foreground were doing such a fine job of running the world, any God was needed behind the scenes at all. Gottfried Leibniz, a contemporary of Newton, already noticed this: "Sir Isaac Newton says that space is an organ, which God makes use of to perceive things by. But if God stands in need of any organ to perceive things by, it will follow, that they do not depend altogether upon him, nor were produced by him" (1715). If divine laws and the laws of physics have become hopelessly entangled such that God looks like an abstract force at work in the natural world, why not collapse the two together? Is it not a more thoroughgoing and critical science to reduce Newton's law-standing-for-God down simply to the law itself? Therefore, rather than "God keeps the planets in motion by the universally present force of gravity," one should simply claim that "gravity keeps the planets in motion." From Leibniz down to the 20th century's Carl Sagan and Stephen Hawking, this reduction has seemed sufficient to erase any need to reference God.

II. A MODERN HISTORY OF ATHEISTIC REDUCTIONS

We have now begun to glimpse just what Nietzsche's madman was proclaiming in the streets. It now remains to inquire briefly into the forms some of these modern atheisms take.

It is important to note at the outset that in reading the texts of the famous modern atheists, one finds that none of them are purely negative in their appraisals of religion. Their arguments never stop at "God does not exist" but go on to say, "What people call God is really X." That is to say, God properly so called *is not,* but X truly is, and *its* existence requires little or no proof. The negative denials, then, actually take the form of *re-placements.* In the following sampling of some of the more prominent atheistic reductions, we will examine the critiques and locate "the values for X" that constitute the positivism of these arguments. The implicit question these discussions raise is this: Is there no great distance between theism and atheism after all?

A. *Materialist Philosophy: God Is an Anthropological Projection.* In 1841 Ludwig Feuerbach published a highly influential philosophy of religion called *The Essence of Christianity.* The text had an impact on both atheistic Marxism and major strands of theology in the 20th century. Feuerbach's argument is, in a single sentence, that the essence of religion is the essence of humanity. When humans posit a belief in a transcendent God, they are not believing in God at all. They are projecting their own nature outward, onto the heavens, and believing in that.

The negative aspect of Feuerbach's claim is the more obvious. Religion is *nothing more than* human consciousness writ large. Religious confidence that God is something that transcends the believer is impossible to sustain: the *object* of belief never reaches beyond the *subject.* "Such as are a man's thoughts and dispositions, such is his God; so much worth as a man has, so much and no more has his God. Consciousness of God is self-consciousness, knowledge of God is self-knowledge" (1989 [1841], 12).

Feuerbach's critique was launched in large part in response to the most influential Protestant theologian of the first half of the 19th century, Friedrich Schleiermacher. According to Schleiermacher, the "proof" of religion is found in the consciousness of the human being and, in particular, in the deep undeniable feeling of dependence that lies in the heart of each individual. If we understood this feeling better, Schleiermacher says, we would see it as a "God-consciousness," a God-shaped hole in our human experience. That such a hole exists, he claims, is not a matter for debate. Introspection—a deep and honest self-searching—will reveal to each individual that underlying all self-confidence and abilities is this "feeling of utter dependence."

Schleiermacher's proof from experience is recognizably a repetition of the theistic formula that begins from a neutral space in the attempt to find enough evidence to demonstrate the reality of a divine being. In this case, introspection is the necessary means to discovery. If the introspector does his or her work critically, he or she will uncover within a feeling that points outside of him or her to a transcendent being. Yet once again, this argument is only a short step away from atheism: if a feeling points unproblematically to *something* on which we depend, what is keeping us from substituting a term for God into the equation? Why not say that individuals feel a dependence on humanity? After all, Schleiermacher's theology is at heart an anthropology (*God* is to be found in a *human* feeling). Why not draw the conclusion, with Feuerbach, that theology is *nothing but* anthropology? If Schleiermacher is right, Feuerbach says, then atheism is the secret of religion itself.

There is, however, also a positive side to Feuerbach's critique, as he himself insisted. His project was not at all to *abolish* religion but to reveal its true essence. Unlike animals, he says, who can be conscious of themselves and others only individually, humans have the unique ability to make their own species an object of thought. In being conscious of humanity as such, the individual consciousness has before it the essence of something greater than itself. Faced with his or her own limitations, an individual nonetheless remains conscious of his or her species-essence and thus of the infinite creative capacity in which he or she shares. This species-essence becomes the true site of religious affections that are wrongly identified with a transcendent God. Humanity becomes the true seat of the name "God." "Let it be remembered," says Feuerbach, "that . . . religion itself, not indeed on the surface, but fundamentally, not in intention or according to its own supposition, but in its heart, in its essence, *believes in nothing else than the truth and divinity of human nature*" (1989 [1841], xvi).

The notion of an unchanging species-essence was ironically, in Feuerbach's day, the central thesis of natural theologians who considered the unalterable design of organisms to be proof for the existence of a divine designer. Pre-Darwinian evolutionary hypotheses were already challenging the idea that a static biological essence determines individual characteristics, and the notion of a species-essence is now almost universally considered untenable. Moreover, the idea that this species-essence might be hard-wired into the consciousness of each of its individual members, at least for humans, renders Feuerbach's thesis problematic. What are the grounds for suggesting that a human being is conscious not only of himself or herself but of the infinite creative capacity of human essence? Has Feuerbach done anything more than replace the God-shaped hole in the human heart with a species-shaped hole?

Karl Marx, who accepted from Feuerbach the notion that religion is simply a human projection, nonetheless believed him to have failed precisely in this resort to species-essence. What Feuerbach succeeded in doing, Marx said, was not abolishing the religious sphere but exalting the secular into its own sort of transcendence. "The secular foundation lifts itself and establishes an independent realm in the clouds," argues Marx, thereby constituting a "self-contradiction of this secular basis" (1888,

305). The idea of a species-essence inherent in each individual human being turns out, then, to be an abstraction. Despite his best efforts, Feuerbach was not describing a "real" human condition at all. He was describing an idealistic secular theology available only for those who put faith in such abstractions.

For his own part, Marx held that religion is wholly a human construction. It arises when humans find themselves in situations in which illusion is preferable to reality. For instance, when humans become the property of others, as happens in particular in capitalistic societies, they turn to illusion (1844b). Members of the working class (the proletariat), confined to play roles of servitude in order to survive, spend their entire lives creating products that are immediately taken from their hands and exchanged to bring profit to the business owners in the higher classes. Marx describes this condition as *alienation:* to have one's own lifework—and therefore one's life—exchanged on the market for the profit of another. Religion takes the form of a passive protest against these oppressive forces. Under the unbearable weight of reality, religion hopes for a better world. "Religion," says, Marx, "is the sigh of the afflicted creature, the soul of the heartless world, as it is also the spirit of spiritless conditions. It is the *opium* of the people" (1844a, 286).

We must not overlook Marx's own version of quasi-religious optimism, however. The positive thrust of Marxism is its unwavering confidence in *critical philosophy.* If conditions of labor and social injustice produce religion, Marx emphatically affirmed that religion's rigorous critique would abolish the need for this opium and establish a society in which alienation ended. "The criticism of religion ends with the doctrine that man is the highest being for man" (1844a, 287). This critique would take the form of the identification *and denial* of alienation by putting the theories of social justice into practice. Marx referred to his atheistic materialism as "the poetry of the future" (1852)—a call to the kind of revolutionary activity that would actually create an earthly paradise. Marxist's practitioners, we might say, were secular evangelists preaching their gospel of an earthly heaven and going forth with confidence that their active criticism would answer philosophy's call to change the world.

Despite their differences, Feuerbach and Marx both believed that religion is an illusion of the masses, and both saw as their task the unmasking of this situation. What men and women commonly call God is a projection of their desire to escape the confines of their own finitude and exist within something greater. Feuerbach, we might say, believed that "something greater" is available simply and universally as the essence of the species called *homo sapiens.* Marx believed that "something greater" must (and *can*) be created by the force of practical and critical philosophy.

B. Sociology: God Is Social Cohesion. More than half a century after Marx wrote his *Theses on Feuerbach,* sociologist Emile Durkheim was working out a theory of religion from a different angle. Most philosophers of religion, he said, develop a theory by analyzing a particular idea of religion *as if it were religion itself.* They never ask whether their particular idea really is the essence of religion or simply the manifestation of a particular religion with which they happened to be familiar. Durkheim proposed that a real analysis of religion be critical especially of the idea itself. To discover what is common to all religions, one should proceed by examining the simplest forms of religion available and assume that the more complex represent advancements on the universal theme.

Accordingly, Durkheim in his *The Elementary Forms of the Religious Life* (1912) turned to the totemic worship of Australian aboriginal tribes. He claimed aboriginal religion to be "the most primitive and simple religion" in the contemporary world (although, it should be noted, Durkheim himself never traveled to Australia). Totemic societies like those of Australia are characterized by belief in clan-specific divinities that come to be symbolized by a particular object in the natural world—most often a plant or animal. This divinity manifests itself in sacred objects, which appear in three sites: first, as the plant or animal itself, second, as human-constructed representations of that object—"totems"—and, finally, as the individuals of the particular society. If the divine figure of a particular intratribal clan is a kangaroo, the object of religious belief will be the kangaroos, the totemic objects (emblems, body decorations, images on coins), and finally the members of the tribes will even refer to themselves as "kangaroos." These three levels of divine manifestation create a society that is strongly bound together in a shared religious practice. Tribal cohesion is stronger, according to Durkheim, even than bloodlines.

This last observation is the case largely because of a further characteristic of these native Australian tribes. The totem takes the form of an authority figure, and each member must obey the moral imperative to live for the good of the totem/clan. At the same time, however, this "moral ascendancy" also creates a sense of empowerment. As each member of a clan considers himself or herself in some sense a real manifestation of the totemic being, membership in a clan entails a certain heightened psychic and moral energy. Emotions, already stirred up by the level of commitment and self-awareness of an individual, play off the similar commitments of the others. The beliefs of the group are exponentially stronger as a whole than are those of any of its members. Durkheim finds support for this group psychology outside aboriginal Australia in such events as the Crusades, in which the energy and commitment of a crowd is obviously greater than the sum of the energy and commitment of its individuals.

"Because [the individual] is in moral harmony with his comrades, he has more confidence, courage and boldness in action, just like the believer who thinks that he feels the regard of his god turned graciously towards him" (1915, 211).

Durkheim claimed that the phenomenon he outlined could be witnessed in the modern world, not only in religious communities, but also in nations. One's country becomes a sort of impersonal divine figure represented totemically by a flag and embodied most strongly by the individuals of that country. Moreover, the "moral effervescence" of citizens is clearly seen in the abstract notion of "patriotism," especially in time of war. Young men and women are not called to die for a piece of cloth or even strictly for their neighbors. They are called to die for their country. In all such cases, the "form of the religious life" can be clearly seen. Individuals feel themselves to be a part of something that exceeds them, and, both out of moral duty and heightened energy, they act for the good of their society.

Unlike the militant tone of Feuerbach and Marx, Durkheim's text is highly implicit in its atheistic reduction. Indeed, a reader might often find himself or herself caught up into the analysis of totemism and forget where the real thrust of the study lies: the religious life, from its most primitive roots to its most complex expression, is ultimately misguided. Every social group bound together by specific rites and beliefs is actually nothing more than a repetition of totemism. That which societies call God is the society itself projected onto the heavens. The sociological study of totemism simply serves as an occasion to observe this mistake at its root. "In order to understand an hallucination perfectly, and give it its most appropriate treatment," says Durkheim, "a physician must know its original point of departure" (7). Modern religions represent nothing more than a complex form of this age-old social practice.

Religion, however, is not *simply* hallucination. Durkheim couches his atheism in the terms of a radical liberalism: "In reality, then, there are no religions which are false. All are true in their own fashion: all answer, though in different ways, to the given conditions of human existence" (3). The force that overwhelms an individual from within is real: it is society. The clan member is, of course, wrong in believing that this strength flows from the plant or animal, but these totems nonetheless become for him or her the personification of the moral force of the society. Religion, then, is quite right in its chief notion: "It is an eternal truth that outside of us there exists something greater than us, with which we enter into communion" (226). Religious folks are simply wrong to project the referent of this "something" into the supernatural or transcendent. Cultic practices are not meaningless, because their *apparent* function is to attach the believer to God. But they *actually* serve to bind an individual to his or her society.

For Durkheim, sociology itself is a "positive science," whose task is the analysis of cultures to reveal something about *humanity as such*. Ultimately, Durkheim is forced to take one of two positions: either he must admit that his research in Australian totemism is an analysis of social bonds in *certain religious communities,* or he must leap out of grounded science into speculation and reduce *all religions* to this single "primitive form." Given this option, Durkheim's move is clear: "If we have taken [totemism] as the subject of our research, it is because it has seemed to us better adapted than any other [religion] to lead to an understanding of the religious nature of man, that is to say, to show us *an essential and permanent aspect of humanity"* (1-2). Like Feuerbach, then, Durkheim makes uncritical assumptions about the essence of humanity, and, in spite of his claim to go beyond such arguments, ends up accepting his discovery as somehow a paradigm for the essence of religion itself. It is beyond the bounds of his considerations, for instance, that humanity itself might be something besides a permanent grouping and that "society" may not be a static category. Contemporary sociologists, in fact, are generally resistant to these very essentialisms.

The positive substitution of Durkheim's negative verdict on the question of God is that "God" is a name given to the glue that binds religious communities together—not simply certain communities in certain contexts, but each and every religious community that will ever be. In the conclusion of his work, Durkheim argues against the Marxist notion that religion is bound to disappear. He believes that as societies grow stronger, the need for social cohesion and moral zeal from within will only increase and so will the commitment and energy of its religious life.

C. Psychoanalysis: God Is Neurosis. Around the turn of the 20th century, Sigmund Freud, the father of psychoanalysis, developed an elaborate theory of religion that borrowed substantially from the research of Feuerbach, Marx, and Durkheim. Like them, he believed religion to be a human projection but not primarily of a species-essence, alienated self, or need for social cohesion. Instead, Freud believed religion to be about the guilt, fear, and insecurity that were formerly repressed and dormant in the human psyche. An individual's conscious self (ego), according to Freud, when faced with overwhelming obstacles to the fulfillment of its own wishes, responds with a controlling mechanism (superego) that buries these wishes in the unconscious (id). The buried memories return, however. And when they do, they take on perverse and neurotic forms. Religion, for Freud, is the name of certain tendencies resulting from this "return of the repressed." The most important repression is the libido of infant sexuality.

This theory begins with the celebrated (and infamous) Oedipus complex, according to which boys pass through an early stage of infant sexuality. In this stage, the boys' connection to their mothers takes the form of sexual arousal. The father enters this relation at first as rival for the love of the mother. But later, because of his vast advantage in strength, the father becomes the feared avenger. Fear of the father is centrally a fear of castration, and the child responds (wisely) by repressing his love for his mother. The period of repression lasts through childhood and into early adolescence, at which time the sexual desire returns, though transformed. Now the child is dominated not by an attachment to the mother but by an identification with the victorious father. The "image of the father" proceeds with his own sexual exploits, repeating the cycle by instilling fear in all his competitors (Freud, 1939).

The actual "discovery" of Freud's most famous theory is highly suspicious, as a letter to a close friend demonstrates: "I have found in my own case too [the phenomenon of] being in love with my mother and jealous of my father, and I now consider it a universal event in early childhood." Freud's vivid imagination seems to run wild after his "discovery." Already we see Freud's self-evident positivism, which suggests that everyone experiences the wish-fulfillment and repression mechanism that he (perhaps) discovered in his own memory.

In order to turn the Oedipus complex into a theory of religion, Freud relied on a version of the same precritical biological hypothesis that Feuerbach supported, namely, that individuals somehow encapsulate their entire species. Freud began with the supposition that each individual recapitulates the species' history. He went on to an exotic speculation that took the form of a universal Oedipus narrative. In humanity's prehistory, he speculated, society consisted of "primal hordes"—groups of women dominated by single males. These males banished all other males, including their own offspring (1913). The single male had, of course, all sexual rights to the women of the horde. At the dawn of history, the speculation continues, the sons of the father rose up and destroyed the father, consumed his body, and took the women of his horde as their own. They each assumed the role of the father. Of course, now there were many, and the earlier autocratic structure of social cohesion was no longer possible. The fragmented image of the father and the threat of social collapse that it brought, as well as the guilt felt by the sons for the murder, led to the projection of the father's image on a totem animal. The totem, according to Freud, was simultaneously the symbol of the tribe and of the father figure. To honor the father as well as to ensure the coherence of the group, the society instituted a festival during which the sacred animal could be killed and eaten, just as the sons had consumed the father.

Religion for Freud, therefore, consists in the recapitulated participation in this prehistoric event. The father figure, who was first of all feared and respected, then envied, and finally overcome, is the one before who all stand guilty. Buried deep with the id of each member of the human race is this fear, envy, and guilt that constantly seeks an image of the father on which to project itself. All the neurotic rituals of world religions (especially, though not exclusively, the Christian sacrament of communion) can be traced back to the totemic practices of this primeval horde.

That Freud would be criticized for the unscientific character of his hypothesis will come as no surprise. His writings often have the character more of elaborate fictions than scholarly theories. For our purposes, the positive character of his atheism should already be clear. First, he requires the same biological essentialism that we saw in Feuerbach and Durkheim. Further, his exotic narrative serves to replace faith-narratives that are no more far-fetched. In place of the transcendent God of his own Jewish tradition, Freud places the primal murdered father. In place of the temple cult of ancient Israel, he places the ritualizing of neurosis. Finally, the "universal key" of all psychic activity is found, famously, in libido and wish-fulfillment. Religion is ultimately the fulfillment of a (prehistoric) wish to identify closely with our fathers, which itself is the fulfillment of a wish to penetrate our mothers.

D. Natural Science: God Is Universal Law. In the Western Hemisphere, especially in the United States, Charles Darwin's *The Origin of Species by means of Natural Selection* (1859) tops most lists of atheistic manifestos. The godless-universe hypotheses that trace their heritage to this text have outlasted the others which we have discussed. Darwinism stands in mainstream culture as a widely accepted argument against the existence of God. The irony of this observation is that atheism is nowhere mentioned or even implicitly defended within the pages of Darwin's book. At the time of its publication, its author was struggling between the Anglican heritage of his family and the deism of British intellectual culture. While it is true that later publications, especially *The Descent of Man* (1871) began to draw out atheism as a logical conclusion of his thesis, even here Darwin could never identify himself unequivocally as an atheist.

The thesis of the *Origin* is remarkably simple: all of the species currently populating the earth have emerged as a result of an endless struggle for survival. As all organisms are in constant competition for a limited supply of food, water, oxygen, and space, nature will favor those who are born with chance variations offering advantages in this struggle. Woodpeckers, for instance, depend upon their ability to bore into trees in order to reach the worms inside. If a handful of worms in a particular generation happen to have a natural tendency to nest deeper in the trees than their parents, it will be more difficult for the woodpeckers to reach them. And, all other factors remaining consistent, these worms will tend to increase at a greater rate than the others. If a handful of woodpeckers happen to be born with longer and sharper beaks, this results in an advantage in the quest for the now deeply burrowing worms. However, the increase in the latter will be matched by an increase in the former. Assuming that those who eat more will live longer and reproduce more offspring, these conditions will result, after a number of generations and in this particular setting, in a significant alteration in the design of worms and woodpeckers. This is the process that Darwin names *natural selection*. By this method, he speculates that "probably all organic beings which have ever lived on this earth have descended from some one primordial form, into which life was first breathed" (1968 [1859], 455).

The religious implications of Darwin's thesis are obvious: if the biological world evolves by chance variations and the selective power inherent in reproduction, God is not needed to keep things running. This thesis still leaves room for deism, however, according to which God created the world as a sort of perpetual machine and then steps aside. Passages from the *Origin* certainly sound deistic. The rejection of deism, however, is also hinted at by Darwin.

The key to arguments against the existence of God is to be found not in the arguments or texts themselves but in the theological precursors to the atheistic positions. In this respect, Darwin is a paradigm case. Raised on a tradition of British natural theology, he claimed once to have "practically memorized" the central text of this tradition, William Paley's *Natural Theology*. Founded very much in line with Newtonian science, this tradition taught that finding God in the face of nature simply required rigorous investigation and strict adherence to scientific method. Even more than this, however, natural theologians believed that classic attributes of God, such as benevolence, could also be discovered in the way in which the world functions. This belief is illustrated in the subtitle of Paley's text: *Evidence for the Existence and Attributes of a Deity, Collected from the Appearance of Nature*.

If this neutral space is one's starting point (as it was for Darwin); however, it is not difficult to see how the conclusion might be less stable than it appears. For a proof of God's goodness from the goodness of nature is simply waiting for a researcher to come along and *disprove* the same conclusion. This in effect is what Darwin's *Origin* did for the tradition in 1859. In what would appear to be a direct confrontation of natural theology's optimism, he says,

We behold the face of nature bright with gladness, we often see the superabundance of food; we do not see, or we forget, that the birds which are idly singing round us live on insects or seeds, and are thus constantly destroying life; or we forget how largely these songsters, or their eggs, or their nestlings, are destroyed by birds and beasts of prey; we do not always bear in mind, that though food may be now superabundant, it is not so at all seasons of each recurring year (116).

In spite of his own theological confusions, Darwin was already convinced that most proofs of God from the ways of nature require a certain blindness toward the realities of the world. His exhaustive research attempts to correct the situation. Darwin's *Origen* thesis, however, was not entirely pessimistic. His final judgment on the essence of religion was that it marked an early precritical stage in humanity's evolution. Furthermore, it was bound to be *replaced by* science (1871).

The science that would replace religion, however, also has its share of uncritical baggage. First, modern science depends upon a preestablished demand that the natural world is *not* directed to any supernatural end. One must adhere to a scientific method that, while claiming to be purely objective, only counts certain responses as legitimate. Even more, however, we should note again that the very notion of universal law under which Darwin strove to bring the biological sphere was Newton's. And natural law functioned for Newton as the parameters for a theistic universe.

CONCLUSION

This chapter began with the paradoxical proclamation of Nietzsche's madman: not "there is no God" or "God is a figment of our own imaginations," but "God is dead . . . and we have killed him." The madman gives us not so much an argument as an observation. Nietzsche himself had his arguments against the claims of faith—especially Christianity—and explains his atheism in terms similar to both Marx and Darwin. Nietzsche believed religion to be a weakness, an "answer" to life's questions for those who are neither confident to think for themselves nor brave enough to face the harsh realities of the world. Religion, he was fond of stating, is a stage in the evolution of humanity that is bound to be transcended by the "overman"—the one who can rise above the "herd" and seize the reins of his or her own existence.

Nietzsche recognized, however, that the overman is the exception. That one might "rise above" implies that there are still the masses down below, those who prefer to be led by the hand. In this tone, another fictional character, his famous Zarathustra, who comes down from a cave on a mountain and proclaims the news of God's death, offers the following cynical commentary on the reception of his message:

> Verily, I may have taken a hundred words from you and the dearest toys of your virtue, and now you are angry with me, as children are angry. They played by the sea, and a wave came and carried off their toy to the depths: now they are crying. But the same wave shall bring them new toys and shower new colorful shells before them. Thus they will be comforted; and like them, you too, my friends, shall have your comfortings—and new colorful shells (1966 [1892], 96).

This is a prophet with no grand visions about his sermons changing the world. Even if humans give up on the God of their mothers and fathers, he seems to say, they will find new gods, new "toys," that will not long evade their childlike fingers.

We might employ these words of Zarathustra as commentary on the brief history traced in this chapter. New toys, or new *idols,* as Zarathustra also says, emerge: human essence, a poetry of the future, society as such, sexual impulse, universal law. This is the case even for Nietzsche himself, whose bizarre account of the capabilities of the overman is perhaps the most optimistic and "idolatrous" of all.

The question might be whether these figures are properly called atheists at all. Is it not perhaps more to the point to characterize them as "radical" theists, who carry out the implications of theism to an end that their forebears were unwilling to go? Perhaps the decisive moment in the emergence of arguments against God's existence is the point at which faith-narratives gave way to the laboratory-like environment of secular science. As soon as God was a mathematical hypothesis, it was no great leap to offer in place of God a series of algebraic substitutions. There are but new colorful shells washed up on the shore at the feet of children who were not yet finished crying over the one that the tide took away from them.

Texts for Further Reading

Altizer, Thomas J. J. *The Gospel of Christian Atheism.* Philadelphia: Westminster, 1966.

Anselm. *Proslogion* (1076). Trans. F. S. Schmitt. *A Scholastic Miscellany: Anselm to Ockham.* Ed. Eugene Fairweather. Philadelphia: Westminster, 1956.

Aquinas, Thomas. *Summa Theologica* (1256-1276), 3 vols. Trans. Fathers of the English Dominican Province. New York: Benzinger Brothers, 1947.

Ayer, A. J. *Language, Truth and Logic.* 2d ed. New York: Dover, 1946.

Brooke, John Hedley. *Science and Religion: Some Historical Perspectives.* Cambridge: Cambridge University Press, 1991.

Darwin, Charles. *On the Origin of Species by Means of Natural Selection* (1859). Ed. J. W. Burrow. London: Penguin, 1968.

———. *The Descent of Man and Selection in Relation to Sex* (1871). Princeton, Princeton University Press, 1981.

Durkheim, Emile. *The Elementary Forms of the Religious Life* (1912). Trans. J. W. Swain. London: Allen and Unwin, 1968.

Feuerbach, Ludwig. *The Essence of Christianity* (1841). Trans. George Eliot. Buffalo, N.Y.: Prometheus, 1989.

Freud, Sigmund. *Moses and Monotheism* (1913). Trans. Katherine Jones. New York: Vintage, 1939.

_____. *Totem and Taboo* (1939). Trans. James Strachey. New York: Norton and Company, 1962.

_____. *The Future of an Illusion* (1927). Trans. James Strachey. New York: Norton and Company, 1961.

Leibniz, Gottfried. "Mr. Leibniz's First Paper" (1715). *The Leibniz-Clarke Correspondence.* Ed. H. G. Alexander. New York: Philosophical Library, 1956.

Mackie, J. L. *The Miracle of Theism: Arguments for and against the Existence of God.* London: Oxford University Press, 1982.

Marx, Karl. *Contribution to the Critique of Hegel's Philosophy of Right* (1844a). Trans. T. M. Knox. In *The Marx-Engels Reader.* 2d ed. Ed. Robert C. Tucker. New York: W. W. Norton, 1978.

_____. *Economic and Philosophic Manuscripts of 1844* (1844b). Trans. Martin Milligan. In *The Marx-Engels Reader.* 2d ed. Ed. Robert C. Tucker. New York: W. W. Norton, 1978.

_____. *The Eighteenth Brumaire of Louis Bonaparte* (1852). New York: International Publishers, 1975.

_____. *Theses on Feuerbach* (1888). In *The Marx-Engels Reader.* 2d ed. Ed. Robert C. Tucker. New York: W. W. Norton, 1978.

Milbank, John. *Theology and Social Theory: Beyond Secular Reason.* Oxford: Blackwell Publishers, 1990.

Nielsen, Kai. *Naturalism without Foundations.* Buffalo, N.Y.: Prometheus, 1996.

Nietzsche, Friedrich. *The Gay Science* (1882). Trans. Walter Kauffman. New York, Vintage, 1974.

_____. *On the Genealogy of Morals* (1887) and *Ecce Homo* (1908). Trans. Walter Kauffman. New York, Vintage, 1967.

_____. *Thus Spoke Zarathustra* (1892). Trans. Walter Kauffman. New York: Viking, 1966.

Placher, William. *The Domestication of Transcendence: How Modern Thinking About God Went Wrong.* Louisville, Ky.: Westminster John Knox Press, 1997.

Proudfoot, Wayne. *Religious Experience.* Berkeley: University of California Press, 1985.

Russell, Bertrand. *Why I Am Not a Christian.* New York: Simon and Schuster, 1957.

Webster, Richard. *Why Freud Was Wrong: Sin, Science, and Psychoanalysis.* New York: Basic-Books, 1995.

Westphal, Merold. *Suspicion and Faith: The Religious Uses of Modern Atheism.* Grand Rapids: Eerdmans, 1993.

SECTION II

DIVINE ATTRIBUTES

Introduction to Section II

Robert J. Thompson

◆

Human investigation into the nature of the divine often follows closely on the heels of the first glimmering awareness that the divine exists. Rare indeed would be the person who acknowledged the existence of God but cared not what qualities God possessed. It is fitting, then, that this section that deals with the nature of the divine follows the section concerning what manner of justification there might be for belief in the divine's existence. Here the reader will find the concept of *God* filled out; qualities assigned and meaning given to the essence of the being that is said to be.

In "Divine Love," Thomas Jay Oord reflects on the simple assertion that "God is love." Seeking to better understand the kind of love that is being affirmed of God and whether it is being affirmed accidentally or essentially, Oord focuses on the work of two important theologians, Augustine of Hippo and John Wesley, while also turning to the helpful distinctions found in the Greek understanding among the various types of love: *agape, eros,* and *philia.* Ultimately, Oord acknowledges that the simple claim that "God is love" is far more complex than it looks at first blush, but he also argues that the investigation is well worth the effort.

In "Divine Power," Kevin Timpe seeks to settle the age-old question of God's power. By clarifying the ambiguities inherent in the expression "all," Timpe focuses the reader's attention to the salient issues surrounding the claim of divine omnipotence. Timpe considers several contemporary attempts to dissolve the tension between divine power and, for example, the limits of the rational, by losing reference to omnipotence altogether in favor of a more benign power. Finally, Timpe ends his treatment with an investigation of how various formulations of power can affect other qualities of the divine.

In "Divine Presence," Bryan P. Stone begins his exploration with a series of questions, including the thorny issue of the relationship between divine presence and the divine as person. After evaluating various forms of Christian theism, Stone finally argues for an understanding of divine presence and person that embraces the mysterious transcendence of the immanent God-as-Spirit.

In "Divine Knowledge and Relation to Time," Amos Yong tackles the difficult issue of divine foreknowledge and human freedom. After clearly staking out the landscape, Yong turns to the nature of time and God's relation to time. Yong emphasizes the incongruities within the biblical text itself, regarding God's knowledge and human freedom before offering several possible resolutions. He remains aware, however, that each has its own problems and that there is no abatement on the horizon in the debate over divine knowledge and human freedom.

In "Divine Holiness," Michael Lodahl wrestles with the word-concept "holiness" and wonders whether or not such a concept is open to philosophical definition. Lodahl begins his treatment with Rudolf Otto's impressive contribution to the subject, what Otto called the *mysterium tremendum* of the divine, coupled with critiques of Otto's helpful but ultimately truncated picture of holiness. Included both as critique and as important in its own right are the work of Karl Barth and the journey that his own understanding of holiness took from an extreme affirmation of transcendence to a more convivial understanding of transcendence and immanence in partnership with one another. Ultimately, Lodahl turns to another characteristic, divine love, to better understand divine holiness. When viewed in relation to love, holiness ceases to be an emphasis on divine separation or absence and becomes a mysterious nearness and presence.

In "Divine Trinity," Samuel Powell addresses a topic that is often overlooked by philosophers of religion. In his treatment, Powell emphasizes the Trinitarian work of Thomas Aquinas and G. W. F. Hegel while keeping in mind three significant issues that permeate the philosophy of religion: the relationship between reason and revelation, the legitimacy of religious language, and the human potential to know the divine. Powell finds that Aquinas and Hegel have important differences with respect to these three issues but that they agree on the importance of considering the Trinity when addressing the God question. A failure to consider the Trinity when considering the philosophy of religion, Powell argues, is finally a failure to seek to know God as God is.

Divine Love

Thomas Jay Oord

◆

"God is love," writes the author of 1 John (4:8, 16). At least in their devotional expressions, Christians throughout the centuries have claimed that these three words, "God is love," represent the core of how they understand divinity. But the notion that deity and love are inextricably linked is not an exclusively Christian one. Theists of other religions have at least implicitly affirmed the meaning of this simple sentence.

Some philosophers and theologians have ascribed love to God, because they—having been influenced by Anselm of Canterbury (1033—1109)—regard love as a perfection necessary to that being than which nothing greater can be conceived. The greatest conceivable being must love perfectly. When someone in antiquity wished to ascribe perfect love to the greatest conceivable being (God), the words "impeccable" or "omnibenevolent" might be used. Today, philosophers often speak of divine love as "a maximal perfection" vital for conceiving of the maximally perfect being.

This chapter examines the meaning of "God is love." In this examination, various definitions, traditions, theories, and issues are addressed. Presupposed throughout is the affirmation that divine love is maximally perfect.

I. Defining Love and God's Relationship to Love

Ascertaining what someone means by the word "love" is almost as difficult as ascertaining what someone means by "God." As Mildred Bangs Wynkoop has said, love is a notoriously ambiguous "weasel word" (1972). Part of the problem is that, for those who speak English, the one word "love" conveys meanings that other languages employ a variety of words to convey. Sometimes love is understood as a powerful emotion involving an intense attachment to an object and high evaluation of it (e.g., "I love Jerusalem"). Sometimes love is understood to involve active interest in securing the well-being of the other (e.g., "When I feed hungry children, I show that I love them"). Sometimes love is understood essentially to involve relationships involving mutuality and reciprocity (e.g., "Their love for each other grew through years of honest give-and-take interaction"). In addition, because love can be variously defined, philosophers and theologians often speak of various types of love, e.g., *agape, eros,* and *philia.*

Further confusion arises when one fails to identify clearly a love's quality or appropriateness. One prominent philosophical tradition, stretching back at least to Plato and Aristotle, classifies any action whatsoever as a loving action. The quality of each love in this tradition, however, is based upon each love's proper or improper status. If one loves properly, this love is a virtue; if one loves improperly, such love is a vice. The tradition that identifies loves in this way might be called the "virtue and vice" love tradition.

By contrast, sometimes love is used to describe *only* what is proper, righteous, or supremely good. Love in this sense is never connected with improper action. The tradition that understands love as synonymous with righteous action might be called the *"hesed"* love tradition. *Hesed* is a Hebrew word often translated by biblical scholars as "steadfast love." To love with *hesed* is necessarily to love properly.

Christians should note that biblical writers employ both of these love traditions in various ways when speaking of creaturely love.* Given the assumption that divine love is maximally perfect, however, the important distinction between the *hesed* and the virtue-and-vice love traditions applies only to creaturely love. God's love is always proper, because God always acts rightly. Or, as stated earlier, divine love is maximally perfect. Unless otherwise indicated, then, "love" will be used in this chapter as the *hesed* tradition does.

Even after establishing from which love tradition one is speaking, fundamental questions about love itself are not yet solved. Perhaps most fundamentally, what is love? How should love be defined? While many people use the word love and place a high level of honor and value upon it, very few take the time to define love.

For the purposes of this chapter, love is defined as acting intentionally, in sympathetic response to the actions of others, to attain the highest degree of overall well-being given the degrees of ill and well-being possible for a particular act (Oord). This definition is rather brief, but further explanation and expansion of this way of understanding love will be proffered throughout the remainder of this chapter.

Having noted various understandings of love and having defined love briefly, let us return to questions about God's relationship to love. Are God and love identical? Should love and God be equated? Is it just as

---

*For example, the virtue and vice love tradition is illustrated in 2 Tim. 4:10, Rom. 12:9, and 2 Cor. 6:6, among other passages. The *hesed* love tradition is illustrated in Hos. 11:8, Exod. 34:14, and Deut. 5:9, among other passages.

proper for someone to say, "God is love," as it is to say, "love is God?" One way to address these questions is to consider a classic question posed by Plato: Is God good, or is good God? For our purpose, the question might be posed in this way: Is some action loving *only* because God does it, or does God do some action because it *is* loving?

Some philosophers and theologians answer these questions by denying that God is responsible to a standard that, in any way, transcends Godself. To say that God's actions cannot be measured by a transcendent standard of what is loving means that *whatever* God decides to do is loving. Some action is loving merely because God has decided to do it. This answer to the question implies, for instance, that God never commits an evil act, *only* because nothing God does can be called "evil." This answer entails the claim that God's will comes prior to God's loving nature. What should be called "loving" is so because God has chosen to call it "loving." A philosophical tradition called "nominalism" supports this contention that the divine will precedes the divine essence.

When responding to the answer that an action is loving *only* because God says so, critics typically argue that this makes divine love entirely arbitrary. God cannot be said to have any reason for what God wills—except that God wills it. Furthermore, if God arbitrarily decides what counts as loving, the claim "God is love" becomes unintelligible. If there exists no standard that, in some way, transcends or logically precedes the divine will whereby God's actions can be judged as loving or unloving, it makes no sense to judge God's actions as loving. Instead of "God is love," say critics, one should say "God is whatever God arbitrarily decides to be." Gottfried Leibniz (1646—1716) expresses this criticism in this way: "If we say that things are good by no rule of goodness beyond the will of God alone, we thoughtlessly destroy, I feel, all the love and glory of God. For why praise Him for what He has done if He would be equally praiseworthy for doing the opposite?" (1956, sec. 2)

A second answer to the question of God's relation to love is the affirmation that love, even divine love, must be measured by a standard that, in some sense, transcends or logically precedes the divine will. Those holding this position typically claim that what makes God different from other individuals—and why one should claim "God is love"—is that God perfectly and everlastingly meets this standard of love. God does not arbitrarily decide what is love and what is not. Instead, deity meets the perfect standard of love, because doing so is an aspect of God's essence or nature. God's greatness is tied to divinity's incessant actualization of the loving actions this standard measures. Charles Hartshorne (1897—2000) advocates this answer: "An ideal is not good because God arbitrarily wills it, nor are his acts good because they express goodness as something nondivine; they are good, as our acts . . . are good, because of an abstract ideal antecedent to each such act; however, this ideal is not antecedent to God but [is] his eternal and unchangeable purpose. . . . We and God serve the same ideal; but in us it is our glimpse of God's essence" (1953).

Critics of this second position claim that, if God's actions must be measured by a standard unestablished by deity, God cannot be said to be the ultimate Creator of all things, including abstractions. After all, to claim that God is responsible to an abstract standard that deity did not establish assumes that some standard transcends or logically precedes, at least in some way, even God. God must create all, say such critics, which includes creating abstract principles, definitions, standards, or ideals.

The foregoing discussion of the divine will and essence often leads philosophers and theologians to wonder whether God loves voluntarily or involuntarily. Are God's expressions of love solely a product of the divine will, or is love an aspect of the divine essence and thus obligatory to deity? In the manner of Anselm, one might ask, which conception of God is greatest: (1) A God who chooses to love because the divine will is primary, or (2) a God who must love because love is essential to God, and God could no more cease loving than cease to be? Philosophers often use the words "contingency" and "necessity" in such questions: Is divine love contingent (may or may not be) or necessary (must be)?

Those who believe that the greatest conceivable being loves contingently claim that their conception of divinity is greater. A God who incessantly *chooses* to love is greater than a deity who must love. A being who everlastingly loves voluntarily, despite being able to do otherwise, should be considered the greatest conceivable being. A God who necessarily loves should not be praised. After all, we do not praise someone for doing what he or she could not refrain from doing.

Those who believe that the greatest conceivable being loves necessarily claim, of course, that their conception of deity is greater. A God whose essence involves love is greater than a God whose essence does not. Those who affirm this position say that, "God is love," entailing that love resides as a necessary property of the divine essence. A God who chooses to love could, theoretically at least, choose not to love. The greatest conceivable being, however, could no more stop loving than cease to exist. Perfect love, like perfect existence, is a necessary or essential property of the greatest conceivable being's essence or nature.

A combination of these positions might also be offered in which divine love has both necessary and contingent aspects. *That* God loves is a necessary aspect of the divine essence, and thus God loves involuntarily. *How* God loves, however, is contingent upon the experiences God has with others. The voluntary element of divine love is exhibited in this contingent aspect of divine love. This proposal allows one to affirm both the constancy and variability of a personal, maximally perfect Lover. It also provides a conceptual basis for praise of God's contingent decisions of *how* to love while affirming love's necessary role in the divine essence.

II. DIVINE LOVE IN SCRIPTURE AND RELIGIOUS TRADITIONS

Various sacred books and religious traditions attest to the significance of divine love. For most of this section, we will address the role of divine love in the Bible and Christian tradition. The emphasis upon Christian doctrines of divine love is warranted, according to Irving Singer, because "whatever Christians may have done to others or themselves, theirs is the only faith in which God and love are the same" (1984 [1966], 159). At the end of this section, however, we will also address the role love plays in some other religious traditions.

In the books that comprise the Old Testament, God is recorded as repeatedly expressing love to a chosen people. Biblical writers characterize divine love, *hesed,* as "steadfast;" God expresses *hesed* in the establishment of covenants with Israel. *Hesed* can be relied upon (Deut. 5:10; 7:9-13), and *hesed* is everlasting: "With everlasting love I will have compassion on you, says the LORD your Redeemer" (Isa. 54:8). "I will heal their faithlessness," the God of Hosea says, "I will love [*hesed*] them freely" (Hos. 14:4, RSV). Israel believes that the proper response to this loving God should be to love in return. Responsive love is no more evident than in the *shema*: "Hear, O Israel: the LORD our God is one LORD; and you shall love the LORD your God with all you heart, and with all your soul, and with all your might" (Deut. 6:4-5, RSV). Although some of the actions attributed to God by Old Testament writers are seemingly unloving, the preponderance of biblical passages witness to a loving deity.

Love enjoys greater prominence in the New Testament. While the writer of 1 John explicitly states that "God is love" (4:8, 16), other New Testament writers at least implicitly acknowledge the integral connection between God and love. Old Testament writers considered God's love to be primarily, though not exclusively, expressed to the chosen nation of Israel. New Testament writers, by contrast, witness to divine expressions of love to all people and even all creation. John's gospel explains this by saying that "God so loved the world that he gave his only begotten son" (John 3:16, KJV). According to New Testament writers, God reveals divine love most profoundly in Jesus: "God proves his love for us in that while we still were sinners Christ died for us," writes the apostle Paul (Rom. 5:8, NRSV).

In some way and to some degree, creatures are to express love analogous to the perfect love expressed by God. Creatures are able to love because God has first loved them (1 John 4:19). The letter to the Ephesians urges readers to imitate God by loving (5:1-2), and Paul claims that the greatest way his Corinthian readers could respond to God was to pursue love (1 Cor. 13:13; 14:1). Jesus elevates to primary status two love commands found in the Old Testament: "'You shall love the Lord your God with all your heart, and with all your soul, and with all your mind.' This is the greatest and first commandment. And a second is like it: 'You shall love your neighbor as yourself.' On these two commandments hang all the law and the prophets" (Matt. 22:37-40, NRSV).

Love has enjoyed widespread prominence in the writings—especially devotional literature—of Christians for 2,000 years. The following is a list of Christians whose technical writings on love have been influential (following each person's name is the century in which he or she lived): Marcion (second), Origen (third), Gregory of Nyssa (fourth), Augustine (fifth), Dionysius (sixth), Peter Abelard (12th), Bernard of Clairvaux (12th), Thomas Aquinas (13th), Francis of Assisi (13th), Julian of Norwich (14th), Martin Luther (16th), John of the Cross (16th), Teresa of Avila (16th), Francois de Fenelon (17th), John Wesley (18th), Jonathan Edwards (18th), Fyodor Dostoyevsky (19th), Søren Kierkegaard (19th), Walter Rauschenbusch (20th), Paul Tillich (20th), Martin Luther King Jr. (20th), Karl Rahner (20th), Martin C. D'Arcy (20th), Anders Nygren (20th), and C. S. Lewis (20th). In the following paragraphs I briefly sketch ideas about divine love found in the formal theologies of two very influential love theologians: Augustine and John Wesley.

Augustine of Hippo (354—430), more than any other early Christian philosopher, afforded love a central place in his reflections about God and creatures. With regard to creaturely love, Augustine was heavily influenced by the virtue-and-vice love tradition. According to him, all human love includes an element of desire; love is a kind of craving. God placed this craving in creatures so that they would desire the divine.

The object upon which a creaturely love is fixed determines that love's validity. When a creature fixes his or her love on God, Augustine calls this love *"caritas"* (from which is derived the English word "charity"). When a creature fixes his or her love upon created things rather than the Creator, Augustine calls this love *"cupiditas"* (from which is derived the English word "cupidity"). The difference between *caritas* and *cupiditas* is one of object: "Love, but see to it *what* you love," says Augustine (2000 [394], 90-31-5).

In a further discussion of proper love, Augustine employs the Latin verbs *frui* and *uti*. *Frui* means "to enjoy" something for its own sake; *uti* means "to use" something for the sake of something else. When combined with *cupiditas* and *caritas,* four possible relations emerge: (1) right enjoyment (enjoyment of God); (2) wrong enjoyment (enjoyment of the world);

(3) right use (use of the world); and (4) wrong use (use of God). All disorder in existence stems from improper creaturely love.

Augustine asks rhetorically about the nature of God's love in reference to his *frui* and *uti* scheme: "Does God love us in order to use us or in order to enjoy us?" (1958 [395], 1-31-34). Augustine replies to his own question by arguing that because deity is self-sufficient and the sum of all good, God does not enjoy us. Although the thought of God using us has its difficulties, Augustine feels compelled to claim that God does so. After all, admits Augustine, "if He neither enjoys nor uses us, I am at a loss to discover in what way He can love us" (1958 [395], 1-32-35).

Augustine's doctrine of divine love has Trinitarian underpinnings. God is lover, love, and beloved in Trinity. The Trinity's inner life is molded by the love with which God ceaselessly loves Godself in contemplation and enjoyment of deity's own perfection. In short, the inner life of the Trinity is the life of absolute love (Augustine 1990 [399-422]).

John Wesley (1703-91), an 18th-century British theologian, considered love God's primary property. Love is God's "reigning attribute," said Wesley, "the attribute that sheds an amiable glory on all his other perfections" (1975c). "It is not written 'God is justice,' or 'God is truth' . . . "but it is written, 'God is love'" (1975d [1773], 10:227). Furthermore, Wesley argues, "love is the end of all the commandments of God. Love is the end, the sole end, of every dispensation of God, from the beginning of the world to the consummation of all things" (1975a [1750], 5:462). John Wesley could agree with an oft-repeated phrase in one his brother's hymns: God's name and nature is love.

Wesley's central theological concept for understanding how God expresses love to creatures has been called the doctrine of "prevenient grace" (or "responsible grace"). Prevenient grace refers to God's loving action that comes before and makes possible creaturely response. In love, God inspires, enables, or empowers creatures to respond freely; deity does not coerce or overpower. God's loving influences "are not to supersede, but to encourage, our own efforts," wrote Wesley (1975c). The doctrine of prevenient grace supports Wesley's rejection of predestination (predestination can be defined as the belief that God alone chooses some to be eternally saved but others to be eternally damned), because Wesley believed that creatures can freely cooperate with or reject God's loving call for salvation.

Wesley believed that the Bible supported his conviction that divine love is expressed to *all* individuals. He refers to several supporting scriptural passages in a sermon he titled "On Working Out Our Own Salvation"—

> Some great truths . . . are to be found in all nations: So that, in some sense it may be said to every child of man, "he hath showed

thee, O man, what is good; even to do justly, to love mercy, and to walk humbly with thy God." With this truth he has, in some measure, "enlightened every one that cometh into the world." And hereby they that "have not the law," that have no written law, "are a law unto themselves." They show "the work of the law,"—the substance of it, though not the letter—"written on their hearts," by the same hand which wrote the commandments on the tables of stone: "Their conscience also bearing them witness," whether they act suitably thereto or not.

The implication Wesley draws from reason and scripture is that

> Every one has some measure of that light, some faint glimmering ray, which, sooner or later, more or less, enlightens every man that cometh into the world. And every one, unless he be one of the small number whose conscience is seared as with a hot iron, feels more or less uneasy when he acts contrary to the light of his own conscience. So that no man sins because he has not grace, but because does not use the grace which he hath. Therefore . . . it is possible for you to "love God, because he hath first loved us;" and to "walk in love," after the pattern of our great Master (1975b, 3:206).

Wesley summarizes this conviction that creatures love when they respond appropriately to the Being whose essence *is* love, when he says that "love existed from eternity in God, the great ocean of love. Love had a place in all the children of God, from the moment of their creation. They received at once, from their gracious Creator, [the ability] to exist and to love" (1975a [1750]).

Christians are not the only believers to ponder the relationship between God and love. Mohammed (570—632) spoke of divine love, and the benevolence of deity has a place in Islamic traditions. Divine love, according to the Qu'ran, is reserved for particular types of individuals: those who are virtuous. "Allah loves the righteous," Mohammed writes in the Qu'ran (3:77). "Allah loves those who put their trust in him" (3:160), and "Allah loves those who turn to him often and Allah loves those who are clean and pure" (2:223). Love as obedience and devotion is the proper response of the righteous.

Hindu traditions offer a wide variety of love doctrines. Partly because Hinduism is not essentially monotheistic, however, it is not easy to identify well the character of divine love as understood by Hindus. Perhaps the most significant love notion in Hinduism is found in the *bhakti* love union of creatures with God. The sacred writings of the *Bhagavad-Gita* point to a personal deity (Krishna) who protects and masters affectionately. During medieval times, a famous *bhakti sutra* was titled the *Way of Divine Love*. Attributed to an ancient figure named "Narada" mentioned in the *Upan-*

ishads, the *sutra* includes these words: "Work that we perform as service to the lord creates love and devotion in us. This love and devotion, in turn, bring wisdom; and at last, guided by this wisdom, we surrender ourselves to the Lord of Love and meditate upon him" (Mohler 1975, 50).

Of course, the connection between God and love is nonexistent in some religious traditions, because such traditions are essentially nontheistic. For example, although Mahayana Buddhists consider love (*karuna*) an important discipline, this love is confined to creaturely actions. The Buddhist loves by not harming others (*ahimsa*) and by promoting the good of all beings through practicing the *dharmas.*

Confucianists Mo Tzu (6th century B.C.) and Mencius (4th century B.C.) identified creaturely expressions of love with a universal heavenly love. Although neither of these Confucianists espoused belief in a maximally perfect Being, both argued that creatures can love, because, as Mo Tzu states, "heaven loves the whole world universally" (Mohler 1975, 6). Similarly, Taoists such as Lao Tzu taught that an indefinable, supremely powerful world soul exists who is at least partially loving.

III. Types of Divine Love: Agape, Eros, and/or Philia?

Having briefly examined the role of love in Christian and some non-Christian traditions, we turn to examine various types of love. Scholars often attempt to classify love by referring to these various love-types. Three Greek words are typically used: *agape, eros,* and *philia.* Although other Greek words indicate aspects of love, most scholars agree that the meanings of these other love words can be subsumed under these three types. This section examines these love-types and considers God's relation to them.

Despite the diverse meanings *agape* possesses in the New Testament, contemporary Christians have uniquely embraced this love-type word. Gene Outka observes that *agape* is almost uniformly the referent for any alleged distinctiveness in Christian love (1972). However, the definitions, conceptions, and characterizations Christians give *agape* vary widely. Theological systems, metaphysics, phenomenology, anthropology, psychology, church confessions, biblical studies, and other factors account for this vast definitional and conceptual diversity.

The emphasis upon *agape* as the distinctly Christian love is a relatively recent phenomenon. It was Anders Nygren's mid-20th-century book *Agape and Eros* that initiated interest in *agape* and the love-types (1957 [1930]). The following list contains some of the prominent ways that Nygren characterizes *agape.* According to him, *agape* is

- Unconditioned, spontaneous, groundless, or unmotivated
- Indifferent to, but creative of, value

- Love directed toward sinners
- The sole initiator of creaturely fellowship with God
- In opposition to all that can be called self-love
- Sacrificial giving to others
- Divine love, not human love

Critics have rejected, for one reason or another, virtually every characterization of *agape* made by Nygren. For instance, if *agape* is understood as the only appropriate love for Christians and if *agape* opposes all that can be called self-love, there exists no basis for Christians to love themselves in healthy and appropriate ways (Singer 1984). If the only appropriate love for Christians is sacrificial giving to others, Christians do not love when receiving from others (Williams 1968). If *agape* is exclusively divine love, there exists no basis upon which to talk about creaturely *agape;* therefore, if biblical writers are correct that *agape* is connected to salvation, some form of predestination seems implied (Outka 1972). Nygren's emphasis upon *agape* as the only appropriate Christian love, say many critics, neglects legitimate Christian *philia* (D'Arcy 1964, Vacek 1994) and Christian *eros* (Avis 1990, Vacek 1994).

Both scholars and the general public characterize *agape* often as "unconditional love." Gene Outka, for instance, points to *agape's* unconditional character in his endorsement of Karl Barth's understanding of *agape* as love expressed "in utter independence of the question of [the other's] attractiveness" (Outka 1972, 208). When love expressions are not dependent upon the other's attractiveness, these expressions are not *conditioned* by the other's state of being. They are unconditional.

The problem with speaking of divine *agape* as "unconditional," however, is that one can easily become confused as to whether *"agape"* refers to a *mode* of action or a love *type*. Scholars sometimes use *"agape"* in the modal sense to refer to the necessary fact *that* God loves. *Agape* as a mode of action refers to the "whether" question; the modal answer *agape* provides is that God loves necessarily. To say that God loves necessarily is to say that, no matter what the other's state, God inevitably expresses love to the other.

By contrast, *agape* as one type of love refers to the "why" question. The "why" question is a contingent love-type question, and the answer *agape* provides distinguishes it from the other contingent love-types, *eros* and *philia*. Confusion can be reduced if we do not use the word *"agape"* to claim that God loves necessarily and use the word *"agape,"* instead, to compare one contingent type of love to others.

In the contingent type sense, divine *agape* might be best defined as love that promotes well-being when responding to activity generating ill-being. In theological terms, divine *agape* is inextricably linked with creaturely sin. The answer to the "why" question provided by divine *agape* is that God, when confronted with sin, condemns creaturely wrongdoing while promoting and inspiring creaturely love.

We turn now to address *eros*. Given the way in which *eros* and "erotic" are popularly conceived, perhaps it is wise to note early that, in the philosophical sense, *eros* only occasionally refers to sexual matters. Plato, for instance, understood *eros* to be one's intense desire for a beautiful or valuable other (Osborne 1994). The other that is desired may be an object, idea, or individual. *Eros* is fundamentally oriented around acquisition of what one deems worthwhile. Unlike *agape*, which is expressed in repulsion to actions generating ill-being, *eros* responds affectionately to the value perceived in the other. In sum, *eros* might be defined as love that promotes well-being by affirming and enjoying what is valuable.

While *agape* has been almost universally acknowledged to be a divine love-type, *eros* is often thought not to be associated with divinity. One Protestant Christian tradition rejects *eros* as a divine love, because this tradition considers humans to be totally depraved and creation to be utterly fallen (Nygren 1957 [1939]). God would have no reason to affirm or enjoy others who are now essentially worthless, says this tradition. Another powerful tradition has rejected *eros* as a divine love, because this tradition assumes that divine perfection implies that God lacks all desire. Desire connotes lack or need, and a God who is maximally perfect, says this line of reasoning, would have no lack or need (Augustine 1958 [395]). According to this tradition, a maximally perfect God may give to others, but deity has no desires and does not receive from others.

Those who affirm *eros* as a divine love-type respond to these arguments in a variety of ways. To the tradition emphasizing total depravity, adherents of divine *eros* theology either reject the notion that creatures are totally depraved or affirm the intrinsic value of all creatures by virtue of God's having created them good. To the tradition speaking of God as perfect and thus without need, adherents of divine *eros* argue that maximal perfection involves perfect desiring and receiving. Our conception of a maximal human lover is not of someone detached and without desire; a great lover is someone who desires appropriately and who is appropriately influenced by others. The maximally perfect lover must be a maximally perfect giver *and* maximally perfect receiver, say advocates of divine *eros* theology (Hartshorne, 1941).

Issues pertaining to divine *agape* and *eros* arise in philosophical discussions of divine altruism and egoism. Egoistic actions can be defined as those actions done with the intent to further one's own interests. Egoism is often equated with selfishness. Some argue that God is selfish because He creates the universe out of divine desire for companionship. Others argue that God creates creatures because He wants to be worshiped or glorified. In either case, God's motivation for creating is egoistic, which means that divine love includes selfish aspects.

Some argue that divine love is purely altruistic; God always loves unselfishly. Altruistic actions can be defined as those actions done with the intent exclusively to further the interest of others. Altruism is often equated with complete unselfishness. Some argue that God demonstrates altruism in creating the universe, because, although God needs no one, God creates others for their own sake. God creates all things by pouring out love, and this creating has as its motivation the good of others. Sometimes theologians call this outpouring, altruistic, divine love *"kenotic"* in reference to a biblical passage describing the self-emptying actions of Christ Jesus (Phil. 2:7).

Charles Hartshorne has argued that divine love is both perfectly altruistic and perfectly egoistic (1941). That is, there is no divine egoism, in the sense of self-interest, in tension with the ultimate good of the whole. And there is no divine altruism, in the sense of other interest, in tension with the ultimate good of God. While creaturely egoism or altruism may conflict because creatures neither give to nor receive from all others, omnipresence and omniscience afford deity the prefect concurrence of egoistic and altruistic motivations. Among other things, this implies that God's creation of the universe is both selfish and unselfish. God's motivation for creating the universe is the desire to act both for the benefit of others and for the benefit of himself.

The third love-type, *philia,* might be defined as love that promotes well-being by acting to establish deeper friendships with others. Of the three love-types, *philia* most calls attention to interrelatedness and community. While *agape* and *eros* imply that an other exists, intense expressions of *philia* depend upon a heritage of interpersonal activity promoting mutual well-being.

The idea that God expresses *philia* to creatures has received greater attention in recent times. Although biblical writers spoke of friendship between God and humans, divine *philia* for the universe was infrequently stressed in the technical philosophical and theological writings of yesteryear. Three particular notions in Aristotle's conception of friendship likely prevented theologians and philosophers from emphasizing the *philia* relations creatures enjoy with God. Aristotle argued that (1) friendship requires friends to be relatively equal, (2) friendship requires that friends be near, and (3) friends must be relatively similar. "It is not possible to define exactly up to what point friends can remain friends," claims Aristotle, "but, when one party is removed to a great distance, as God is, the possibility of friendship ceases" (1941 [330bc], 1159a4).

Contemporary responses to Aristotle include the following arguments. First, our experience shows that deep friendships can develop, for instance, between individuals of unequal financial, political, or educational status. If inequality fails to prevent creatures from developing friendships, many scholars wonder why inequality should prevent God and creatures from developing friendships. Second, unless one claims that a personal God is dissimilar to personal creatures in every possible way, some similarities must exist between deity and mortals. The apostle Paul's notion that Christians ought to imitate God by loving reveals his belief that similarities between God and creatures exist (Eph. 5:1). Third, those who claim that God is immanent in the world suggest that deity and creatures are not separated or removed from one another. If God is omnipresent, God cannot be unrelated to others. Therefore, creatures are sufficiently close to God for friendship relations to occur.

The discussion of divine *philia,* coupled with the earlier discussion of love as a necessary or contingent divine attribute, leads many philosophers and theologians to ponder issues surrounding God's relations with the universe. Some have argued that, if love is a necessary or essential property of God and if love requires relations to others, God must be essentially relational (Williams 1968). In other words, love relations are essential to divinity.

The argument that God lovingly relates with others clashes with philosophies that envision God as unaffected by others and unchanging in all ways. Greek stoics, for instance, most admired emotionless and unsympathetic acts, and the stoic influence upon doctrines of God has been evident through the ages. Aristotle's notion of God as the "Unmoved Mover" inclined many philosophers, including Thomas Aquinas, to conceive of God as entirely self-sufficient. Aquinas claimed that God is pure act without potentiality, which meant that deity can neither be affected by others nor change in any way (1981 [1265-74]).

Those who reject the notion that deity is totally unaffected and unchanging in all ways argue that love requires God to be affected by those whom He loves. In other words, the phrase "God is love" necessarily implies that deity undergoes some change (Williams 1968, Vacek 1994). Those who are argue that God changes also typically argue that, in another sense, God is unchanging. The fact *that* God loves will never change; this necessary fact refers to love as a property of the divine essence. But *how* God loves changes depending on the circumstances as He is affected by give-and-take relationships with others.

A question arises for those who consider relational love essential to deity: If God loves others necessarily because love requires relations with others, was there ever a time in which others did not exist for God to love?

In other words, has God ever existed alone? By endorsing the view that God voluntarily created the universe out of absolutely nothing *(creatio ex nihilo)*, classic Christian theology has explicitly denied that God has always loved others who had been created. But if one affirms *creatio ex nihilo* and its implication that, at one time, God existed without others, how can "God is love" refer to a necessary characteristic of a relational God?

One answer to this question takes the form of a God-others hypothesis called "pan-en-theism" (which literally means "all in God"). Panentheism (or "theocosmocentrism") can be roughly defined as the view that God dwells in and with all creation, but deity transcends and is more than the created order. Most important for our present concern is the panentheistic idea that God has always existed alongside some created order or another and that He has always lovingly related to these others (Hartshorne 1948, Taylor 1986). If God has always existed alongside others, that deity has been creating, and if God lovingly relates to these others, love can be coherently conceived as a necessary characteristic of divinity. Critics of this version of panentheism, however, argue that the panentheistic hypothesis undermines God's sovereign independence.

Another answer to the question "How can 'God is love' refer to a necessary characteristic of a relational divinity if God once existed without others?" is based upon a particular conception of the Trinity. This answer says that God has always had others with which to relate, because the Persons of the Trinity have always been interrelated (Karl Rahner in Taylor, 1986). The Father, Son, and Holy Spirit exchange love everlastingly, which means that love can be coherently conceived as a necessary characteristic of divinity. Critics of this Trinitarian answer, however, argue that this God is not essentially related to *others,* only to Godself. Other critics argue that, if the Trinity really *does* contain others, this is in tritheism not monotheism.

CONCLUSION

God is love. Although one might not expect a three-word sentence to entail complexity and difficulty, each term in the sentence "God is love" entails such. This brief chapter reveals that the issues involved in ascribing love to God are numerous. But wrestling with these issues can be a rewarding venture.

Texts Cited or Recommended for Further Study

Aquinas, Thomas. *Summa Theologica.* Westminster, Md.: Christian Classics, 1981 (1265-74).

Aristotle. *Nicomachean Ethics.* Trans. W. D. Ross. Bks VII and IX. In *The Basic Works of Aristotle.* Ed. Richard McKeon. New York: Random House, 1941 (330bc).

Avis, Paul. *Eros and the Sacred.* Harrisburg, Penn.: Morehouse, 1990.

Augustine. *Expositions on the Psalms.* In *The Works of Saint Augustine.* New York: New York City Press, 2000 [394].

_____. *On Christian Doctrine.* New York: Liberal Arts, 1958 (395).

_____. *On the Trinity.* In *The Works of Saint Augustine.* New York: New City Press, 1990 (399-422).

D'Arcy, Martin Cyril. *The Heart and Mind of Love, Lion and Unicorn: A Study in Eros and Agape.* Cleveland: World, 1964.

Hartshorne, Charles. *The Divine Relativity: A Social Conception of God.* New Haven: Yale University Press, 1948.

_____. *Man's Vision of God.* Chicago: Willet, Clark and Co., 1941.

_____. *Philosophers Speak of God.* Chicago: University of Chicago Press, 1953.

Kierkegaard, Søren. *Works of Love.* Trans. Howard and Edna Hong. New York: Harper and Brothers, 1962.

Liebniz, Gottfried. "Discourse on Metaphysics." In *Philosophical Papers and Letters.* Ed. and trans. Leroy E. Loemker. Chicago: University of Chicago Press, 1956.

Mohler, James A., S. J. *Dimensions of Love: East and West.* Garden City, N.Y.: Doubleday, 1975.

Nygren, Anders. *Agape and Eros.* Trans. Philip S. Watson. New York: Harper and Row, 1957 [1930].

Osborne, Catherine. *Eros Unveiled: Plato and the God of Love.* Oxford: Clarendon Press, 1994.

Outka, Gene. *Agape: An Ethical Analysis.* New Haven: Yale University Press, 1972.

Plato. *Symposium* and *Phaedrus.*

Singer, Irving. *The Nature of Love: Plato to Luther.* Vol. 1, 2d ed. Chicago: University of Chicago Press, 1966, 1984.

Soble, Alan. *Eros, Agape, and Philia.* New York: Paragon, 1989.

_____. *The Structure of Love.* New Haven: Yale University Press, 1990.

Stone, Bryan P. and Thomas Jay Oord. *Thy Nature and Thy Name Is Love: Wesleyan and Process Theologies in Dialogue.* Nashville: Kingswood, 2001.

Taylor, Mark Lloyd. *God Is Love: A Study in the Theology of Karl Rahner.* Atlanta: Scholars, 1986.

Tillich, Paul. *Love, Power, and Justice: Ontological Analyses and Ethical Applications.* New York: Oxford University Press, 1963.

Vacek, Edward Collins. *Love, Human and Divine: The Heart of Christian Ethics.* Washington, D.C.: Georgetown University Press, 1994.

Wesley, John. (a) "The Law Established Through Faith." In *The Works of John Wesley.* Oxford: Clarendon Press, 1975-83; Nashville: Abingdon Press, 1984- [1750].

_____. (b) "On Working Out Our Own Salvation." In *The Works of John Wesley.*

_____. (c) *NT Notes* 1 John 4:8 & Phil. 2:12-13. In *The Works of John Wesley.*

_____. (d) "Predestination Calmly Considered." In *The Works of John Wesley* [1773].

Williams, Daniel Day. *The Spirit and the Forms of Love.* New York: Harper and Row, 1968.

Wynkoop, Mildred Bangs. *A Theology of Love: The Dynamic of Wesleyanism.* Kansas City: Beacon Hill Press of Kansas City, 1972.

DIVINE POWER
Kevin Timpe

━━━━━━━━━━━━━ ◆ ━━━━━━━━━━━━━

In 1616 the Inquisition ordered Galileo to refrain from teaching Copernican astronomy on the grounds that it was philosophically and scientifically indefensible, and because this astronomy was considered a theological heresy. Among the many objections raised against Copernican heleocentrism (the view that the earth orbits the sun) was the allegation that it contradicted the Church's teachings. Both the consensus of the Church fathers and the holy Scriptures, it was claimed, clearly taught that the sun moved and that the earth was stationary, not vice-versa. The theological objection to Copernican heleocentrism was based upon the claim of divine omnipotence, and it took the following form:

1. God is omnipotent.
2. If God is omnipotent, God can create the universe in any way God wishes.
3. If God wishes, God can create a universe in which the sun orbits the earth, despite all the astronomical evidence that might suggest otherwise.
4. Heleocentrism asserts that the earth orbits the sun based upon all the astronomical evidence.
5. Therefore, heleocentrism contradicts divine omnipotence.

Thanks to this way of thinking, Galileo was forbidden to defend or teach publicly the doctrine that the earth moved in orbit around the sun. As a result, he refrained temporarily from promoting heleocentrism.

While the format of this argument does not logically prove that heleocentrism is true or false, it does demonstrate the importance of divine omnipotence for the Church's teachings. What it means to be "omnipotent," however, is not easily ascertained. Thomas Aquinas noted in the *Summa Theologiae* that "all confess that God is omnipotent; but it seems difficult to explain in what His omnipotence precisely consists: for there may be doubt as to the precise meaning of the word 'all' when we say that God can do all things" (q. 25, a. 3). In the following pages I will attempt to outline some of the standard ways philosophers have understood divine omnipotence. I will also show how one's understanding of this doctrine influences what one can say regarding other issues in the philosophy of religion.

The doctrine of omnipotence is most frequently used in theological or philosophy of religion discussions. Omnipotence is almost always used in reference to a divine being who is usually thought both to exist by necessity and have this nature necessarily. "God is supposed to have [omnipotence], like all of his other attributes, essentially, meaning that it is logically or conceptually impossible that God exist without having this attribute," notes Richard Gale. "His possession of omnipotence is an example of a *de re* necessity, because it follows from his nature, not our way of referring to God, that he has it" (1991, 18). If God is necessarily omnipotent, the theological and philosophical importance of omnipotence is obvious. The theist's attempt to understand the exact nature and magnitude of God's power is far from being mere philosophical speculation. This being the case, it becomes essential to understand what is meant when one says "God is omnipotent."

I. FOUR MEANINGS OF OMNIPOTENCE

In order for a definition of divine omnipotence to be acceptable, it must meet at least the following two criteria:

1. The definition must satisfactorily preserve God's omnipotence, and
2. The definition must also exclude all beings that are not properly considered omnipotent.

While the first criteria is obvious, the second is equally important in order for the concept of omnipotence to be coherent. A definition of omnipotence that results in *falsely* ascribing omnipotence must be discarded or revised. While most theists agree with these two criteria, they disagree as to the need for additional criteria; e.g., logical consistency, philosophical coherence, and continuity with theological orthodoxy. The definitions that philosophers and theologians have given omnipotence throughout history tend to fall into a few major categories that reflect the perceived need for these additional criteria.

In this section I will evaluate four major ways in which omnipotence has been defined. For purposes of convenience, I have given each way a title that reflects the main thrust of its position.

Absolute Omnipotence

The first and broadest understanding of omnipotence might be called *absolute omnipotence*. Simply stated, this position holds that God can do "absolutely anything." While this may initially seem to be what most theists intend to convey when they claim that God is omnipotent, this position is beset with a myriad of problems. For this reason, very few theologians and philosophers have embraced absolute omnipotence.

One notable philosopher who accepted absolute omnipotence is

René Descartes. Descartes makes it clear why he holds to such a strong understanding of divine omnipotence: "In general we can be quite certain that God can do whatever we are able to understand, but not that He cannot do what we are unable to understand. For it would be presumptuous to think that our imagination extends as far as His power" (letter to Mersenne, 15 April 1930). He writes elsewhere, "I turn to the difficulty of conceiving how God [could have] . . . made it false that the three angles of a triangle were unequal to two right angles, or in general that contradictions could not be true altogether. It is easy to dispel this difficulty by considering that *the power of God cannot have any limits, and that our mind is finite*" (letter to Mesland, 2 May 1644, emphasis added).

When one considers the broad direction of Descartes' philosophy found in his books *Meditations* and *Discourse on Method,* one can better understand why he defends *absolute omnipotence.* Because God establishes all the laws of nature and mathematics, it follows that these laws are dependent upon God. If they are dependent upon God, Descartes thinks, it follows that God can change them if God so wills. Elsewhere, Descartes writes that divine omnipotence means that God could do anything, even if it seems contradictory to the human mind. God can

a. make a circle in which all the radii are not equal,
b. create a mountain that exists without a valley,
c. make it possible that $2 + 1$ does not equal 3.

Few philosophers, however, have been willing to agree with Descartes and embrace *absolute omnipotence* because of the difficulties involved with the position. If the gap between the human and the divine is as wide as Descartes suggests, and if finite humans cannot comprehend *anything* about God, there is no way for humans to reason philosophically or theologically at all. One can affirm that the human intellect is not able to fully comprehend God, because the human understanding is limited without having a gulf between deity and creatures as wide as Descartes thought was necessary.

On this definition of omnipotence, one can see why some have argued that omnipotence itself is incoherent and thus must be discarded. According to *absolute omnipotence,* God would be able also to do the following actions:

a. create a married bachelor
b. create a square circle
c. create a statue that is both constituted entirely of gold and constituted entirely of wax
d. bring about a state of affairs in which $2+2=4$ and $2+2=5$.

Yet all of these are impossible, for they involve contradictions.

One of the most famous examples used to attack omnipotence is the paradox of the stone. The paradox is formed around whether or not God can create a stone that is so heavy that even God cannot lift it.

If God can do absolutely anything, God must be able to create the stone in question. Yet, as soon as one grants that God can create such a stone, the problem arises that there is an action that God cannot do, i.e., lift that stone. This paradox is frequently used as an argument against the existence of an omnipotent being on the ground that omnipotence is incoherent. In other words, argue critics, the notion of an omnipotent being is logically inconsistent.

The paradox of the stone is one example of an atheological argument, the point of which is to reveal an internal inconsistency in the theist's conception of God. The atheological argument begins with propositions that the theist would supposedly accept. It then attempts to demonstrate, without the addition of any additional premises that the theist could reject, that these initial premises necessarily result in a contradiction within the theist's understanding of God. The critic who raises this argument is attempting to show that one cannot ascribe omnipotence to God (or any other being), because the notion of omnipotence itself is incoherent and self-defeating.

A common response to the paradox of the stone is to deny the concept of *absolute omnipotence*. The problem with *absolute omnipotence* is that it entails the claim that God can do what is logically impossible. If this is true, one should not expect to be able to understand the divine being at all, because human understanding presupposes certain logical laws. One of the most fundamental of these laws is the law of noncontradiction, which states that *it is impossible for a thing to both be and not be in the same respect at the same time.* As noted by Aristotle over 2,000 years ago, if one does not accept the law of noncontradiction, one cannot argue or speak intelligibly at all. The theist who embraces *absolute omnipotence* must be prepared to abandon logic when thinking about the divine being. While some theists think that *absolute omnipotence* is the only way to protect the transcendence of God, doing so has the unfortunate consequence of rendering all theological and philosophical discourse about God worthless. "To say that God is so powerful that he can do the logically impossible is not pious nor reverential; it is just confused," argues Thomas Morris. "If we insist that God can do the logically impossible, we find that if we were to attempt to describe the results of his so doing, we violate the conditions under which, and under which alone, we are able to engage in coherent discourse of describing reality" (1991, 66f). For these reasons, most theistic philosophers reject *absolute omnipotence* in favor of a more restricted understanding.

Logical Omnipotence

Because *absolute omnipotence* renders philosophical and theological reflection problematic, theists often embrace other, more restricted, understandings of the scope of divine power. Some embrace what might be called *logical omnipotence,* which states that God can do anything that is logically possible. According to logical omnipotence, God need not be able to do logically contradictory events, although this limitation in no way detracts from divine omnipotence. For example, in response to the paradox of the stone, one who believes in *logical omnipotence* could reply that "creating a stone so heavy that God cannot lift it" is not a logically possible task.

Although he does not ultimately hold to this position, Thomas Aquinas correctly captures the essence of *logical omnipotence* in the *Summa Theologiae*:

> If . . . we consider the matter aright, since power is said in reference to possible things, this phrase, "God can do all things," is rightly understood to mean that *God can do all things that are possible;* and for this reason He is said to be omnipotent. . . . Everything that does not imply a contradiction in terms, is numbered amongst those possible things, in respect of which God is called omnipotent: whereas *whatever implies contradiction does not come within the scope of divine omnipotence,* because it cannot have the aspect of possibility. Hence it is better to say that such things cannot be done, than that God cannot do them (q. 25, a. 3, emphasis added).

According to *logical omnipotence,* it is not a limitation of God's power to say that deity cannot do what is logically impossible.

Most theists also agree that even an omnipotent being cannot change the past. According to the standard understanding of time, if an event *e* happens at time *t,* for any time after *t* it is a necessary fact that *e* occurred at *t.* This is what is known as the "necessity of the past." If the past is necessary, it would be logically impossible for any being, even an omnipotent one, to bring it about after *t* that *e* did not occur at *t.* Aquinas develops this line of argumentation saying that "some things . . . at one time were in the nature of possibility, whilst they were yet to be done, which now fall short of the nature of possibility, when they have been done. So is God said not to be able to do them, because they themselves cannot be done" (q. 25, a. 4, ob. 2).

Some have suggested that *logical omnipotence* does not go far enough in qualifying what should be meant by divine omnipotence. Consider the following list of actions, all of which are logically possible:

    a. having an essential physical nature
    b. lying

c. breaking a promise that one has previously made

d. committing suicide

e. committing an immoral action

f. sinning

Even from just this short list, one quickly sees that it is easy to describe logically possible actions that many believe God cannot do. While *logical omnipotence* avoids some of the problems inherent in *absolute omnipotence,* logical omnipotence has some problems of its own. For example, while many Christians assert that it is possible for God to assume a physical nature (i.e., the Incarnation), the dominant Christian belief has been that God is immaterial. If this is so, having a physical nature cannot be part of God's essence. Some theists have also argued that the Christian faith collapses unless it is impossible for God to lie or break promises (see Num. 23:19; Ps. 89:34). Likewise, if God loves perfectly, it would not be possible for God to sin, even though committing sin is logically possible to do. Furthermore, if one believes, as most theists do, that necessary existence is a perfection, and God has all perfections, God could not bring about God's own nonexistence.

Divine Nature Omnipotence

What I call *divine nature omnipotence* directly addresses many problems raised against *logical omnipotence.* This understanding of omnipotence is directly connected with the other attributes predicated of God (e.g., omnibenevolence, necessary existence, and omniscience). Whereas *logical omnipotence* limited God's power to actions that are possible to do, *divine nature omnipotence* further limits divine power to actions that a being with a certain nature (and all the attributes that nature involves) could do. This excludes actions that, "although it is logically possible that some being do them, God cannot do them while retaining his nature (i.e. his other essential properties)" (Swinburne, 164).

However, saying that "an omnipotent being can do anything that a being with a certain nature (and all the attributes that nature involves) can do" can be interpreted narrowly or broadly. Broadly speaking, one could affirm this third omnipotence criterion (the other criteria were listed above):

A being is omnipotent *if and only if* that being has the power to do whatever he or she is logically possible for a being with that nature to do.

If this is what one means when he or she says a being is omnipotent, almost any being could be omnipotent. This would, therefore, violate the second criterion given at the start of this chapter regarding omnipotence. Consider this example: A being is not "said to be omnipotent because he can do all things which are possible for him to do," argues William of Ockham, because "it would follow that a minimally powerful being is omnipotent. For suppose that Socrates performs one action and is not capable of performing any others. Then one argues as follows: 'He is performing every action which it is possible for him to perform, therefore he is omnipotent'" (Ockham, 611). The broad formulation of *divine nature omnipotence* is problematic. For this reason, a second, narrower definition of *divine nature omnipotence* is given:

> A being is omnipotent *if and only if* that being has the power to do whatever it is logically possible for a *perfect* being to do.

In this way one avoids the problem with the previous thought, because only beings who can do whatever a perfect being could do are omnipotent. Because theists usually believe that God is the only perfect being (that than which nothing greater can be conceived), only God would be omnipotent.

Yet in order for one to say what an omnipotent being could do according to our last statement, one would have to be able to answer the following question: What exactly is the nature of this perfect being? At worst, the statement is circular; at best, it necessitates a clearly developed doctrine of God.

One could even ask if this statement properly preserves *divine* omnipotence. I can imagine a fictitious being named Allison who has equal power with God but is not limited in the exercise of her power by any other attributes. Allison can do anything that God can do, but Allison could also do additional actions such as sin, lie, or cause needless suffering, because she is not limited by the attribute of perfect love. It would seem that Allison would then have more power than God.

A standard reply to this objection is found in the doctrine of divine simplicity. This doctrine states that God's attributes are aspects of God's one nature. Because God is identical with God's own properties, and they all require each other, no being could have one of the divine attributes (such as omnipotence) without having them all. This means that no individual other than God could have any of these properties.

When discussing the divine nature, Thomas Aquinas gives a long list of things that God cannot do even though omnipotent. This list contains the claims that God is unable to change, fail, be weary, forget, repent, violate the law of noncontradiction, or act contrary to the divine will. Thomas argues that, while God cannot do these things, such a limitation does not detract from divine omnipotence or perfection. There is no detrimental effect on the nature of God, because God is limited only by God's own nature.

In order to understand better how God might be qualified by the divine nature, consider a being who is both omnipotent and necessarily good. While sin is logically possible for many beings (a fact all too common among humans), God could not sin, because doing so would be contrary to God's nature (James 1:13). If God is necessarily good, there is a whole range of actions that God cannot do without implying any limitation on divine power.

Along the same lines, many Wesleyans describe the nature of God as self-giving and self-revealing love and maintain that the power of God is limited to those actions that are compatible with perfect love. Divine power becomes nothing else than the divine power of love, rather than some capricious or indefinable ability to do any action. According to this view, God would do only those actions wherein divine love is expressed. If God's essential nature is divine love, the questions regarding what God can do become questions about the possibilities of divine love.

Synergetic Power Omnipotence

Finally, some theists claim that the phrase "God is omnipotent" does not mean that God can do anything, even when this is understood according to the limitations discussed above. Instead, they think that saying a being is omnipotent merely means that this being is the most powerful being among other beings who also possess a degree of power. According to what might be called *synergetic power omnipotence,* an omnipotent being has the greatest amount of power that it is possible for any one being to have. Because this power is expressed synergistically, however, an omnipotent being cannot entirely control the power actions of others. For instance, while God may be able to bring it about that I drink a cup of tea, God cannot unilaterally determine that I *freely* choose to drink tea. If God unilaterally forces me to drink, my action is no longer free. All individuals, whether divine or creaturely, necessarily possess at least some degree of power, which implies that they also possess a degree of freedom. This means that God cannot entirely control the actions of others, but God acts synergistically with creatures.

Some theists, however, do not think that a being with *synergistic power omnipotence* is powerful enough to be a being worthy of worship. If God does not have power to control entirely particular circumstances of history, to what degree does God have power over the overall course of history? *Synergistic power omnipotence* implies that God cannot ensure the occurrence of those plans made by deity that involve the decisions of creatures. This notion at least seems to be contrary to some biblical portrayals of divine power.

II. CRUCIAL ISSUES PERTAINING TO OMNIPOTENCE

The problems with the various formulations of the doctrine of omnipotence have led some philosophers and theologians to abandon omnipotence in favor of other ways of expressing divine power. Joshua Hoffman and Gary Rosenkrantz, for example, deny that God is omnipotent at all and prefer to ascribe "maximal power" to deity. A maximally powerful being (similar in many ways to a being with *synergistic power omnipotence*) is one whose power cannot be exceeded by that of another being. This does not entail that a maximally powerful being could bring about any state of affairs, thereby avoiding some of the problems associated with *absolute omnipotence.*

Hoffman and Rosenkrantz also argue that the doctrine of maximal power protects human freedom from encroachment by divine power. It does not follow "that a being with *maximal power* can bring about whatever any other agent can bring about. If a can bring about s, and b cannot, it does not follow that a is *overall* more powerful than b, because it could be that b can bring about some other state or states of affairs which a cannot" (Hoffman and Rosenkrantz, 230). This would allow the theist to avoid some problems associated with saying that God is omnipotent.

Peter Geach offers another alternative for conceiving divine power. Geach distinguishes between the philosophical doctrine of "omnipotence" on the one hand and the scriptural teaching of "almightiness" on the other. Whereas the first is taken to mean "the ability to *do* everything," the latter means "having power *over* all things." Geach believes that theology must think in terms of God's almightiness, rather than God's omnipotence, because all understandings of omnipotence involve logical difficulties. "When people have tried to read into 'God can do everything' a signification not of Pious Intention but of Philosophical Truth," says Geach, "they have only landed themselves in intractable problems and hopeless confusions; no graspable sense has ever been given to this sentence that did not lead to self-contradiction or at least to conclusions manifestly untenable from the Christian point of view" (1977, 4). Given these problems, he thinks "we may well cry out with Hobbes: 'Can any man think that God is served with such absurdities?'" (Ibid., 4). Geach believes that conceiving of divine power in terms of almightiness avoids the problems of omnipotence while still affirming basic theistic beliefs about divine power.

Richard Gale largely agrees with Geach. Gale cautions against forcing the scriptural portrayal of God's power to fit into the philosophical and theological category of omnipotence. He argues,

> The idea of redesigning our concept of God might strike some as blasphemous. This becomes less shocking when it is realized that the concept of God that is the target of an atheological argument is

that of the theologian, which is a highly theoretical concept that is as distant from the somewhat anthropomorphic concept of God in the Scriptures as is the physicist's concept of a table from that of the ordinary person. . . . The basic problem that a theological concept of God faces is that of over metaphysicalizing God so that he no longer is a person and thereby becomes religiously unavailable (1991, 4).

It should be noted that the truth of Gale's words may be acknowledged without also separating philosophy from theology so that philosophy no longer has applicability to Christian faith.

For Christians, the biblical witness pertaining to divine power must be taken seriously. One must be very careful, however, when taking a biblical text or set of texts and extrapolating a theological or philosophical doctrine from them. Although there is biblical authority for including omnipotence among the divine attributes, Scripture nowhere offers a systematic account of God's power. It is a matter of interpretation regarding what the various biblical statements on divine power exactly imply, particularly given the fact that no part of scripture deals explicitly with omnipotence in the way with which omnipotence is dealt in philosophical debates. "There is considerable room for conceptual reform here," Gale argues along these lines, "since the theologian's notion of God's omnipotence is a theoretical reconstruction of the biblical notion of God Almighty" (1991, 19). Philosophical understandings of God, while perhaps being based upon scripture, should not be equated with Scripture itself.

As noted earlier, the position that one takes regarding the exact interpretation of divine omnipotence has dramatic effects on other philosophical and theological issues. Frequently this involves an apparent contradiction between omnipotence and other divine attributes. While the impact of omnipotence on some of these attributes has been mentioned earlier, the topic warrants a more detailed analysis.

A frequently mentioned example of how one's notion of omnipotence affects how one understands the other divine attributes is the problem of evil. The problem can be stated as such:

1. If God exists, God must be omnipotent (i.e., be all-powerful), which means that deity would *be able* to prevent genuinely evil occurrences.
2. If God exists, God must be omnibenevolent (i.e., love perfectly), which means that deity would *want* to prevent genuinely evil occurrences.
3. However, genuine evils occur.
4. Therefore, God must not exist.

While this issue is covered in more detail elsewhere in this volume, it is necessary to mention it in order to illustrate the importance of how one conceives divine omnipotence. According to the first premise, God, as omnipotent, is purported to have the power to prevent evil. Furthermore, as omnibenevolent, God surely would want to prevent all evil. If God has both the power and desire to end evil, the argument implies, surely God would do so. Because few people defend the proposition that genuine evils never occur, it would seem that either premise 1 or premise 2 must be abandoned or modified. Gale notes that the understanding of omnipotence in 1 is usually restricted, because modifying 2 seems to detract from God's being worthy of worship and obedience (Gale, 2). While it is not my intention to deal thoroughly with the problem of evil here, it is quite clear how central divine omnipotence is to the problem. Without omnipotence as a premise, there would be no problem. To claim that God is omnibenevolent and that God wishes to get rid of evil but cannot because God is unable allows one to explain the occurrence of genuine evil more easily.

Not only does one's doctrine of omnipotence make a difference in regard to the problem of evil and theodicy, but it also has direct influence upon the doctrine of divine goodness. According to at least some interpretations of omnipotence as outlined earlier (e.g., *absolute omnipotence* and *logical omnipotence*), an omnipotent divine being must possess the ability to do evil and/or sin. Such positions are rejected by many theists, however, because of their drastic theological ramifications. It seems intuitively true that any divine being worthy of worship and praise would not knowingly cause evil or commit sin.

As noted in the brief discussion of synergetic divine omnipotence, how one conceives of divine power affects how he or she can coherently conceive of human freedom. Christians have traditionally held that God, through creating humans in God's own image (Gen. 1:26ff), endowed them with free will. The exercise of that freedom is an essential part of what it means to be human. However, many Christians also profess that God has sovereign control over earthly events and the outcome of earthly history. If, on the one hand, all things do in fact work according to a divine plan and nothing can thwart this plan (Job 42:1ff), exactly how much freedom do humans have, and what type of freedom is it? If, on the other hand, humans really do have significant freedom, how can God be said to be in total control of earthly history?

J. L. Mackie refers to what he calls the "paradox of omnipotence" when addressing this problem. Mackie wonders whether an omnipotent being can unilaterally create a creature that this omnipotent being subsequently cannot control. According to him, a proper understanding of omnipotence precludes God having the ability to create unilaterally a creature over which He cannot subsequently exercise control. Mackie contends that this paradox of omnipotence reveals that Christianity is inconsistent to the extent that it attempts to affirm both the traditional notion that God is omnipotent and also that human beings are significantly free (1982, 160).

How can the theist reconcile divine omnipotence and creaturely freedom? A variety of answers are given to this question, and each entails beliefs about how much control God has in a world containing free beings. At one end of the spectrum, some philosophers and theologians embrace a position called compatibilism, which states that, even if God governs the world deterministically according to divine power, this detracts in no way from creaturely freedom. On the other end of the spectrum are those who think that God cannot unilaterally bring about any event in a world containing free beings. Two main alternatives on this second end of the spectrum provide nontraditional proposals for how divine omnipotence and creaturely freedom might be coherently conceived. These alternatives are found in process and feminist philosophical theologies.

Process philosophy of religion, as developed from the thought of Alfred North Whitehead and Charles Hartshorne, stands in sharp contrast with the traditional philosophical approaches of the west. At the heart of this contrast is a different understanding of divine power. Whereas traditional doctrines of divine power entail the claim that God does, or at least could, unilaterally or coercively bring about any state of affairs, process thought believes that divine expressions of power are persuasive. Whitehead argues that "the doctrine of an aboriginal, eminently real, transcendent creator, at whose fiat the world came into being, and whose imposed will it obeys, is the fallacy that has infused tragedy into the histories of Christianity and Mohametanism" (Whitehead, 519). Similarly, Hartshorne claims that "no worse falsehood was ever perpetrated than the traditional concept of omnipotence. It is a piece of unconscious blasphemy" (Hartshorne, 18).

In contrast, process theism advocates an understanding of divine power in which God influences all that happens rather than determining any particular state of affairs. God is still all-powerful, although this means that God has the highest conceivable form of power and that divine power extends noncoercively to all things. "God has power uniquely excellent in quality and scope, and in no respect inferior to any coherently conceivable power. In power, as in all properties, God is exalted beyond legitimate criticism or fault finding" (Hartshorne, 26). Hartshorne believes, however, that "omnipotence" has been so misused that the word should be dropped altogether.

Some feminists have criticized the traditional understanding of omnipotence. The question of divine power is not so much about the scope of God's power but the *kind* of power God possesses. While there is no single feminist perspective regarding divine omnipotence, many feminists consider the Christian tradition's understanding of power as male-biased.

These feminists theologians and philosophers claim that the masculinization of God has resulted in the idolatry and deification of male power. The problem does not lie just within the masculine language the tradition has typically used when referring to God. Rather, the problem is found in the underlying content of the concept of God that accompanies that language when one conceives of God primarily according to male stereotypes.

Feminist critiques also tend to focus on the social and political consequences of the traditional understanding of divine power. The problem here is not primarily with the position's metaphysical or theological ramifications but with its moral adequacy. Understanding power in terms of coercive might and dominance ultimately results in a tyrannical conception of God that is not worthy of worship. Consider, for example, the words of Dorothee Soelle:

> As a woman I have to ask why it is that human beings honor a God whose primary attribute is power, whose prime need is to subjugate, whose greatest fear is equality. . . . What kind of a God is that, whose major interests have to be described in these terms? A being who is addressed as "Lord," a being whom his theologians have to describe as all-powerful because he cannot be satisfied with being merely powerful? The most important criticisms that an incipient feminist theology has to make of the current dominant theology are directed against these phallocratic fantasies, against the accumulation of power and the worship of power. . . . Why should we honor and love this being, and what moral right do we have to do so if this being is in fact no more than an outsized man whose main idea is to be independent and have power? (1984, 97).

By reconceiving God in feminine images, feminist theologians and philosophers hope to overturn the social consequences of elevating domination and control, such as oppression, exploitation, and violence. Instead, feminists suggest that power should be developed in terms of care and responsibility. The God-world relationship characterized by divine power could then be reconceived in images of a mother who carries a child in her womb rather than in terms of a king and his kingdom. As with process philosophy, this would result in an understanding of divine power based in love, persuasion, and empowerment, rather than coercion.

CONCLUSION

This essay outlines some of the main doctrines of divine power, showing how various qualifications might be needed to correct perceived problems with other doctrines of omnipotence. Both for the Christian, in particular, and the theist, in general, the doctrine of divine power is central to a coherent conception of God. I have shown that a myriad of issues must be addressed when formulating an adequate doctrine of divine power for philosophy of religion.

Sources and Recommended Reading

Aquinas, Thomas. *On the Power of God.* Trans. the English Dominican Fathers. Westminster, Md.: Newman Press, 1952.

_____. *Summa Theologiae.* Trans. the English Domincan Fathers. Westminster, Md.: Newman Press, 1947.

Basinger, David and Randall Basinger, eds. *Predestination and Free Will: Four Views of Divine Sovereignty and Human Freedom.* Downers Grove, Ill.: InterVarsity Press, 1986.

Case-Winters, Anna. *God's Power: Traditional Understandings and Contemporary Challenges.* Louisville, Ky.: Westminster John Knox Press, 1990.

Davis, Stephen T. *Logic and the Nature of God.* Grand Rapids: Wm. B. Eerdmans Publishing Co., 1983.

Descartes, René. *The Philosophical Writings of Descartes.* Vol. III, *The Correspondence.* Trans. John Cottingham, Robert Stoothoff, Dugald Murdoch, Anthony Kenny. Cambridge: Cambridge University Press, 1984.

Flew, Antony. "Divine Omnipotence and Human Freedom." In *New Essays in Philosophical Theology.* Ed. Antony Flew and A. C. MacIntyre. London: SCM, 1963.

Flint, Thomas P., and Alfred J. Freddoso. "Maximal Power." In *The Existence and Nature of God.* Ed. Alfred J Freddoso. Notre Dame, Ind.: University of Notre Dame Press, 1983.

Frankfurt, Harry. "The Logic of Omnipotence." *Philosophical Review* (1964) 73, 262-63.

Gale, Richard M. *On the Nature and Existence of God.* Cambridge: Cambridge University Press, 1991.

Galileo. *Galileo on the World Systems: A New Abridged Translation and Guide.* Trans. and ed. Maurice A. Finocchiaro. Berkeley, Calif.: University of California Press, 1997.

Geach, Peter. *Providence and Evil.* Cambridge: Cambridge University Press, 1977.

Hartshorne, Charles. *Omnipotence and Other Theological Mistakes.* Albany, N.Y.: State University of New York Press, 1984.

Hoffman, Joshua, and Gary Rosenkrantz. "Omnipotence." In *A Companion to Philosophy of Religion.* Ed. Philip Quinn. Blackwell Companions to Philosophy. Oxford: Blackwell Publishing, 1997.

La Croix, Richard. "The Impossibility of Defining 'Omnipotence.'" *Philosophical Studies* (1977) 32.2, 181-90.

Mackie, J. L. *The Miracle of Theism: Arguments for and Against the Existence of God.* Oxford: Clarendon Press, 1982.

Morris, Thomas. *Our Idea of God: An Introduction to Philosophical Theology.* Notre Dame, Ind.: University of Notre Dame Press, 1991.

Ockham, William. *Ockham: Opera Theologica.* Vol. 4. Ed. Gerald Etzkorn and Francis Kelly. St. Bonaventure, N.Y.: St. Bonaventure Press, 1979.

Pike, Nelson. "Omnipotence and God's Ability to Sin." *The American Philosophical Quarterly* (1969), 208-16.

Plantinga, Alvin. "Does God have a Nature?" In *The Analytic Theist: An Alvin Plantinga Reader.* Ed. James Sennett. Grand Rapids: Wm. B. Eerdmans Publishing Co., 1998.

Raitt, Jill. "Structures and Strictures: Relational Theology and a Woman's Contribution to Theological Conversation." *Journal of the American Academy of Religion* (1982) 50, 3-17.

Savage, C. Wade. "The Paradox of the Stone." *The Philosophical Review* (1967) 76, 74-79.

Soelle, Dorothee. *The Strength of the Weak: Toward a Christian Feminist Identity.* trans. Robert and Rita Kimber. Philadelphia: Westminster Press, 1984.

Swinburne, Richard. *The Coherence of Theism.* Rev. ed. Oxford: Clarendon Press, 1993.

Whitehead, Alfred North. *Process and Reality: An Essay in Cosmology.* Corrected edition. Ed. David Ray Griffin and Donald W. Sherburne. New York: Free Press, 1978; Orig. ed. 1929.

Wierenga, Edward. *The Nature of God.* Ithaca, N.Y.: Cornell University Press, 1989.

DIVINE PRESENCE
Bryan P. Stone

"May the Force be with you."

Thus says Obi-wan Kenobi in his now-classic benediction to Luke Skywalker in *Star Wars*. But how is the Force present in the world? Obi-wan describes it as "an energy field created by all living things. It surrounds us. It penetrates us. It binds the galaxy together." Still, that leaves a lot of questions unanswered. Fortunately, *Star Wars* is just a movie, and there is no pressing need for us to comprehend its universe. Yet most religious people throughout history have taken quite seriously the question of how the divine is present in, with, and to the world. How is it that we should speak of God's influence not only in the universe but also in human life?

In some religious traditions—most of them ancient but several of them quite vital even today—the presence of the supernatural is conceived of as operating through nature itself. In these traditions, otherwise "inanimate" objects are taken to be spiritually alive or "animated" by the divine. For these *animistic* religions, the whole world is understood to be full of sacred presences with which humans may learn to live in harmony and from whose power humans may benefit. So, for example, Japanese Shinto holds that various *kami* (gods, or sacred powers) are present in natural objects, such as rocks, mountains, or trees. Shinto employs rituals both to appease these *kami* and to reverence them. Likewise, in some Native American traditions and in some tribal religions in Africa and elsewhere, shamans or spirit-mediums are believed to hold the power to connect individuals and entire communities with the sacred powers in and around them.

These animistic traditions rarely think of sacred powers in nature as personal deities. Rather, they think of them as supernatural forces or presences. In the case of *polytheism* (literally, a belief in "many gods"), however, these powers take on personal characteristics and are situated within a larger pantheon of gods. The most well known of these gods appears in ancient Roman and Greek literature. Still, the activity of these individual gods is fairly limited to a particular region or to particular aspects of nature or human interaction. So, for example, Zeus causes lightening and Poseidon causes earthquakes. For the Greeks, Aphrodite is the goddess of love, while for the Romans it is Venus. It is likely that even Judaism, which is rigidly monotheistic, may have early on held to at least a "descriptive polytheism," whereby it would have acknowledged the existence, presence, and power of other gods without actually worshiping them.

In contrast to animists or polytheists, *monotheists* believe strictly in one god. So, for example, the writer of Deuteronomy insists that "the LORD is our God, the LORD is one!" (6:4, NASB). Likewise, in the New Testament we are told that there is "one God and Father of all who is over all and through all and in all" (Eph. 4:6; 1 Tim. 2:5). For Muslims, too, "God is one God. There is no god but He" (Qu'ran 2:163).

Monotheists are often referred to simply as *theists,* because they believe that God exists, in contrast to *atheists,* who do not believe that God exists. There is, however, great variety in how theists understand the relationship of God to the world. Most theists believe that God is omnipresent; i.e., they believe that God is in all places at all times. Consider the following words from John Wesley, the 18th-century British evangelist and founder of Methodism, in a sermon in which he is commenting on a particular passage from Jesus' Sermon on the Mount:

> But the great lesson which our blessed Lord inculcates here, and which he illustrates by this example, is that God is in all things, and that we are to see the Creator in the glass of every creature; that we should use and look upon nothing as separate from God, which indeed is a kind of practical atheism; but with a true magnificence of thought survey heaven and earth and all that is therein as contained by God in the hollow of his hand, who by his intimate presence holds them all in being, who pervades and actuates the whole created frame, and is in a true sense the soul of the universe (1991, 516-17).

But just as theists generally believe in God's omnipresence (or universality), so most theists also hold to God's individuality and can even speak of God in "personal" terms as an individual with whom relationship is possible. God is one who loves us, listens to us, and responds to us. Of course, God is not merely one individual among others, not even the greatest among these, but rather *the* individual. God is the only "universal individual" whose existence is both necessary and boundless and in whom everything finds both its ultimate source and final end (Ogden 1996, 98-99). Likewise, to speak of God as personal is not to say that God is a "person" in the ordinary sense that word is used, which usually includes (a) finitude and (b) gender. But to say God is personal is to agree with Martin Buber that "the relation to a human being is the proper metaphor for the relation to God" (1970, 151) so that God is to be addressed as a "You" rather than an "It." As Grace Jantzen puts it, "although God is the supreme mystery, and hence all our predicates stand in need of qualification in their application to him, he is a personal mystery, not less" (1984, 15).

The pressing philosophical questions become: How we are to construe God's presence in the world as both universal *and* individual? How is it that the One whom theists claim is present everywhere and at all times can also be present personally? Is, for example, the relationship between God and the world one of intimacy or is it more external and remote? Do God and the world influence one another or is the influence unilateral? Does God act in the world persuasively or, instead, coercively? Given that this personal God is the creator of the world, how is God related to the world? Should we imagine God's relationship to the world as that of a carpenter to a table? Or is it more like that of a mother to a child? Is God related to the world like a soul to a body, or the sun to its rays of light?

I. TYPES OF THEISM

In response to these questions, it is possible to distinguish four major positions that have come to predominate among theists over time: (1) pantheism, (2) deism, (3) classical theism, and (4) neoclassical theism (also sometimes referred to as "panentheism" or "process theism"). Although there are considerable differences between each of these positions, it is possible to view all of them as forming something like a continuum along which there are other mediating positions. Each of the four positions attempts to answer the question of how God is both individual and universal. Each offers its own model of how God, as creator of the world, is related to the world. Each is distinctive in the way it conceives of, on the one hand, God's *transcendence,* distinctiveness, or "other"-ness from the world and, on the other hand, God's *immanence* in, proximity to, or identification with the world.

The first position, *pantheism,* affirms the total immanence of God in the world such that any distinction between the two is removed. God is simply identified with the world. For that reason, some consider pantheism as but another form of atheism and perhaps not even monotheistic at all. There is clearly no distinct creator or transcendent deity here. Pantheism is monistic in that it conceives of only one thing, force, or substance that is ultimately real. It avoids mind/body, God/world, and spirit/matter dualisms by collapsing these distinctions altogether. Indeed, one of the most powerful beliefs of pantheism is the unity of all things, and often this arises from a mystical experience of the world in which distinctions recede into the background in the presence of a single all-inclusive divine reality. So, for example, the Advaita Vedanta philosophy of Hinduism holds that there is only one nondualistic reality: Brahman. To understand oneself truly is to realize that the self *is* Brahman. Furthermore, this one ultimate reality is generally understood to be impersonal. It is important to note, however, that there are significant streams of Vedantic thought that construe this single ultimate reality as a personal and worshipful supreme being. Some streams even understand various gods and goddesses to be incarnations or "avatars" of the one supreme being.

Pantheistic conceptions of the God-world relationship have influenced several varieties of monotheistic religion over the centuries. The Neoplatonist philosophers of the third through sixth centuries—most notably Plotinus (CE 204/5-70)—held to a view of creation that borders on pantheism. Plotinus argued that the world emanates from "the One" in a way that is similar to the way heat or rays of light emanate from the sun. For Plotinus, the One, as transcendent source, remains unchanged and is not merely spread out in a pantheistic way. The One "proceeds" or "flows out" and generates other levels of being. Still, there is a necessity to this emanation—creation is not a voluntary act of a personal deity—and thus later conceptions of the God-world relationship that borrow from this worldview tend to be pantheistic (for example, the Jewish form of mysticism known as "Kabbalah").

If pantheism erases or at least blurs the line between God and the world by conceiving of God as wholly immanent in the world, *deism* lies on the other end of the theistic spectrum by construing God's relationship with the world as far more remote and external. Especially popular in America and Western Europe in the 17th and 18th centuries, deism flourished in a period when there was enormous confidence in the power of reason not only to prove the existence of God but also to grasp the character of the moral and natural laws that God set up to govern the universe. Deists had little use for the notion of a special revelation, whereby God should intervene in the world to reveal truths otherwise inaccessible by our senses and our reason. It would hardly be fair that the most important truths about the nature of the world and the way we ought to live should be available only to those who have access to special revelation. Instead, the knowledge of God is generally available and utterly rational. It is worth noting that democracies were being born in this period. Reason was considered far more suitable to democratic ideals than other sources of authority, because reason was more universally reliable as a path to truth. Indeed, many of the founders of the United States (such as Benjamin Franklin, Thomas Jefferson, and George Washington) held beliefs that were essentially deistic. Even the Declaration of Independence holds that the truth of human equality is "self-evident."

The mere fact that deists trusted in reason does not mean that they did not believe in the Bible, although some deists did reject those portions of Scripture that seemed inexplicable to reason. Miracles, for example, do not really fit a deistic worldview, because miracles require the suspension of an orderly, predictable universe and rely, instead, upon a God who intervenes from time to time in earthly affairs. Most deists simply tried to interpret the Bible to show that its truths, far from being irrational or incomprehensible, were perfectly reasonable. One can detect this concern in the titles of two of the most important deistic books of the time: John Toland's *Christianity Not Mysterious* (1696) and Matthew Tindal's *Christianity as Old as Creation* (1730).

Knowing even this much about deism, it is not too difficult to see how many deists would interpret God's relationship with the world as somewhat detached and distant. Although God created the world, God was not thought to maintain a constant guiding or sustaining presence in the world. Instead, the world might be imagined as a large clock that, having been wound up by the watchmaker, is capable of running on its own. This does not mean that God does not love the world. Rather, God lovingly created the world according to natural laws that are for our benefit. Likewise, we need not speak of God's immanence in the world other than through the regularity and rhythms that God has put into place.

Some interpreters of Islam compare Islamic understanding of God with deism. Muslims typically believe it dangerous to think of God as being encountered directly, although God may be known through divine laws. For example, Islam strictly forbids representations of the deity, because such representations necessarily idolize and lift the contingent, human, or ordinary features of our world to the level of deity. God, contend Muslims, is far beyond the human imagination. There are, however, more mystical forms of Islam, such as Sufism, that encourage spiritual paths toward a more immediate encounter with God—although God nonetheless remains ineffable. And unlike deism, Islam believes that the truth about God cannot be known through reason. God can be known only through special revelation and through prophets such as Moses, Jesus, and, most perfectly, Mohammed.

In contrast to both deism and pantheism stands *classical theism,* the belief that God is distinct from the world but nonetheless present and active in the world as creator, governor, and sustainer. God is the one unique, eternal, and ultimate reality who is all-powerful, omniscient, self-sufficient, and unchanging. Clearly, classical theism is the most widespread conception of God among monotheists. In fact, most Christians, Jews, or Muslims would simply consider it the orthodox view of God. And yet classical theism is shaped deeply by philosophical commitments outside each of these traditions. These philosophical traditions go back as far as Plato and Aristotle (some four centuries before Christ), and these commitments continued in the Neoplatonists of the third through sixth centuries after Christ. The very fact that many theists consider this view of God to be orthodox, despite the fact that it often conflicts with the portrayals of God in their own sacred texts, reveals the extent to which all three major monotheistic traditions have been shaped by the Platonic philosophical tradition.

For classical theism, God is "perfect," by which is meant "complete" and self-sufficient. God needs nothing and is completely independent. God does not need the world, and God would be the same God whether or not any world was to exist at all. Just as Plato identified perfection with that which is unchangeable (or "immutable"), so also, for classical theism, God cannot change or be changed. If God could change in any way, He would not be perfect or complete.

All this does not mean that classical theists regard God as unrelated to the world. However, God's relationship to the world is essentially external. Here it is important to distinguish between two types of relations: external and internal. If I enter a kitchen where a hot apple pie has just been taken out of the oven, I have an internal relationship to that pie. I am different, because I will usually grow hungry for a slice of the pie whose aroma tantalizes me. The pie (*qua* pie), however, is unchanged by my presence. The internal relationship is not mutual. The pie's relationship to me is external, because I make no internal difference to the pie. Or, consider two pool balls bumping into each other. In their bumping, they have only an external relationship to one another. Only their location relative to one another has changed. They themselves have not changed substantially from the pool balls they once were. Individuals, however, are another kind of thing altogether. Our mere presence or absence can change internally those with who we are in relationship.

For classical Greek philosophy—and the theism that has been shaped by it—God's relationship to the world is wholly external to God, which means that the world in no way essentially affects or changes God. To admit the contrary, say classical theists, is to admit that God is not already as perfect as God might be. For classical theism, there are no possibilities for God that are not already realized. One should certainly never talk about God being "enriched." God is completely self-sufficient. God may act upon the world, but deity cannot be acted upon by the world. As Aristotle argued, God is the "unmoved mover"—the one who sets all things in motion and influences all that is. But God is not likewise moved or influenced by anything. So also, for classical theism, God does not exist in time, for time is meaningful only when change occurs. To say that God is eternal, therefore, does not mean that God exists in "all" time (understood as endless duration), but rather it means that God exists in "no" time or "outside of" time.

These classical superlatives may sound like high praise when applied to God: God is perfect; God is complete; God can do anything; God needs nothing; God is unbound by time. Consider one of these claims as a specific example: God is unchanging. Apart from such an attribute, it is difficult to see how one could worship God or depend upon God. Certainly what sets the theistic deity apart from the fickle deities of ancient polytheism is that God is not capricious, whimsical, or untrustworthy. God is a rock upon which we can build our lives (Ps. 18:2) and in whom we can place our trust. As Mal. 3:6 reports, "I the LORD do not change." Likewise, in the Epistle of James, we read, "Every good thing bestowed and every perfect gift is from above, coming down from the Father of lights, with whom there is no variation, or shifting shadow" (1:17, NASB).

And yet in a number of critically important ways, classical theism does not do justice to many of the central theistic claims about God, especially those found in the Bible pertaining to the quality of God's relationships with human beings. The God of the Hebrews is one who is said to be alive and active in history, rather than standing outside it. God is portrayed as a deity who, for example, can even have a change of mind based on the repentance of human beings (Jon. 3:10) or in response to petitions such as those of Amos (7:4-7) or Abraham (Gen.18:22-33). Consider the following exchange between Moses and God:

> Then Moses entreated the LORD his God, and said, "O LORD, why does Your anger burn against Your people whom You have brought out from the land of Egypt with great power and with a mighty hand? . . . Turn from Your burning anger and change Your mind about doing harm to Your people. Remember Abraham, Isaac, and Israel, Your servants to whom You swore to Yourself, and said to them, 'I will multiply your descendants as the stars of the heavens, and all this land of which I have spoken I will give to your descendants, and they shall inherit it forever.'" So the LORD changed His mind about the harm which He said He would do to His people (Exod. 32:11-14, NASB).

Perhaps such stories can be written off as merely anthropomorphic representations of God (i.e., treating a nonhuman as if it were human) not to be taken literally. But there remain serious philosophical and theological questions about the God of classical theism that bear critical scrutiny. Indeed, it is difficult to make much sense of prayer if there is no sense in which God changes or can be changed. Some theists are fond of saying that prayer changes us but not God. While this is a clever way of exempting God from change, it does not comport well with biblical examples of prayer that are quite literally petitions that expect particular responses from God. It may sound like high praise to claim that God is self-sufficient and unchanging in all ways, but one is left with a God who cannot really be affected by others or experience joy and suffering. For if God did suffer with us, God's emotional state would, in some sense, be dependent upon us. It would therefore be possible for us to affect a change in God. For this reason, classical theism has always insisted that, properly speaking, God cannot suffer. Even the very basic claim that we "matter" to God cannot, strictly speaking, be true for classical theism. Nothing "matters" to God. If it did, God would be changeable. It is impossible to "matter" to someone without that someone's being changed in some way.

For these and a number of other reasons, *neoclassical theism* proposes a view of God that, while similar to classical theism, differs from it in crucial ways. Neoclassical theism (or "panentheism") expresses the notion that God's relationship with the world is dynamic and, to some extent, mutual. While classical and neoclassical theism agree on the scope of God's relations—God is related to literally everything—neoclassical theism insists that these relations are internal, making a real difference both to God and the world. As we have seen, classical theism denies internal relations in the case of God. And here lies an essential difference between the two conceptions: for classical theism, nothing truly makes a difference to God while, for neoclassical theism, everything makes a difference to God. Charles Hartshorne, one of the most important of the neoclassical philosophers, puts the matter this way: "A personal God is one who has social relations, *really* has them, and thus is constituted by relationships and hence is relative" (1948, x). Not only is God social, says Hartshorne, but supremely so.

The difference between these two conceptions of deity has dramatic implications for how God's involvement in the world is imagined. Classical theism might envision God's relationship to the world as that of a carpenter to a table or as a potter to clay. Neoclassical theism, on the other hand, would be more comfortable with the previously mentioned description of God by John Wesley as an "intimate presence . . . who pervades and actuates the whole created frame, and is in a true sense the soul of the universe" (1991, 516-17). This, of course, does not mean that Wesley was a neoclassical theist. But clearly the God-world relationship in neoclassical theism is just this intimate, much more so than is allowed by classical theism. What happens in the world affects God and really matters to God; it even changes God to some extent. God could not be love otherwise. The very fact that God is love—that God unfailingly and unsurpassingly shares the joys and sufferings of the world—is precisely what does not change about God. Thus, there is a sense in which neoclassical theism wants to affirm that God is immutable (unchanging), but only inso-far as God could never fail to be loving. That is, God could never fail both to be enriched by all and to respond adequately to all. God can, therefore, be said to include the world into God's own being (it really "matters" to God). It is for this reason that neoclassical theism is also referred to as *panentheism*—literally, "all is *in* God," in contrast to pantheism, for which "all is God."

Neoclassical theism rejects the classical conceptions of divine im-mutability, independence, and self-sufficiency, not because they are alto-gether wrong, but because these conceptions are only partially true. They emphasize only part of what needs to be said about God. Perhaps "rock" is a good metaphor for God in some respects, but not in every respect. Rocks may be reliable, but they are not very loving, forgiving, listening, or responsive in times of trouble. Consider the following argument from Hartshorne: "Suppose . . . a man says, 'I can be equally happy and serene and joyous regardless of how men and women suffer around me.' Shall we admire this alleged independence? I think not. Why should we admire it when it is alleged of God?" (1948, 44)

That God should change in response to what happens in the world, according to neoclassical theists, is not a sign of weakness or a lack of perfection. Perfection is not to be measured "quantitatively" such that it does not admit of increase or alteration. It is to be measured qualitatively in terms of appropriateness to the situation. There is nothing admirable about human beings who have become so utterly independent, insulated, and isolated that they can neither rejoice with those who rejoice or mourn with those who mourn. So also, there is nothing majestic or worshipful about a God who is unmoved when the creation experiences joy and suf-fering. The problem with classical theism, argues Hartshorne, is that it was as much Greek as it was Christian, Jewish, or Islamic. It was "an incorrect translation of the central religious idea into philosophical categories" (1948, vii).

What neoclassical theism argues for, therefore, is a conception of God that is "di-polar" (Whitehead 1978 [1929], 345). God both influ-ences the world and is influenced by the world. God is a source of all that exists and yet also a recipient of all that exists. God is immutable in one respect and mutable in another respect. God is independent of the world (God will be God regardless of any particular world to which God is relat-ed) and yet dependent upon the world (God genuinely experiences the world and is changed by that experience). God is free, and yet God does not have complete control over the way in which God will be influenced. God is not a coercive dictator; rather, God leads the world through beauty and persuasion. God influences the world by providing aims requiring our free response. Alfred North Whitehead, generally acknowledged as the most important philosophical source of this type of theism, says that this vision of God "does not emphasize the ruling Caesar, or the ruthless moralist, or the unmoved mover. It dwells upon the tender elements in the world, which slowly and in quietness operate by love. . . . Love neither rules, nor is it unmoved" (1978 [1929], 343).

How might we go about evaluating these very different ways of conceiving divine presence and influence in the world? How, if at all, are we to ask about their meaning and truth? Clearly, we will not be able to validate one or the other on the basis of empirical observation. And yet at the same time our experience of the world does shape our understanding of the God-world relationship. In a prescientific era, "natural" phenomena such as lightning, thunder, tides, disease, or the movement of the sun, moon, and stars were readily explained with reference to supranaturalistic forces or deities. With the advent of Newtonian physics, mechanistic laws of cause and effect prevailed and influenced a more deistic account of how God acted in the world. Today, however, newer discoveries in relativity theory and quantum mechanics have taught us that reality is not made up of static substances—inert, lifeless atoms that merely act upon one another—but rather interrelated and dynamic force fields, wave-particles, and quanta of energy such that reality takes on the characteristics more of an event rather than a collection of "things" or "substances." To many, a neoclassical theism now appears to fit better with this more dynamic, organic, and social view of reality.

In addition to thinking about how our understanding of the God-world relationship corresponds to our experience, theists who wish to commend their position to others will naturally be concerned to think through the rational credibility and coherence of each view. For example, do the claims of a particular position entail any self-contradictions? Are the claims coherent and intelligible? Insofar as a theist is not one solely on philosophical grounds but also (or even primarily) on religious grounds, he or she may also ask about the compatibility of each position with the core texts that are held to be authoritative in one's own particular religious tradition. A Christian will certainly be concerned to ask whether this or that view of God's presence in the world corresponds faithfully to the way biblical writers generally represent God. The same would be true for a Jew in the case of the Hebrew Scriptures or for a Muslim with regard to the Qu'ran.

The criterion of "worshipfulness" may well end up serving as the most important measure for judging whether this or that view of God's presence is religiously satisfying. If, on the one hand, God is identified too closely with the world, God's majesty and sovereignty may be obscured. The net result may be that the sense of human dependency upon God necessary for worship is thereby eroded. This is a criticism that is sometimes made against neoclassical theism. Perhaps a God with no coercive power to change the world unilaterally is not, after all, a God worthy of worship. If, on the other hand, God's relationship to the world is too remote or is wholly external, there may be little sense that we can approach God in prayer and worship. An overly transcendent God may provide little reason for us to believe that any of our actions really matter to God.

II. THE SPIRIT AND DIVINE PRESENCE

The most common biblical expression for speaking about God's presence in the world is "Spirit"—an incredibly rich term both theologically and philosophically. In the Hebrew Scriptures the word for Spirit, *ruach,* is synonymous with "breath," "wind," or "air." Such imagery is provocative as a way of describing God's presence and agency in creating, sustaining, guiding, liberating, and transforming. Early in the Book of Genesis we find God's Spirit blowing over the surface of the waters as the agent of creation (1:2). Likewise, it is God's Spirit that is blown into the nostrils of human beings making them "living beings" (2:7). It is this continued "breath" in our lives that upholds us: "The Spirit of God has made me, And the breath of the Almighty gives me life. . . . If He should gather to himself His spirit and His breath, all flesh would perish together, and [humanity] would return to dust" (Job 33:4, 34:14-15, NASB).

The Spirit represents God's activity in particular situations and in specific instances and individuals. It is God's Spirit who endows certain persons with distinct gifts and abilities, and this Spirit anoints chosen persons for special callings and purposes. The Spirit is the source of leadership ability (Num. 11), prophetic visions, and speech (Is. 61:1ff). God can even be spoken of as "coming upon" individuals such as prophets and judges. In fact, the future Messiah is portrayed as one who will be especially endowed with the Spirit (Isa. 11; 42:1-4). In rabbinic literature, the word *Shekhinah* is used to describe God's presence, or literally "dwelling" (Exod. 25:8), so that God's nearness is even further emphasized. New Testament writers portray the Spirit as God's active presence that not only dwells in us but in which we are to dwell (Rom. 8:9; Eph. 2:22) and by which we are called to walk (Gal. 5:25).

The Spirit is also a way of talking about God's universal and inescapable presence that is far beyond any personal, private, or communal experience of God. As the Psalmist writes, "Where can I go from Your Spirit? Or where can I flee from Your presence? If I ascend to heaven, You are there; If I make my bed in Sheol, behold, You are there. If I take the wings of the dawn, If I dwell in the remotest part of the sea, Even there Your hand will lead me, And Your right hand will lay hold of me" (Ps.

139:7-10, NASB). It is precisely this universality of God's presence and activity in Jewish history that created a tension, as Michael Lodahl notes, "between God's presence among the people Israel and their intuition that God must also be present and active in the world and peoples outside Israel" (1992, 57). It is likewise this universality of the Spirit that in the New Testament becomes the basis not only for Christian unity (Eph. 4:3-4) and a creative liberty that stands against all deadening legalism (2 Cor. 3:17) but also for an inclusiveness and equality that defies any sort of elitism based on heredity, race, status, or power.

This dual emphasis in the biblical notion of God's Spirit is instructive for philosophical reflection on divine presence from a theistic standpoint. Spirit can be used as shorthand both for God's discernible and intimate presence and, at the same time, for God's mysterious "otherness." On the one hand, God's presence may be sought and invoked through disciplines such as fasting, prayer, worship, works of mercy and justice, or meditation. It is a life-altering gift that, while always somehow present, can yet break in and transform human beings in powerful ways—with the prophetic hope that some day the Spirit will be "poured out" on all persons (Joel 2:28-29). On the other hand, God's presence is creative and mysterious, often defying rational constructs and definition. Like the wind, the Spirit "blows where it wishes" (John 3:8, NASB). It may in no sense be manipulated, as with Simon the magician, who sought to buy the gift of the Holy Spirit from the apostles (Acts 8:9-24).

Fidelity to the metaphor of "Spirit" in talking about divine presence and agency requires us to abandon strictly mechanical accounts of causation and to think beyond the debilitating subject-object dualism of classical Western thought. Indeed, one of the most engaging aspects of the Spirit as a clue to how we might understand divine activity in the world is its function in pointing us to God as the presence of hope and novelty. Often in the Bible the Spirit represents God's presence as a down payment or "first fruits" of the future toward which God is leading the world. Here we discover that the divine is present not as much as a force from the ancient past but as a future aim and hope.

A theism that makes room for the divine presence as a "call forward" (Cobb 1969, 45), rather than as a sanction of the established past or a unilateral determination of the present, will have radical implications for how we live our lives on a daily basis. That God "acts upon" the world (if we can even use that way of talking) not by mechanical coercion but by "inspiration" (literally by "breathing into") affirms creaturely dignity, freedom, and creativity. As John Cobb Jr. says:

> The Creator-Lord of history is not the all-determinative cause of the course of natural and historical events, but a lover of the world

who calls it ever beyond what it has attained by affirming life, novelty, consciousness, and freedom again and again. . . . The Holy One is not the primordial sacred which transcends and annihilates all separateness and individuality through mysterious and dehumanizing cults, but the immanent-transcendent Ground of life and creativity which calls us ever forward in and through the ordinary events of daily life and the often terrifying occurrences of human history (1969, 65-66).

As properly abstract as is the question of God's relationship to the world, perhaps we can also begin to see some of the implications of how we construe this relationship for such central moral concerns as, for example, contemporary ecological issues. A negative assessment of the material world, born largely of the Platonic dualism of body and soul, heavily shaped the classical Western philosophy's stress upon God's separation and independence from the world. It would have been utterly inconceivable that the divine could be sullied by the physical world, much less that the world might actually be imagined as in some sense genuinely affecting God. The world and the physical body were construed as distractions from that which is ultimate, divine, and eternal. Today, however, there is a new openness among theists in the West to a more organic and relational worldview that finds God intimately involved in creation while nonetheless remaining the mystery and depth of creation. The world, including not only human life but all plant and animal life as well, may be valued in its own right as something that enriches God. Therefore, the world is something to be treated and tended with respect.

For a Christian theist, who is committed to understanding the divine as having been incarnated in the very physical "stuff" of this world, classical dualisms between soul and body, spirit and matter, God and world simply will not do. These dualisms were inherited largely from philosophical sources alien to Judeo-Christian commitments anyway. There are some things that a Christian theist may learn from other religious and philosophical perspectives about how we should speak of divine presence. The respect for the natural ecosphere found in Native American religious traditions, for example, stands in stark contrast to the exploitation of the planet in those parts of the world where Christianity has predominated for nearly two millennia. The difference in attitude toward the ecosphere is fundamentally related to the very different ways that God's relationship to the world has been envisioned in each tradition. And yet, within Christian theism's understanding of God's presence as "Spirit," there are clearly resources that offer hope for a new and liberating theism. There are resources for a theism that preserves God's transcendence without reducing the world to insignificance and one that preserves God's immanence without elevating the world to the status of deity itself.

Bibliography

Buber, Martin. *I and Thou.* Trans. Walter Kaufmann. New York: Charles Scribner's Sons, 1970.

Cobb, John B., Jr. *God and the World.* Philadelphia: Westminster Press, 1969.

Hartshorne, Charles. *The Divine Relativity: A Social Conception of God.* New Haven, Conn.: Yale University Press, 1948.

Heron, Alasdair I. C. *The Holy Spirit.* Philadelphia: Westminster Press, 1983.

Jantzen, Grace. *God's World, God's Body.* Philadelphia: Westminster Press, 1984.

Lodahl, Michael Eugene. *Shekhinah/Spirit: Divine Presence in Jewish and Christian Religion.* New York: Paulist, 1992.

McFague, Sallie. *Models of God: Theology for an Ecological, Nuclear Age.* Philadelphia: Fortress Press, 1987.

———. *The Body of God: An Ecological Theology.* Minneapolis: Fortress Press, 1993.

Ogden, Schubert M. *Doing Theology Today.* Valley Forge, Penn.: Trinity Press, 1996.

Wesley, John. Sermon 23, "Upon Our Lord's Sermon on the Mount: Discourse the Third." *The Works of John Wesley.* Bicentennial Edition. Ed. Albert C. Outler. Nashville: Abingdon Press, 1991 (510-30).

Whitehead, Alfred North. *Process and Reality.* Ed. David Ray Griffin and Donald W. Sherburne. New York: The Free Press, 1978.

DIVINE KNOWLEDGE AND RELATION TO TIME

Amos Yong

◆

I. INTRODUCTION

The problem of divine foreknowledge and creaturely freedom can be stated as follows:

1. God knows all things—past, present, and future.
2. If God knows the future, the future is determined.
3. If the future is determined, my future acts are predetermined.
4. If my future acts are predetermined, I am not truly free or responsible for those acts.
5. Yet God, as judge, holds me accountable for my actions.

The question of how divine foreknowledge and creaturely freedom are related has drawn the sustained attention of Christian philosophers and theologians over the centuries. (Space constraints prohibit discussion of Jewish, Islamic or Hindu responses to this issue, although these religious traditions offer substantive contributions to this topic that merit attention.) One solution to this question is to deny premise 5 above. In other words, someone may either deny that God will someday judge sinners for sins committed or deny that God presently judges sin. But to deny creaturely accountability and divine judgment, say critics, indicates one's failure to consider adequately the biblical notions of divine love and wrath, eternal punishment, God's repugnance toward sin, and moral responsibility.

Someone could "solve" the problem by understanding the predetermination of 3 and 4 as compatible with creaturely freedom. This solution is called *compatibilism,* and compatibilists generally define freedom as doing what one wishes to do apart from external hindrance. What someone wants to do is determined by what he or she likes or dislikes, what options are available, the causal factors preceding a decision, or the outcomes expected or desired. In this case, a person's future sins are predetermined by a person's predilection to sin. This can be known by God, say compatibilists, without the knowledge undermining a person's responsibility for having committed these sins.

A third solution to the problem relies upon a more robust doctrine of freedom, which emphasizes self-determination. *Incompatibilism,* also known as *libertarianism,* defines freedom in terms of an agent possessing both the capacity and the opportunity to choose between alternative, pos-sible, future options. Given this libertarian notion of freedom (which pro-ponents claim is both intuitive and necessary for moral responsibility), the foreknowledge-freedom dilemma is understood differently. For libertari-ans, the question arises as to whether or not God can know with certainty the future contingent acts of free creatures if these creatures are truly free.

Each of these responses is related to how one understands claims 1 and 2 above. But how should these claims be understood? For instance, what is it that God knows? How does God know what God knows? Does God know the future, and if so, what is the nature of this knowledge? Does God know only the past and present as actual and the future as con-sisting of possibilities? Is the future a determined portion of eternity, an un-determined aspect of time's flow, or perhaps only causally and contingent-ly determinable?

In this essay I begin by addressing questions about time, eternity, and the future. Following this, I proceed to the heart of this essay, which in-cludes the question of God's relationship to time and eternity. In the final section, I turn to the proposed solutions to the divine foreknowledge—creaturely freedom dilemma.

II. TIME, ETERNITY, AND THE NATURE OF THE FUTURE

Questions regarding the nature of time, eternity, and the future are the focus of this segment. Two dominant models for understanding the relationship between time and eternity have emerged in Western civiliza-tion. I refer to them as the "Parmenidean" and the "Heraclitan" models after ancient Greek philosophers Parmenides (ca. 515—450 B.C.) and Her-aclitus (ca. 540—475 B.C).

The Parmenidean model emphasizes the eternal now. Parmenides reasoned that all change registered by sense experience must be illusory, because it is impossible for something nonexistent to begin existing. Being must therefore be eternal, changeless, and accessible only to thought. In its Platonic and Neoplatonic forms, the Parmenidean model of time can be understood either as the moving image of eternity (Plato) or as the sub-jective anticipation and memory of the soul (Augustine). Past, present, and future are temporal manifestations and expressions of what eternally in-variably is. Things do not actually come into or pass out of existence. The Parmenidean model can also be understood negatively, in which eternity consists of the removal of time entirely (Plotinus). Or it can be conceived of positively, in which eternity consists of the entirety of time's together-ness (Boethius' *totum simul*). The Parmenidean model inclines toward a deterministic understanding of what we think of as temporal processes.

The Heraclitan model, by contrast, emphasizes the ontological reality of temporal passage. Heraclitus's saying "You cannot step into the same river twice" highlights the experience of time's flow. In the Aristotelian form of the Heraclitan model, time is synonymous with sequence. Time is understood as the means of measuring physical motion. The Heraclitan model understands eternity as the beginningless and endless duration of time. Aristotle was thus inclined to see the universe as endlessly existing, with particular things coming into and fading out of existence. Because time's flow is constitutive of reality, our experience of temporal passage is indicative of the way things really are. This model inclines toward an indeterministic understanding of temporal processes.

So which one of these models is correct? Everyday experience tends to confirm the reality of temporal passage (Heraclitan). However, mystics in most religious traditions suggest that humans are sometimes able to transcend temporal experience (Parmenidean).

How one understands the nature of time affects what one thinks about the future. The Parmenidean model regards the future as already actual and predetermined. Those who believe that creaturely actions cannot change the future, i.e., *fatalists,* hold this position. The Parmenidean model also appeals to compatibilists who believe that the future is not random or haphazard but determined by past and present events. For the Heraclitan model, however, the future is understood as not yet actual, undetermined (or determinable), and at least partially open. Heraclitans believe that past and present do not totally determine what will occur in the future. The future emerges from a complex of factors, they claim, including causal influences from the past, novel action on the part of free agents in the present, and, perhaps, even random and spontaneous events.

III. GOD, TIME, AND ETERNITY

Not surprisingly, the Parmenidean and Heraclitan models of time and eternity have theological counterparts. Application of the Parmenidean model to theology results in an eternal, nontemporal, or timeless God. Application of the Heraclitan model leads to a sempiternal, pantemporal, or everlasting God. In what follows, I elaborate on the strengths and weaknesses of these theological models. Before proceeding, however, I offer a brief exegetical digression to explain why this issue resists an obvious biblical answer.

Biblical scholars are divided on how to understand the biblical concept of "eternity." Oscar Cullmann has argued that divine timelessness, or what I have called the Parmenidean notion of eternity, is a nonbiblical, Platonic intrusion into Christian theology. The biblical understanding of eternity (the prevalent words are *olam* in the Hebrew Bible and *aion* in the Greek New Testament) is "endless time," says Cullman. Eternity should be understood as pantemporal; it is "the linking of an unlimited series of limited world periods, whose succession only God is able to survey" (1964, 46). Cullmann proposes that the biblical concept of time is linear, and linear time should be preferred to the Hellenistic concept of cyclical time.

James Barr claims, however, that Cullmann argues primarily on the basis of biblical word studies, and this makes Cullmann's work methodologically flawed. Theological conclusions should be derived from the syntactical complexes of the biblical data, Barr says, rather than the etymological or lexical data abstracted from their contexts. Cullmann has read into the Bible his own views of time and eternity, says Barr, and the result is a distorted understanding (1962).

Who is correct? It is best to admit that the biblical evidence is ambiguous on this issue; passages can be interpreted as supporting either model. For instance, the divine name revealed to Moses in Exod. 3:14 can be understood either as "I am who I am" (a Parmenidean reading) or "I will be who I will be" (a Heraclitan reading). Also, "Jesus Christ is the same yesterday and today and for ever" (Heb. 13:8) can be interpreted as either describing an eternal Christ or pointing to Christ's everlasting constancy. (Other "Parmenidean" texts include Eccles. 3:11; John 8:58; and 2 Pet. 3:8. "Heraclitan" passages are said to include Exod. 15:18; Ps. 90:2; 102:25-27 [referred to in Heb. 1:10-12], Isa. 40:28; and Mic. 5:2.)

If the Bible can be interpreted to support either view, how should one conceive of God's relationship to time and eternity? The Parmenidean model understands God as eternal in the sense of timeless or nontemporal, and proponents of this conception generally argue that God created time. As created, time is a function of the physical world and thereby subject to God. As eternal, God transcends the world and experiences the fullness of life all at once. Divine eternalism also coheres to and is indissolubly bound up with other classical doctrines of God such as divine immutability, impassability, simplicity, and perfection.

The Heraclitan model conceives of God as pantemporal, sempiternal, or everlasting. On this view, God either exists everlastingly and experiences duration and succession just as creatures do, or God experiences God's own temporal framework of duration and succession. The fact that God is omnipresent and without beginning or end distinguishes divinity from creatures: God experiences time in its fullness by relating temporally to temporal things; creaturely experiences of time are discontinuous, marred by finitude, and limiting.

A good way to assess the theological strengths and weaknesses of both models of time and eternity is to examine what opponents have said about them and to examine how adherents respond to these criticisms. The remainder of this segment will be given to exploring these matters.

A. Objections to God as Nontemporal

First, critics of the notion that God essentially exists outside time (nontemporally) point out that this notion should be considered in connection with the classical doctrine of divine immutability. Many contemporary thinkers admit that the doctrine of divine immutability is both unnecessary to the Christian faith and represents a distorting intrusion of Platonic philosophy into Christian theology. Furthermore, critics contend one should not equate temporality and change with imperfection. Those who believe God is nontemporal typically respond to these criticisms in one of two ways. Either proponents argue that today's pantemporal theisms are a by-product of modern philosophical commitments, or they attempt to defend divine immutability as biblically warranted and historically central to Christian theology.

Second, critics of the notion that God is nontemporal argue that a timeless God is unable to know temporally tensed propositions such as "It is raining now" or "It is raining today." A nontemporal God cannot know these propositions, because these propositions "can only be entertained by certain persons or at certain times" (Pike 1970, 175). Eternalists have responded to this criticism by arguing that while divine knowledge does not include temporal relationships, because God relates eternally to all temporal realities, God knows all that can be known about temporal realities and relationships from God's eternal perspective. Although the temporal perspective plagues human knowers, it cannot be debilitating for the divine knower, because the divine knower is not temporal.

A third objection to conceiving God as nontemporal is that a timeless God cannot be a personal God. A personal being acts, knows, remembers, anticipates, conceptualizes, deliberates, intends, and so forth, say critics, and these actions all presume temporal experience. Eternalist proponents are quick to point out, however, that appearances are deceiving. For example, knowing something should be distinguished from coming to know something. Knowing requires only that a cognitive relationship exists between knower and known. It does not require that such a relationship be mediated temporally.

Fourth, critics of eternalism claim that envisioning God as nontemporal poses problems for the Christian doctrines of creation and providence. The charge here is that a timeless God cannot create, sustain, or relate to a temporal world, because worldly things come into and fade out of existence. Most eternalists respond by admitting that statements such as "God creates," "God sustains," or "God experiences" need to be qualified when one embraces the eternalist model. But even a nontemporal God does these things only analogously (similar to and yet different from) to the way that we do them. The medieval claim that creatures are not literally present to God but only "represented in the mind of God," argue non-temporalists, is still preferable to the pantemporalist alternatives.

Responses to the previous criticism raise a fifth objection: the problem of religious language. Eternalists appear to evacuate all assertions about God's actions and responses to the world, because the words involved are used in highly stretched senses with regard to God. By contrast, pantemporalists need not resort to such stretching of scriptural language. Eternalists counter that no one, not even pantemporalists, consistently uses religious and theological language literally.

Even though theological language is not always taken as literal, say critics, a sixth objection follows: a timeless God is not religiously accessible. The nontemporal God, who only acts upon the world without being affected by it, is never personally affected by actions of free creatures. How, for example, can it be coherently maintained that God *responds* to petitionary prayer? Eternalists generally respond to these criticisms by claiming that God's response to free creatures is already logically present within His one eternal creating and sustaining act. This means that prayers are simultaneously heard and answered in God's single eternal act.

Last, critics of eternalism charge that the notion of a timeless God is incoherent. "An interesting consequence of the view that all temporal things and events coexist with God in the eternal present," says Delmas Lewis, "is that they all thereby have an eternal, and so timeless, mode of existence" (1988, 78). Timelessness entails God's simultaneous knowledge of all happenings that, in turn, translates into the simultaneity of all things. It is incoherent, say critics, to claim that sequential events are also simultaneous. Eternalism's proponents insist, however, that their critics' reasoning is flawed. God knows temporal things as temporal, not eternal. Temporal things have a timeless mode of existence vis-à-vis God, yet temporal things also exist temporally vis-à-vis their created relationships.

In sum, defenders of eternalism believe that their critics privilege temporality and, therefore, attempt to understand eternity in temporal categories. The more adequate approach to understanding God's relation to time, say proponents of eternalism, requires us to step out of temporalistic language and categories.

B. Objections to God as Temporal

Objections to the view that God is pantemporal (or "sempiternal") are also vigorous. As noted occasionally above, some eternalist responses function simultaneously as objections to pantemporalism. The following paragraphs contain criticisms of pantemporalism and responses to those criticisms by pantemporalism's proponents.

First, meditative mystics, throughout the ages, witness to their experience of time's suspension. Critics of pantemporalism argue that this evidence undermines claims often made by pantemporalists that time stands still for no one. Pantemporalists, however, are suspicious of claims derived from presumed altered states of consciousness. One should not consider the language of the mystics as straightforward analyses of time and eternity, they reply. Rather, this language points to a subjective encounter with God that is, as mystics admit, finally ineffable. If truly ineffable, this is no argument against pantemporalism.

Critics of pantemporalism argue that, since Augustine, many in the history of Christian thought have believed that time was created with the world. If so, a second objection to pantemporalism is that the Christian tradition regards God as responsible for creating time rather than being subject to it. Pantemporalists often reply to this objection by pointing to a Christian tradition, which began with Aristotle and included early Christians such as Clement of Alexandria and Origen, that alleges that the world itself is everlasting. One should not appeal to a consistent Christian tradition when contending that God creates time, because the tradition allows for diversity on this point.

Third, critics of pantemporalism claim that, if created things need to be sustained through time due to their temporality, a temporal God also needs to be sustained. Pantemporalists typically respond to this objection by reminding critics of how one should conceive of time itself. Time is not just another "thing" that needs to be integrated into the whole. On the contrary, time is better understood adverbially to characterize the temporalistic nature of things. Things, as well as God, do not exist *in* time, say pantemporalists. Rather, both God and things exist temporally.

A fourth criticism of pantemporalism is that temporality is, by nature, limiting. A temporal God is a limited God, because such a deity suffers loss as time passes away. On this count, pantemporalism falls short of Anselm's definition of God as "something than which nothing greater can be conceived." The defense pantemporalists generally give this criticism is that Anselm's definition, which supports the classical doctrine of divine immutability, results in a static and, therefore, inadequate God. By contrast, pantemporalism conceives God to be the greatest being precisely because God is an active individual surpassable by no one but deity. To say that God is able to surpass God's self implies that temporality is not limiting but enabling.

Fifth, critics of pantemporalism contend that saying "God experiences time" is problematic. Is it the case that God experiences time exactly as humans do? If so, this is a univocal (literal) claim that blurs the transcendence of God. If not, saying "God experiences time" is either an analogical (similar) claim, which is difficult to conceive of at best, or an equivocal (entirely disimilar) claim, which is meaningless at worst. An impasse arises when pantemporalists admit that they mean to speak literally about God experiencing time, because nontemporalists believe that talk about God's relation to time cannot be literal.

IV. GOD'S KNOWLEDGE OF THE FUTURE

So far, we have examined (1) two metaphysical models of time, (2) their relationships to eternity, and (3) God's relationship to both models. When we turn to address the question of God's knowledge of the future, it seems that nontemporal theologies affirm that God knows the future, while pantemporalist theologies do not. There are some important exceptions and subtle nuances, however, to this general assumption.

In what follows, I examine five models answering the question of whether or not God knows future contingent events. Classical theism and Molinism are eternalist models that affirm God's knowledge of future contingents. On the other side, process theology and open theism (or "classical free-will theism") argue that God knows only future possibilities but does not know with certainty which possibilities will become actual. In the middle is the Ockhamist model, which attempts a response to this issue without making commitments to God as either nontemporal or pantemporal. I will begin, as I did in the previous segment, by surveying what the Bible says about God's foreknowledge.

The verb "foreknow" (Greek, *proginosko*) and the noun "foreknowledge" (Greek, *prognosis*) are applied to God five times in the New Testament: Acts 2:23; Rom. 8:29; 11:2; 1 Pet. 1:2, 20. Historically, two interpretations of these texts have been dominant. Classical theists—the patristic fathers, the medieval theologians, the Scholastics, and the Reformers as well as those in subsequent and contemporary periods who follow these traditions—interpret these texts as expressions of God's making inviolable eternal and personal commitments to individuals whom God elects. Arminians, however, generally understand the elect in these passages to refer to groups rather than to individuals. The latter position believes that God's election of groups, rather than individuals, preserves God's initiative without sacrificing an individual's freedom and responsibility to respond to divine grace.

These biblical texts have not historically raised questions about God's knowledge of the future. Instead, the driving problem has been to reconcile creaturely freedom with God's eternalist knowledge. Pantemporalism, which has emerged as a strong theistic model only during the last 100 years or so, combines an advocacy of libertarian freedom with a critique of eternalism to arrive at a denial of God's foreknowledge of the future. In many ways, then, the issue at stake concerns as much the nature of human freedom as the nature of God's foreknowledge. Given these generalizations, we proceed to survey the proposed solutions to the problem of God's knowledge of future contingent events.

A. Classical Theism and Eternal/Willing Knowledge

"Classical theism" is a label that holds together diverse Christian thinkers spanning more than a millennium. For purposes of the topic at hand, classical theists are those who, following Augustine, Boethius, Anselm, and Thomas Aquinas, deny that, strictly speaking, God has "foreknowledge" of any future event. They deny that there can even be a "fore," because an eternal God sees the pasts, presents, and futures of temporal things all at once in the divine now.

Boethius (480—524) was the first to apply directly the notion of divine eternity to resolve the divine foreknowledge-creaturely freedom dilemma. He reasoned that because God's eternal now immediately embraces past, present, and future, God's knowledge of the future had to be understood as a "never-ending presence" rather than as previsioning or seeing beforehand. Boethius, however, recognized that, on one level, God's knowledge of future contingents threatened creaturely freedom and responsibility. In order to preserve freedom and responsibility, he distinguished between simple and contingent necessity. Simple necessity is the kind of necessity that follows by definition, such as "all humans are mortal." Contingent necessity does not follow by definition; if follows from a thing's characteristics. God's knowledge of future contingent events does not, in the contingent sense, erase creaturely freedom, because such knowledge does not *cause* those contingent events to occur. Boethius concluded that free future contingents do not "cause" God to know something so that the content of what God knows changes in time's flow. He claimed, instead, that God knows temporal realities immediately through God's infinite, eternal life and presence. God knows past, present and future, not in their own temporal modalities, but in God's own eternal now (1969, bk. 5, ch. 6).

Thomas Aquinas (1225-74) granted that, from the temporal perspective, the future is indeterminate and hence has no truth value. Yet, said Thomas, God knows what is unknowable in itself, because the future is not future to God's eternity. The future is present to God's eternal now. In his discussion of God's knowledge (*Summa Theologica* 1.14), Thomas defended, among other things, the following theses: that God necessarily and perfectly knows things through God's own effective, causal, and intellective essence; that God knows future contingents, because "they are subject to the divine sight in their presentness" (1.14.13); that God's knowledge of other things derived from their exemplification in the infinite divine essence; and that God's knowledge is invariable.

John Duns Scotus (ca. 1265—1308) also wrestled with the problem of how God can know future occurrences. Part of his contribution to the issues involved his denial that God possessed temporalistic freedom. God cannot be free temporally, because of divine nontemporality. This nontemporality is implied in the doctrines of divine simplicity and immutability, for the implications of these doctrines denied successive acts of the divine will. With regard to human freedom, Scotus argued that the human will is determined, if only in part, by the object of desire and the intellect. It remains debatable whether Scotistic freedom is compatibilistic or libertarian.

Generally, then, classical theists affirm at least the following two assertions: that God knows the future according to God's eternal perspective, and that God's necessary knowledge of future contingents does not compromise their causal contingencies. Classical attempts to solve the divine foreknowledge-creaturely freedom dilemma are certainly alive and well today. Rather than reiterating the litany of charges against these assertions and theories, it will be more fruitful to continue exploring the various historical alternatives developed by those dissatisfied with the classical responses.

B. Ockhamism and Contingent Knowledge

William of Ockham (ca. 1285—1348) also attempted to understand God's knowledge of future contingents as genuinely contingent, but yet determinate, certain, and necessary. Ockham admitted that *how* God necessarily knows future contingents was a mystery. Yet he opted for the classical eternalist answer. Ockham insisted on affirming God's contingent willing, which led many of his interpreters to understand him as affirming that divine willing *followed* future contingents rather than determining them. In other words, God's willing contingently meant that God's will and knowledge follow from what actually happens. For example, if Amos is in New York today, God wills and knows that. But, if Amos happens to be in Boston today, God wills and knows that instead.

The success of Ockham's argument hinges on a hard fact vs. soft fact distinction. A *hard fact* is one that is solely about the past—i.e., "Amos Yong was born in 1965"—and is therefore accidentally necessary (my parents may have decided against having children in 1965). A *soft fact,* on the other hand, concerns future contingents—i.e., "Amos Yong was born before he published his second book." After all, I might decide one book is enough, and there is always the possibility that all publishers will reject the manuscript of a second book. Given that the publication of my second book is contingent and may not in fact occur, this statement might never be true. Applied to God's knowledge of the future, the hard fact-soft fact distinction preserves creaturely freedom and yet insists that whatever creatures decide to do, God knows that necessarily.

The question this raises, however, is whether the entire notion of backward causation implied in Ockham's theory is plausible. Is it possible that what I decide to do in the future has retroactive implications for what God knows now? Many philosophers consider retroactive causation an entirely dubious notion. Most Ockhamists, however, deny that their theory involves changing the past. In fact, we do not "change" the past just as we do not "change" the future. The future is whatever will be, and in that sense, is unchangeable. But free creatures can bring about God's past states of knowledge.

Not so fast, insist the critics of Ockhamism. William Hasker, for example, distinguishes three meanings of talk about our "power over the past" in decreasing order of logical strength: A causes B; A brings about B when A occurs; if A were to occur, then B would occur, where "there is a *relation of counterfactual dependence* between A and B" (1989, 105, italics orig.). But, he continues, "counterfactual dependence by itself tells us remarkably little about the nature of the relationship between the events in question" (1989, 106). Are A and B identical? Does the latter entail the former? Is there causal dependence or is necessary consequence involved? Hasker argues that "with respect to our power over God's past beliefs, the distinction between counterfactual power over the past and power to bring about the past collapses: it is a distinction that fails to distinguish" (1989, 111).

A final objection to the Ockhamist position should be considered. It seems as though the hard fact vs. soft fact distinction for God's knowledge fails ultimately, because the statement "Amos believed yesterday that he would write his second book next summer" states a hard fact about my belief yesterday. Now, I might turn out to be wrong, but it is necessarily true that I believed that yesterday, and the fact that I believed that will never change. God's knowledge, however, is not only unchangeable; necessarily, it is inerrant. The Ockhamist notion of changing past truth-values may, therefore, turn out to be trivial, because there remains a sense in which we can have causal effects on our future but can't change the past knowledge of an omniscient being.

C. Molinism and Middle Knowledge

Middle knowledge, also called "Molinism," derives from the efforts of a 16th-century Jesuit, Luis de Molina (1535—1600), to affirm God's sovereignty as well as the libertarian freedom of creatures. Molina began with the conviction that God has knowledge of *counterfactuals* of freedom—what free creatures would do under hypothetical circumstances, or circumstances that never become actual. God chooses to bring about a certain state of affairs based on God's middle knowledge. *Free knowledge* then follows from God's decision to bring about particular sets of circumstances. Free knowledge is divine knowledge of what *will* happen given that state of affairs. Molina claims that middle knowledge allows for genuine libertarian freedom on the part of creatures and yet preserves God's prerogative to actualize only those circumstances that God desires or permits. In order to understand and assess the viability of this claim, I examine four objections raised against middle knowledge and Molinist responses to these objections.

First, say critics, middle knowledge posits passivity in God against the medieval consensus of God as first cause. Molinists respond to this criticism by affirming God as first cause, because if God had not chosen to create the world, it would not be. Of course, God's choice to create just this world flows from divine middle knowledge of all possible worlds and of the counterfactuals of creaturely freedom in those possible worlds, but this does not negate the fact that God did not need to create and yet chose to do so.

But, critics wonder, if God is the only efficient cause and what is known is nonexistent at the moment of middle knowledge, how then is middle knowledge possible? Following the medieval thinkers, advocates respond that Molina believed divine middle knowledge to be innate rather than derived from the counterfactuals of freedom.

The second objection claims that the divine will seems to be separate from divine knowledge, thus undermining the medieval doctrine of divine simplicity. If, for example, divine middle knowledge includes God's own free decisions, there is an infinite regress between God's freedom and God's knowledge. There is an infinite regress because God's decisions to create would depend on God's knowing the counterfactuals of freedom, and that would depend on God's decisions to create, and so on, *ad infinitum*. Molinists counter that to separate God's knowledge from God's will this way is to confuse the logical moments of God's knowledge with progressive ontological states of divine reality.

Third, critics argue, the middle knowledge notion of libertarian freedom commits the original sin of putting creatures on ontological par with the creator, because free creaturely actions at least constrain God's creative options. Doesn't this put God at the mercy of free creatures? Molinists respond to this objection with counter moves aimed at securing libertarian freedom without compromising divine power. First, because libertarian freedom is only a necessary condition for and not an efficient cause of salvation, it does not undercut the notion of salvation as a gift. Second, the abridgement of divine power does not impugn God's omnipotence, because it is a matter of logical necessity that God cannot actualize worlds corresponding to a false counterfactual of creaturely freedom (cf. Craig 1991, 271-74).

But, fourth, does the Molinist account provide for a viable theodicy? Is not the God of middle knowledge still responsible for all the evils in this world by choosing to actualize circumstances that God knows through middle knowledge will eventuate in evil? Inevitably, Molinists appeal to God's long-term goals for creation and the divine wisdom's capacity to accomplish those goals in and through the evils that God does allow.

In summary, advocates of middle knowledge believe that they have countered most, if not all, objections. Further, they believe the advantages of middle knowledge over other models are immense. Most middle knowledge proponents believe that the burden of proof lies on detractors of middle knowledge to provide a more satisfying alternative to the fore-knowledge-freedom dilemma.

D. Process Theology and Present Knowledge

Molinism clearly tends toward a nontemporal rather than pantemporal conception of God. Up until the emergence of the process metaphysics of Alfred North Whitehead in the 20th century, a systematically formulated philosophical alternative to Neoplatonic eternalism had never been fully developed. Central axioms to Whitehead's philosophy include the ontological reality of time's flow, the interrelatedness of all things, and the creative novelty inherent in each and every actuality. Things are thus defined as the (self-) becoming of events. Eternity is understood as the endless process in which events come to be. The created order consists of an everlasting procession of what Whitehead calls "cosmic epochs" with neither a beginning *creatio ex nihilo* nor an end to time. In this scheme of things, creaturely freedom is libertarian rather than compatibilistic.

For process theology, God is pantemporal. Divine infinity is understood as God's everlastingness. God's perfection is no longer conceived solely in static or immutable terms. Instead, as supreme being, God is unsurpassable except by God's self. This does not, of course, undermine divine perfections. God is the supremely temporal and relational reality by which the world is both held together and lured toward its future. By this, process thinkers affirm God's activity in the world as persuasive love rather than coercive force. God is persuasive because all actualities possess varying degrees of power to actualize themselves. The God envisioned by process theists is, therefore, supremely personal and relational: God lovingly and intrinsically relates to the world, influences the course of the world's events, responds to the world, is sometimes taken by surprise at the world's novel turns, is elated at the world's developments, and is disappointed by its tragedies.

It is not surprising to find that process thinkers understand divine omniscience to involve God's knowing all that is logically possible to know. Given the pantemporalness of the divine life, God has *present knowledge* —knowledge of all there is to know at that time. This knowledge includes knowledge of the infinite past, the actual present, all determined future events (to be brought about by the laws of nature, and so on), and all possibilities whatsoever. This excludes, however, God's knowledge of future contingent events. To say this is not to say that God's knowledge is limited, because process theists still affirm that God is omniscient. It is only that the nature of what is knowable has been circumscribed. The ongoing emergence of new realities by the creative process results in God's knowledge increasing. Divine omniscience is perfect, and yet surpassable only by itself. Given libertarian freedom, however, even God cannot know with certainty which future contingent events will become actual events. God's "foreknowledge" of what will occur is God's "best guess," subject to confirmation or correction by the creative process. Because God knows the past and present exhaustively, however, God can often predict with uncanny accuracy what will occur in the future.

Critics of process thought have focused more on divine agency and power rather than divine knowledge. At issue is a basis for eschatological optimism given the process theological framework. If God's knowledge of the future is neither determinative nor conclusive, how can anyone have confidence that God's best intentions for the world will not be thwarted? God cannot *guarantee* the eschatological consummation inferred in some biblical passages. If God cannot exhaustively know the details surrounding future contingents, how can accurate predictive prophecies be given? Because many of these questions apply also open theism as well, discussing how open theists answer their critics may shed light on a process response.

E. Open Theism, or Classical Freewill Theism

Open theism is a specifically evangelical construal of divine pantemporalism that has emerged only in this last generation. Many open theists consider themselves to be articulating a more "consistent Arminianism" by following out the logic of human responsibility and free will. Open theism shares with process theism emphases on divine pantemporalism, God's genuine relationship with and responsiveness to the world, libertarian creaturely freedom, the future as unreal now and at least partially undetermined, and divine omniscience defined as knowledge of all that is knowable.

The philosophical argument of open theists has been presented in this form:

1. To be God is to be omniscient.
2. If actions are free, knowledge of them has to be contingent on their being done.
3. If God *has* to know them, such knowledge would be necessary (a tautology).
4. If such were necessary, they would not be contingent (from 3).
5. But 4 contradicts 2.
6. Therefore, God is not omniscient.
7. But 6 contradicts 1.
8. Conclusion: God is omniscient, but such omniscience is necessarily defined as *not having to have* knowledge of free actions (cf. Kvanvig 1986, 17).

Open theists are divided, however, on whether this "not having to have" is a present voluntary self-limitation or an ontological limitation based upon a past voluntary decision. The former means God specifically limits divine foreknowledge of future contingents (e.g., Pinnock 1986) while the latter means that, in the beginning, God knowingly took a risk in creating free agents.

Open theists also question classical metaphysics, specifically the classical construal of how God relates to the world. William Hasker writes:

[T]he most difficult aspect of the [classical] doctrine to accept is the one that [is] called "the problem of the presence of time in eternity." It seems inescapable . . . that if God is eternal, he knows us only by contemplating in eternity his own unchangeable "similitudes," "images," or representations of us. . . . I can tell myself that an eternal God can still cause there to exist in time all of the events that we experience as his historical interventions, as his gracious presence in our lives, and the like. But that God . . . knows us, and relates to us, only as the eternal representations in his own essence —this is a hard doctrine. I cannot keep myself from thinking . . . that it is far better if God has "immediate awareness" of fact. . . . And if . . . in order to have immediate awareness of temporal facts, God must himself be temporal, then so be it. To make the other choice leaves too great a distance between the God who is affirmed theologically and the God who is known through Scripture and experience (1989, 184).

While these philosophical-theological "arguments" may be debated, open theism's understanding of divine omniscience is best understood as driven by its prolonged engagement with the biblical text. Open theists point, for example, to texts that speak of God finding things out, deity being surprised—not expecting the choices and actions of free agents, and God changing God's mind. Yet open theists also see Scripture as affirming God's specific intentionality regarding certain aspects of the future, such as the person and work of Christ or God's eschatological plans. They therefore repeatedly emphasize the need to hold both sets of texts in tension. The future is therefore partly open, contingent on creaturely freedom, and partly closed, determined in advance by God. It is important to note, however, that with regard to the open future, God knows not only all possibilities but also the probabilities attached to those possibilities. For open theists, only this preserves both creaturely freedom and divine sovereignty. Because of God's perfect knowledge of probabilities, God can anticipate and outmaneuver free creatures to accomplish the divine objectives without subverting libertarian freedom. Such an ingenious and wise God is, on open theist accounts, more worthy of worship and adoration than the classical deterministic God.

But does not the open theist doctrine of omniscience and the corresponding insistence on libertarian freedom undermine eschatological confidence? The same questions posed to process theists arise here. Open theists answer by emphasizing the attribute of divine power, not divine knowledge, as the foundation for eschatological optimism. Although God's cosmic blueprint is general and not specific, we should not underestimate God's ability to cope with contingencies. Assurance regarding the future is not grounded on God's foreknowledge (or lack of it, as the case may be) but on God's character as revealed in Scripture (cf. Sanders 1998, 228-35).

CONCLUSION

The contemporary debate over whether God has foreknowledge and, if so, how that is compatible with creaturely freedom shows no signs of abating. As shown in this chapter, the question of God's relationship to time and eternity and the definition of creaturely freedom are at the heart of this problem. What the Bible says on this topic has, both in the past and in the present, been read through particular philosophical, theological, and interpretive lenses.

Works Cited or Recommended for Research

Anselm. "The Harmony of the Foreknowledge, the Predestination, and the Grace of God with Free Choice." In *Anselm of Canterbury,* Vol. II. Ed. Jasper Hopkins and Herbert Richardson. Toronto and New York: Edwin Mellen Press, 1976. 179-224.

Aquinas, Thomas. *Summa Theologica,* esp. Part I, Qs. 10 and 14.

Augustine. *The Confessions,* esp. Book 11.

Barr, James. *Biblical Words for Time.* London: SCM Press, 1962; and Naperville, Ill.: Alec R. Allenson, Inc., 1962.

Boethius. *The Consolation of Philosophy.* Trans. V. E. Watts. Harmondsworth, England: Penguin Books, 1969.

Craig, William Lane. *The Only Wise God: The Compatibility of Divine Foreknowledge and Human Freedom.* Grand Rapids: Baker Book House, 1987.

_____. *The Problem of Divine Foreknowledge and Future Contingents from Aristotle to Suarez.* Leiden and New York: E. J. Brill, 1988.

_____. *Divine Foreknowledge and Human Freedom. The Coherence of Theism: Omniscience.* Brill's Studies in Intellectual History 19. Leiden and New York: E. J. Brill, 1991.

Cullmann, Oscar. *Christ and Time: The Primitive Christian Conception of Time and History.* Rev. ed. Trans. Floyd V. Filson. Philadelphia: Westminster Press, 1964.

Eddy, Paul R. and James K. Beilby, eds. *Divine Foreknowledge: Four Views.* Downers Grove, Ill.: InterVarsity Press, 2001.

Flint, Thomas. *Divine Providence: The Molinist Account.* Ithaca, N.Y.: Cornell University Press, 1998.

Ganssle, Gregory E., ed. *God and Time: Four Views.* Downers Grove, Ill.: Intervarsity Press, 2001.

Griffin, David Ray, ed. *Physics and the Ultimate Significance of Time: Bohm, Prigogine, and Process Philosophy.* Albany: SUNY Press, 1986.

Hasker, William. *God, Time, and Knowledge.* Ithaca, N.Y., and London: Cornell University Press, 1989.

Helm, Paul. *Eternal God: A Study of God without Time.* Oxford: Clarendon Press, 1988.

Kvanvig, Jonathan. *The Possibility of an All-Knowing God.* New York: St. Martin's Press, 1986.

Leftow, Brian. *Time and Eternity.* Ithaca, N.Y., and London: Cornell University Press, 1991.

Lewis, Delmas. "Eternity, Time and Tenselessness." *Faith and Philosophy* 5 (1988): 72-86.

Lucas, John R. *The Future: An Essay on God, Temporality, and Truth.* Oxford and New York: Blackwell, 1989.

Molina, Luis de. *On Divine Foreknowledge: Part IV of the* Concordia. Trans. Alfred J. Freddoso. Ithaca, N.Y., and London: Cornell University Press, 1988.

Ockham, William. *Predestination, God's Foreknowledge, and Future Contingents.* 2d ed. Trans. Marilyn McCord Adams and Norman Kretzmann. Indianapolis: Hackett Publishing Co., 1983.

Padgett, Alan G. *God, Eternity and the Nature of Time.* New York: St. Martin's Press, 1992.

Pike, Nelson. *God and Timelessness.* London: Routledge and Kegan Paul, 1970.

Pinnock, Clark. "God Limits His Knowledge." In *Predestination and Free Will: Four Views of Divine Sovereignty and Human Freedom.* Ed. David Basinger and Randall Basinger. Downers Grove, Ill.: InterVarsity Press, 1986. 141-62.

Plantinga, Alvin. "On Ockham's Way Out." In *God, Foreknowledge, and Freedom.* Ed. John Martin Fischer. Stanford, Conn.: Stanford University Press, 1989. 178-216.

Robinson, Michael D. *Eternity and Freedom: A Critical Analysis of Divine Timelessness as a Solution to the Foreknowledge/Free Will Debate.* Lanham, Md.: University Press of America, 1995.

Sanders, John. *The God Who Risks: A Theology of Providence.* Downers Grove, Ill.: InterVarsity Press, 1998.

Scotus, John Duns. *God and Creatures: The Quodlibetal Questions.* Trans. Felix Alluntis and Allan B. Wolter. Washington, D.C.: Catholic University of America Press, 1975.

Swinburne, Richard. *The Coherence of Theism.* Rev. ed. Oxford: Clarendon Press, 1993.

Wolterstorff, Nicholas. "God Everlasting." In *God and the Good: Essays in Honor of Henry Stob.* Ed. Clifton Orlebeke and Lewis Smedes. Grand Rapids: Wm. B. Eerdmans Publishing Co., 1975. 181-203.

Yates, John C. *The Timelessness of God.* Landham, Md.: University Press of America, 1990.

Zagzebski, Linda. *The Dilemma of Freedom and Foreknowledge.* New York and Oxford: Oxford University Press, 1991.

Divine Holiness

Michael E. Lodahl

◆

The word-concept "holiness," or "the holy," occupies a critical place in philosophical reflection upon religious belief, practice, and experience. It highlights the utterly unique and otherworldly character of the object of religious devotion and worship. In other words, "holiness" is the term that denotes the radical and thorough difference between (a) normal, everyday objects and experiences and (b) that sacred reality that human beings attempt to address, appease, or obey in their religious practices. Therefore, "holiness" in Jewish and Christian holy writ and tradition corresponds neatly with the meanings associated with the more purely philosophical term, *transcendence*.

When God is called holy (Heb., *qadosh*) in the Hebrew Scriptures (e.g., Lev. 19:2; Isa. 6:3), such descriptions primarily connote that God is utterly distinct and thoroughly different from the created world and its creatures. God is in a class of His own! But words such as "distinct" and "different" and categories such as "class" do little justice to what is implied by *qadosh*. These words pale in comparison to the majestic awe-fulness and even strangeness that experiences of the Holy evoke as described in the sacred writings of many religious traditions. In fact, all words must, by definition, pale in the presence of holiness, for the notion of "holiness" refers to an unspeakable and indescribable mystery infinitely beyond, and yet fundamentally upholding, all creaturely realities. No wonder "holiness" is such a difficult concept to grasp—if it can be rationally grasped at all.

I. Rudolf Otto's Concept of the Holy

In his 1917 publication *The Idea of the Holy,* German philosopher of religion Rudolf Otto provided one of the most important and formative contributions to a philosophical appreciation of holiness. Otto began his book by acknowledging the important role of rationality in religious belief:

> It is essential to every theistic conception of God, and most of all to the Christian that [a conception] designates and precisely characterizes Deity by the attributes Spirit, Reason, Purpose, Good Will, Supreme Power, Unity, Selfhood. The nature of God is thus thought of by analogy with our human nature of reason and personality; only,

whereas in ourselves we are aware of this as qualified by restriction and limitation, as applied to God the attributes we use are "completed", i.e., thought as absolute and unqualified (1917 [1923], 1).

Otto argued that the concept of God we construct by extrapolating from our own "rational" selves is, not surprisingly, rational in nature. In other words, the attributes of this deity can be grasped by the intellect, analyzed by thought, and even defined. Here, in fact, lurks Otto's implied criticism: we (especially Christians) have tended over time to create a concept of the deity that is little other than the human being writ large—and a decidedly rational human being at that.

Our tendency to imagine God in our own image has, of course, been observed by philosophers at least as far back as the pre-Socratics. More recently, Ludwig Feuerbach (1804-72) built his critique of Christianity (and religious belief in general) around this very tendency. Feuerbach certainly found plenty of evidence for his criticism in 19th-century theology and philosophy. The highest value of the philosophical and political tradition we call the Enlightenment was the power of human reason. It is not terribly surprising that in such a milieu God would be conceived as an eminently reasonable deity. Writing as an heir of the rational religion of Western European Christendom, Otto maintained—quite possibly with tongue in cheek—that "we [Christians] count this the very mark and criterion of a religion's high rank and superior value, that it should have no lack of *conceptions* about God. . . . Christianity not only possesses such conceptions but possesses them in unique clarity and abundance, and this is . . . a very real sign of its superiority over religions of other forms" (Ibid.).

Otto wrote these words at precisely the time that human reason was suffering its most telling blow: the World War of 1914-18. Only in the wake of such vast violence and bloodshed and only in the sobering acknowledgement that reason's capacity for technology was being put to the use of creating bigger and more efficient killing machines could Western man (and we *do* mean "man" in this instance) begin to perceive the cracks in the artifice of Enlightenment rationality. Human beings no longer seemed so unambiguously reasonable. Only now could Europeans begin to appreciate their darker prophets of the 19th century who had stood alone denouncing the pretensions of human goodness, human reason, human optimism, human godlikeness. Such prophets include Søren Kierkegaard, Fyodor Dostoyevsky, and Friedrich Nietzsche.

The point here is not so much that Otto challenged the dominant (but crumbling) liberal notion of human rationality. The point is more that the sociohistorical context in which he wrote *The Idea of the Holy* was already becoming amenable to explorations of the irrational, the darkly unpredictable, the dangerous and even frightening dimensions of human experience—including religious experience. In such a context, theoreticians of religion found themselves resonating with his argument that rationalistic interpretations of religious belief and experience were blind to the essence of "holiness" as including the inexpressible. Therefore, while Otto freely admitted that "the holy" had generally come to be identified with the "completely good" or moral perfection, he believed that there was a much more primordial sense of "the holy." This sense was without its moral moment and rational aspect.

It was this different "moment" in the concept of holiness, an originary and primordial "moment," that Otto sought to isolate and evoke in his readers. "It will be our endeavor," he wrote, "to suggest this unnamed Something to the reader as far as we may, so that he may himself feel it" (Ibid., 6). Despite its being beyond words, Otto coined the term "numinous" (from the Latin *numen*) as a pointer toward the experience he sought to evoke. *Numen* connotes divine or otherworldly power or presence, particularly as associated with a specific place, person or event. For Otto, this experience of the numinous created a feeling, or awareness, of awesome terror and overwhelming mystery in the human. He called this the *mysterium tremendum*: "the presence of that which is a *Mystery* inexpressible and above all creatures" (Ibid., 13). And yet, argued Otto, this awe-inspiring *mysterius tremendum* also often fascinates and attracts us at the same time. This possibility of being terrified and tantalized at the same time is, thought Otto, at once the strangest and most noteworthy phenomenon in the whole history of religions. He writes:

> The daemonic-divine object may appear to the mind an object of horror and dread, but at the same time it is no less something that allures with a potent charm, and the creature, who trembles before it, utterly cowed and cast down, has always at the same time the impulse to turn to it, nay even to make it somehow his own. . . . [H]e feels a something that captivates and transports him with a strange ravishment, rising often enough to the pitch of dizzy intoxication (Ibid., 31).

It is not difficult to cite biblical examples of the sort of experience that Otto termed the *mysterium tremendum et fascinans*—an awareness of a mysterious "Wholly Other" that both overwhelms and attracts at one and the same time. We read of "a deep and terrifying darkness" that descended upon Abram in his experience of divine assurance that the promise of many descendants would be fulfilled (Gen. 15:12ff). We read of the "thunder and lightning," the "thick cloud on the mountain," and the "blast of a trumpet so loud that all the people who were in the camp trembled" at the foot of Mount Sinai (Exod. 19:16ff). We read of Isaiah's Temple vision, where "the pivots on the thresholds shook at the voices of those who called, and the house filled with smoke. And I said, 'Woe is me! I am lost, for I am a man of unclean lips, and I live among a people of unclean lips; yet my eyes have seen the King, [Yahweh] of hosts!'" (Isa. 6:4-5, NRSV). In fact, Otto devoted an entire chapter of his classic book to "The Numinous in the Old Testament."

While Otto believed that in Jesus we see the consummation of a process tending to rationalize, moralize, and humanize the idea of God, he insisted that "it would be a mistake to think that such a rationalization means that 'the numinous' is excluded or superceded in the New Testament" (Ibid., 85). Think of Peter falling at Jesus' knees and begging him to "Go away from me, Lord, for I am a sinful man!" (Luke 5:8, NRSV). Remember Jesus' inner circle of disciples on their faces in abject fear on the Mount of Transfiguration as the voice from the cloud thundered down upon them. Then, there is the warning of the Epistle to the Hebrews, "It is a fearful thing to fall into the hands of the living God" (10:31, NRSV) or, from the same document, "Our God is a consuming fire" (12:29, NRSV). Otto comments upon the latter proposition, thoroughly laced as it is with the *mysterium tremendum:* "Here the adaptation of Deuteronomy 4:24, 'The Lord is a consuming fire' into 'Our God is a consuming fire' gives a contrast whose effect enhances the horror of the saying" (Ibid., 87). Otto apparently meant that it is all the more terrible that this "consuming fire" is *our God*—the One to whom we draw near "with reverence and awe" (Heb. 12:28)—and not some theoretical deity-in-general.

The sort of experience to which Otto alludes is, to be sure, not restricted to biblical faith. Primal religions thrive on a profound human sensitivity to the awesome and mysterious powers of nature (Abram 1996). The testimony of Muhammad is replete with the prophet's terror and utter confusion concerning the origin and nature of the voice that shook him and called him to "Recite!" the words addressed to him in the seclusion of a dark cave. But perhaps the most dramatic example of Otto's category of "the numinous," the *mysterium tremendum et fascinans,* is found in the Eleventh Book of the Hindu classic *The Bhagavad Gita.*

The story told in the *Gita* is set on a battlefield. Prince Arjuna is preparing to lead his troops into a battle against an army that includes friends and relatives. Can he do it? Can he wreak violence upon his own kin? He seeks counsel from his charioteer, who is, in fact, the god Krishna mercifully disguised as a mere human being. The charioteer provides a series of arguments goading Arjuna into fulfilling his caste duties as a soldier, and as the dialogue continues, it dawns upon the prince that this is no ordinary charioteer. Finally, in a crucial moment not entirely unlike Moses' request to see the glory of God (Exod. 33:18) or Job's insistence upon an audience with the Almighty, Arjuna asks to behold the "divine form" of Krishna. The disguised deity, as we should properly expect, replies to Arjuna, "But you cannot see me thus with those human eyes. Therefore, I give you divine sight." Arjuna is given eyes to see the unspeakable:

> Suppose a thousand suns should rise together into the sky: such is the glory of the Shape of the Infinite God. . . . Then was Arjuna, that lord of mighty riches, overcome with wonder. His hair stood erect. He bowed low before God in adoration, and clasped his hands, and spoke:
>
> Universal Form, I see you without limit,
> Infinite of arms, eyes, mouths and bellies—
> See, and find no end, midst, or beginning. . . .
> At the sight of this, your Shape stupendous
> Full of mouths and eyes, feet, thighs and bellies,
> Terrible with fangs, O mighty master,
> All the worlds are fear-struck, even as I am. . . .
>
> All my peace is gone; my heart is troubled. . . .
>
> Therefore I bow down, prostrate and ask for pardon . . .
> I have seen what no man ever saw before me:
> Deep is my delight, but still my dread is greater.
> Show me now your [previous] Form, O Lord, be gracious (Prabhavananda and Isherwood 1987, 113-19).

Otto's analysis of the primordial experience of the holy as *mysterium tremendum et fascinans* finds no more fitting illustration than this. Arjuna is overwhelmed by the wondrous beauty and all-encompassing power of the divine Form, and in the same moment he is utterly stricken with terror in beholding the Wholly Other: *Deep is my delight, but still my dread is greater.*

It is important to keep in mind that Otto did not claim that this experience comprises the entirety of the human meeting with the holy. Our attempts to understand and explain the sacred, together with our quest to know and to do the good, are also elements of this encounter. It was, however, Otto's burden to demonstrate that these rational and moral dimensions of the religious quest are later developments in human religious history and, for all of their importance, should not be allowed to eclipse or subsume the primal encounter with the terrifying mystery of the "wholly other." If Otto's analysis is correct, then Arjuna's vision of the Divine Form in the *Bhagavad Gita* certainly stands out as a virtually perfect portrait of the human "feel" for the Numinous.

The importance of Otto's contribution should not obscure the criticisms that his work has undergone. While he may have offered a telling critique of liberalism's rationalistic and moralistic "man" (*and* deity), his isolation of an experience of *mysterium* is nevertheless clearly a product of the liberal assumption of a "religious *a priori*" in the human psyche. Forty years after the publication of *The Idea of the Holy,* Mircea Eliade proposed that Otto's work was still valuable but that Otto's concentration on the irrational element of religion was ultimately too narrow. Eliade would focus instead on what he called "the sacred in its entirety," i.e., as "the opposite of the profane" (1957, 10). More recently, Ninian Smart has argued that Otto's account "seems to be less successful in dealing with the contemplative mystic, such as the Buddha and Shankara, than with the prophet and the worshipper" (1979, 13). Smart argues that

> [T]he Buddha did not—judging from the scriptural reports—feel himself to be confronted by an Other. For him there was no *tremendum;* he did not bow down in awe before a Wholly Other. . . .

> It also happens that in the Upanishads and in some other phases of the Hindu tradition, there is a sense of the identification of the eternal Self with the ground of being, Brahman. . . . It is not a matter of experiencing a Wholly Other, still less a personal Object of devotion (Ibid., 15).

No reader should be troubled by the apparent contradiction between what Smart writes of Hindu religious philosophy and what we have already explored in the *Bhagavad Gita.* Like any great religious tradition and probably more than most other traditions, the term "Hinduism" represents an incredibly rich and vastly diverse set of ideas and practices. The main point is that Eliade and Smart, among a host of others, have effectively pointed out various blind spots in Otto's work.

We have nonetheless given considerable space to understanding Otto's analysis for the simple reason that, more than any other in the past century, he has influenced sophisticated theological and philosophical reflections upon the category of the holy. To a considerable extent, he rescued the concept from banality by reintroducing the notion of the awe-ful and overpowering mystery of a realm, as he puts it, "inherently 'wholly other', whose kind and character are incommensurable with our own, and before which we therefore recoil in a wonder that strikes us chill and numb" (1923, 28). Otto's classic is a powerful preventive against turning "holiness" into nothing other than "moral purity." Later in the chapter, we will attempt to determine what role should be reserved for the category of "moral purity" in our reflections upon holiness. But first we turn to the most dramatic *theological* proponent of divine holiness in the 20th century.

II. KARL BARTH'S INSISTENCE UPON THE "WHOLLY OTHER"

It is instructive to consider Otto's exploration of the *mysterium tremendum et fascinans* in company with Karl Barth's "turn to the Subject." In this case, the "Subject" of whom Barth speaks is the Absolute Subject, the Transcendent God, the Father of our Lord Jesus Christ. Both Otto and Barth longed to distance the category of holiness from the merely human. Both insisted upon the Wholly Otherness, the utter strangeness, of the Holy One vis-à-vis the world. Perhaps Otto was not so outspoken as Barth, but one readily suspects that he too had his deep reservations about the self-confident morality and rationality of late-19th- and early-20th-century European cultures. Neither was interested in seeing religious faith reduced to theology or ethics.

And yet there is this decisive and differentiating factor: Otto was certain that he had discovered, and isolated, a common strand of religious experience in a variety of otherwise quite disparate religious traditions. The experience of the numinous, he argued, was there to be discovered, to be read about and even encountered, in a host of religious texts and practices from throughout the world and its history. The obvious implication is that, for Otto, this *mysterium tremendum* was an authentically *human experience* of the Holy, and thus in some measure amenable to the human structures of knowing. It was, in a word, somehow *immanent* within human consciousness, or at least susceptible to human awareness. Certainly in this regard, Otto was heir to the liberal tradition whose seeds lay in the Enlightenment and Romanticism, flowering in a 19th-century European theology that was, in Barth's judgment, *"religionistic, anthropocentric, and in this sense, humanistic"* (1960, 39).

If Barth could be sympathetic to Otto's concern to respect the distance and difference between God and the human, his early theology made little room for Otto's approach that gave such credence to the notion of a universally widespread human awareness of, and response toward, the holy. Despite their differences, Otto, Eliade, and others like them "all locate ultimately significant contact with whatever is finally important to religion in the prereflective experiential depths of the self" argues George Lindbeck (1984, 21). Karl Barth was eminently suspicious of this locale! The Barthian "take" on holiness, in other words, would be to "out-*mysterium*" Otto's *mysterium tremendum*, to wrest the category entirely out of the grasp of human subjectivity.

One of the most fascinating texts in which Barth describes and analyzes his own early (post–World War I) concern to champion a radical reading of divine holiness is his 1956 address "The Humanity of God." In the opening paragraphs, Barth as elder statesman looks back upon his early years as one of the leaders of neoorthodoxy:

> I should indeed have been somewhat embarrassed if one had invited me to speak on the humanity of God—say in the year 1920, the year in which I stood up in this hall against my great teacher,

Adolf von Harnack. We should have suspected evil implications in this topic. . . . What began forcibly to press itself upon us about forty years ago was not so much the humanity of God as His *deity*—a God absolutely unique in His relation to man and the world, over-poweringly lofty and distant, strange, yes even wholly other (38, 37).

What Barth calls God's *deity* is essentially what we have been exploring under the category of *holiness*. Barth insists that it was only with this newly discovered emphasis upon the absolutely unique *deity* of God that he, and others like him, could properly function as "theologians, and in particular, preachers—ministers of the divine Word" (Ibid., 41). As Barth looks back, he is convinced that "we were certainly right" in this insistence that the path trod by thinkers in the liberal tradition was "a blind alley." Barth lists Otto as one of several thinkers who were simply "shifting around within the complex of inherited questions" when what was actually needed was "a change in direction" (Ibid.).

Yet with a maturity, humility, and humor that generally come most naturally to the elderly, Barth proceeds to confess that "we were at that time only partially in the right":

What expressions we used—in part taken over and in part newly invented!—above all, the famous "wholly other" breaking in upon us "perpendicularly from above," the not less famous "infinite qualitative distinction" between God and man, the vacuum, the mathematical point, and the tangent in which alone they must meet. . . . How we cleared things away! And we did almost nothing but clear away! . . . Where did we really go astray? (Ibid., 42-44).

Barth answers his own question with yet another question: "But did it not appear to escape us by quite a distance that the *deity* of the *living* God . . . found its meaning and its power only in the context of His history and of His dialogue with *man*, and thus in His *togetherness* with man?" (Ibid., 45). Barth had always proclaimed in his theology the central role of Jesus Christ as God's revelatory and reconciliatory Word in human history. But even that role, Barth suggests in "The Humanity of God," had been somewhat shrouded in his early thought by a more comprehensive and fundamental vision of divine otherness. Only with considerable time did the theologic of the incarnation make sufficiently deep inroads into his theology. "In Jesus Christ there is no isolation of man from God or of God from man. . . . Jesus Christ is in His one Person, as true *God, man's* loyal partner, and as true *man, God's*" (Ibid., 46). The orienting concern of Barth's theology had shifted over a period of four decades from a position of "wholly otherness"—or, as he put it, "the swallowing of immanence by transcendence" (Ibid., 43)—toward a position of "partnership" grounded in the person and work of Jesus Christ.

The movement in his thinking that Barth describes is instructive. His early insistence upon the holiness or "deity" of God interpreted as radical transcendence, while perhaps understandable and even necessary in the ashes of the First World War, was ultimately vulnerable to questions of adequacy to the Christian gospel. As we have seen, in fact, this was the essential reason behind Barth's transition in thought over the decades of the first half of the 20th century. "God's deity is thus no prison in which He can exist only in and for Himself. . . . It is when we look at Jesus Christ that we know decisively that God's deity does not exclude, but includes His *humanity*" (Ibid., 49). In light of the doctrine of the incarnation and the attendant gracious offer of God to become a true "partner" to humanity, it is only reasonable to question the adequacy of understanding the category of holiness, at least from a Christian perspective, as denoting sheer otherness. To put the question simply, does not the gospel of Jesus demand a richer, more nuanced interpretation of the holy?

On the one hand, the gospels certainly offer glimpses of the experience of *mysterium tremendum* of which Otto wrote. Earlier in this essay, for example, I alluded to the experience of the inner circle of Jesus' disciples on the Mount of Transfiguration. It is worth our noting that the gospels do not present this visionary experience of the disciples, wherein they witnessed the glorified Jesus in company with the eschatological vanguard of Moses and Elijah, as having inspired a particularly marked sense of the *mysterium*. Peter's brash words may reflect the second element, the *fascinans* that bedazzles and attracts. It was not until "suddenly a bright cloud overshadowed them, and from the cloud" a voice spoke, however, that the disciples "fell to the ground and were overcome by fear" (Matt. 17:5-6, NRSV). It is critical to appreciate that the presence of Jesus did not, in this case, automatically dispel or immediately neutralize the disciples' awe-ful fear in the shadow of divine glory. Nonetheless, Jesus "came and touched them, saying, 'Get up and do not be afraid'" (17:7, NRSV). Thus we discover in the text both an overwhelming divine presence that terrifies the human—*and* the human presence of Jesus who inspires courage and calm.

Perhaps this gospel narrative, found in each of the synoptics, may lend us some operative insights into the issue of divine holiness and the gospel. Apparently Jesus himself is not overwhelmed by the heavenly voice from the cloud. In fact, he functions as one who bestows peace and calm to these disciples overwhelmed by the divine *mysterium*. If the bright cloud and heavenly voice are tokens of divine holiness drawing near and, in so doing, terrifying mortal creatures, then what sort of holiness does Jesus embody? Further, it is eminently significant that the voice directs the disciples' attention to Jesus, to "listen to him!" (v. 5, NRSV)—and that when the disciples, emboldened by Jesus' calming influence, finally look up they see "no one except Jesus himself alone" (v. 8, NRSV). It is almost as though we are viewing a visual parable of the very process that Otto described: the movement in religions from the terrifying experience of the Numinous toward a rationalizing and moralizing of the holy.

Yet we occasionally get glimpses of the *mysterium tremendum* in Jesus' own persona as proclaimed by the gospels. Luke writes that in Peter's initial meeting of Jesus, the erstwhile fisherman "fell down at Jesus' knees, saying, 'Go away from me, Lord, for I am a sinful man!'" (Luke 5:8, NRSV). The disciples could be "filled with great awe" (Mark 4:41, NRSV) at the sight of Jesus' wondrous works, and even "amazed" and "afraid" simply at the sight of Jesus' determined strides toward Jerusalem and death. The examples could be multiplied, but the point is that the Gospels are certainly capable of presenting Jesus in ways that are consonant with Otto's category of nonrational holiness. Thus, Jesus and the gospel should not at all be thought to represent nothing but a process of rationalization (i.e., holiness as readily graspable by reason) and moralization (i.e., holiness as readily achievable by behavior).   ·

We nonetheless return to the fact that the Gospels obviously present Jesus as a mediating figure, a humanizing factor in the encounter between divine holiness and human frailty. If indeed Jesus is God's "holy servant" (Acts 4:27, 30, NRSV), then his person, words, and works may very well demand of us a radical rethinking of the category of "the holy."

III. HOLINESS AND THE THEO-LOGIC OF THE GOSPEL

Although in the strictest sense only God is holy, according to the sacred writings of both Jews and Christians, this Holy One seeks to create a holy people (Lev. 19:1-2; 1 Pet. 1:15-16). As mentioned at the outset of this chapter, the primary connotation of the Hebrew term usually translated "holiness," *qadosh*, is "separateness" or "withdrawal." Because for the Hebrews Yahweh alone is God (Deut. 6:4-6), Yahweh is holy: the Deliverer and Guide of the Hebrew people is utterly separate and set apart from other (false) gods and all creaturely things. By the same token, anything set apart by God for divine purposes could also be considered holy, e.g., the Sabbath day, the tithe, the priesthood, the altars and their sacrifices, the entire people of Israel. Because of the presence of the holy God calling him to lead the Israelites out from Egyptian slavery, even the ground under Moses' feet was deemed holy (Exod. 3:4-6). We might term this *holiness as separation,* wherein people or objects become holy by virtue of being set apart or separated from mundane or ordinary purposes and associated with the holy deity. This type of holiness is manifested in the typically priestly concern to separate clean from unclean, healthy from diseased, sacred from profane, divine from creaturely.

There is clearly also an ethical element in *qadosh*. God's holy people Israel are not simply to be a separate and distinct nation, but they are also to embody their distinctiveness by such behaviors as feeding the poor and the stranger (Lev. 19:9-10), telling the truth to one another (vv. 11-12), and dealing with one another in justice and honesty (vv. 15, 35-36). Indeed, this people is called not only to "love your neighbor as yourself" but to "love the alien as yourself, for you were aliens in the land of Egypt: I am [Yahweh' your God" (vv. 18, 34, NRSV). We might term this *holiness as compassion*. It is manifested in the typically prophetic concern to seek justice, rescue the oppressed, defend the orphan, and plead for the widow (Isa. 1:17).

It would be a mistake to assume that *holiness as separation* (traditionally designated "ceremonial holiness") and *holiness as compassion* (traditionally designated "ethical holiness") are mutually exclusive. It is obvious that these streams of teaching are intertwined in the Old Testament. Nonetheless, it is not difficult to see how they might also enter into real tension with each other: does not the ideology of *separation* seem, at least on the face of it, to mitigate against *compassion*?

This tension, in fact, appears to have been an important element in the opposition Jesus encountered during His ministry. Although it is a gross error to assume that all Pharisees of Jesus' (or any) era were alike or that they all agreed with one another, or even that all Pharisees would have been opposed to Jesus' teaching, it is evident that the Pharisees generally understood themselves as champions of "holiness as separation." Marcus Borg comments,

> Holiness as the cultural dynamic shaping Israel's ethos had originated as a survival strategy during the exile and afterward as the Jewish people pondered their recent experience of destruction and suffering. They were determined to be faithful to God in order to avoid another outpouring of the divine judgment. Moreover, as a small social group—a conquered one at that, bereft of kingship and other national institutions—they were profoundly endangered by the possibility of assimilation into the surrounding cultures. Such has been the fate of most small social groups throughout history. The quest for holiness addressed both needs. It was the path of faithfulness and the path of social survival (1991, 87).

Borg's points should be well taken. Not all Pharisees (or "holy ones") were hypocrites by any stretch of the imagination. It generally appears that they had the spiritual and physical well-being of the Jewish people at heart. It appears also that the Pharisees believed that Israel's best chances for survival as the people of God depended on their maintaining high standards of separation, or what Borg calls "the politics of holiness." Their most dramatic method of practicing "the politics of holiness," we learn from both the Gospels and the rabbinic lore later gathered in the Talmud, occurred in their table fellowship: Pharisees would not sit down to dinner with anyone they deemed unclean, sinful or not fully observant of the laws of Moses.

Jesus, on the other hand, practiced a radically open table fellowship that included "tax collectors and sinners" (Luke 5:30: 15:1, NRSV). This practice offended the Pharisees precisely because it presented a stiff challenge to their practice of holiness. His sabbath healings—each of which could easily have been performed on the next day instead—were further affronts to their understanding of holiness as separation, because the Sabbath was to be a day separated, set apart, from the rest of the days of the week. As the synoptic gospels present Jesus' ministry, it is clear that Jesus practiced holiness-as-compassion and thereby threatened the Pharisees' very reason to be. Further, we read, especially in the gospel of Luke, that Jesus peppered his interactions with Pharisees with unsettling interrogations:

Is it lawful to cure people on the sabbath, or not? . . .

Ought not this woman, a daughter of Abraham whom Satan bound for eighteen long years, be set free from this bondage on the sabbath day? . . .

But woe to you Pharisees! For you tithe mint and rue and herbs of all kinds, and neglect justice and the love of God; it is these you ought to have practiced, without neglecting the others (*Luke 14:3; 13:16; 11:42*).

Two further examples from Luke's Gospel should suffice to make the point. If Lev. 19:2 called the people of Israel to "be holy, for I [Yahweh] your God am holy" (NRSV), Luke's version of the same command has Jesus calling his disciples to "be merciful, just as your Father is merciful" (6:36, NRSV). Then, in one of the most famous of Jesus' parables, unique to Luke, Jesus describes an outcast Samaritan who is "moved with compassion" toward a roadside victim while official representatives of Jewish Temple holiness-as-separation had kept their distance on the other side of the road (10:25-37). There can be no question that the Synoptic Gospels, and Luke especially, present Jesus' ministry as radically undercutting the dominant Pharasaic practice of holiness as separation.

Thus we return to our earlier question: must these two modes of holiness, separation and compassion, be interpreted so as to exclude one another? How do the biblical claims that God is holy *and* that God is love (1 John 4:8, 16) relate to one another? If God is so holy as to be utterly distinct, the "wholly other," separated essentially from the creaturely and the unclean, how can God also be the compassionate, outpouring love that Jesus both spoke of and embodied?

A number of Christian theologians, particularly those of the Wesleyan theological tradition, have conjoined the apparently tensional categories of holiness and love in the phrase "holy love." In so doing, they follow John Wesley's insistence upon self-emptying love as the essential character of God, and they appeal to the adjective "holy" as the modifier of the primary and more central term "love." It is not always clear, however, just how these thinkers propose to unite "holy" and "love." Certainly the solution does not lie in attempting to "balance" the two terms, as though the adjective "holy" is there simply to keep anyone from becoming overly enthusiastic about God's love! Neither will it do to pit the two terms against one another, as though God is sometimes "holy," distant, and wrathful and other times "love."

In his systematic theology *Grace, Faith and Holiness,* H. Ray Dunning appears to have approximated what I would suggest is the most satisfying interpretation of the phrase "holy love," although he left the possibility largely underdeveloped. For Dunning, holiness implies separateness or otherness. It "serves as the barrier [against] reducing theology to anthropology" and protects against "obliterating the distinction between the human and the divine" (1988, 194, 193). Therefore, even while one may lay claim to the Johannine proposition that "God is love," the modifier "holy" serves as a reminder that this "love" that "God is" cannot be simply equated with, or reduced to, human conceptions or experiences somehow associated with "love." God's love is not reducible to human loves. "We have noted," writes Dunning, "that the unique character of God in Christian theology is love. But love is susceptible to being reduced to human sentimentality. Therefore, even the central declaration of Christian faith about God must be qualified as 'holy love'" (Ibid., 194).

Dunning's suggestion begs further interpretation. First, the love with which God is identified in the first epistle of John is actually described quite simply as laying down one's life for others, just as Christ "laid down his life for us" (1 John 3:16, NRSV). This laying down of life is further elucidated in decidedly practical terms of sharing one's material goods with those in need (3:17). In this, love has received its divine definition, according to Christian faith, in the sacrificial living and dying of Jesus of Nazareth. How might the modifier "holy" function in this connection? It would appear that the simplest, most economical interpretation of "holy love" would be something along these lines: The self-giving, outpoured *love* we see in the gospel portrait of Jesus is the very nature of God—and this love is *holy* because, utterly unlike even the best of human loves, it knows no limits and has no boundaries. What "sets God apart" *as the Holy One* is that only God's love is utterly and ineffably boundless. In the lyrics of Charles Wesley, "Love Divine" excels all other loves precisely because it (He) is "all compassion; Pure, unbounded love"!

"Pure, unbounded love" *is* God's holiness, God's radical otherness, because no other love is as pure (unmixed with other motives or means) or as unbounded (without restriction as to merit) as God's is. There is no boundary that the holy God cannot or will not transgress for the sake of the beloved creature. Holiness as separation in this case does not mean that God is insulated from the creature or the unclean any more than Jesus in his earthly ministry was insulated. Rather, in this case, holiness as separation means that *no other self-giving love, no other kenotic compassion, is anywhere near the love that God is:* God *alone* occupies the class of self-giving love and compassion without limits. If this is so, divine holiness is a radically indescribable holiness that draws near in infinite ("no limits") compassion to the creaturely realm. This holiness is *defined precisely* by its wildly exorbitant generosity as self-giving, other-receiving love.

We should now be able readily to see a clear parallel here to the movement in Barth's thinking explored earlier in this chapter. Barth's transition from an early emphasis upon what he termed God's "deity" to his later emphasis upon God's covenantal "partnership" with human beings was rooted, as we have seen, in his deepening appreciation for the implications of Christology. "How could God's deity exclude His humanity, since it is God's freedom for love and thus His capacity to be not only in the heights but also in the depths, not only great but also small, not only in and for Himself but also with another distinct from Him, and to offer Himself to him?" (1978, 49). Just as Barth suggests that "God's deity" is essentially "God's freedom for love," so we have suggested that the category of "holiness" may be best interpreted, at least by Christians, as God's "pure, unbounded love."

But can we go full circle and return in these reflections to Otto's analysis of the holy? Certainly a *boundless* love is "wholly other" than our experience of our own, or of others', love. If there is One who is "all compassion," surely this One is unlike anything or anyone else in the world. This kind of love would be altogether strange, fundamentally alien to our mundane experience, and more than a little overpowering. Further, if this love is, as Dante wrote, "the Love that moves the sun and the other stars," its power and beauty truly attract and terrify us in the same moment.

Finally, let us return to a biblical passage alluded to early in this chapter. In Isa. 6, the prophet describes a visionary experience in the Temple in which the sense of *mysterium tremendum et fascinans* is palpable. The glory of Yahweh fills the house, angels chant the holiness of God, and the prophet is overcome by the sense of his own inadequacy and uncleanness. The entire passage (6:1-8) evokes a sense of the utterly unusual and unusually fearsome presence of God. By all appearances, this deity is thoroughly separated from the everyday and infinitely set apart from the unclean creaturely realm: "Holy, holy, holy is Yahweh of hosts!" The angelic chorus, however, does not end there. Instead, the cherubic song seems to suggest the tantalizing possibility that the overwhelmingly intense experience of God in the Temple is, at least in principle, possible anywhere and any time. God's holiness is not a withdrawing *from* but a drawing near *to* the creature; not a qualitative distance *from* but an intimate communion *with* the world; not absolute separation but utterly mysterious inflowing: "The whole earth is full of God's glory!"

Texts for Further Reading

Abram, David. *The Spell of the Sensuous: Perception and Language in a More-than-Human World.* New York: Pantheon, 1996.

Baillie, John. *The Interpretation of Religion: An Introductory Study of Theological Principles.* Nashville: Abingdon, 1928.

Barth, Karl. *The Humanity of God.* Atlanta: John Knox, 1978.

Bhagavad Gita, The Song of God. Trans. Swami Prabhavananda and Christopher Isherwood. Hollywood, Calif.: Vedanta, 1987.

Borg, Marcus. Jesus: *A New Vision—Spirit, Culture, and the Life of Discipleship.* San Francisco: HarperSanFrancisco, 1991.

Dunning, H. Ray. *Grace, Faith, and Holiness: A Wesleyan Systematic Theology.* Kansas City: Beacon Hill Press of Kansas City, 1988.

Eliade, Mircea. *The Sacred and the Profane: The Nature of Religion.* New York: Harper and Row, 1957.

Jones, O. R. *The Concept of Holiness.* New York: Macmillan, 1961.

Kierkegaard, Søren. *Training in Christianity.* Trans. Walter Lowrie. Princeton, N.J.: Princeton University Press, 1967.

Lindbeck, George A. *The Nature of Doctrine: Religion and Theology in a Postliberal Age.* Philadelphia: Westminster, 1984.

Oden, Thomas. *The Living God.* San Francisco: Harper and Row, 1987.

Otto, Rudolf. *The Idea of the Holy: An Inquiry into the Non-Rational Factor in the Idea of the Divine and Its Relation to the Rational.* Trans. John W. Harvey. Oxford: Oxford University Press, 1923.

Powell, Samuel M., and Michael E. Lodahl, eds. *Embodied Holiness: Toward a Corporate Theology of Spiritual Growth.* Downers Grove, Ill.: InterVarsity, 1999.

Schleiermacher, Friedrich. *On Religion: Speeches to Its Cultured Despisers.* Trans. Richard Crouter. Cambridge: Cambridge University Press, 1988.

Smart, Ninian. *The Philosophy of Religion.* Oxford: Oxford University Press, 1979.

PART II, SECTION VI

DIVINITY IN TRINITY

Samuel M. Powell

◆

The purpose of this chapter is to introduce the idea of the Trinity. Although it is not common to see the Trinity discussed by philosophers of religion, some very important philosophers have done so. Two of these are Thomas Aquinas (1224-74) and Georg Wilhelm Friedrich Hegel (1770—1831). Thomas's discussion of the Trinity and related topics is found in the work popularly known as the *Summa Theologica* (1945 [c. 1270]). Hegel's thoughts on the Trinity appear in several of his works, especially the *Lectures on the Philosophy of Religion* (1985 and 1988 [1828]). This chapter will study Thomas's and Hegel's understandings of the Trinity by looking at three issues of great importance in the philosophy of religion: reason and revelation, language used of God, and human knowledge of God.

I. REASON AND REVELATION

The first thing to note is a distinction Thomas Aquinas makes between natural theology and revealed theology. He asserts that there are two categories of true statements about God. Truths of the first category cannot be discovered or proved by natural human reason. For Thomas, the doctrine of the Trinity falls into this category. This type of truth can be given to us only by God's revelation in the Bible. Truths of the second category can be discovered and understood by human reason, even without the aid of special revelation. For Thomas, this category includes such statements as "God exists," "God is one," and "God is eternal." These statements are the subject of that part of philosophy known as natural theology. Naturally, there is some overlap between the truths of revealed theology and the truths of natural theology. For example, Thomas believed that the existence of God can be proved by human reason and is also revealed in Scripture. However, he asserted that there can be no philosophical proof of the truths that exceed human reason. Because the Trinity is one of these truths, Thomas strenuously objected to all attempts at proving this doctrine by philosophical means (part 1, question 32, article 1).

Thomas's assertion that the Trinity cannot be proven by natural reason rests on the distinction between God's eternal, inward life and God's creative actions directed toward the universe. God's eternal, inward life is the Trinity, and the distinction of the Trinitarian persons and the unity of God's nature characterize it. However, when it comes to God's creative activity toward and in the world, we have no basis for distinguishing the Trinitarian persons from one another. This is because, according to Thomas, human reason can know of God only what it can infer from the fact that God is the first cause of the universe. Because Thomas held that the Trinity in its *unity* creates the world (1.32.1), knowledge of God the Creator does not yield knowledge of the distinction of Trinitarian persons. Reason can know nothing about God's eternal and inward essence, and therefore reason can know nothing about God's Trinitarian life (1.12.14). It is easy to see from this line of argument that, for Thomas, belief in the Trinity is a matter of faith and not reason, of theology and not philosophy. Although the doctrine of the Trinity does not contradict human reason (1.32.1), it does go far beyond reason's powers of comprehension.

Although human reason can neither discover nor comprehend the Trinity, philosophical reasoning still makes a contribution. Philosophy can help us understand in a limited way the doctrines that have been revealed. Although revealed theology does not use human reason to prove matters of faith, Thomas contends that it can use reason to *clarify* certain aspects of the faith (1.1.5). This clarifying task is evident in the way in which Thomas represents the Trinity. He notes that the Son (or "the Word") is said to proceed from the Father. Thomas uses philosophical analysis to understand the nature of this procession. He argues that this divine procession is like the act of intellect in the human mind. This likeness rests on the fact that, when humans exercise their intellect, the result is a concept. This concept is then signified by spoken words (1.27.1).

In this argument, Thomas draws an analogy between, on the one hand, the act by which the Father eternally begets the Word and, on the other hand, the forming of a concept from an act of human intellect. In both cases there is an agent: the Father begets; the human mind thinks. In both cases there is a result: the Word proceeds from the Father; the concept proceeds from the mind. Further, in both cases the result mirrors the agent. The Word is the image of the Father; the concept reflects the mind. In this way, Thomas gives philosophical elucidation to the relation between the Father and the Word. The matter is similar in the case of the Holy Spirit. In the human mind there are two operations: that of the intellect and that of the will. As the concept proceeds from the intellect, so love proceeds from the will (1.27.3). And just as the Word is analogous to the mind's concept, so the Holy Spirit is analogous to the mind's love.

To a limited extent, says Thomas, we can understand the Trinity, because it is analogous to our minds and the activities of our minds. According to Thomas, this analysis does not constitute a proof of the Trinity. The doctrine's truth rests on the authority of revelation. Nevertheless, he believed that the philosophical analysis helps to clarify certain aspects of the doctrine.

George W. F. Hegel's response to this distinction between reason and revelation is simple: he rejected it. Hegel's philosophy is a consistent attempt to show that all distinctions of this sort are faulty and misleading. The problem, Hegel suggests, is that our thinking often takes things that are whole, artificially analyzes them into parts, and then wrongly sets the parts in opposition to one another. The result is that the artificial parts appear to be, if not contradictory, at least utterly distinct from one another. Hegel argues that this is exactly what has happened in theology. The knowledge of God, which in human thinking is a unity, has been divided into separate compartments named "reason" and "revelation." These compartments have been separated from one another until they seem to have little to do with each other and until there is a significant danger of their falling into contradiction.

The way to overcome this tendency of our thinking, Hegel proposes, is to think in a different and more elevated way. He calls this way of thinking "dialectics." What is dialectical thinking? It is often simplistically represented as the belief that one idea (the thesis) gives rise to the opposite idea (the antithesis) and that this opposition is resolved by a third idea (the synthesis), which preserves the truth of the first two. There is enough truth in this picture to make it useful. However, it does not fully convey how dialectical thinking works.

Hegel's point is that, if we reflect on any given idea, eventually and necessarily we are led to reflect on another idea that is contrary to the first. Quite often we are satisfied to leave this opposition as we find it. We simply grant that there are two ideas that are related but contrary, and we allow them to remain in their opposition. Some of us will affirm the first idea, others the second idea. Each side believes that attains the truth. Each side, however, is mistaken, because each of these ideas is in fact a one-sided and therefore incomplete aspect of the whole truth. Our everyday sort of thinking cannot grasp this whole truth, because it sees only the opposition between the ideas and cannot see their unity. Our normal thinking also fails because it customarily conceives of the truth as something simple and seamless. On the contrary, Hegel asserted, the truth is complex, because it is a unity of opposites. The ideas, which appear to be opposed to one another, turn out to be a unity. We can begin to see the unity only by noting that, when we reflect on either idea, our thought is necessarily led to the other idea. For Hegel, truth is the whole that encompasses ideas that are contrary. Error occurs when we one-sidedly focus on the opposition. Consequently, knowledge is a movement of thought in which we grasp the whole that is the truth.

One way to grasp Hegel's point is with an illustration. When we consider a seed becoming a plant, we are tempted to treat the seed as a distinct entity in itself and to treat the plant as another distinct entity in itself. What Hegel wanted us to see is that both seed and plant are merely two phases in a larger movement of life. The concrete reality in this case is the whole movement from seed to plant. Considered in themselves, seed and plant are abstractions from and momentary aspects of this living movement. It is Hegel's opinion that our everyday understanding of things cannot grasp the truth about the living process, because it focuses on the difference between seed and plant. Only dialectical thinking can grasp the living movement and the unity as the fundamental reality (1988, 424).

This illustration of the living entity indicates that for Hegel what is truly real is the unity that embraces distinctions and oppositions. Thinking in the truest sense is the thinking that grasps not only the distinctions and oppositions between things but also the unity that embraces them. This is dialectical thinking.

Perhaps now it will be clear why Hegel rejected Thomas's understanding of the relation between reason and revelation. Our customary thinking, exemplified by Thomas Aquinas, holds that human reason is one distinct thing and that revelation is another. It accepts the distinction and leaves the two in their difference and opposition. We are normally happy if the two do not overtly and destructively contradict each other. But dialectical thinking finds problems with this separation.

The first problem is that the natural theology that results from abstract human reasoning about God is quite empty of content (1988, 207), because abstract reason cannot accept the concept of distinctions in God. It attributes a unity to God, but this unity is not the true unity of the Trinity. This unity is rather abstract and simplistic, and it lacks distinctions. In our reasoning thus about God, we discard all distinctions within God. The result is an abstraction of thought that falls far short of the truth about God. Consequently, Hegel is very critical of natural theology (1988, 485).

The second problem concerns the way in which revelation is often represented. According to the view to which Thomas gives classical expression, revelation differs from reason. It comes to us from God. Revelation communicates knowledge about God that we otherwise could not have. It exceeds the ability of human reason. In Hegel's estimation, however, such an idea of revelation is as one-sided and abstract as the customary ideas of reason and natural theology. Its principal fault lies in the assumption that revelation communicates to us truths about God that are above the powers of reason. Once again, something (revelation) is being set in opposition to something else (reason) as though the two have nothing to do with each other.

Hegel argued that revelation has nothing to do with the kind of abstract reasoning that produces an abstract natural theology. But, he asserted, revelation is not different from *true* reasoning. The true reasoning he has in mind is dialectical thinking. Dialectical thinking coincides with revelation, because it apprehends unity amid distinctions and because God the Trinity is the ultimate illustration of unity amid distinctions. The Trinitarian unity of God is a unity that embraces distinctions—the distinctions of the Trinitarian persons. In dialectical thinking, we know God as God truly is, because we know God as having Trinitarian distinctions. God is revealed in dialectical thinking, because to think dialectically is to think in a way that parallels God's nature. As a result, God is no longer a mystery and is not above reason. Instead, God is fully revealed. In this way, Hegel believed that he had shown that neither reason nor revelation can be without the other. Reason without revelation is empty; revelation is fully open to dialectical reason.

Of the two views of reason and revelation, Thomas's and Hegel's, which is to be preferred? On the whole, it must be admitted that there are problems with Thomas's view. It treats revelation as a factual content that has been miraculously lodged in the Bible. All the emphasis falls on the idea that in revelation God communicates certain important facts that we could not otherwise obtain. Revelation, in this sense, is purely informational. Hegel asserts that revelation is God's being open to us and becoming known by us. In the traditional view, information is given. In Hegel's view, God's own self is given.

At the same time, there is something disturbing about Hegel's assertion that human reason can comprehend God. An assertion at odds with general religious sentiment raises our suspicion. Is there a way of preserving Hegel's insights without accepting the full extent of his claims?

A means of resolving the dispute between Thomas's and Hegel's views presents itself if we appeal to the Biblical representation of God, whereby, even in the revelation of deity, God remains at least partially hidden. For example, Deuteronomy states, "[Remember] the day you stood before the LORD your God at Horeb. . . . Then the LORD spoke to you from the midst of the fire; you heard the sound of words, but you saw no form—only a voice" (4:10, 12, NASB). This passage reminds us that the presence of God is associated paradoxically with God's distance from us and divine hiddenness. This principle can also be found in the New Testament. For instance, although Jesus Christ is the revelation of God, we are reminded that even in this revelation, "No one has seen God at any time" (John 1:18, NASB). Jesus is the revelation of God, but he is so in a way that is veiled to ordinary understanding. Revelation, according to the Bible, is God's coming to us and being present to us. But this is a presence that does not remove the distance that separates God from us. Thomas's view is most certainly on the right track when it cautions against believing that God is fully present to us in our knowledge. Hegel has erred by identifying our capacity to know God conceptually with His revelatory presence. God's presence is always given with God's distance. The revealed God is at the same time the hidden God.

Thomas is correct that we cannot comprehend God conceptually. Hegel is correct that revelation is more than the communication of information; it is God's becoming open to us. The strengths of both views can be preserved if we think of revelation not in terms of the communication of information but instead as the presence of God to us, a presence that maintains God's distinction and distance from us.

II. HUMAN LANGUAGE ABOUT GOD

Philosophers and theologians have recognized for centuries that human language is not fully adequate for talking about God. Augustine offers a classic statement of this inadequacy in his book on the Trinity. In discussing the use of technical terms such as "essence" and "substance" to describe the Trinity, he makes the following observation:

> For the sake of speaking of things that cannot be uttered, [in order] that we may be able in some way to utter what we are able in no way to utter fully, our Greek friends have spoken of one essence, [and] three substances. . . . And provided that what is said is understood only in a mystery, such a way of speaking was sufficient, in order that there might be something to say when it was asked what the three [Trinitarian persons] are (Book 7, chapter 4).

Augustine's statement is a frank reminder that our words about God fall far short of describing God in a fully adequate way.

Following the lead of Augustine, Thomas Aquinas developed an innovative way of understanding language about God. His way is based on the idea of analogy. He began by noting that there are two ways of misunderstanding our language about God. First, we may think that words have exactly the same meaning when applied to God that they have in ordinary contexts. For example, if we say that a certain human person is wise and that God is wise, we may believe that this human person and God are wise in precisely the same way. But this belief would be mistaken, argues Thomas, because human wisdom is in no way comparable to God's wisdom (1.13.1). Second, we may hold that the same word, when applied to God and to creatures, has two completely different meanings. For instance, when we say that this human person is good and then say that God is good, we may mean that because God is infinite and transcendent, His goodness is totally different from human goodness. The consequence of this would be that we could make no affirmations about God. Thomas rejects this conclusion (1.13.5).

The alternative that Thomas proposed is that words have analogous meanings (1.13.5). By "analogy" he means that there is a relation of similarity between God and creatures based on the fact that God is the Creator. Something of God's nature passes over into the created world, and this enables us to know something about God from meditating on phenomena in the world. For example, although God is wise in a way that surpasses our comprehension, we can confidently and truly affirm, Thomas argued, that God is wise. Because God's nature is infinite, we cannot know what God's wisdom is like. However, because any positive characteristic that creatures possess must be rooted in the Creator's nature, true statements about God are possible. Such statements are not merely metaphorical. Although Thomas admitted that the Bible does occasionally speak metaphorically of God (1.1.9)—for example, God is called a rock— he held that it also speaks of God properly and truly whenever it ascribes to God some nonbodily quality. When it does speak properly and truly of God, it speaks analogously (1.13.3).

For Thomas, our knowledge of the Trinity proceeds along these same lines. Terms such as "Father" and "Son," when applied to God, are said properly and truly; they are not metaphors (1.33.2). Although the second person of the Trinity is truly said to be a Son, our language here is still analogical and taken from our experience of things in the world.

Hegel had quite a different understanding of the language we use for God. He believed that such language is highly picturesque. Take, for example, the Trinitarian language of Father and Son. Hegel agreed with Thomas that these terms are taken from everyday family life (1985, 283). The difference between Thomas and Hegel on this issue is not so much about the source of such language as about its significance. For Thomas, language taken from everyday life and applied to God is being used analogously and, therefore, legitimately. For Hegel, on the contrary, there is something very misleading about such picturesque language taken from natural family relations. In his opinion, such terms are unsuitable for thinking about God. To see why this is the case, it is necessary to understand his view of religious language and picture-thinking.

Picture-thinking, for Hegel, combines thought and images. For example, the Trinitarian language of Father and Son employs family images. In this case, an aspect of our everyday life has been used to depict God. At the same time, although picture-thinking employs images, it is still a form of thinking. In it, we are thinking about God, because God is not an object directly experienced through sensory perception. God is neither seen nor heard nor felt. Instead, argues Hegel, God is for us an object of thought, even in picture-thinking.

For Hegel, religious picture-thinking is a paradigm case of thinking that falls short of dialectical thinking. For example, when we use picture-thinking to reflect on the Trinity, we have the terms Father and Son drawn from family life. But as pictures or images, these terms characterize the Father and the Son only in their difference from each other. Although the ancient creeds remind us that the Father and Son are one, people who think in pictures do not really grasp the unity. They cannot get past the Father and Son distinction (1988, 149).

Although picture-thinking grasps the truth about God dimly, according to Hegel, it does not rise to the clarity of dialectical thinking. On the one hand, religious picture-thinking is an authentic knowledge of the truth. When the religious community confesses, for example, that God is Father and Son, it has affirmed and knows that truth about God. On the other hand, the truth is not comprehended in an intellectual form that is appropriate and adequate in picture-thinking. Only through dialectical thinking can we know the truth adequately, because only in dialectical thinking do we grasp the unity that embraces difference (1988, 152-54). Only in dialectical thinking does the pattern of our thought parallel the pattern of truth itself and of God's nature. Whereas in picture-thinking we simply acknowledge that God is Father and Son, in dialectical thinking we know that God is not simply Father and Son in their distinctness but, instead, is the unity that embraces the difference between Father and Son. In dialectical thinking, we see that God is a unity amid distinction.

It was Hegel's belief that dialectical thinking is philosophy in the proper sense. If we are to ascend to an adequate knowledge of the truth, argued Hegel, we must go beyond the picture-thinking that characterizes religious belief and adopt a philosophical standpoint. Only in dialectical thinking, and that means in philosophy, do we finally know the truth as the truth should be known. As a result, Hegel asserted that philosophy is an improvement on religious knowledge and language. Of course, Hegel was not suggesting that philosophy is a *substitute* for religion. He understood very well the historical importance of religion. He also acknowledged that religion was the first and is the most universal way in which God is known. Nonetheless, it is only in dialectical thinking that God is known adequately. Religious picture-thinking is seriously flawed due to its inherent inability to comprehend unity amid differences.

The philosophies of Thomas Aquinas and Hegel both agree that language applied to God is necessarily a matter of images. Both acknowledge that such language is not fully adequate. However, they disagree about why religious language is not fully adequate. Thomas believed that because God is infinite, the human mind cannot comprehend deity. As a result, all human words fall short of adequately depicting God. Hegel, although acknowledging that God is infinite, would disagree with Thomas's premise that we cannot comprehend God. For Hegel, the infinite is not that which is incomprehensible. Instead, the infinite is that which is not limited by anything external to itself. It is therefore comprehensible by means of dialectics.

What conclusions can we reach concerning language about God? For one thing, we must acknowledge the large area of agreement between Thomas and Hegel. Both affirm that the words we use to portray God are taken from our daily experience and are therefore severely limited. It will always be important to keep this in mind in order to prevent a naive use of the Bible and other religious literature. Religious literature such as the Bible is used naively when its declarations about God are taken at face value and accepted without further thought. However, even brief reflection on religious texts will convince us that the Bible and other religious sources have described God with words that are challenging. Sometimes these words are obviously anthropomorphic, as when God is said to have a right hand. Others are plainly metaphorical, as when God is said to ride on the clouds as on a chariot. In all of these cases, it is necessary to go beyond the literal meaning of the words and acknowledge that, although there may well be some sense in which these words describe God, there are important senses in which they do not describe deity. We must use human language, but we must also recognize the limitations of this language.

III. THE KNOWLEDGE OF GOD

As already noted, Thomas believed that there are two main ways in which God can be known. First, we can know God by the exercise of our reason as we reflect on the created world. Such reflection leads, for instance, to knowledge of God as first cause (1.2.3). Of course, the amount of knowledge about God that can be inferred in this way is limited. It does not lead us to knowledge of the living God disclosed in Scripture. Nevertheless, this knowledge is reliable and important. The second way in which we can know God is by means of revelation. Because human intellect is weak and because some truths about God are necessary for salvation, God revealed certain vital doctrines, most of which are incomprehensible and must be accepted in faith (1.1.1). As noted previously, the doctrine of the Trinity is an example of a revealed truth (1.32.1).

According to Thomas, whether our knowledge of God is gained through human reasoning or through revelation, that knowledge is analogical. This is another way of saying that in this life it is impossible for us to know the essence of God. The reason for this is that the way in which we know depends on our human nature. In this life we are souls joined to bodies. Our knowledge depends on physical perception. As a result, we have a direct knowledge only of material things (1.12.11). We can know God only to the extent that material things bear a likeness to deity as a result of being created by God. This means that our knowledge of God is limited to God's causal activity.

In order to appreciate Hegel's view of our knowledge of God, it is necessary to have some understanding of his historical situation. Hegel set himself against two important theological movements of his day: the enlightenment and pietism. Enlightenment theology, better known as deism, was founded on the belief that God is the Creator. Pietism was a religious movement that at times found little theological value in thinking and philosophy. Instead, pietism valued the direct experience of God in religious feeling.

Hegel's evaluation of enlightenment theology rests on his judgment that it consists in thinking about the idea of God by means of abstract human understanding. As we have seen, Hegel approved of applying human thought to the idea of God. At the same time, Hegel held that, instead of thinking of God dialectically, the enlightenment theologians limited themselves to employing what he called the "understanding." Understanding is a form of thinking that, like picture-thinking, falls short of dialectical reasoning. It lacks the capacity to grasp unity amid distinction. As a result, it could not accept the doctrine of the Trinity, for it is precisely distinctions within God that the enlightenment and its view of unity could not tolerate. For enlightenment theologians, God was nothing more than an abstract idea. Enlightenment thinkers, having denied distinctions and concreteness to God, had to conclude that God is ultimately unknowable (1988, 485).

Hegel's critique of pietism proceeded along different lines. He complained that pietism elevated human subjectivity (i.e., religious experience) to such a degree that all objective knowledge such as we find in doctrines is made impossible. By downplaying the importance of doctrines, pietism risks losing the objective truth that resides in religious faith. Pietists accepted the distinction between faith and reason that Thomas adopted. A major difference was that Thomas has a favorable attitude toward reason, while pietists did not. The final result, in Hegel's estimation, is that pietistic theology came to resemble enlightenment theology, because, in both cases, the idea of God was stripped of all content (1988, 486). Both fell short of the dialectical reasoning necessary to comprehend the idea of God.

In opposition to these two views, Hegel proposed that God is knowable. Against the pietists he argued that God is properly an object of thought and conceptual comprehension. Against the theology of the enlightenment he asserted that God is more than just a mystery. God is knowable because God is a unity that embraces distinctions, and because dialectical thinking is the thinking that comprehends this kind of reality. Hegel believed that all this is exactly what the doctrine of the Trinity says about God. It states that God is not a solitary being. God is instead three persons who are a unity. Of course, Hegel believed that the historical doctrines represented this truth about God in the form of picture-thinking. But picture-thinking too easily suggests that the Trinity is three separate individuals. What one should do is translate the truth of the doctrine from picture-thinking into the clear concepts of dialectical thinking.

Dialectical thinking about God involves three steps. In the first step, God is known as an object of thought. In the second, God is known by means of physical perception. Third, God is known in the Christian community in the subjective certainty of its reconciliation with God (1985, 271-73). The fact that God is known in these three ways is not dependent on some aspect or quality of human nature. It depends instead on the being of God. In other words, this threefold division of knowledge is associated with the fact that God is a Trinity.

First of all, God is known as an object of thought. By object of thought, Hegel did not mean human opinions about God or abstract conceptions of God. Instead, he meant that we can know God as God truly is in eternity (1988, 417). The eternal or ontological Trinity is God the Trinity as existing eternally before and apart from the created world. (This is contrasted with the economic Trinity, which is the Trinity as it enters history as God the Father, Jesus the Son, and the Holy Spirit.) For Hegel, the important point is that the idea of God, apart from any relation to creation or history, already contains within itself unity amid diversity. God's eternal life embraces difference in such a way that unity and identity are not compromised by the difference. This is indicated in the traditional doctrine of the Trinity by asserting that the Father begets the Son and that Father, Son, and Spirit are all God. The idea of the Father begetting the Son points to the self-differentiating aspect of God. The doctrine that both Father and Son are God and possess the same divine nature indicates the unity that is not compromised by the self-differentiating movement of God's Trinitarian life. The living unity of the Trinity is indicated in the traditional doctrine that asserts that the Holy Spirit is the bond of love that unites Father and Son (1988, 418).

Jesus Christ is a second way in which God is known. In Jesus Christ, God is revealed as an object of physical perception. In Jesus Christ, people of ancient times beheld in the form of an individual human being humanity's alienation from God and its unity with God. God was, as it were, sensibly present. Of course, the picture-thinking of religious doctrine has tended to represent this unity by means of very concrete images that are not completely appropriate. These images do not fully convey the truth of Jesus Christ and his place in the self-differentiating movement that is God. For this truth, we must, Hegel argued, adopt the philosophical standpoint of dialectical thinking (1988, 454-55).

The third way in which God is known is in subjective certainty or, in other words, faith. This corresponds, in biblical terms, to the Church's life in and through the Holy Spirit. Here human knowledge of God is not so much a matter of thought (as in the first form of the knowledge of God) as it is a matter of conviction. The sensible presence of God, i.e., the historical Jesus Christ, is no longer available to be physically perceived. As a result, God can no longer be known in the second way. After the death of Christ, however, the knowledge of God through perception was replaced by a higher sort of knowledge in the Spirit. Although it was necessary that the self-differentiating movement of otherness take the form of an individual (Jesus Christ), it was also necessary for humanity to transcend this sensible presence in favor of a universal form of the knowledge of God. The sensible presence of Christ could bring conviction only for those who could physically perceive Him. The Spirit, however, is a universal form of knowledge. In the Spirit, the certainty of reconciliation formerly based on the sensible presence of God has been replaced by a certainty based on the inward witness of the Holy Spirit. As a consequence, Hegel argued, the universality of faith has risen above the particularity of history. Historians may interpret the gospel story in a historical way, but faith apprehends the spiritual truth of that story and knows it with an inward immediacy (1988, 472-73).

According to Hegel, however, even this third way of knowing suffers from a certain limitation. Although in it the religious community possesses the truth, its members continue to represent God by means of picture-thinking. They continue to think of God as a being who is up in heaven and distinct from the world. They think of reconciliation simply as forgiveness of sins. They have not yet comprehended the full implications of reconciliation with God. One more step is necessary, and that step is to realize that the unity of God with humanity goes far deeper than picture-thinking. Philosophy, i.e., dialectical thinking, is this further step.

Through philosophy, we come to realize that God and humanity together constitute a unity amid diversity. Although humanity is not God and God is not humanity, there is a fundamental unity between them that escapes picture-thinking. Dialectical thinking grasps this unity by knowing that the finite world, including humanity, is a moment in the life of God. The world is not outside God; rather, it is a part of God's life. Religious picture-thinking represents God and the universe as two distinct entities just as it represents the Trinity as three distinct individuals. Faith knows the truth that God and the world are reconciled, but it knows this faith in the inadequate form of picture-thinking. Only in philosophy do we attain the perfect unity of truth and the conceptual form of truth. Consequently, philosophy is the pinnacle of human knowledge. In philosophy, God, who is the truth, is fully present and revealed.

Thomas and Hegel present us with quite different views of the knowledge of God. They agree that the human mind can know the essence of God; however, they disagree dramatically on the question of when humans attain to this knowledge. For Thomas, such knowledge is impossible as long as the soul is joined to the body. For Hegel, this knowledge is already available now through dialectical thinking. For Thomas, revelation discloses that God is a Trinity; however, we still have only analogical knowledge of how God is a Trinity. For Hegel, through dialectical thinking we rise above analogical knowledge of God.

Some today find good reasons to prefer Hegel over Thomas. Thomas's view rests on a difference between God's outward activity (in which there are no Trinitarian distinctions) and God's inward essence (in which there are Trinitarian distinctions). This difference makes God's inner life appear to be something that, apart from revelation, is enclosed and unknowable. In the presence of a firm distinction between two things, where the two are regarded as being utterly different, the dialectical thinker seeks to find an underlying unity. Dialectical thinking's suspicion about this inner-outer distinction is reinforced when we note that Thomas's distinction is associated with the belief that revelation consists essentially in God's imparting information to us about God's inner life. Because there seems no entirely convincing reason to regard this as the correct understanding of revelation, there also seems to be no entirely convincing reason to claim that God has a mysterious inner life that is utterly incomprehensible to human reason.

Of course, this is not to say that the word "mystery" cannot be validly applied to God. In fact, the concept of mystery provides a very important corrective to Hegel's philosophy. There is general agreement among philosophers that Hegel overextended himself in believing that we can comprehend the Trinity and all other things by dialectical thinking. What is needed is an account of the knowledge of God that maintains the strengths of dialectical thinking while acknowledging that human reason can never cognitively comprehend the idea of God fully.

The solution to this problem lies in shifting the meaning of revelation. Both Thomas and Hegel represent revelation in cognitive terms. For Thomas it is the imparting of information. For Hegel it is linked to the rational comprehension of the idea of God. If we define revelation different-ly, then a way may be found to improve on both Thomas and Hegel. As suggested previously in this chapter, revelation might be better thought of as the presence of God among us, a presence that preserves God's dis-tance. The moment of revelation is God's truly being among us. However, God is not among us as an object or process that can be inspected and analyzed. God, instead, may appear among us as a Trinitarian life in which we are summoned to participate.

If we adopt this view of revelation, Hegel's insight into the impor-tance of dialectical thinking seems correct. In revelation there are two things that are both distinct and united: the divine life and the human community. On the side of difference, we recognize an important distinc-tion between God and humanity. It would be naive and foolish simply to identify them. At the same time and on the side of unity, revelation brings about our unity with God through participation in the divine Trinitarian life. In revelation, the Trinity is not simply a being that is distinct from us. It is, instead, a life into which we enter and participate. There comes to be a unity between us and God. Perhaps we should think of God as the sort of being who invites our participation.

CONCLUSION

Thomas Aquinas and Georg W. F. Hegel present us with two sophisti-cated philosophical analyses of the Trinity. Although they share points of agreement, they also differ profoundly on such matters as the relation be-tween reason and revelation, the nature of language used to describe God, and the character of our knowledge of God.

What is more important than the particular theories of Thomas and Hegel is that the doctrine of the Trinity has a significant place in the phi-losophy of religion. It is true that the great majority of philosophers of reli-gion, even those with strong theological commitments, fail to consider the Trinity in their ruminations on God. This essay argues, however, that it is a mistake to do so. Human awareness of God that seeks to be knowledge must know God as God is. This means that the form of thinking that we use in connection with God must conform to divine mode of being.

References and Recommended Reading

Augustine, "On the Holy Trinity. I *A Select Library of Nicene and Post-Nicene Fathers of the Chris-tian Church*. Vol. 3. d.Philip Schaff. Grand Rapids: Wm. B. Eerdmans Publishing Co., 1978.

Davies, Brian. *The Thought of Thomas Aquinas*. Oxford: Clarendon, 1993.

Erickson, Millard. *God in Three Persons: A Contemporary Interpretation of the Trinity*. Grand Rapids: Baker, 1995.

Fackenheim, Emil L. *The Religious Dimension in Hegel's Thought*. Bloomington, Ind.: Indiana University Press, 1968.

Gunton, Colin. *The One, The Three and the Many: God, Creation, and Culture of Modernity.* New York: Cambridge University Press, 1993.

———. *The Promise of Trinitarian Theology.* Edinburgh: T & T Clark, 1991.

Hankey, W. J. *God in Himself: Aquinas' Doctrine of God as Expounded in the Summa Theologiae.* Oxford: Oxford University Press, 1987.

Hegel, Georg Wilhelm Friedrich. *Lectures on the Philosophy of Religion.* Vol. 3. Ed. Peter C. Hodgson. Trans. R. F. Brown et al. Berkeley, Calif.: University of California Press, 1985.

———. *Lectures on the Philosophy of Religion.* One-volume edition: "The Lectures of 1827." Ed. Peter C. Hodgson. Trans. R. F. Brown et al. Berkeley, Calif.: University of California Press, 1988.

Kretzmann, Norman and Eleonore Stump, eds. *The Cambridge Companion to Aquinas.* New York: Cambridge University Press, 1993.

LaCugna, Catherine Mowry. *God for Us: The Trinity and Christian Life.* San Francisco: HarperSanFrancisco, 1991.

Lauer, Quentin. *Hegel's Concept of God.* Albany, N.Y.: State University of New York Press, 1982.

Leupp, Roderick. *Knowing the Name of God: A Trinitarian Tapestry of Grace, Faith, and Community.* Downers Grove, Ill.: InterVarsity Press, 1996.

Lonergan, Bernard. *The Way to Nicea: The Dialectical Development of Trinitarian Theology.* Trans. Conn O'Donovan. Philadelphia: Westminster Press, 1976.

Lorenzen, Lynne Faber. *The College Student's Introduction to the Trinity.* Collegeville, Minn.: Liturgical Press, 1999.

McCarthy, Vincent A. *Quest for a Historical Jesus: Christianity and Philosophy in Rousseau, Kant, Hegel, and Schelling.* Macon, Ga.: Mercer University Press, 1986.

Moltmann, Juergen. *The Trinity and the Kingdom: The Doctrine of God.* Minneapolis: Fortress, 1993.

Powell, Samuel M. *The Trinity in German Thought.* Cambridge: Cambridge University Press, 2000.

Rahner, Karl. *The Trinity.* New York: Herder and Herder, 1970.

Thomas Aquinas. *Basic Writings of Saint Thomas Aquinas: Volume One [Summa Theologica].* Ed. Anton C. Pegis. New York: Random House, 1945.

Ware, Kallistos. *The Orthodox Way.* Crestwood, N.Y.: St. Vladimir's Seminary, 1981.

Yerkes, James. *The Christology of Hegel.* Albany, N.Y.: State University of New York Press, 1983.

Zizioulas, John D. *Being as Communion: Studies in Personhood and the Church.* Crestwood, N.Y.: St. Vladimir's Seminary Press, 1985.

◆ SECTION III ◆
OTHER ISSUES

INTRODUCTION TO SECTION III

Michael E. Lodahl

◆

Philosophical reflection upon the convictions and practices of faith communities, especially those of Christianity, has raised a host of thorny intellectual problems. The most representative of these problems are explored in this part of the book.

In Section I, "Faith and Reason," Henry W. Spaulding undertakes a historical survey of the options that theologians and philosophers of religion have explored regarding the complicated and contested relationship between careful, critical reasoning and the claims and practices attributed to a revelatory source. From Tertullian and Kierkegaard to Thomas Aquinas and Paul Tillich, Spaulding suggests that, in the end, we find that no amount of philosophical deliberation frees us of the necessity of assumptions rooted in some "faith" or another.

Thomas Jay Oord guides the reader through the thickets and thistles of the problem of evil in Section II, "Theodicy." The question of why there is so much pain and suffering in a world reputed to have been created by a good, loving and all-powerful deity has been one of the most troubling for theistic believers. This problem of evil is certainly one of the most ready objections to belief offered by atheists, agnostics, and other critics of faith traditions. The careful reader will detect Oord's preferred solution to this problem.

In Section III, T. Scott Daniels helps the reader to wrestle with the issues of religious ethics. Daniels points out that deliberations concerning right and wrong are always undertaken within the overarching context of some "transcendent reality," though this reality need not be conceived in religious or theological terms. Despite the inherent difficulties that plague most ethical dilemmas, Daniels concludes on a confident note that "we find truth together on our journey" and thus that our quests to determine and to do the right are not undertaken alone.

Though Western philosophical reflection has traditionally sought to illuminate the true, the good, and the beautiful, Kenton Stiles in his essay "Aesthetics and Religion" (Section IV) bemoans the relative lack on attention to the category of beauty among philosophers of religion. Stiles points to a recent growth of interest in a religious aesthetic, however, and he celebrates this renewal as an indicator of "a power that manifests itself in the birth of the human spirit."

A relatively new item of discussion at the table of philosophy of religion is the issue of exactly *who* sits at the table! The overwhelming majority of the participants in the discussions of the past have been white males. In her essay "Do Race and Gender Matter?" (Section V), Christina Gschwandtner carefully shows exactly why. Her essay demonstrates the critical importance of social and historical location in all human reflection. Gschwandtner reports that the oppressive dominance of the white male voice has tended to silence all other voices, and she suggests what must now be done to address this situation.

Mark Mann addresses one of the most pressing issues confronting theologians and philosophers of religion in our increasingly shrinking world in "Religion and the Challenge of Religious Pluralism" (Section VII). Mann surveys models that have dominated much of the reflection on interreligious relations, and he argues that a particularly Wesleyan approach to the issue will operate from a confidence in the working of God's prevenient grace throughout the world and in every culture. A Wesleyan approach will look for ways to reflect upon other traditions in ways that foster greater respect and love, and it will happily recognize that those other traditions will have their own distinctive ways of interpreting us!

In "Philosophy and the Afterlife," Eric Manchester surveys the philosophical arguments both for and against the proposition that human beings, in some way, survive their physical deaths. In the final analysis, he points us toward Thomas Aquinas as a monumental figure in addressing this issue: Aquinas inherited and assumed a dualism of mortal body and immortal soul but was careful to wed this notion to the biblical teaching about the resurrection of the body. This teaching tends to move us toward a fuller, more holistic understanding of the human being than the more typical body—soul dualism.

FAITH AND REASON

Henry W. Spaulding II

The paths of faith and reason often diverge and converge in the Christian tradition. This phenomenon is apparent in the pages of the New Testament, and it persists to contemporary discussions in philosophy of religion. The apostle Paul in 1 Cor. 1:20 asks, "Has not God made foolish the wisdom of the world?" (NRSV). He responds to his own question: "God's foolishness is wiser than human wisdom, and God's weakness is stronger than human strength" (1:25, NRSV). The sentiment of these verses is reflected in the succeeding generations of the Christian tradition. For example, Tertullian asked, "What has Jerusalem to do with Athens?" He was concerned about "human and demonic doctrines, engendered for itching ears by the ingenuity of that worldly wisdom that the Lord called foolishness, choosing the foolish things of the world to put philosophy to shame" (Helm, 61).

One might conclude that theologians are universally suspicious of reason and philosophy. However, such is not the case. In fact, the language of philosophy has historically proven useful for theological reflection. The language of faith and the language of reason often have traveled the same path. For example, John Scotus Erigena (810-77) wrote that "true philosophy is true religion, and that true religion is true philosophy" (83). The purpose of this chapter is to examine some of the issues and proposals for coming to terms with the winding paths of reason and faith.

I. PRELIMINARY QUESTIONS

Many issues arise in the discussion regarding the relationship between reason and faith. Most will be treated in our examination of the discussion's major contributors. There are, however, two important questions that require special attention.

Is reason sufficient?

Reason obviously is utterly necessary for philosophical reflection. Perhaps no one is more identified with reason than Socrates, the main character in Plato's *Republic*. Socrates trusted reason instead of the senses, and he sought to reason toward eternal realities that alone provide understanding. The so-called Socratic method, which is virtually synonymous with philosophical reflection, involves posing questions to those who claim to have wisdom. The Socratic method shaped philosophy's character, because this method consists of reason, argument, and criticism. Any opinion for which one can give reasons is admissible in philosophy, but once a claim has been supported by an argument, subsequent criticism must then engage the argument. Those who place a high degree of confidence in reason tend to think that humans are capable of conducting life and finding happiness on rational terms. The fate of Socrates, who was put to death by the "good" men of Athens, might call this conclusion into question.

Reasoning involves making arguments, which often includes eliminating inadequate assumptions or inferences. One can locate at least three meanings for reason, each with a bit more narrow understanding. First, reason is that which aims "to discover truth and avoid error" (Miller 1999, 151). Here the hope is that reason is capable of discovering coherence and defining a reasonable standard. Second, reason is identified with "the natural use of our cognitive faculties in our interaction with the natural world" (Ibid., 152). When reason is understood in this way, it is distinguished from the senses, even if it does not deny their value. Third, reason is identified with the rules of logic. This understanding of reason is really about the highest standards of rationality that are found in the region of formal logic. Some suggest that logic by itself diminishes the horizon of human knowledge, even as it attempts to clarify what can be talked about. Reason is best understood as a disciplined activity of the intellect, which seeks to grasp and order truth.

The challenge of the sufficiency of reason for understanding reality comes from several fronts in Western philosophy. While it is not possible to account for all of these challenges fully, it is important to note a few. One of the most important comes from empiricism. Empiricism maintains that all reliable knowledge comes from sensory experience rather than reason alone. David Hume (1711-76), an important 18th-century empiricist, makes a distinction between impressions and ideas. Impressions are experiences or a matter of fact; ideas are copies of an experience and connected to reason. Hume is ruthless in his opposition to those who attempt to order knowledge rationally. Reason should be distrusted, because it tends to produce images of the world that reflect the bias of the philosopher.

Another challenge to the sufficiency of reason comes from Friedrich Nietzsche (1844—1900). Nietzsche argues that reason is really more about power and less about the scientific search for truth. This message has reverberated into the 20th century in the work of Michel Foucault. It illustrates a clear dilemma for those who think of reason as somehow the place of objective truth.

Ultimately, the question regarding the sufficiency of reason comes down to its capacity to grasp and define reliably anything outside experience. Traditionally, this attempt of reason to describe the unexperienced is called "metaphysics." The metaphysical question has many faces in the history of Western philosophy. For example, Aristotle understood metaphysics to be connected to the necessity of the Unmoved Mover. If the strict rules of logic guide thinking and experience has no place, then some contend that we will never suppose the existence of God, immortality, or miracles, for example.

Reason can have a broader meaning, even though some humility about the sufficiency of truth claims is required. Some restrict reason's role to assessing the validity of truth claims rather than attempting to define a nonempirical class. But one must be willing to admit that the limits to reason may relate to the nature of reality. Maybe there is no class of things beyond experience. Maybe it is dangerous to act as if there is. We must look closely at this issue as we examine the major contributions in the next section.

Does faith need to be disciplined by reason?

The previous segment contained arguments for why reason might not be sufficient, in and of itself, to establish some of the most cherished claims of faith. Even if this conclusion is accepted, it does not necessarily mean that reason is unimportant. But what does faith have to do with reason? In order to answer this question, a definition of faith must be proffered.

The writer of the letter to the Hebrews provides one of the best-known definitions of faith: "Faith is the assurance of things hoped for, the conviction of things not seen" (11:1, NRSV). The writer reports of men and women who have acted with such assurance and conviction. R. G. Collingwood provides another definition: "Faith is a habit of mind which accepts without criticizing, pronounces without proving, and acts without arguing" (1968, 122). The difference between the activities envisioned by these definitions of faith is evident. Hebrews affirms an understanding of faith that moves one to action and sustains one in the face of opposition. It is linked to the traditions of people who have lived a particular faith. Collingwood defines a particular posture regarding rational and/or scientific investigation. The activities envisioned here are mostly negative, i.e., not criticizing, not proving, and not arguing. Any investigation of faith and reason must somehow account for both of these understandings.

Faith has many other meanings. It can be equated with trust. When "faith" is used in this manner, it might find expression on the lips of an evangelist who invites people to accept Jesus as their personal Savior. Such faith is wrapped up with personal piety and the delicate tissues of spirituality. Sometimes "faith" is used to refer to the teaching of a particular religious tradition. When faith is so understood, it is often used by those who seek to pass along beliefs from person to person and generation to generation. "Faith" can also refer to a particular set of cognitive truths, or it can refer to a feeling that cannot be substantiated by reason (i.e., is noncognitive). "Faith" can be interpreted either to be a gift of God or a human way of knowing.

There are many images of faith in the literature of philosophy and theology. Perhaps no image is any more compelling that the one provided by Søren Kierkegaard (1813-55) in *Fear and Trembling*. He juxtaposes the story of Abraham and the story of Agamemnon. Both men are faced with the decision about sacrificing a child. Yet it is Kierkegaard's conviction that Abraham faces the situation with an advantage—faith. It is faith that makes it possible to face the momentous decision with hope instead of resignation. When things are understood in this fashion, the value of reason can be called into question. What value did reason have for Abraham when faced with the decision to sacrifice Isaac? For some, faith is the only thing capable of offering guidance in such a situation.

When considering the meaning of faith, especially as it relates to reason, crucial questions emerge: Is reason a stepping-stone to faith? Does reason operate in a realm apart from faith? Is it possible for something to be true for reason and not for faith? These questions are important for understanding how faith and reason are related. If one believes in God as the source of truth, then all that is true comes from God. Thus, faith embraces everything. Put another way, the language of faith is a master discourse. When things are understood in this way, there can be no independent space for reason alone. There is only one space, and it is filled with God.

The very nature of an informed and religious life requires a sustained and rigorous reflection on the relationship between faith and reason. Lazy or thoughtless separation of reason and faith must be avoided. Equally, all attempts to submerge faith under reason are inadequate. Any attempt to diminish the importance of reason for a faithful life must be understood as ill-advised. Paul Tillich, an influential philosophical theologian of the 20th century, worked creatively on the boundaries of reason and faith. He argued that "anyone standing on the boundary between theology and philosophy must necessarily develop a clear conception of the logical relation between them" (1966, 55). Tillich's approach allows for a creative and critical engagement between faith and reason.

Considered from this perspective, the question becomes "Can reason discipline faith?" The answer is "yes," and the evidence for this answer is both historical and logical. Even a cursory look at the Christian tradition reveals the many convergences of reason and faith. The central indication of the importance of reason for faith is logical. One illustration of this logicality is creation. Central to the Christian faith is the conviction that God created a visible world. It is reasonable to expect that one could locate, in the very texture of the world, some evidence of God. Reason corresponds to the God who is revealed in creation; this might be called "graced" rationality. It is this understanding of reason that finds its place in the narration of faith. Admittedly, this is a more modest use of reason than certain modern theories desire, but it is no less rigorous. Yet it might prove to be most helpful.

II. MAJOR CONTRIBUTIONS

According to Nicholas Wolterstorff, "the task of implementing the vision of the Christian scholar . . . requires . . . all the qualities of the competent, imaginative, and courageous scholar" (107). We will now turn to a brief examination of some who have struggled to face these issues with an informed faith. We will consider in this section three general proposals regarding faith and reason.

Reason alone is sufficient

One side of the discussion concerning the relation of faith and reason has affirmed the near-exclusive value of reason. There are many examples of this, but none is as clear as that offered by W. K. Clifford (1845-79). Clifford tells of a ship owner who contemplates sending a ship to sea. The problem with the ship, however, is that it might not be seaworthy. The ship's owner believes the ship might make the voyage, but he also entertains real doubts. He decides to act on his belief that the vessel is seaworthy. But the ship sinks. Clifford believes that when we see the matter in this way, it is clear that it is always wrong to act with insufficient reason/evidence. Applying this to religion, Clifford argues that it is always wrong, even immoral, to act on a belief without sufficient reason or evidence. This is sometimes called "evidentialism."

Clifford's argument is dependent upon the nearly total separation of reason and faith. It is also dependent upon the conclusion that reason is always superior to faith. This dependence upon reason is illustrated in the thought of Baruch Spinoza (1632-77), who argues that revelation/faith/piety is an important way to know but that philosophy/reason is the path to secure understanding. This understanding of faith and reason is analogous to the relationship between folk medicine and modern medicine. Folk medicine has a place for some; it even includes a subtle wisdom. It may even be fine to follow some of this practical wisdom when we have a cold or headache. But very few people seriously believe that folk medicine is as worthwhile as modern medicine. If we are really sick, we want the more reliable treatment; we want a properly trained physician. In the same way, reason is superior to faith for Spinoza. Any proposition that cannot be clearly established by reason must be held with some measure of suspicion. The adequacy of this conclusion, however, is dependent upon what life looks like in such a world. We might ask whether or not the assumption that modern medicine is always better can be properly warranted. Perhaps there is a subtle wisdom that modernity missed by its dismissal of all folk medicine. Similarly, it just might be that the logic of faith is adequate even in the face of strong rationalism.

Let us suppose that a couple is walking along the mall hand-in-hand. The woman looks into the eyes of the man and asks, "Do you love me?" He responds, "Yes, I love you!" What he does not know is that she is taking a philosophy of religion course. She has read Clifford and knows it is wrong to accept anything as true that cannot be warranted by reason alone. She also knows that her agnosticism must turn to absolute doubt if he cannot rationally establish the claim "I love you." Not many of us would want to be in the shoes of this man walking down the mall. The very importance of the question begs for an answer, but there are no indisputable grounds for the woman to believe the truth claim of the man.

This illustration happens within the world assumed by all those who believe that reason is alone sufficient. Would anyone ever be married in such a world? Would anyone ever accept another's declaration of love? Would Abraham walk up the mountain with Isaac? The answer is "no." But what else falls when the standard is set so high? Some believe that religious belief itself is denied by what is called strong rationalism or evidentialism. Almost everyone would agree that to accept the declaration of another as truth and then be wrong could lead to terrible results, but can someone's declaration ever be justified sufficiently in the court of reason alone? It is not that reason is unimportant. The question is whether reason is the only or even the best tool for determining the truth of the assertion "I love you."

Faith is sufficient

The limitations of reason lead some to suggest that there might be other grounds for justifying religious claims. Generally, there are two positions that need to be placed under this rubric. The first is usually referred to as voluntarism and/or pragmatic justification. This point of view says that a proposition's warrant is its usefulness. We will look at Blaise Pascal and William James as examples of this position. The second position is usually referred to as "fideism." This position rejects altogether the capacity of reason to warrant religious belief. Faith is all one needs to justify religious convictions. As examples of this position, we will look at Søren Kierkegaard and Ludwig Wittgenstein. Their positions are treated together, because they share a common conviction that faith is enough. And they share the view that reason cannot be sufficient.

Blaise Pascal (1623-62) asks, "[Who] will blame Christians for being unable to give a reason for their belief, because they profess a religion that cannot be explained by reason?" (183). Pascal understands that one cannot rationally assert the existence of God. Yet the answer one gives to the question "Does God exist?" has eternal significance. In fact, it is the very importance of the question that suggests our need to decide correctly. Pascal argues this in the form of a wager: If God does not exist, and we affirm that God *does* exist, we have lost little. But, if God *does* exist, and we claim that God does *not,* we have lost everything. Given Pascal's assumptions, it is obvious that the wisest decision is to affirm the existence of God. It is not only our capacity to justify rationally a truth claim that determines the usefulness of a proposition—we must determine the consequences of such a proposition.

William James (1842—1910) provides another response to strong rationalism in an important essay titled "The Will to Believe." James argues that "faith based on desire is certainly a lawful and possibly an indispensable thing" (150). He rejects the notion that it is possible or even advisable to make judgments on purely rational grounds. According to James, we need to decide certain things because they are important and useful. One ought to be free to believe a proposition without having to satisfy rationalist criteria.

Two things seem to be important for James. First, reason is not capable of resolving some of our most important questions. Second, reason has no right to be the ultimate arbitrator. One has the freedom to believe, because that belief renders us better off. This is at the heart of pragmatic justification. James studied religion and found that religion is part of how some people put their life together. Considering this, the rationalist has no right to require the believer to prove in the court of reason what he or she believes. Going back to the couple in the mall, the woman should be able to believe that the man loves her without having to satisfy rational criteria. After all, as James says, "a rule of thinking that would absolutely prevent me from acknowledging certain kinds of truth if those kinds of truth were really there, would be an irrational one" (152).

Pascal treats faith as a wise gamble in light of the difficulty of satisfying the criteria of rationalism. James treats faith as a possible and useful response. Religion may not be on firm rational ground, but there is living proof that it works. In both cases, the justification for belief reflects doubts about the sufficiency of reason. Yet they do not doubt seriously the importance of reason as a disciplining function for faith, even as they both assert the importance of faith for the believer.

Søren Kierkegaard understands faith to be a journey and not as some intellectual consent or approximation. He wraps his understanding of faith within the practice of faith. In *Concluding Unscientific Postscript,* he defines faith as "the objective uncertainty due to the repulsion of the absurd held fast by the passion of inwardness, which in this instance is intensified to the utmost degree" (19). In *Philosophical Fragments,* Kierkegaard compares Socrates and Jesus and concludes this comparison by stating that while Socrates could only attract the learner, Jesus has the capacity to change the condition of the learner. The condition of the learner must be changed because of the learner's inability to discover the truth. It is not possible to penetrate the unknown with the resources of reason alone. One must assume another organ: faith.

How would Kierkegaard's thought help the woman to answer the man in the mall? First, the enormity of the question of love would never be lost on Kierkegaard. Second, he might advise that any declaration of love, or acceptance of such a declaration, is made intelligible within the practice of hope made possible by faith. Had the woman read Kierkegaard, she would at least understand that matters of love are really about faith instead of reason. There is no evidence that will indisputably establish the assertion of love.

Ludwig Wittgenstein (1889—1951) was a 20th-century philosopher who began his philosophical career with a bias toward reason alone but ended it by embracing a fideist point of view. The only book he published in his lifetime is titled *Tractatus-Logico-Philosophicus.* Two statements, one at the beginning and the other at the end of this book, suggest Wittgenstein's importance for our discussion. The first statement suggests that, although he has said all that can be said about fundamental problems of philosophy, he believes that little can be said and even this little is unimportant. The second statement comes at the end of the book when he observes that he has climbed a ladder and kicked it away. Taken together, these statements indicate profound questions about the capacity of reason to talk about what is really important. As his posthumous *Philosophical Investigations* indicates, Wittgenstein gives priority to "language games" or "forms of life" for determining the meaningfulness of propositions. He doubts that reason can justify what is most important in life. He states that "perhaps one could convince someone that God exists by means of a certain kind of upbringing, by shaping his life in such and such a way" (85e). Faith cannot be justified by reason. Rather it must be lived, taught, and maybe even caught. At the very least, the first move is never rational argument.

This segment's claim that faith is sufficient for religion can be taken in at least two different ways. First, the claim that "faith is sufficient" can mean that one's own beliefs define and guide his or her life. This same logic can apply to all the areas of life, whether it is explicitly religious or not. This understanding of the sufficiency of faith can apply to the belief that God exists or to the affirmation of love. Second, "faith is sufficient" can be understood as the belief that, ultimately, reason applies only to a certain kind of proposition. This means that faith is about the kind of proposition that is linked to performance, to concrete decisions and deeds. For example, Kierkegaard says that the Christian faith is about a journey and that the meaningfulness of Christianity's truth claims are tied to the quality of life arising from the faith. When one says, "Love your neighbor as you love yourself," a way of life is affirmed that cannot be captured entirely by reason. But does a "faith as sufficient" perspective require the woman in the mall to believe the man who says, "I love you," just because he says it? Some believe that God's love is like this. God is love, just because God said it. Because love in these instances seems arbitrary, a strict fideism may be inadequate.

Reason and faith are compatible

The two general positions regarding the relationship between faith and reason already surveyed share at least one characteristic: each position believes it does not need the other. Those who hold that reason is sufficient believe that faith is not necessary for true understanding. Those who hold that faith is sufficient believe that reason is so limited that it has no basis upon which to exclude the capacity of faith to define truth. A careful look at these two views suggests that a third option might be necessary. This third option affirms that faith and reason are compatible.

The view that faith and reason are compatible will be examined by looking at five specific individuals. Thomas Aquinas represents the height of medieval thought regarding this matter. Immanuel Kant had high hope for reason, but came to allow faith an important function. Paul Tillich takes up the logic of Kant and G. W. F. Hegel and presents a compelling image of how faith and reason are compatible. Alvin Plantinga rejects both evidentialism and fideism in favor of the epistemic value of basic religious beliefs. Finally, this section will conclude with a brief treatment of contemporary theologian John Milbank's thought on this subject. Each of these individuals makes contributions to the discussions that are uniquely important. Yet together they all agree that reason and faith are mutually compatible.

Thomas Aquinas (1225-74) is one of the more important contributors to the position that faith and reason are compatible. While Thomas's philosophical theology is far too vast to capture in a paragraph or two, it is important to discuss some aspects of his work. In general, we can say that there are two interpretations of his view of the relationship of faith and reason. The first interpretation says that Thomas understood reason to have some capacity for defining truth, but ultimately it must give way to faith for its completion. In fact, Thomas says, "there are . . . some truths about God that are open to the human reason; but there are others that absolutely surpass its power" (59). Those who interpret Thomas this way talk about two modes of truth: those of reason and those of faith. A second interpretation of Thomas holds that one mode of truth subsumes the other. According to this interpretation, faith subsumes reason. Thomas says that "the truth that the human reason is naturally endowed to know cannot be opposed to the truth of the Christian faith" (62-63). Those who hold this interpretation of Thomas locate all of life in one realm, that of theology and faith. Reason is one way of knowing within the realm of faith. Understood in this way, the truths of reason never contradict the truths of faith.

Thomas Aquinas lived in an intellectual world far different than ours. For him, the central problem was not how to justify the existence of God. It was how to justify the existence of humans. For him, everything flows out of the reality of God. Understood in this way, it is easy to see how reason could be subsumed under revelation. Thomas understood reason to be a less intense form of revelation, but it is revelation all the same. While this may seem to be naïve in the light of modern philosophy, there are those who see a subtle sophistication in this point of view.

Immanuel Kant (1724—1804) attempted to arbitrate between the Continental Rationalists (Descartes, Spinoza, Leibniz) and the British Empiricists (Locke, Berkeley, Hume). One way to understand Kant's philosophy is to begin by noting that he accepted empiricism's fundamental assertion that all true knowledge comes from experience. Yet he believed that empiricism was limited in providing a full account of reality. Therefore, he uses reason to regulate ideas that cannot be verified either rationally or empirically. Kant argued that analytic, a priori propositions can be justified by appealing to reason alone. But he believed that synthetic, a posteriori propositions require experience for justification and can only be approximated. The first claim is a rationalistic one, and the second claim is more empiricist in orientation. Kant argues that some propositions cannot be enclosed by reason but need reason in order to be responsibly discussed. Propositions pertaining to God, world, and self are not strictly rational but are dependent upon reason for illumination. In short, the complexity of life suggests the compatibility of reason and faith.

Kant's fullest treatment of the relationship between reason and faith is found in his book *Religion Within the Bounds of Reason Alone*. Throughout this book, Kant argues for the necessity of reason for the life of faith. "Without reason," he argues, "no religion is possible" (163). Kant's view of reason, human freedom, morality, and duty is not necessarily hostile to revealed religion. But the ultimate goal is a religion that only reason can sustain.

Paul Tillich (1886—1965) is another philosopher of religion who holds the view that reason and faith need not contradict one another. Tillich argues that philosophy/reason is interested in the *structure* of being. Theology/faith is interested in the *meaning* of being. He says further that reason is detached, while faith is involved. Reason looks at the whole, while faith looks at what concerns it most. In other words, reason connects to the universal logos, while faith is interested in the concrete logos (1951, 22-28). According to Tillich and in much the same way as Thomas Aquinas, the concrete logos never finally contradicts the universal logos.

Tillich's understanding of faith is developed in *Dynamics of Faith*. The most basic meaning Tillich gives faith in this book is "ultimate concern." To be ultimately concerned is to be being grasped by something that concerns us ultimately. "A faith which destroys reason," he argues, "destroys itself and the humanity of man" (76). In fact, "there is no conflict between faith in its true nature and reason in its true nature" (80). It should be noted that, although some have incorrectly interpreted Tillich's understanding of faith as disconnected from the Christian tradition, such a reading is unnecessary.

Alvin Plantinga offers another important contribution to the discussion regarding the relationship between reason and faith. The view he develops is called "Reformed epistemology," which is so termed because of its relationship with philosophical theology in the Reformed tradition. Plantinga calls into question the idea that only reason is capable of providing appropriate evidence for knowledge. "A person can perfectly well know something," says Plantinga, "even if he can't demonstrate it in this fashion to everyone else" (331). The claims of faith can be understood as basic without having to appeal to the court of reason for ultimate justification. In fact, knowledge is not restricted to what all rational people will accept as true. Yet Plantinga is clearly not arguing that a religious person is warranted to believe whatever he or she is inclined to believe. In other words, faith is not about getting away with as much as is possible. Rather, it is the acknowledgment of "the right use and proper functioning of our epistemic capacities" (336).

It is not difficult to connect Plantinga and Kierkegaard regarding reason and faith. Both seem to believe that reason cannot be understood as providing the only true path of knowledge. For Kierkegaard, the unknown cannot be objectified and enclosed by reason. The terrain is just too thick for human reason to penetrate. Plantinga takes this to a more sophisticated level, perhaps, when he suggests that general acceptance of rational people should not be understood as the ultimate warrant for belief. What

Plantinga seems to do is to place arguments within the rubric of Christian experience in the community of faith. Religious experience is usually not counted as important in the discussion of reason and faith, but, according to Plantinga, this reveals a weakness in the rationalist argument. Accordingly, reason serves a certain ordering function within the human epistemic capacity. This view allows a certain compatibility between reason and faith.

The final example of the position that faith and reason are compatible is found in a movement called "Radical Orthodoxy." A central person in this new movement is John Milbank. One area that concerns Milbank is the relationship between reason and faith. He calls into question attempts to separate these two. Milbank rejects the notion that anything exists apart from theology/faith. In fact, he argues that secular reason represents a misstep for the Christian faith. Like Thomas Aquinas, Milbank suggests that theology is a master discourse under which everything else must be understood.

The seriousness of Milbank's approach is evident in his call for a counterontology. This move is intimately tied to a Trinitarian ontology that refuses to appeal to a Greek metaphysic for its language and structure. The practice of the faith is the rubric by which reality is structured. It emerges in the liturgy of the Church and spills into the world as pronouncement. Perhaps in this way we can begin to understand the relationship of reason and faith. For Milbank, it is the discourse evident in faith that subsumes all other discourses, including reason. Faith does not reject reason, but faith cannot be reduced by reason. Rather, Milbank calls for a situating of reason within the practice of faith. Such an understanding of reason might be called "graced rationality." This term makes an important clarification, namely, that within the very fabric of the Christian faith an order emerges.

These five contributions attempt to make a space for reason and faith in the hope of a more adequate understanding. They answer the question regarding the adequacy of reason by suggesting that reason is not adequate in itself. Reason is a help for understanding, but it can help only in the context of something more adequate. Religious experience, left to its own, leaves little capacity for determining the difference between what is true and what is false. A critical rationalism can accept the sensibilities of the believer, even as it holds those very sentiments accountable to a larger field of understanding. This view seems to respect the importance of holding faith and reason together within a reflective faith.

CONCLUSION

After looking at some of those who have reflected on the converging and diverging paths of reason, some concluding remarks are necessary. First, it may be that reason is insufficient to guide a person through the complexity of life. There may be too many decisions in life that resist rational analysis. We may face a fork in the road, and no amount of reason/ analysis seems capable of determining which course to take. Second, it may be that faith needs reason to guide it through the often-too-seductive paths of subjectivity. After all, when we face the fork in the road, we are not alone. We stand in the grand tradition of those who have walked this path. While the faith of a child links us to the kingdom of God, it is the mature faith of an adult that prepares us for the challenges of life. Understanding these paths is important for all men and women who yearn for a faith that endures. It is not a task for timid or lazy people. Once engaged, it enriches all of life.

The ancient maxim of "faith seeking understanding" envisions such a life, affirming the importance of both reason and faith. The notion that faith seeks understanding is found in many religious traditions, but it is especially woven into the texture of the Christian faith. Faith without reason cannot possibly stand in the face of life's complexity. Reason without faith is sterile. Both components are necessary to fully appreciate the genius of the ancient inclination for faith to seek understanding.

Cited or Recommended

Abernethy, George, and Thomas Langford, ed. *Philosophy of Religion: A Book of Readings.* 2d ed. New York: Macmillan, 1968.

Aquinas, Thomas. "Summa Contra Gentiles." *Philosophy of Religion: Selected Readings.* Ed. Michael Peterson, William Hasker, Bruce Reichenbach, and David Basinger. New York and Oxford: Oxford University Press, 1996.

———. *Summa Theologica.* London: Eyre and Spottiswoode; New York: McGraw-Hill for Blackfriars, 1964.

Collingwood, R. G. *Faith and Reason: Essays in Philosophy of Religion.* Ed. Lionel Rubinoff. Chicago: University of Chicago Press, 1968.

Delaney, C. P., ed. *Rationality and Religious Belief.* Notre Dame, Ind.: University of Notre Dame Press, 1979.

Eriugena, John Scotus. "On Predestination." In *Faith and Reason.* Ed. Paul Helm. New York and Oxford: Oxford University Press, 1999.

Flew, Antony, R. M. Hare, and Basil Mitchell. "Theology and Falsification." *New Essays in Philosophical Theology.* Ed. Antony Flew and Alasdair MacIntyre. London: SCM, 1955.

Helm, Paul, ed. *Faith and Reason.* New York and Oxford: Oxford University Press, 1999.

James, William. "The Will to Believe." *Exploring the Philosophy of Religion.* 4th ed. Ed. David Stewart. Upper Saddle River, N.J.: Prentice Hall, 1998.

Kant, Immanuel. *Religion Within the Limits of Reason Alone.* Trans. Theodore M. Greene and Hoyt H. Hudson. New York: Harper and Brothers, 1960.

Kierkegaard, Søren. "Concluding Unscientific Postscript." *Philosophy of Religion.* 2d ed. Ed. George L. Abernethy and Thomas A. Langford. London: Collier-Macmillan, 1968.

Kung, Hans. *Does God Exist? An Answer for Today.* Trans. Edward Quinn. New York: Vintage, 1981.

Miller, Caleb. "Faith and Reason." *Reason for the Hope Within.* Ed. Michael J. Murray. Grand Rapids: Wm. B. Eerdmans Publishing Co., 1999.

Pascal, Blaise. "The Pensees." *Faith and Reason.* Ed. Paul Helm. New York and Oxford: Oxford University Press, 1999.

Peirce, C. S. "The Fixation of Belief." *Philosophical Writings of Peirce.* Ed. Justus Buchler. New York: Dover, 1955.

Plantinga, Alvin. "On Reformed Epistemology." In *Philosophy of Religion: Selected Readings.* Ed. Michael Peterson, William Hasker, Bruce Reichenbach, and David Basinger. New York and Oxford: Oxford University Press, 1996.

———— and Nicholas Wolterstorff, eds. *Faith and Rationality.* Notre Dame, Ind.: University of Notre Dame Press, 1983.

Rosenberg, Jay. *The Practice of Philosophy: A Handbook for Beginners.* Upper Saddle River, N.J.: Prentice-Hall, 1996.

Steward, David. *Exploring the Philosophy of Religion,* 4th ed. Upper Saddle River, N.J.: Prentice-Hall, 1998.

Swinburne, Richard. *Faith and Reason.* Oxford: Oxford University Press, 1981.

Tessier, Linda. *Concepts of the Ultimate.* New York: St. Martin's, 1989.

Tillich, Paul. *Dynamics of Faith.* New York: Harper and Row, 1957.

————. *On the Boundary: An Autobiographical Sketch.* New York: Scribner's, 1966.

————. *Systematic Theology.* Vol. 1. Chicago: University of Chicago Press, 1951.

Wittgenstein, Ludwig. *Culture and Value.* Trans. Peter Winch. Chicago: University of Chicago Press, 1980.

————. *Philosophical Investigations.* 3d ed. Trans. G. E. M. Anscombe. Englewood Cliffs, N.J.: Prentice Hall, 1958.

————. *Tractatus-Logico-Philosophicus.* Trans. D. F. Pears and B. F. McGuinness. London: Routledge, 1921.

Wolterstorff, Nicholas. *Reason Within the Bounds of Religion.* 2d ed. Grand Rapids: Wm. B. Eerdmans Publishing Co., 1984.

Section III, Part II
Theodicy
Thomas Jay Oord

◆

A theodicy justifies (*dikay* [justice]) one's belief that God (*theo* [deity]) exists despite the occurrence of evil (*theo* + *dikay* = theodicy). From the earliest of times, individuals have attempted to explain why God permits evil. Modern adherents of the three great monotheistic religions—Christianity, Islam, and Judaism—are especially interested in the work of theodicy. Many today, both members and nonmembers of these religious traditions, regard the problem of evil as *the* most serious intellectual challenge to monotheism (Davis 1981).

I. The Problem of Evil Argument

The problem of evil has been presented in various ways. As early as the sixth century B.C., the prophet Jeremiah pondered why the innocent suffer and the wicked prosper (Jer. 12:1). And, even today, we still wonder, "Why do bad things happen to good people?" In recent centuries, the problem of evil is often presented in the form of an argument. David Hume presents the problem of evil succinctly as such: "Is [God] willing to prevent evil, but not able? Then he is impotent. Is he able, but not willing? Then he is malevolent. Is he both able and willing? Whence then is evil?" (1779).

Although theodicists (i.e., those who construct theodicies) have primarily been interested in a theoretical answer to this problem, some have suggested other solutions. For instance, some have argued that figuring out an adequate theoretical answer is not the point of the problem of evil. Instead, they claim, one should be concerned *only* with acting to overcome or prevent evil (Phillips 1977). The time spent formulating a theoretical answer, they say, is time better spent ridding evil from the world. Others have suggested that the problem is solved when one realizes that God feels ("suffers") all creaturely pain and suffering. Christians, in particular, have pointed to the cross of Christ to justify why evil occurs despite God's being omnipotent and omnibenevolent (Moltmann 1993). The Cross is the supreme evidence that God suffers with creatures in the midst of their suffering.

Although these alternative solutions contain helpful elements for analyzing some aspects of the problem of evil, this chapter will not concern itself with them. It will concentrate instead upon the problem of evil's theoretical aspect while supposing that theoretical concerns influence the way we all actually live. If theory and practice are mutually influential, the

201

theories offered here will imply certain practices, and our practices will influence which of these theories we find preferable.

For the purposes of this chapter, the problem of evil is presented in this argument:

1. If God exists, God must be omnipotent (i.e., all-powerful), which means that God would *be able* to prevent genuinely evil occurrences.
2. If God exists, God must be omnibenevolent (i.e., love perfectly), which means that God would *want* to prevent genuinely evil occurrences.
3. However, genuine evils occur.
4. Therefore, God must not exist.

In addressing the various answers given the questions raised by the problem of evil, I will attend to the above statements in reverse order.

4. God must not exist.

In the technical sense, a thoroughgoing atheist is not personally interested in theodicy. In other words, if one has already concluded that God does not exist, he or she would feel no deep need to propose an answer that justifies God's existence despite the occurrence of evil. This does not mean that atheists are uninterested in acting to prevent genuinely evil occurrences. It only means that those who have made up their mind that God does not exist on grounds other than the problem of evil are not likely to become theists should an adequate theodicy be presented to them.

It appears as though many modern atheists deny that God exists, however, primarily because of the problem of evil. For those who choose to believe that God does not exist because they know of no adequate solution to the problem, the work of theodicy takes on personal relevance.

It is also true that some thoroughgoing theists do not take seriously the problem of evil's conclusion: "God must not exist." If someone has already concluded that God exists and will not address sincerely any argument or evidence that suggests otherwise, such a person will feel no deep need to propose an answer that justifies God's existence despite the occurrence of evil. Critics of this position argue that addressing the problem of evil from a privileged, *a priori,* foundation is irresponsible. The question of God's existence, or at least the nature of divine attributes in question, cannot be arbitrarily set aside as unimportant.

The problem of evil presents intellectual and existential challenges to the belief that God exists. Both believers and nonbelievers alike must take these challenges seriously.

3. Genuine evils occur.

Most people affirm that genuinely evil events occur—at least, most affirm this in their initial reflections. There is good reason for this affirmation. If we were to examine the 20th century alone, we would find numerous atrocious and pain-filled events: genocide and ethnic cleansing, random murder, wide-scale local and world wars, pointless executions, indifference to the poor and disenfranchised, sexual abuse of children, exploitation and oppression of women, the Cambodian "killing fields," the slaughter of millions in Soviet-controlled countries, racism, rampant disease and malnutrition, napalm and atomic bombings, AIDS infestation, drug addiction, ecological violence, terrorism, torture chambers and medical "experimentation," incest, rape, and, perhaps most famously, the Jewish holocaust of World War II. The victims of these evils number in the hundreds of millions. Many of these atrocities appear to be genuinely evil and therefore comprise some of the evidence for affirming that genuine evils occur.

Many philosophers who claim that evils occur distinguish between two main types: moral and natural. Moral evils are caused by the decisions of moral agents, particularly humans. Natural evils are caused by nonmoral factors, e.g., floods, volcanic eruptions, or earthquakes. Distinguishing between moral and natural evil is important for theodicists who argue that the decisions of moral creatures are the only events that produce genuine evil.

In an important sense, however, distinguishing between moral and natural evil is not necessary when considering the problem of evil argument as laid out here. At issue here is the question why God does not prevent genuine evil—whether such evil be the result of improper decisions of persons or the result of natural nonpersonal forces. However, some theodicies are affected by the moral/natural distinction, and this will become apparent later in this essay.

We have noted that almost everyone affirms the occurrence of evil. A few individuals and religious movements, however, have explicitly claimed that evils do not occur, because evil (and good) is purely subjective. When someone calls an event "evil," say these people, all that should be concluded is that the person doing the calling considers an event undesirable. For such people, evil is a matter of personal taste and has no objective reality. Therefore, it makes no sense to talk about evil events.

Augustine offers a subtle but highly influential denial that genuinely evil events occur. He contends that what we call "evil" is only the privation of the good that God creates. Evil has no ontological status. To call a being "evil" merely entails that one has identified an imperfect being. Because only God is perfect, any nondivine being is necessarily imperfect. But imperfection should not be equated with evil; it is merely the absence of perfect goodness. This line of reasoning leads Augustine to conclude that nothing is genuinely evil. Or, as he concludes in his prayer, "To Thee (O God) there is no such thing as evil."

The more common denial of evil arises from the common acknowledgement that at least *some* painful events are required if overall greater good is to be secured. This position is sometimes called the "greater goods defense." For instance, most mothers would not call the pain and suffering they endure when bearing children "evil," because the joy of holding their newborns exceeds any previous discomfort. In other words, this joy is a greater good than the pains of labor. Or consider the suffering that college students must endure when completing a 20-page term paper assigned them. At least in theory, the good that will emerge as each student completes this assignment will be greater than the pain the assignment inflicts. Although some students may lightheartedly complain that the professor "did an evil thing" by assigning the paper, most realize that the assignment is meant for their good.

Childbearing women, students who endure the demands of college professors, and others illustrate that some painful events are "instrumental" evils. Instrumental evils are painful or atrocious events that, when considered from the larger perspective, contribute to the greater good. Pain, suffering, and even death can be instrumental for attaining greater overall well-being. The apostle Paul refers to instrumental evil when claiming that "suffering produces endurance, and endurance produces character, and character produces hope" (Rom. 5:3-4, NRSV). God is justified in permitting instrumentally evil events, because such events bring about a greater amount of good than what could have been secured had these events not occurred.

Instrumental evils differ in kind, however, from genuine evils (or "gratuitous evils"). Genuinely evil events are events, all things considered, without which the universe would have been better (Griffin 1989). To say it another way, while instrumental evils establish a greater degree of overall well-being than what could have been established had they not occurred (or at least are neutral), genuine evils produce a greater degree of overall ill-being than what could have been established had some other events occurred. Genuine evils are evil events that no one has morally sufficient reasons for promoting or permitting. No one who loves perfectly wishes to permit the production of greater overall ill-being.

The crucial questions to be addressed, then, are these: Are all painful and atrocious events of our world instrumentally evil, or are some occurrences genuinely evil? Do all painful and atrocious things that happen in this universe ultimately contribute to the greater good? Or would the universe have been better, all things considered, had some possible events taken place other than these painful and atrocious ones?

The answer one gives to these questions makes all the difference when constructing a theodicy. If all painful and atrocious evil events are instrumental evils, the problem of evil can be easily solved. If every event has secured greater overall well-being, a loving God is justified in permitting every evil. But if someone considers an event to have been genuinely evil, a theodicy is needed.

One might claim, however, that because humans are localized and limited—rather than omnipresent and all-inclusive—humans are not capable of "considering all things." The implication might be that humans are not capable of judging which events are genuinely evil and which are not. The only individual who *could* consider all things, one might claim, would be God; i.e., only God can decide whether genuinely evil events ever occur. After all, the cognitive capacities of creatures presumably pale in significance to the cognition of divinity.

Furthermore, humans often disagree when assessing whether or not certain events are genuinely evil. What one person considers a genuine evil, another person may consider instrumental to some greater good. While the death of hundreds of millions in the 20th century may appear genuinely evil, for instance, someone might argue that these deaths have actually been good. After all, they have prevented the over-population of our planet.

Three responses are given to the claim that nothing genuinely evil ever occurs. First, the redemptive themes of the three great monotheistic traditions seem to suppose the occurrence of genuinely evil events. Christianity, for instance, seems to suppose the reality of genuine evil, because if no events were genuinely evil, Jesus' actions to secure salvation would be unnecessary.

Second, it is very difficult to take certain events, for instance, the rape of a small child, and believe that the world would not have been a better place in the absence of such events. In other words, when looking squarely in the face of some specific atrocity of which circumstances and choices made by those involved are known, most people find it difficult to maintain that the world would not have been better had some other possible actions occurred.

The third response given to the claim that nothing genuinely evil ever occurs is the argument that *all* people have, at some time, regarded some event to be genuinely evil. David Griffin notes that even if we verbally deny the occurrence of genuine evil, we affirm by the way we act our more basic belief that genuine evils occur (1989). We all reveal by our emotions, attitudes, and actions our common belief that not everything that has happened is the best that could have happened. Our sense of guilt for failing to help someone in pain or distress, for instance, illustrates this commonsense notion. Because all persons suppose in their actions that genuine evils occur, says Griffin, a theodicy denying the reality of genuine evil (e.g., Augustine's) cannot be adequate.

Before leaving the discussion of instrumental and genuine evil, it would be wise to address a notable issue. The apostle Paul has written in Rom. 8:28 that God works for the good in all things. This verse can be interpreted to mean that whether the evil is genuine or instrumental, God is active to bring at least *some* good out of pain and suffering. The verse can also be interpreted to mean that God *requires* all painful events so that greater good could be gained. To say that God requires all painful events is to deny genuine evil. Denying genuine evil implies that all painful and atrocious occurrences are instrumental for attaining the greater good. To say that God can use, but does not require, evil events, however, is to claim that God can wring some good even out of the genuinely evil events that God did not want to occur. The difference between these two interpretations is enormous.

2. If God exists, God must be omnibenevolent (i.e., loving perfectly), which means that God would want to prevent genuinely evil occurrences.

The Book of 1 John includes these words twice: "God is love" (4:8, 16). Philosophers and theologians sometimes attempt to capture the meaning of this statement by referring to God as "omnibenevolent." Others, perhaps influenced more by Anselm's definition of deity as that than which nothing greater can be conceived, have said that God loves "perfectly" or "maximally." Still others simply ascribe to God absolute moral goodness. Typically implied in each of these descriptions are the claims that (1) God never commits a genuinely evil act, and (2) God always acts to secure greater overall well-being by both promoting actions that result in well-being and preventing actions that result in ill-being.

Perhaps, however, theists have been too quick to ascribe perfect love to deity. Some, particularly theists who suffered through the Holocaust of World War II, have concluded from their personal experiences that God either sometimes acts in an evil manner or does not always have the production of overall well-being in mind. This seems a plausible conclusion if (1) God exists, (2) at least some Holocaust events were genuinely evil, and (3) God has the power to prevent genuinely evil occurrences. Those espousing such a "protest" theology, then, either explicitly or implicitly deny divine perfect love.

Critics of this protest position typically argue either that their own religious tradition requires that God be considered perfectly loving or that God must be considered perfectly loving if God is a maximally perfect being. In either case, critics also claim that a morally imperfect God is unworthy of worship. Such a God is not deserving of one's unqualified devotion.

Some have concluded on biblical grounds that God must have a "dark" side, because deity is the source of all events, which includes genuinely evil ones. For instance, the writer of Lamentations asks rhetorically, "Is it not from the mouth of the Most High that good and bad come?" (3:38, NRSV). In Isaiah, Jehovah is quoted as saying, "I make weal and create woe; I the LORD do all these things" (45:7, NRSV). The Psalmist pleads with God, "You have put me in the depths of the Pit, in the regions dark and deep. Your wrath lies heavy upon me, and you overwhelm me with all your waves . . . . O LORD, why do you cast me off? Why do you hide your face from me?" (88:6-7, 14). This last phrase is taken by some as a basis for understanding God as hidden (the Latin phrase is *"Deus absconditus"*). Because God is sometimes the source of evil and/or sometimes hidden, biblical writers lament that God fails to come quickly, if at all, to rescue oppressed peoples.

A critic's response to passages of Scripture that depict God as evil, "dark," or hidden typically involves the claim that biblical writers are describing how they *personally* experience God. Such biblical writers are not describing the actual being, essence, or character of God. One's personal perceptions of God may be flawed for any number of reasons. At other times, say critics of this position, the depiction of God as evil is better understood as one's experiencing the *natural* negative consequences that come when one rejects the possibilities of love a perfectly loving God offers. To choose less than love often entails experiencing pain and suffering.

Some have said that although God's love is perfect, what God calls love is not analogous in any way to what humans call love. In other words, what we regard as loving activity, God does not. God says His ways are not our ways (Isa. 55:8). God's ways are infinitely more complex than ours, it is argued, and this infinite separation between deity and creatures means that divine love is infinitely different from creaturely love.

Critics of the position that God's love is in all ways disanalogous to creaturely love remark that such a position makes the central Christian claim "God is love" meaningless. After all, if God's love is entirely disanalogous to human love, one may as well say, "God is xakjano." If we have no idea of what "xakjano" means, it makes as much sense to claim that God is that as it does to claim that "God is love." Furthermore, having no clue as to the nature of perfect divine love means that one cannot know if he or she imitates God when loving (Eph. 5:1-2). While critics acknowledge that God's love likely differs in degree and scope because He is everlasting and omnipresent, they argue that divine love must not differ in kind from creaturely love.

1. If God exists, God must be omnipotent (i.e., be all-powerful), which means that God would be able to prevent genuinely evil occurrences.

The word "omnipotent" is highly ambiguous. Although it literally means "having all power" or "all-powerful," philosophers and theologians have used the word to mean diverse things in reference to God. In order to simplify the discussion, many talk about divine power as "maximally perfect," because a maximally perfect being (God) would have maximally perfect power. But to what does omnipotence as maximally perfect power amount?

First, for some, to say "God is omnipotent" amounts to saying that God is the omni-cause. In other words, God is the *only* cause in the universe. "By the omnipotent God," says Martin Luther, for instance, "I do not mean the potentiality by which he could do many things which he does not, but the active power by which he forcefully works all in all." If divine omnipotence is understood in this way, God is the direct cause of all genuine evil. Critics obviously contend that this notion of divine omnipotence makes divine love untenable if such love involves the allegation made previously: "God never commits a genuinely evil act."

Second, many philosophers and theologians have understood "omnipotent" merely to entail God's *capacity* to be omni-causal at any given time. This understanding involves God's ability to control totally any set of circumstances should He choose to do so. However, God has voluntarily granted power (which is necessary for freedom) to creatures so that they may also act as causes. God essentially possesses all power, but creatures possess power on loan from God. Deity has become self-limited while retaining the capacity to veto (i.e., withdraw or override) creaturely power.

Advocates of this position, sometimes called the "classical freewill defense" (or "accidental freewill theism") believe their position addresses most of the issues in the problem of evil. This defense is preferable, they believe, because the genuine evil of the world can be understood to have been caused by creatures, not by God. Deity is not the direct cause of evil, and responsibility for life's pain and suffering should be placed upon the shoulders of creatures who have used their God-given power wrongly. God always uses divine power lovingly; creatures sometimes use God-derived power in evil ways.

Critics of the classical freewill defense contend that this option does not get God off the hook. God is still ultimately culpable for evil, they claim, because He did not *prevent* genuine evil from occurring. Being perfectly loving involves both promoting events that secure well-being and preventing events that produce ill-being. The God who essentially possesses all power—but is usually self-limited—should give up these self-imposed limitations, become unselflimited, and act to prevent genuinely evil occurrences. In sum, the God of the classical freewill defense, say critics, does not love perfectly. This God voluntarily chooses not to prevent genuine evils from occurring.

Third, for some philosophers and theologians the claim that "God is omnipotent" merely means that God is the most powerful being (i.e., mightiest) in the universe. The power of God is the maximal amount of power any one being could possess, but other individuals may also possess power—even power vis-à-vis God. This position, "essential freewill theism," claims that both God and creatures essentially possess some power. This power cannot be completely overridden, withdrawn, or vetoed by anyone, because all beings *necessarily* exert some power. Under this hypothesis, say its advocates, one may claim that the genuine evil of the world has been caused by creatures who use their power wrongly, and not even God has the capacity entirely to prevent creatures from committing genuinely evil acts.

Critics of this third understanding of omnipotence and its implications typically claim that this conception does not ring true to their religious intuitions. The God who does not essentially possess all power and who cannot withdraw or override entirely the power of creatures seems stunted. The deity of this conception just seems too limited.

Almost all professional philosophers and theologians are prepared to admit that God must be understood to be limited in some ways. Very few believe that God can perform logically impossible tasks, for instance. Most admit that God cannot make a square circle, cannot cause $2 + 3$ to equal 914, and cannot create a rock so big that even God could not lift it. Performing logically impossible tasks is not possible for *any* being. So, if the maximally perfect being is unable to do the illogical, this limitation is not serious.

Many philosophers and theologians also admit that God is limited to doing only those things that conform to the divine nature. For instance, because the actions of a maximally perfect being would, by hypothesis, always be perfectly loving, such a being would be unable to love imperfectly. God's goodness also involves limitations, because divinity is unable to sin. (For example, although one biblical writer reports Jesus as saying that all things are possible for God [Matt. 19:26], which seems to deny that God has any limitations, another writer argues that it is impossible for God to lie [Heb. 6:18], which acknowledges divine limitation.) Finally, if the divine nature includes necessary existence, then it is also impossible for God not to exist.

In sum, although what is meant by the claim "God is omnipotent" varies from person to person, most philosophers and theologians are prepared to make qualifications to explain more explicitly what they mean when speaking of divine power.

II. PROMINENT CONTEMPORARY THEODICIES OR ANSWERS TO THE PROBLEM OF EVIL

Having addressed the various statements in the problem of evil as presented here, I will conclude this essay by addressing some contemporary theodicies that play a prominent role in current discussions. In doing so, I will occasionally make references to material that has been presented thus far. In addition, criticisms of these contemporary theodical options will be noted.

Mystery and Incomprehensibility

One of the prominent answers to the problem evil, given by both novices and experts alike, is that humans are essentially incapable of grasping a solution to the problem of evil. Why God permits evil, despite being all-powerful and perfectly loving, is an unfathomable mystery. Although some philosophers and theologians appeal to mystery on theological grounds, some appeal to mystery because they are profoundly aware that human minds are limited. Those who argue the latter are saying that the problem of evil cannot be solved due to our cognitive limitations: the human mind is not able to apprehend all of the relevant data surrounding the issues of theodicy.

A solution to the problem of evil remains incomprehensible, say many, because God remains utterly incomprehensible for humans. Claiming that God is utterly incomprehensible for humans is not something new. Negative or "apophatic" theology has been around for more than a thousand years. But a resurgence of such thinking has emerged during the last half of the 20th century and spilled over into the 21st. God is too immense and too elusive for any human systems or words, say advocates of what might be called the "mystery" answer to the problem of evil. Furthermore, as certain thinkers have argued, what one accepts as rational, linguistically proper, or religious is strongly influenced by unconscious factors as well as social ideology (Taylor 1990). In fact, one should always be suspicious of the underlying power implications of any proposal to solve the problem of evil. Advocates of the mystery answer conclude, then, that the problem of evil argument, with its statements about who God is or what God does, is doomed to remain insoluble.

Critics of the mystery/incomprehensibility position raise several objections to this problem of evil response. Some argue that a loving God who is omnipotent would have the desire and the ability to reveal information about himself so that He would not remain *utterly* incomprehensible. Unconscious factors and societal ideology would not stop this God. Furthermore, such a God would have the desire and ability to reveal the reasons for why genuine evils are permitted. The limitations of the human mind would not be a limitation to an omnipotent God who, out of love, wished to reveal something about these all-important matters.

Many Christian critics also argue that the Bible has given humans at least a glimpse of who God is. For instance, biblical writers claim that God has been revealed in Jesus of Nazareth. Furthermore, according to scripture, nature reveals important aspects of deity to everyone (Rom. 1:19-20). Finally, those who claim that God is utterly incomprehensible usually continue to speak about God as though they really *do* know something about divinity. In other words, their actions contradict their claim that God is utterly incomprehensible. While many critics of the incomprehensible/mystery "solution" admit that humans cannot completely comprehend God and, therefore, one's statements about deity should be provisional, many also argue that one ultimately cannot remain undecided about the issues resting at the heart of the problem of evil.

John Hick's Soul-Making Explanation

John Hick's contemporary answer to the problem of evil, which takes its basic idea from the second-century Christian theologian Irenaeus, is often called a "soul-making" theodicy. Hick believes that what God most desires is for each human to become virtuous, i.e., to build character. Although God could have "injected" these virtues in humans, He would rather these virtues be formed by free creaturely decisions. After all, says Hick, those virtues that have been formed in humans through their own "right decisions in situations of challenge and temptation, are intrinsically more valuable than virtues created within [humans] ready made and without any effort on [their] own part." This means, according to Hick, that God chose not to create humans "as already perfect beings but rather as imperfect creatures who can then attain to the more valuable kind of goodness through their own free choices." The evils of life faced by such imperfect beings are not only inevitable because the world is imperfect, but God permits these evils to engender human growth into moral self-consciousness and personal responsibility.

According to Hick's scheme, evil occurrences are necessary for the development of moral virtues. This can be illustrated by considering the virtue of compassion. In order for humans to develop certain types of compassion, it seems logically required that certain types of evil occur. As humans respond compassionately to the suffering of others, for instance, the process of becoming more virtuous can occur. This process is rarely completed on earth, however. Therefore, this "soul-making" procedure must continue beyond bodily existence until, as Hick claims, "sooner or later, in our own time and in our own way, we shall all freely come to God" (Hick, in Davis 1977).

Many criticisms have been proffered to Hick's theodicy. A typical criticism is called the "evidential problem." Although a certain amount of evil appears necessary if a certain amount of good can be attained, the actual amount of evil in the world exceeds what is required for procuring this good. The vast amount and varieties of evil, say Hick's critics, are not necessary for the amount and diversity of good present. Admittedly, gauging amounts and degrees of good and evil is difficult. But critics wonder why a Creator, whose power is not limited by anything other than what is logically possible and consistent with the divine nature, did not do a better job in creating our world so that an appropriate balance of good and evil would have emerged.

A second criticism of Hick's theodicy involves questioning God's purposes. Critics contend that Hick's line of reasoning, which says that evil is required for the development of certain moral virtues, makes a secondary good into a primary good. For example, Hick considers the "having compassion for those who suffer from evil" virtue of primary importance, while the absence of evils that would be required to develop this compassion virtue is of secondary importance. But what should be of primary importance is the absence of evil, contend critics, not the development of virtues. A being that loves perfectly would be more interested in preventing genuine evil altogether than promoting evil-contingent virtues. After all, respond critics, this world would have been a better place had no one needed to develop the "compassion for sufferers of evil" virtue.

Third, if God has allowed all past pain and agony in order to produce what is the greatest good—human character—then there have never been painful or destructive events that have made the universe, all things considered, worse than it might have otherwise been. In other words, say critics, there has never been any event that is genuinely evil. Hick admits as such: "What now threatens us as final evil will prove to have been interim evil out of which good will in the end have been brought" (1978). The problems Hick's theodicy faces when it denies that genuinely evil events occur were mentioned earlier.

Alvin Plantinga's Freewill Defense

Alvin Plantinga has become well known in philosophical circles for his contribution to the problem of evil question. Plantinga has argued that, contrary to previous speculation, there are no logical inconsistencies in the problem of evil as typically stated. "The existence of God is neither precluded nor rendered improbable by the existence of evil," says Plantinga (1983). To affirm that God is omnipotent and omnibenevolent, while also affirming that evil events occur, does not amount to a logical contradiction.

Plantinga uses Gottfried Leibniz's "possible worlds" line of reasoning to argue that it is logically possible that an omnipotent and omnibenevolent God exists despite the occurrence of evil events. A world with free creatures is more valuable than a world in which creatures had no freedom. But freedom to do right, argues Plantinga, always entails the correlate possibility of doing wrong. There are no possible worlds in which creatures are free and yet entirely determined by God to do good. In other words, it is logically impossible for God to create free creatures and also guarantee that these creatures will refrain from evil. Because creating free creatures is morally superior to creating creatures without freedom, God did the most loving thing by creating a world with the potential for evil. In other words, in any possible world that God could create, it is logically necessary for free creatures to have the *opportunity* to make genuinely free decisions among various morally conditioned options.

Plantinga is not arguing that all evil is required so that creatures can know the difference between good and evil. Such an argument would be weak, because the actual amount of evil that has occurred in recorded history is much greater than what would be necessary for humans to make such a good/evil differentiation.

J. L. Mackie has responded critically to Plantinga's possible worlds scenario. Mackie wonders why God would be unable to create persons in such a way that they would always freely choose the good. If God is all-powerful in every possible world, God ought to be able to create a world in which people invariably choose rightly. Plantinga's response to Mackie is that God cannot both determine that people choose rightly and also create people that are genuinely free. Creating free yet entirely determined people is logically impossible for anyone, including God. Most philosophers and theologians side with Plantinga over Mackie in this argument.

As helpful as Plantinga's contribution of showing that no logical inconsistencies are present in the problem of evil argument is, many critics contend that the fundamental issues of theodicy are not logical ones. In fact, say detractors, Plantinga has not even offered a theodicy. A theodicy involves offering an answer to the problem of evil that is not just logically *possible* but also evidentially *plausible*. Just because the logical aspect of the problem of evil has been solved this does not mean that the evidential aspect is resolved. In fact, it does not seem plausible, say some critics, that a loving God would create *any* world if the best possible one must contain the unspeakable horrors and atrocities witnessed in the previous century.

Others criticize Plantinga's proposal because it implies that God is self-limited. While it may be logically impossible for a creature to be genuinely free and entirely determined by God, there is nothing logically contradictory in God choosing to withdraw or constrain the freedom of those who perpetrate evil. The best of all possible worlds would seem to include God's occasional unilateral determination of evil creatures—if God were metaphysically able to do so—to prevent innocent victims from suffering genuine horrors. After all, sometimes our most loving actions involve constraining the freedom of criminals so the innocent do not suffer. Why should God's love be entirely different from ours when it comes to constraining the freedom of criminals? In short, argue critics, it does not seem plausible to ascribe perfect love to Plantinga's self-limited God, because this deity does not occasionally become unselflimited in the name of love.

David Ray Griffin's Metaphysical Laws Hypothesis

The final prominent contemporary theodicy considered here is proffered by process theist David Ray Griffin. This process theodicy involves a reconception of divine power to account for creaturely freedom. As Griffin states, "My solution dissolves the problem of evil by denying the doctrine of omnipotence fundamental to it" (Griffin, in Davis 1981, 105). This denial of classical omnipotence and therefore reconception of divine power is required, argues Griffin, because inadequate formulations of divine power are traditionally accepted. In this scheme, God's power is perfect. However, the perfect power ascribed to divinity does not make God indictable for genuine evil. Most, if not all, creatures who have misused the power they possess are indictable. Deity cannot prevent the misuse of power, because God cannot unilaterally determine any occurrence in the universe.

Griffin speculates that God's inability to determine creaturely decisions unilaterally is an inability based upon eternal metaphysical laws. It is not an inability based upon divine self-limitation. The metaphysics Griffin finds most adequate requires that creatures possess self-determinative power (freedom) that cannot be withdrawn or overridden by others, including God. God cannot circumvent this eternal metaphysical law, because He did not create it. Or, as Griffin states, "the process theodicy that I am presenting . . . hinges upon the notion that there are metaphysical principles which are beyond even divine decision" (1976). Griffin advocates a form of essential freewill theism.

God does bear a measure of responsibility, in Griffin's hypothesis, for the intensity of pain and suffering experienced by creatures. God is responsible for bringing our present world to its complex present state, including the creation of such complex creatures as humans. This complexity allows for profound expressions of love and beauty, but it also allows for the possibility that profound evils could occur. Although responsible for guiding creation to its current degree of complexity, God is *not* indictable for failing to prevent genuinely evil events from occurring. Creatures are indictable for genuinely evil events, because they have misused their own power. Metaphysical laws prevent even God from taking all power and freedom away from creatures that misuse freedom. Griffin solves the problem of evil, then, by denying that God is able to prevent genuinely evil occurrences.

The recurring criticism of this position attacks Griffin's hypothesis that God did not create the metaphysical laws that govern actual existence. Although some theists have acknowledged that God could not have created the metaphysical laws to which His own essence is subject, most have argued that part of what it means for God to be the world's creator is that He created the metaphysical laws that govern what it means to exist.

Accepting Griffin's proposal also requires one to reconceive what it means to call God "Creator." Unlike the God of traditional Christian theology, the creative God envisioned here has always been creating out of a realm of nondivine actualities. This hypothesis undermines the classic Church doctrine that God voluntarily created the world out of absolute nothingness (or *"creatio ex nihilo"*). Many critics are not willing to give up this time-honored doctrine pertaining to God's capacity to create unilaterally.

CONCLUSION

In addressing the main issues of theodicy, this chapter offered various explanations for why it might be that evil occurs although a loving and powerful God exists. Upon reading about the issues and alternatives involved, readers will hopefully find themselves more attracted to one option over others. If it is true that our theoretical answers to the problem of evil influence the practical way we actually live, the impact of this exercise will be significant.

TEXTS FOR FURTHER READING

Augustine. *The Confessions of St. Augustine.* Ed. and trans. J. K. Ryan. Garden City, N.Y.: Image Books, 1960.

Basinger, David. *The Case for Free Will Theism.* Downers Grove, Ill.: InterVarsity Press, 1996.

Bertocci, Peter. *The Goodness of God.* Washington, D.C.: University Press of America, 1981.

Davis, Stephen T. *Encountering Evil: Live Options in Theodicy.* Philadelphia: John Knox, 1981.

Griffin, David Ray. *Evil Revisited: Responses and Reconsiderations.* Albany, N.Y.: State University of New York Press, 1989.

———. *God, Power and Evil: A Process Theodicy.* Philadelphia: Westminster, 1976.

Hick, John. *Evil and the God of Love.* 2d ed. New York: Harper and Row, 1978.

Hume, David. *Dialogues Concerning Natural Religion* (1779). Indianapolis: Hackett, 1980.

Inbody, Tyron. *The Transforming God: An Interpretation of Suffering and Evil.* Louisville: Westminster John Knox, 1997.

Leibniz, Gottfried. *The Theodicy: Abridgment of the Argument Reduced to Syllogistic Form* (1710).

Luther, Martin. *Luther's Works.* Ed. N. Pelikan and H. T. Lehman. St. Louis: Chalice. 33.

Mackie, J. L. *The Miracle of Theism: Arguments for and Against the Existence of God.* Oxford: Oxford University Press, 1982.

Moltmann, Jurgen. *The Crucified God: The Cross of Christ as the Foundation and Criticism of Christian Theology.* Minneapolis: Fortress, 1993.

Phillips, D. Z. "The Problem of Evil: A Critique of Swinburne." *Reason and Religion.* Ed. Stuart C . Brown. Ithaca, N.Y.: Cornell University Press, 1977.

Pike, Nelson. *God and Evil.* Englewood Cliffs, N.J.: Prentice-Hall, 1964.

Plantinga, Alvin. *God, Freedom and Evil.* Grand Rapids: Wm. B. Eerdmans Publishing Co., 1983.

Taylor, Mark C. *Tears.* Albany, N.Y.: State University of New Press, 1990.

Religious Ethics

T. Scott Daniels

I. Defining Ethics

The discipline of ethics involves *critical thinking about moral judgments* concerning the *kinds of things that people do* and the *sorts of persons people are* in light of *transcendent reality*. Examining closely what each of these key phrases entails can help us grasp better what this sentence means.

Although ethicists are not completely uninterested in feelings, more often than not, feelings matter little to the discipline of ethics. For this reason, the discipline of ethics focuses upon reflection. A psychologist or social scientist might ask a person how he or she feels about abortion or capital punishment, but an ethicist thinks critically about whether an action is right or wrong regardless of how the he or she feels about the subject.

Those engaging in ethical reflection think critically about what people do. What people do, i.e., moral actions, arise in both individual and communal forms. For example, the ethicist asks the individualistic question "Is it right for me to take my own life to end my physical suffering?" But the ethicist must also ask whether or not a society or culture should allow euthanasia (literally "a good death") within its community. The ethicist thinks critically about the moral actions of both the individual and the society.

An area of ethics that is often overlooked is moral character. What kind of people are we, and what should we be? Once again, the ethicist raises these questions on both the corporate and individual level. For example, the ethicist asks, "If I see a person suffering, should I, as a good person, help the person no matter the cost?" But the ethicist must also ask whether a nation should assist the poor or leave its citizens to their own devises.

These first three parts of the definition of ethics might be obvious. But the importance of the phrase pertaining to transcendent reality may not be so obvious. Most ethicists argue, however, that the discipline of ethics requires a reference point. The idea of morality or "rightness" can be measured only by a standard that falls outside our particular moral situations.

Consider the following example. It is the seventh game of the World Series. The New York Yankees are battling the Cincinnati Reds, and the series is tied at three games each. It is the bottom of the ninth inning, the game is tied, the bases are loaded, and there are two outs. Roger Clemens is pitching to Ken Griffey Jr., and the count is three balls and two strikes. Clemens throws a 95-mile-an-hour fastball, and Griffey lets it go by. If the pitch is a ball, the winning run scores. If the pitch is a strike, the game goes to extra innings. How do we know whether the pitch is a ball or a strike? Clemens threw the ball where he expects it to be a strike. Griffey let it go, because he thinks the pitch is a ball. But how do we know which is right? Obviously, we look to the umpire.

In this situation, the umpire, as the arbitrator of the rules of baseball, is the transcendent reality. There are baseball rules that keep this game from being football. For example, the Reds' player standing at second base cannot just decide to run and tackle the pitcher before the pitcher has a chance to throw the ball. The pitcher cannot decide to run all over the field keeping the ball away from the other players. The rules of baseball (and the umpire as the unbiased distributor of the rules) make the game possible. Without the rules that transcend the game itself, we would have chaos.

The same is essentially true of ethics. If we all get together and simply state how we individually feel about the legalization of drugs, we would not have determined what is right or wrong. We would only have discovered how each of us feels. Most ethicists believe that ethics needs a referee or an umpire; ethics can be truly done only in the light of a transcendent reality. But what is that transcendent reality?

II. GOD AS THE TRANSCENDENT REALITY

There are many different ethical theories, and each one seems to point to its own transcendent reality. The *cultural relativist* (e.g., Protagoras, Melville Herskovits) argues that the cultural context in which one finds himself or herself is the transcendent creator of the moral rules for conduct within that culture. *Ethical egoism* (e.g., Thomas Hobbes, Ayn Rand) looks to the individual's needs and desires as the transcendent reality that determines right and wrong. *Utilitarianism* (e.g., Jeremy Bentham, John Stuart Mill) determines the right or the good by measuring the total happiness or pain a decision produces. In the utilitarian system, happiness is the transcendent reality that determines the rightness of our decisions. *Deontology* (e.g., Immanuel Kant) makes reason the transcendent moral reality. If we want to make the right decision, says Kant, we should find the rule at work in any moral situation, universalize it, and then determine whether or not following this rule is reasonable. Although each of these theories differs in what is chosen as the appropriate transcendent reality, each has a transcendent reality that serves as its moral compass or umpire.

All systems of *theistic ethics* have a transcendent reality. For the theistic ethicist, the transcendent reality is the divine. There are many religious traditions, however, and each has a different view or understanding of deity. These various understandings result in different ethical systems. For the sake of space, we will focus on the theistic traditions of Western culture. Most of the moral traditions of the West have their origin, in one way or another, in Christian theism. But even if we narrow our field of inquiry down to religious ethics in Western Christianity, we are left with several religious ethical systems to explore.

The question in Western religious ethics is not "Should we consider God to be the transcendent reality in determining what is right and wrong?" The question, rather, is "How do we understand the word or will of God with regard to moral behavior?" In other words, how is God's moral will *mediated* to human creatures?

Although we could probably think of more, I will explore four major systems or traditions in religious ethics. We turn to those.

A. Natural Law Ethics

In October 1994 Americans were horrified when they heard the report about a double homicide committed by a young South Carolina woman named Susan Smith; she had drowned her two young sons, Michael and Alex, by rolling her car into a lake near Union, South Carolina, with her sons strapped in their car seats. The question asked countless times by countless people the next day was "How can a mother do that to her own children?" What disturbs us about this kind of situation is that it appears to violate something basic in nature: the loving relationship between a parent and a child. To most of us, what Susan Smith did tears at the deepest fabric of who we are.

The above situation points to a reality that one group of religious ethicists call "natural law." For the natural law ethicist, there is a fundamental order to nature that should not be violated. The way things are in creation is the way things ought to be. When we act according to the laws of the creation, things go well for us, and we are doing "right." But when we violate the fundamental laws of nature, we are violating not only the creation but who we are intended to be.

Perhaps the best example of a natural law theorist is Thomas Aquinas (1225-74). Thomas was a highly educated Dominican monk who spent a great deal of his intellectual life wrestling with the relationship between reason and faith. There had been a rediscovery of the philosophical work of Aristotle in his day. Thomas picked up philosophical ideas from Aristotle and brought them into philosophical theology. We don't know God simply through special revelation (God's unique working within history—Scriptural revelation, miracles, Jesus Christ, and so on), argues Thomas, but we also discover a great deal about God by observing the nature of creation.

Thomas is famous for his five ways of proving the existence of God.

The fifth way of demonstrating God's existence is the way of design. "Goal-directed behaviour is observed in all bodies obeying natural laws, even when they lack awareness," argues Thomas. "Their behaviour hardly ever varies and practically always turns out well, showing that they truly tend to goals and do not merely hit them by accident" (1989, 13). God has woven certain laws into nature that determine and shape the way creatures behave. Thomas believed that we can discover much about God by looking at God's work written within nature's blueprint.

Thomas believed that the laws of nature are not derived from nature itself, however. Instead, they are there by the will and decree of God. The Hebrew word for "glory" in the Old Testament is the word *kabod,* which can be translated "heaviness" or "weightiness." When people in the Old Testament, like Moses, saw the glory of God, they understood themselves to be seeing the imprint or fingerprints left by God's weightiness.

What do we learn about God by observing creation? We learn that God is logical; there is a logical order to the creation. Gravity allows us to stay rooted to the surface of the planet. The right mix of oxygen and carbon exists in the atmosphere to make life possible. We live the right distance from the sun to enjoy its warmth—we are neither destroyed by its heat nor frozen by its separation. It is difficult for Thomas to conceive of a more orderly universe than the one God has created. Like God, we are logical and orderly. We reflect this logic when we build homes, plant gardens, write laws, have families, work according to schedules, etc. We reflect the very nature and image of God when we order our lives within the order of creation.

We also learn from creation, according to Thomas, that God is loving. We know this because of the way God supplies creatures with what they need. God has established seasons; the land brings forth the food we need; there is a "circle of life" that allows all of creation to be lovingly sustained. In the same way, we should find the same virtuous balance to our lives that God has established in the creation. We are called as humans to have dominion over the creation in the same way that God has dominion over it. God has certain intentions for creation, and we are "good" when we discover and live according to those intentions. In this sense, we should act "naturally." Humans, as the image of God on earth, are to align their wills with the will of God exhibited in the order of creation.

Not only does Thomas think we should act according to nature, but he is optimistic that we can discover the laws inherent within nature. The language of the United States' Declaration of Independence illustrates Thomas's belief that we can discover the laws of nature. This document states, "We hold these Truths to be self-evident, that all Men are created equal, that they are endowed by their Creator with certain unalienable

Rights." The key phrase in these opening lines is that these truths are "self-evident." Why are they self-evident? For the natural law theorist, the concept of an individual's rights to life, liberty, and the pursuit of happiness are obvious to all, because the Creator has formed the creation in such a way that these laws need no rational defense. They are obvious.

This idea of a natural law has several implications. One is that every person is without moral excuse. The basic and primary laws of God are self-evident within the structure of creation. This explains why some people seem to do much of what Scripture requires even though they have no knowledge of it. What Scripture commands is consistent with the laws of nature, because everyone, to some degree, has access to the law of God.

Another implication is that the state has an obligation, as a kind of divinely appointed authority, to establish and uphold laws that are also in line with nature. The state should punish those who violate the laws of nature, but they should also enact "positive" laws that help us mold our lives to the virtues of nature.

Perhaps it is easiest to understand the natural law theory of religious ethics by placing it within the context of a contemporary issue. How would the natural law ethicist understand human sexuality and its relationship to the Christian ideal of covenantal monogamy within marriage? I imagine the natural law ethicist would respond in some of the following ways.

The first thing we might see in the natural law is the rejection of homosexuality in favor of heterosexuality. In nature, God seems to have created men and women in such a way that they make for "natural" sexual partners. This is especially true if one sees in nature the idea that procreation is one of the intended ends or goals of sexuality. From this perspective, homosexual acts of intimacy are always violations of the natural law.

The natural law ethicist might also argue that we see in the creation a proclivity toward covenantal monogamy within heterosexual relationships. One might point to some of the animal species that mate with one partner for life as evidence of built-in monogamy. (It is dangerous to take this too far. The female praying mantis often bites off the head of its male partner after mating. I would shutter to think that this is the standard for all creation!) A more helpful approach would be to argue that it is within the monogamous relationship between a husband and wife that children are most welcomed. It seems self-evident to the natural law ethicist that the law of marriage is based upon the idea of creating a "home." Families, especially the nuclear idea of the family, are part of the structure of creation. Things just seem to be "working right" in the creation when committed spouses have children and build homes of love. For the natural law religious ethicist, this is what God intended.

Natural law ethics provide valuable aspects for understanding morality. For one thing, this form of ethics provides a conception of *common* morality. This theory helps us understand why some people outside of, or apart from, Christianity act in somewhat Christian ways. Scholars like Thomas also help us to create a place for reason in the Christian life. There is a great deal of God's truth that we can access through reason. This view also opens God up to all people. God is not trying to hide within the confines of a particular religion. He is revealing truth to all people in the light of creation. Natural law ethics helps us to find a balance between the material and spiritual. So much of pre-Thomistic theology rejected creation as evil, but the natural law theorist sees it as part of the good revelation and creation of God. It also recognizes that we have an obligation to write laws and assist others in the care of creation.

Some consider natural law ethics to possess potential problems. One is commonly called the "naturalistic fallacy." Principally associated with the British philosophers David Hume (1711-76) and G. E. Moore (1873—1958), the naturalistic fallacy argues that a "fallacy is committed whenever an argument asserts that, because of certain facts concerning human behavior or the physical world, certain values therefore follow as a consequence" (Porter 1995, 15). Just because things appear to be one way "by nature" does not mean that this is the way things are supposed to be. For example, it appears that "by nature" all acts of sexual intimacy between a man and a woman ought to be at least open to the possibility of conception. But with the invention of various birth control methods in the last century or so, the way things are is not necessarily the way things have to be. And if one argues that sexuality does not necessarily have to be open to procreation, does that view consider homosexuality morally acceptable? This is one of the major problems the natural law theorist encounters when he or she makes nature the mediator of its transcendent reality.

Many see another problem with natural law ethics, and this has to do with the theory's reliance upon human reason. How well does our reason provide access to God? When we see God at work in nature, do we see the real Creator God? Or do we see God through the blurry lenses of our cultural glasses?

The natural law theory does provide several advantages. In it we can find a place to develop a common morality across particular belief systems. In it we also find a God who cares for all creatures. And in it we discover laws that, if lived out, can help us be all that God created us to be.

B. Divine Command Ethics

The American Civil Liberties Union sued Alabama Judge Roy S. Moore in 1995 for opening his court sessions with prayer and posting the

Ten Commandments behind his bench. The situation created a great deal of media stir, and it helped Moore easily win election as the state's chief justice. This raises some interesting issues. If one were a natural law theorist, one might assume that the laws articulated in the Ten Commandments of Exod. 20 are also woven within the fabric of natural life and law. In fact, this is precisely the reason Judge Moore feels convinced that he has a moral duty to keep the Decalogue on his wall. He is there to enforce state laws that derive their essence and moral authority from the law of God. The problem is, however, that Judge Moore can enforce only three out of the ten commands. In his courtroom, one is in trouble if one steals, kills, or bears false witness. But it is legal in this country to have other gods before Yahweh, to dishonor the Sabbath, to use the Lord's name in vain, to make graven images, to commit adultery, to dishonor one's parents, and to covet.

The point is this. Some religious ethicists argue that when we look at nature we get only a small glimpse of God's will. We need to begin not with nature, say these ethicists, but with the explicit commands of God. At the core of the divine command theory of religious ethics (or "theological voluntarism") is the belief that God is the source of moral truth and that He communicates the divine will to humanity via commands. We have a choice as to whether or not we will follow these commands. But right and wrong is determined solely by the commands of God.

Divine command theories are usually based around three propositions:

1. Our creaturely nature obligates us to follow rules that are part of the created order. God, who is not a created being, is not bound by these rules.
2. Good and evil do not exist independently of God. Instead, God creates them just as surely as He creates us.
3. While God's action and decrees may be logical, it is presumptuous for humans to believe that our finite minds can discover this logic (Wilkens 1995, 172-73).

The divine command theory of ethics can often be found, although not exclusively, within the Reformed theological tradition. Much of this association has to do with the Calvinist understanding of humanity as totally depraved. Our sinfulness, our fallen nature, and our consequent total depravity call into question our ability to know or interpret correctly the revelation we receive through natural revelation. Because God is holy, transcendent, and sinless, we must trust the commands we receive from Him.

Some have accused Christianity, when identified with this divine command tradition, of stunted moral development rather than moral superiority. Patrick Nowell-Smith, for example, used Jean Piaget's theory of moral development to accuse divine command ethics of being "infantile."

According to Piaget's theory, we receive commands unquestionably from "above" when we are in a childlike state of moral development. These commands come to us from parental figures in our life. But as we move into adolescent and adult stages of moral development, we begin to question those commands and, in a sense, create a moral life of our own. Nowell-Smith argues that Christianity encourages us to remain moral children by always receiving our moral commands from God "above" and obeying them without question.

Divine command theorist Richard J. Mouw gives a detailed response to Nowell-Smith in his book *The God Who Commands*. Mouw concludes his defense by stating,

> For any pattern of moral decision making to be considered mature, it should presumably be characterized by a willingness to act in the light of the facts as one views them. And the fact is that Christianity views God as being much greater—infinitely greater—than human beings. On such a view of things, a refusal to recognize God's moral greatness would not only be self-deceptive, it would also be, in its own way, a kind of "infantile" discourtesy (Mouw 1990, 13).

Divine command ethics stresses that only as we acknowledge the reality of our dependence, our sinfulness, and our inability to grasp God's ways can we move forward. God's superiority and transcendence over creation is the foundation of divine command ethics.

The Reformed tradition is highly dependent upon the volitionalist views of nominalist philosophers like John Dun Scotus (1266—1308) and William of Occam (ca. 1280—1347). Prior to the 13th and 14th centuries, most philosophers were considered realists. The realists believed that when we see an object in the material realm (e.g., a cloud), we know what it is, because it reflects its eternal idea (the form of the cloud). The nominalists argued that we call an object by a certain name (a cloud) not because it reflects any eternal reality but because we have agreed to call the object by that certain name. In other words, reality does not conform itself to some eternal idea, form, or norm; we simply name the way we find reality at each moment.

Philosophers like Scotus and Occam blend this nominalism with a high view of God's determining will (volitionalism or voluntarism). The universe is the way it is, for Scotus and Occam, neither because God created it according to some preexisting pattern nor because God created it within the bounds of His own good nature. Deity simply willed creation to be this way. Although God willed for Israel to follow the Ten Commandments, for example, He just as easily could have willed the opposite. Instead of condemning adultery, stealing, and murder, God could have said, "Thou *shalt* kill. Thou *shalt* steal. Thou *shalt* commit adultery." It may be bizarre for us to imagine such a world, yet it is not beyond the power of the sovereign God to have willed such a place to exist. God alone defines what is good and evil.

While admittedly the above examples seem ridiculous, the divine command theorist wants to remind us of our finitude and fallen reason. Mouw argues that

> It is not always easy to ascertain what God's own thoughts might be when it comes to the issues of moral justification. There is an important element of mystery and awe that characterizes a healthy relationship to the God of the Bible; the distance between moral decision making and worship is not always very great in the Christian life. There are good Christian reasons for nurturing a resistance to attempts to "psyche God out" in too much detail in dealing with the issues of ethical theory (1990, 41-42).

In short, the divine command theorist essentially argues that we are arrogant and shortsighted if we believe that we can understand the mind and heart of God. Whatever God decrees is right, and the proper choice for humans is obedience. According to the divine command theorist, we understand who we are and who God is because of His special revelation to us. We are dependent upon the Word of God to know divine commands. This places Scripture at the heart of ethical dialogue.

Critics contend that divine command ethics fails where natural law succeeds. When the divine command theorist ignores the importance of reason, the theorist loses the ability to dialogue across religious traditions or with those who lack religious belief. Dismissing reason raises all kinds of questions about the arbitrariness of God's commands. Do we really want to say that God's commands are good simply because God commands them? Undercutting the role of reason eliminates our ability to evaluate the commands of God.

Another potential problem with divine command theory is the narrow scope of its data. We face many complexities and contexts in the contemporary world that are unfamiliar to Scripture. How should we think about abortion, euthanasia, genetic engineering, technological advancement, or nuclear warfare from a scriptural perspective? There may be passages or commands we use to address these issues indirectly, but none of these contemporary problems are addressed in a specific way in the historical context of Scripture. It seems as though reason must be accessed if we are to understand God's will for our lives in these areas.

C. Situation Ethics

The "situation ethics" theory of morality is met with a negative response in many Christian circles. Few ministers stand in a pulpit and declare that they advocate situation ethics. The reason for this is that we often associate situation ethics with moral relativism. In one situation we might act one way. As soon as the situation changes, we act another way.

Suppose, however, that you were part of a family—like the Corrie Ten Boom family of The Netherlands—who hid Jews so that they would be protected from Nazi extermination during World War II. Suppose that Hitler's soldiers knocked on your door one day and asked if Jews were hiding in your home. How do you respond? If you are a divine command theorist, you are in big trouble. The Scripture very plainly commands us not to lie. But honesty in this situation would mean the extermination of the Jewish people you are hiding. So what should you do?

The answer seems obvious: you lie. You deny that there are Jews in the house and thus save their lives. Why is the answer to this scenario so obvious? Situation ethicist Joseph Fletcher would argue that we know that lying is proper in this circumstance, because there is one Christian law that supercedes all others: the law of love. No matter what situation in which we find ourselves, we must practice the law of love. And practicing the law of love means that we may act differently in different moral situations. Fletcher believes that love is the only thing that is intrinsically good. He argues that

> Christian situation ethics has only one norm or principle or law (call it what you will) that is binding and unexceptionable, always good and right regardless of the circumstances. That is "love"—the *agape* of the summary commandment to love God and the neighbor. Everything else without exception, all laws and rules and principles and ideals and norms are only *contingent,* only valid *if they happen* to serve love in any situation (1966, 30).

It is critical for Fletcher that *agape* love be distinguished from other forms of love in the Greek mind (*eros, storge, phileo*). According to his interpretation, *agape* acts exclusively out of interest for the other. *Agape* does not depend upon the reciprocation of the one loved, and *agape* is open to the stranger and even the enemy.

For the situation ethicist, all laws except one are what we might think of as "rules of strategy." In baseball the pitcher does not intentionally walk the next batter if the bases are loaded. In fact, the rules would tend to dictate that you do everything in your power not to walk the batter— that is, unless the batter is Mark McGwire. Twice during his 70-home-run season Mark McGwire was intentionally walked with the bases loaded. Both times that he was intentionally walked, the opposing team won the game. In ethics, just as in baseball, one sometimes breaks conventional rules to attain the greater good.

Fletcher argued that Jesus provides our greatest example of situation ethics in action. Several times in the Gospels Jesus is accused of breaking not only social convention but also divine commands. In several Gospel narratives, we see Jesus healing or allowing His disciples to pick heads of grain on the Sabbath. In each of these cases, Jesus poses the same question "Which is better, to rest or to do good on the Sabbath?" (author's paraphrase). It seems obvious that it is better to do that which is "good." Fletcher agrees. Most of the time religious laws help us do what is good and loving. But in some situations, doing the loving thing means breaking the laws originally meant to help us. According to the situational ethicist, love is the final authority in all situations.

The situation ethics tradition is helpful in many ways. It fits well in a Wesleyan tradition that emphasizes love as the primary quality of God's character and the perfection of love in us by the power of the Spirit. Situation ethics has an absolute standard, love, and this absolute appears to be a very appropriate one for the Christian life. There is a deep sense in which the law of love fits well with the witness and testimony of Christ. It seems to be right that Jesus places love for others above obedience to law and social convention. Even Paul dismisses longstanding Jewish laws like circumcision for the sake of including Gentiles into the Church.

Situation ethics also provides a way to determine between conflicting laws. The example of the family hiding Jews during World War II is similar to the setting of Philip Hallie's nonfiction book, *Lest Innocent Blood Be Shed*. In Hallie's book the people of Le Chambon find themselves caught during the war between charity and the laws of truth-telling as they work to protect Jews from Hitler. But this conflict is resolved—although not easily—by applying the law of love. When we find ourselves caught between two conflicting laws, we can always do that which is the most loving.

Although there is much to celebrate about the law of love, it also has potential problems. Situation ethics is essentially a form of teleological or even utilitarian ethics. Decisions are made based upon the results of the decision. For the situationist, we should act in a way that lovingly brings about the most good and the least amount of evil. But like other teleological systems, it falls prey to the problem of defining a situation. Do we ever know a situation fully? How far out in time should we estimate the results?

Another potential problem surrounds the definition of love. How do we define or describe what is the loving thing to do? If you have a child struggling with but denying an addiction to drugs, how do you act lovingly toward your child? Some people refer to this kind of situation as an opportunity to display "tough love." But how do we know that, in this case, toughness is loving?

D. Virtue Ethics

The concept of virtue, as a category in which to think about Christian ethics, has become popular in recent decades. The virtue tradition finds its origin in the philosophy of Aristotle. Aristotle believed that all things are moving from what they currently are to what they potentially or teleologically ought to be. Within the acorn, for example, lies the potential of the oak tree. But to become its telos (i.e., end, goal, or purpose), the acorn needs soil, sunlight, and water. Although the acorn responds naturally to these elements, Aristotle might think of these elements as virtues. In human terms, we begin as immature infants both physically and mentally. But within our infantile selves lies the potential of physical and intellectual maturity. To become that which we potentially or teleologically are; however, we must practice certain virtues. Recently, Alasdair MacIntyre and Stanley Hauerwas have articulated a form of virtue ethics for Christianity.

The first thing a virtue ethicist must discover (or rediscover) is a sense of human purpose. The acorn can move and grow only if it "knows" that its ultimate purpose is to become the oak tree. It cannot, for example, grow correctly if it tries to become a fish. In the same way, we humans can flourish and grow only if we first know the goal or purpose of being human. Once we know the purpose of humanity, we can move in that direction. For Aristotle, the human goal is happiness (better translated as contentment or well-being). Aristotle believed that we should practice every virtue that leads to a balanced and contented life.

Philosopher Alasdair MacIntyre argues in his work *After Virtue* that Aristotle's understanding of purpose came from the worldview of ancient Hellenism. Aristotle, argues MacIntyre, lived within an ancient Greek culture that had a fairly unified way of viewing reality. And from this historical understanding of reality, Aristotle derives the notion that happiness is the end of human life. In MacIntyre's view, human beings derive their sense of purpose or telos from their particular worldviews rooted in history and embodied by cultures. In fact, MacIntyre argues that the reason we cannot come to any kind of moral consensus in the contemporary world is that we have been taught by the Enlightenment to be suspicious of cultures and histories. The Enlightenment tried to move away from particular cultures and toward general or "rational" statements about morality. But in the process, Enlightenment scholars simply lost their ability to have any kind of moral debate. Because we live in a world of fragmented worldviews, we live in a morally fragmented world.

Let me illustrate by describing the way in which Americans debate abortion in contemporary culture. When abortion is debated, the pro-life side lines up against the pro-choice side. The pro-life camp argues that all life is sacred and that life begins at conception; therefore, abortion should be abolished. The pro-choice camp argues that everyone has the right to control his or her own body, and a fetus is a part of a woman's body; therefore, a woman has the right to decide what to do with whatever is a part of her body, even her unborn child. Both sides typically become angry in this debate, and little progress is made. Why does this moral debate never seem to get anywhere?

MacIntyre's answer to this questions is that we often fail to recognize that both sides of an issue like abortion are rooted in different histories. For example, the pro-life side is rooted in a tradition that sees God as sovereign over life and death. Life is sacred for this side, because God views life as a sacred gift. The pro-choice side is rooted in the history of democratic or Enlightenment liberalism that understands the rights of the individual are also a sacred and self-evident gift of the divine. So the abortion debate goes on, from MacIntyre's perspective, not because one side doesn't recognize its logical failure or shortsightedness, but because there are two rival histories—two different ways of understanding reality—that come into confrontation with each other over this issue.

Christian ethicists, like Stanley Hauerwas, have taken this MacIntyrean/Aristotelian view and applied it to Christianity. Christians, argues Hauerwas, are "resident aliens" in the world. They are shaped by the unique story (or narrative) of God's creative and redemptive activities in the world. They understand themselves uniquely to be created in the image of God. Yet Christians also realize that they are fallen and in need of redemption. The purpose of the Christian gospel is that we be redeemed by God and transformed in such a way that we, as individuals and as the Body of Christ, begin to "image" God's love in the world.

For Hauerwas, the virtuous practices of the Christian life (charity, faithfulness, worship, prayer, confession, sacraments, and so on) are done so that the telos of Christlikeness might take place in us. As the sun, soil, and water help the acorn to become the oak tree, the Holy Spirit uses virtuous practices of the faith as the means of spiritual transformation.

Let us return to the example of covenantal sexuality. From a natural law perspective, people commit to one another because the formation of family units fits within the structure of nature. From the perspective of the virtue tradition, Christians marry one another so that the covenant they make will become a reflection of the divine covenantal love God has for God's people. Within the practice of marriage, we learn the virtues of kindness, gentleness, patience, unconditional acceptance, and so on. The virtue ethicist might even say that we should not be surprised if the secular culture ceases to value marital monogamy. Christians have a unique worldview that causes them to view marriage as a virtuous practice that assists in achieving human purpose.

CONCLUSION

The fact that we are confronted with so many ethical systems both inside and outside Christianity should not make us question the possibility of arriving at ultimate moral truth. Although the presence of these various systems ought to make us humble as we search for moral truth, it should also remind us that we find truth together on our journey.

Bibliography and Texts for Further Reading

Aquinas, St. Thomas. *Summa Theologiae: A Concise Translation.* Ed. Timothy McDermott. Allen, Texas: Christian Classics, 1989.

Critchley, Simon. *The Ethics of Deconstruction: Derrida and Levinas.* Oxford: Blackwell, 1992.

Fletcher, Joseph. *Moral Responsibility: Situation Ethics at Work.* Philadelphia: Westminster, 1967.

————. *Situation Ethics: The New Morality.* Philadelphia: Westminster, 1966.

Frankena, William K. *Ethics.* 2d ed. Inglewood Cliffs, N.J.: Prentice-Hall, 1973.

Hauerwas, Stanley. *A Community of Character: Toward a Constructive Christian Social Ethic.* Notre Dame, Ind.: University of Notre Dame Press, 1981.

————. *The Peaceable Kingdom: A Primer in Christian Ethics.* Notre Dame, Ind.: University of Notre Dame Press, 1983.

Herskovits, Melville J. *Cultural Relativism: Perspectives in Cultural Pluralism.* Ed. Frances Herskovits. New York: Random House, 1972.

Holmes, Arthur F. *Ethics: Approaching Moral Decisions.* Downers Grove, Ill.: InterVarsity, 1984.

Holmes, Robert L. *Basic Moral Philosophy.* Belmont, Calif.: Wadsworth, 1993.

Kierkegaard, Søren. *Fear and Trembling.* Trans. Howard V. Hong and Edna H. Hong. Princeton, N.J.: Princeton University Press, 1983.

MacIntyre, Aladair. *After Virtue.* 2d ed. Notre Dame, Ind.: University of Notre Dame Press, 1984.

McClendon, James W., Jr. *Ethics: Systematic Theology.* Vol. 1. Nashville: Abingdon, 1986.

Mouw, Richard J. *The God Who Commands: A Study in Divine Command Ethics.* Notre Dame, Ind.: University of Notre Dame Press, 1990.

Murphy, Nancey, Brad J. Kallenburg, and Mark Thiessen Nation. *Virtues and Practices in the Christian Tradition: Christian Ethics after MacIntyre.* Harrisburg, Penns.: Trinity, 1997.

Nielsen, Kai. *Ethics Without God.* London: Pemberton, 1973.

Outka, Gene. *Agape: An Ethical Analysis.* New Haven, Conn.: Yale University Press, 1992.

Porter, Burton F. *The Good Life: Alternatives in Ethics.* 2d Ed. New York: Ardsley House, 1995.

Quinn, Philip L. *Divine Commands and Moral Requirements.* Oxford: Clarendon, 1978.

Ramsey, Paul. *Basic Christian Ethics.* New York: Scribner's, 1950.

Smedes, Lewis B. *Choices: Making Right Decisions in a Complex World.* San Francisco: Harper San Francisco, 1988.

Vacek, Edward Collins. *Love, Human and Divine: The Heart of Christian Ethics.* Washington, D.C.: Georgetown University Press, 1994.

Wilkens, Steve. *Beyond Bumper Sticker Ethics: An Introduction to Theories of Right and Wrong.* Downers Grove, Ill.: InterVarsity, 1995.

SECTION III, PART IV
RELIGION AND AESTHETICS
Kenton Stiles

◆

Michelangelo's famous depiction of the sixth day of Creation stands as a fitting object of inspiration for this study. This Sistine Chapel fresco (1508-12), despite being reproduced *ad nauseum* as an icon of popular culture, presents an image of the intersection of the religious and the aesthetic. In the painting, a reclining Adam reaches out to a muscular and energetic Creator while Eve peeks out from under God's left arm and the folds of an angel-filled cloak. Mortal humanity reaches out to the eternal, and, while the outstretched hands do not quite touch, the image convinces viewers that God's power arcs across the gap. Contact! This representation of God as the source of human inspiration—literally, the genesis of spirit—is simultaneously aesthetic and theological.

Before we get too far into this chapter, some clarification of the word "aesthetics" is necessary. While the word itself is modern (having been coined in 1735 by the German theorist Alexander Baumgarten), the roots of aesthetics are ancient, dating to classical Greek writings on poetry, drama, and other forms of art. An exact definition is difficult to reach, however. It is tempting to offer a circular definition: "aesthetic" pertains to ideas, things, characteristics, or events that have an aesthetic nature. Yet to say that aesthetics pertains to the artistic and beautiful, to nature and the sublime, to the imagination and the act of making, to narrative and tragedy, and even to the dissonant, ugly, and grotesque, we have not yet exhausted its meaning. Aesthetic feelings are also experienced as pleasure when one hits the game-winning home run or as pleasurable pain when watching a pride of lions tear apart its prey in a fascinating documentary film. Perhaps an adequate definition may be that the aesthetic, at its most basic level, is that which engages the human imagination through the senses and reason but does so in a manner that eludes capture or comprehension. At the heart of the aesthetic, then, is a playfulness that enables its full meaning to escape us.

The *classification* of aesthetics, the aesthetic, and aesthetica is a simpler task. These words refer to at least one of the following categories: (1) an area within the discipline of philosophy that includes—but is greater than—the philosophy of art, (2) a type of object, idea, or event, (3) a structured worldview or the architecture of a philosophical system, or (4) a type of rational-sensory experience. This chapter will be primarily concerned with aesthetic philosophy number 1 and its points of contact with religion, as well as how aesthetic philosophy and religion interaction affects how we understand number 3. The other classifications are never far away, however, because actual aesthetic creations and experiences give form to idea and content.

Today, unfortunately, a spirituality in which aesthetics and theology are tightly interwoven seems alien to Westerners. Perhaps it seems alien even to most Christians. While there may be events in which aesthetics and religion intersect or overlap, the common opinion that these are two entirely separate and distinct fields is one that modernist aesthetics has promoted for the last two centuries. As aesthetics and art criticism have become increasingly purist in their primary concern with the processes of abstraction in fine art and the theoretical idealism of performance and conceptual art, discussions of natural beauty and the sublime—topics that formerly provided points of contact with religious thought—rarely occur. Similarly, creativity and artistic genius are now seen as individual or communal capacities, devoid of any origin in divine inspiration. Like Adam and Eve banished from Eden, religion has been banished from the aesthetic garden.

Contemporary secular aestheticians typically find little potential in religious-aesthetic interaction. Notions like beauty, the sublime, metanarrative, and meaning are denied. The "postmodern" world drifts aimlessly in interpretation, relativity, and experience rather than being anchored by universal ideals. There is no value—only values. A postmodern thinker may talk about how layer upon layer of meaning, some of which might be religious, has covered an aesthetic object over time, but all of these layers are still "about" (i.e., external to) the object. Aesthetic interpretation plays around, overwrites, and hides the object with words, while the real center of the whirlpool is loss, emptiness, or absence.

Interest in (re)discovering any point(s) of contact between aesthetics and religion has also increased significantly in the last three decades. Many today consider the spiritual value of art and nature, aesthetic aspects of religious rituals and experience, and aesthetic ideas and structures found in doctrines and theological systems. Nevertheless, it could be said that few of these studies, including some of the most influential, have ever achieved or sustained what could be called a proper theological aesthetics (Brown, *xi-xvi*). In this chapter I will conduct an overview of key figures and periods in the history of Western religious-aesthetic interaction, and I will address a few issues that are relevant to aesthetics and religion today.

I. CONTACT IN HISTORICAL CONTEXT

Writings from the Classical period, both extant and referred to by later thinkers, show the existence of an early interest in religious-aesthetic issues. Pythagoras and his followers, for example, theorize that divine order exists in creation through numerical values, specifically in the ratios of musical tones. Accordingly, certain keys, instruments, and types of melody were thought to influence the human soul directly. Plato discussed numerous religious-aesthetic issues, including the following: the nature of art (e.g., as imitation, beauty, measure, symmetry, and proportion); how art participates in the eternal forms; the moral, political, and religious risks that arts pose; the relation of beauty to being and the divine; and whether or not artistic genius derives from divine inspiration and possession. Aristotle's influence is equally important. Aristotle provides an early focus on the causes and ends of artistic making and experience, proposes the transcendental modes of being (i.e., truth, goodness, and beauty), asks how beauty may be known through particular experience, maintains that certain aesthetic experiences purge and reconstitute the human soul/psyche, and affirms that beauty helps uphold justice and morality. Plotinus developed an extensive aesthetic philosophy of being, maintaining that reality reflects the harmony and symmetry of the many to the universal whole, known alternately as the One, Beauty, or Being.

Medieval Christian thought was shaped profoundly by Classical Greek thought, and it was especially influenced by Plotinus's theory of being as an aesthetic hierarchy emanating from the divine. Augustine's general philosophy of being, for example, set humans just below God and the angelic in a worldly hierarchy. More noteworthy, however, is Augustine's blending of Pythagorean, Plotinian, and Christian aesthetic ideas in his theory of natural existence. In several early works, Augustine advanced a theory in which creation's parts all harmonize with the whole of each other and God. Every created object has an inherent value derived from its internal number, measure, and order. The harmony of an object's properties is a beauty and perfection that correspond to its place in the created order. The loss of any one of these properties, through causing or experiencing evil, sin, ugliness, or pain, simultaneously reduces an object's beauty and diminishes its existence. Such an object becomes exposed to the threat of nonexistence. One of Augustine's most lasting religious-aesthetic contributions is his spiritual autobiography, the *Confessions*. This classic displays the work of a creative genius who filled its pages with moving narratives and beautiful images. Augustine's method was thoroughly aesthetic, and it set a standard for later autobiographies and narratives.

The mystical theology of Denis (Pseudo-Dionysius [5th century A.D.]), elaborated in *The Divine Names, Celestial Hierarchy,* and *Ecclesiastical Hi-*

erarchy, proved to be even more influenced by Plotinus than Augustine's theological aesthetics. Denis's system envisioned heavenly worlds populated with beings emanating from God and the natural world. According to Denis, worldly objects have special referential value: they may directly reflect the beauty of the "Superessential Beautiful" (God), who radiates the cosmos with multicolored and dazzling light, or they may engage the imagination through metaphors that incarnate hidden spiritual truths. Ultimately, the purpose of human existence within this hierarchy of being is religious devotion to and worship of God, because God is the Good and Beautiful. In worship, the divinity descending to the world is met with ascending faith and praise.

Thomas Aquinas' theological aesthetics, while brief, reintroduced Aristotelian philosophy to the medieval world. Of special importance is Thomas's promotion of Aristotle's transcendental modes of being—the true, good, and beautiful—and his promotion of the relationships of reason and matter to form. For Thomas, beauty consists in resplendent form, which emerges as the human mind engages an aesthetic object. Beauty *exists,* then, only when it is *known*—known through the mind's disinterested apprehension of an object's organic form, reflection upon the mental sense-image of its form, and subsequent delight in its resplendence. The term "organic" is significant, because beauty is not an abstraction from form; rather, beauty exists only in the unity of the conditions of wholeness, harmonious proportion, and brightness or clarity. Beauty's perfection in this unity is also the concord of form and function. Thomas' notion of beauty is similar to Denis's metaphysics of divine light with one important exception: while illumination descends from God and is received passively in Denis's aesthetics, in Thomas' system, illumination resides in an object but is incomplete until engaged actively by the human mind.

The commingling of light, beauty, and faith in the mysticism of Bonaventure, the last great aesthetic theologian of medieval Christianity, harmonizes Denis's emanational theology with medieval scholasticism. The foundation of Bonaventure's aesthetic is James 1:17—"Every good and perfect gift is from above, coming down from the Father of heavenly Lights." Bonaventure interprets this verse as identifying light as God's essence and establishes emanation as the created order. He argued that God creates through a fourfold outflow of light: (1) the external light of the seven mechanical arts (i.e., weaving, armor-making, agriculture, hunting, navigation, medicine, and dramatic arts); (2) the lesser interior light of mental perception through the five senses; (3) the higher interior light of rational, moral, and natural philosophy (i.e., grammar, logic, and rhetoric; physics, mathematics, and metaphysics; and ethics, politics, and economics); and (4) the superior light of theology and scripture, which promote spiritual communion with God. The disciplines, which descend from God, create a hierarchy by which the soul returns to God, consummating with the "Beatific Vision." Humanity's chief end is spiritual, but the manner in which one lives—with measure, beauty, and order—is aesthetic.

Hans Urs von Balthasar, author of three separate aesthetic systematic theologies, identifies Bonaventure's late medieval/Gothic era as the developmental apex of Christian theological aesthetics. This is not to say that religious-aesthetic contact ends with the coming of the Renaissance and Reformation. The nature and intensity of the points of contact does begin to change, however. As Renaissance humanism encourages the growth of the arts, letters, and sciences, theology lost its position as the "queen" of the academy.

The birth of the Reformation had negative theoretical and practical effects for aesthetics. Protestantism's strict bibliocentrism—*sola Scriptura*—led theologians to abandon more creative and speculative approaches to philosophical-religious issues. In the churches, antiaestheticism transformed both liturgical space and style. One need only observe the removal of statuary and whitewashing of walls in former Catholic churches, the solemn portraits of Reformers by Hans Holbein, or the moralistic paintings of the Bruegels to appreciate how religious art came to reflect the austere Reformation aesthetic. Even Swiss reformer Ulrich Zwingli, who was an accomplished organist, felt led to remove the pipe organ from his Zurich parish.

The 18th century was a period of remarkable religious and aesthetic activity. Modern aesthetics, as a distinct philosophical discipline, emerged. Developments included the expansion of national art academies and their "classic" styles. Mid-18th-century archaeological discoveries in Rome, neoclassicism's revival of Greek and Roman style, and a resurgence of aesthetic Neoplatonism sparked renewed interest in aesthetics. Cambridge Platonists, led by Anthony Ashley Cooper, Joseph Addison, and Frances Hutcheson, show the Enlightenment's secular influence. While God was still recognized by the Platonists to be the primal cause of natural and artistic beauty, the focus is clearly on art as art.

A notable exception to the "secularization" of aesthetics is Jonathan Edwards. Edwards's theological aesthetics stand as the most original and important American contribution in the history of religious-aesthetic thought. Edwards conceived of God as an artist who creates to express the fullness of divine beauty. Through the "book of Nature," individuals may either revel in natural representations of divine love, beauty, and self-communication, or they may feel repulsed by nature's grotesque and horrifying forms that reveal the demonic. Authentic human existence consists in harmonious living with being itself, other beings, and with the divine Being.

As empiricism undertook more rational and scientific explorations of genius, imagination, taste, beauty, sublimity, and the senses, a movement away from neoplatonic aesthetics occurred. Immanuel Kant became *the* pivotal figure in modern aesthetics and the philosophy of religion. His philosophy of religion included a moral and implied aesthetic-teleological argument for the existence of God. Kant divided thought into rational knowledge, moral desire, and aesthetic feeling. In *Critique of Judgment* (1790), he argues that religious faith is justifiable only when based on moral teleology. What is normally called beauty, Kant asserts, is actually a judgment of subjective taste and self-interest: something is beautiful because it pleases *me* and meets *my* criteria of beauty. The truly beautiful, on the other hand, is both distanced from the human subject and free from rational concepts. While the beautiful has the appearance of conceptuality, what humans experience is actually a "purposiveness without purpose." Kant, however, deflated the popular aesthetic notion of the sublime in his argument that moral beings may transcend awe-inspiring natural occurrences through reason. The only instances of the sublime that the mind cannot transcend are mathematical infinities and "pure" ideas. Notions included among the "pure ideas" include God, freedom, immortality, love, peace, and relation.

The religious and aesthetic abyss that Kant created did not remain empty for long. A group of intellectuals soon brought about the rise of modernist aesthetics joined with liberal Christian theology. Among those at the heart of this return to aesthetics and religion are J. G. Herder, Goethe, August and Friedrich Schlegel, J. G. Fichte, Friedrich Schleiermacher, F. S. Schiller, Friedrich Schelling, and G. W. F. Hegel (Taylor, 20ff.). Their intellectual contributions converge upon the two aesthetic-religious options left by Kant: feeling and idea. In the multifaceted movement known as Romanticism, feelings were of utmost importance, especially when feelings are free, expressive, impassioned, elicited by nature, or directed toward the ideal or infinite. Friedrich Schleiermacher, father of liberal theology, appealed to both feeling and aesthetic intuition as bases for faith in his pivotal work *On Religion: Speeches to Its Cultured Despisers* (1799). He described religion as an intuition of the universe, a "sensibility and taste for the infinite," and an affective vision of "the Infinite in the finite." In his systematic theology, *The Christian Faith* (1825), he described how individuals sense God through a feeling of utter dependence upon "Otherness", calling this relation "aesthetic Religion."

Another consequence of Romanticism is an expansion of the term "religion" to validate all forms of the universal spiritual quest. Both Schleiermacher and Schelling promoted organismic theories. Organismic thinking is one means of countering dualism, of harmonizing the self-conscious individual with the universe, Spirit with Nature, and the rational with the sensual. Romanticism also involved a turn toward the human being as an independent subject and toward nature as a source of aesthetic-religious experience. Romanticism does not divinize nature, generally speaking, but it does find profound religious import in pastoral beauty, picturesque landscapes, and the feelings of wonder that nature elicits.

Idealism, the second major aesthetic-religious movement of the 1800s, pursued the construction of a comprehensive modern philosophy of being. Friedrich Schiller's treatise on human existence, *Letters on the Aesthetic Education of Man* (1795), is an aesthetic anthropology and metaphysics. His primary goal was to promote the aesthetic as the means for overcoming the existential rifts suffered by the world. Because all human culture is "torn asunder," Schiller believed that one must turn to aesthetics and philosophy for a cure. It is only in free and affective play that harmony and true existence can be achieved.

G. W. F. Hegel's philosophical system was even more aesthetic and idealistic than Schiller's, because Hegel proposed that all existence is the living form of "Absolute Idea" or "Universal Spirit" (i.e., God). History is the unfolding of Spirit according to an aesthetic model: Spirit moves in a process of unity, self-differentiation, and the reconciliation of opposites in a new harmony. Within this process, the aesthetic is a significant source for expressing truth and meaning, surpassed only by religion and philosophy. In Hegelian idealism, the transcendent God exists within and through individuals—the universal is present in the particular.

In the 20th century, the final period of this aesthetic-religious survey, modernist and postmodern aesthetic theories preserved secular Western society's bifurcation of religion and aesthetics. Nevertheless, some attempts to bring the religious and aesthetic together met with success. *Written* assessments of such engagement by some who sought to unite the two include Rudolf Otto, Alfred North Whitehead, Martin Heidegger, Paul Tillich, and Urs von Balthasar. I now turn to address some *visual* sources to highlight subtle religious influences within aesthetics that may be unknown to those unfamiliar with contemporary art history.

The two major religious-aesthetic movements in 20th-century Western art are spiritual abstraction and primitivism. The first movement turns to the abstraction of form and image through the use of geometric shapes, intense colors, and symbols in order to represent more pure or "spiritual" forms and ideas. This broadly defined spiritual aesthetic grows today, in part, due to the influence of theosophy, a synthesis of ideas drawn largely from Christian and Asian mysticisms. Noted spiritual abstraction painters, Wassily Kandinsky, Franz Marc, Piet Mondrian, and Paul Klee, were directly involved with theosophical publications and societies. Abstraction's spiritual-material ideals are embodied in the art of the abstract, symbolist, futurist, suprematist, surrealist, and abstract expressionist movements.

Primitivism has a more subtle visual influence on modern art. This cultural ideology, inspired by the exhibition of religious imagery of so-called "primitive" African, Arctic, and Pan-Pacific cultures in European museums, finds expression in the work of many of the century's most prominent artists. A partial list includes painters Gaugin, Matisse, Picasso, Emil Nolde, Klee, Joan Miro, Modigliani, Max Ernst, and Jackson Pollock; sculptors Alberto Giacommetti, Jacques Lipchitz, Henry Moore, Jacob Epstein, and David Smith; and landscape artists Robert Smithson, Michael Heizer, and Richard Long. The "primitive" remains popular even today, because it offers—or is understood to offer—both the artist and society a glimpse of a simpler tribal life and beliefs: a life and set of beliefs that the technological and pessimistic West left behind centuries ago. Inspired by tribal totems and animistic cultic objects, artists find a means of expressing an aesthetic-religious worldview in concrete and unified form.

A third point of aesthetic-religious visual contact is Holocaust and post-Holocaust art. There are many sources of this art, including prisoners' drawings, the camps' architecture of death, video documentaries and popular films like *Schindler's List,* interactive web sites, and postwar Jewish and German art. These works embody their artists' feelings and questions about death and destruction, personal and national guilt, reconciliation and forgiveness, the sacredness of the body and life, the immorality of war, the problem of evil, religious faith and symbolism, religious persecution and tolerance, the perceived absence of God, and divine deliverance. The artworks evoke these same feelings and questions from their viewers, adding sociopolitical significance to their already significant inherent religious value. Holocaust art does not paint a pretty picture for religion to consider. Rather, it depicts a dark abyss. It reveals a negative image of the gap existing between suffering humanity's outstretched hands and an estranged God.

II. CONTEMPORARY CONTACT

A partial story of aesthetic-religious encounter has now been told. The nature and intensity of future contact between the two remains unknown. However, it is both possible and valuable to consider several potential points of contact to the philosophy of religion.

A. Religious Method

Aesthetics is a valid and meaningful religious method at both the practical and theoretical levels. The practical relevance of the aesthetic religious experience, a major subcategory of the philosophy of religion since the publication of William James' pivotal work, *Varieties of Religious Experience* (1902), is undeniable. Religious practice assumes or includes countless aesthetic forms, including vocal and instrumental music, dance, drama, icons, sculpture, stained glass, painting, architecture, and pilgrimages to and processions through sacred spaces. Its continued presence in ritual practice indicates that the aesthetic has enduring value for religion by initiating and enhancing personal experience. Even when religion is practiced in silence, seclusion, or a simple setting, the experience is nevertheless aesthetic.

Works in the philosophy of religion also highlights the common presence of the sublime within religious experience, including Rudolf Otto's *The Idea of the Holy* (1917) and Martin Buber's *I and Thou* (1937). Corporate and individual encounters with the transcendent/God/wholly "Other" elicit sublime feelings of awe, wonder, fear, and mystery. Empirical evidence and practical theory indicate that the aesthetic is an integral part of religious experience when worship is holistic, because holistic worship involves the body's sensing, the mind's knowing, and the heart's feeling.

Aesthetics is also an invaluable methodological resource for theology. This point of aesthetic-religious contact typically expresses itself in three different manners. The first type of engagement is aesthetic theology, which refers to the stylistic method of a given theology. A stylistic approach to theology may be implicit, as in the use of an aesthetic object or idea (e.g., music, beauty, play, or a painting) as an extended metaphor for theological discussion. The theological style may also be explicitly aesthetic, as when ideas assume the concrete forms of poetry, narrative, drama, or song.

The second point of theoretical methodological contact is the use of aesthetics *in* theology. This point of contact is more conducive to traditional constructive theology, because it relates to theological content. A religious system that includes discussions of aesthetic themes would fit within this category. In Christian theology, for example, the following doctrines have particular aesthetic significance: metaphorical theology, trinitarian models, God as Creator, human creativity (i.e., the *imago dei*), christological images, Spirit and inspiration, beauty and holiness, reconciliation (i.e., moral harmony), and ecological ethics.

The third point of aesthetic religious contact is theology *as* aesthetics, also known as theological aesthetics proper. Here form and method are united in a theological system structured on an aesthetic model. Examples of theological aesthetics include Denis's Neoplatonism, medieval emanational theologies, Jonathan Edward's theology, Hegel's Christian idealism, Whiteheadian process theology, von Balthasar's neo-Thomism, and Tillich's existential theology of culture.

B. Religious Language

Human beings, linguists tell us, think symbolically. Our thoughts are a complex system in which symbols, words, and numbers are expressive images—word-pictures—of that to which they refer. Contemporary linguistic theory understands a word to be a symbol or icon, and this has special significance for religion and aesthetics. Language is believed to have a doubly symbolic function in religious and aesthetic disciplines, because these disciplines point to that which cannot be seen (e.g., God, aesthetic ideas, and feelings). Statements about God are even more symbolic, because an infinite God by definition transcends everything finite, which includes language. Any meaningful talk of God must therefore be analogical.

Metaphor lies at the heart of religious language. Metaphor in religious description is a concrete method of analogy consisting of positive statements—for example, "God is a mighty fortress"—and subsequent negations of the analogy's adequacy, such as "God is *not* a mighty fortress; God is more than this." Meaning expresses itself through an image and the alternating play of revealed and concealed truth. The literal meaning of "theology"—"words about God," aptly describes how religious metaphor works: meaning plays *at* or dances *about* its subject-center without becoming exhausted. Or, to use Michelangelo's *Creation* as a metaphor, the analogy reaches out to its subject, making partial contact at certain points but never fully embracing the partner from which it is distanced by an ever-present and infinitely deep gap.

Aesthetic power, in turn, lies at the heart of religious metaphor. Metaphor, after all, is not merely a "literary device." Rather, it is traditionally classified as a form of poetic language, therefore, belonging to aesthetics. One of metaphor's great aesthetic powers is its ability to engage the imagination through dissimilar similarities, to capture the mind's fancy in a to-and-fro playing for meaning amid sense and nonsense. Metaphor's aesthetic play has an endpoint, but it is an end that differs from the precise definitions pursued by logic and science. Religious metaphor ends with feelings, having played itself out to a point of aesthetic-spiritual satisfaction. Humans value metaphor because of its inherent structural beauty as a feeling-form. We judge analogy to be fitting and good despite its rational limitations. Metaphor offers a different and much-needed form of truth and meaning.

Religious language also acts aesthetically at a broader and more primal level. While language in general allows humans to create and communicate meaning to each other, religious language enables individuals to create a worldview. Religious language enables us to define how each "One" relates to the cosmic "Many": to community, to the natural environment, and to the divine. The aesthetic structuring of existence through religious language restores the feelings of harmony and balance that humans seem to lack when confronted by Otherness or the whole of reality. To be able to know and feel one's place in the world is a function of religion. The aesthetic thus operates within the realm of religion not only in religious experience and language but in the religious impulse itself.

C. Aesthetics and the Problem of Evil

Aesthetics offers a powerful and productive response to evil. Aesthetics has special relevance to the problem of evil through theodicy and the prophetic power of art. An aesthetic theodicy is one that attempts to balance evil's reality with God's assumed goodness and power by means of an aesthetic model. A simple form of aesthetic theodicy is emanational dualism, which holds that spirit is good and matter is evil. To escape evil and pain, an individual need only ascend to higher levels of being through spiritual exercises or ascetic practices.

Augustine developed another form of aesthetic theodicy in his earlier Neoplatonic writings. He sees evil as a deprivation of the good through the loss of unity, form, or order. Matter itself is good, but formed matter (e.g., a human subject or a physical object) may misuse, distort, or destroy its order, beauty, and being. Although evil is negative and inevitable, it is nevertheless indispensable for Augustine's theological aesthetic, because beauty can be perceived only when contrasted with evil.

The philosophy of Alfred North Whitehead and its subsequent religious interpretation, process theology, offer a third aesthetic theodicy that solves the problem of evil through aesthetic conceptions of the universe and divine intent. In the process worldview, God and the world are necessary partners in the creative adventure of life. Consequently, God's power is seen as all-influencing rather than all-causing. God acts as a primal lure toward creative beauty. God therefore wills the beautiful more than the moral. In the process aesthetic, God *cannot* prevent the evil resulting from free creaturely choices. But He can use evil as a goad in the world's creative endeavor, spurring it from the ugly and banal toward new harmonies, depths, and intensities.

A fourth type of aesthetic theodicy is the protest one. This theodicy is not necessarily highly ordered or rational. Instead, in the very act of protesting to or against God, this theodicy provides a means for responding to evil. To experience evil and cry out to God is to be a part of the greatest of all dramas: the cosmic battle between evil and good. To enact this drama personally, to revolt and shake one's fist at God, is to find a momentary solution to the problem of evil. This aesthetic theodicy is better psychology than logic, however. It does not explain evil to the point of rational satisfaction. It does, however, allow individuals to work through the feelings evil provokes a process that can be very beneficial. Written protest theodicies have appeared frequently in the aftermath of the Holocaust and human rights movements, but protest theodicies, in general, are as old as the Book of Job. Drama and music, as well as other artistic media, can serve as tools for the catharsis of protest theodicy. Protests against evil dot the landscape of American musical history, for example, and include the spirituals of enslaved African-Americans, the blues of the depressed South, Appalachian folk music, and urban rap.

Just as protests can be aesthetic, so the aesthetic can protest. Art not only has the power to inspire us emotionally to the sublime, but it also has the power prophetically to expose evil to us. When art attacks evil, it also assaults the human viewer at a guttural level. A guttural assault by art can result in unexpected religious import and demand a just response. History has proven art's effectiveness at prophesying against evil. Notable examples of prophetic art are Francisco Goya's drawings of Napoleonic war atrocities, Picasso's *Guernica,* Anselm Kieffer's postmodern German paintings, the war photography of Matthew Brady and Robert Capa, and video footage, narratives, and pieces of art from war-torn nations. Although such art lacks explicit religious imagery or language, this does not deprive the aesthetic of its prophetic power and religious implications. In fact, secular art can be more profoundly religious than art that depicts overtly religious subjects and symbols.

CONCLUSION

Even in the aftermath of modernist and postmodern nonreligious aesthetics, many points of aesthetic-religious contact remain for exploration. In addition to the three areas introduced in the previous section, one might wish to explore some ideas discussed by the authors listed in the ensuing bibliography. These ideas include the nature of artistic making, individual and communal aesthetic tastes, and the aesthetic in religious experience (Brown); aesthetic theories of beauty and the holy in Western and Eastern cultures (Martin); aesthetic divine attributes, the role of human and divine spirit in aesthetic inspiration, and beautiful/sublime visions of cosmic transformation (Sherry); aesthetic beauty as seen from Hispanic, neo-Thomistic perspective (Garcia-Rivera); aesthetic play, the aesthetics of emptiness, and existential disfiguring (Taylor); and the divine foundations of creativity and social transformation (Cobb). As the impact of leading 20th-century theorists continues to be felt and the contemporary renaissance in theological aesthetics retains its vitality, the variety of subjects considered by religious aesthetics will surely expand. Michelangelo's *Creation* suggests that great power exists in the space between the aesthetic and the religious—a power that manifests itself in the birth of human spirit.

Works Cited or Recommended for Further Study

Beardsley, Monroe C. *Aesthetics from Classical Greece to the Present: A Short History.* Tuscaloosa, Ala.: University of Alabama Press, 1966.

Brown, Frank Burch. *Religious Aesthetics: A Theological Study of Making and Meaning.* Princeton, N.J.: Princeton University Press, 1989.

Cobb, John B., Jr. *Christ in a Pluralistic Age.* Philadelphia: Westminster, 1975.

Coleman, Earle J. *Creativity and Spirituality: Bonds Between Art and Religion.* Albany, N.Y.: State University of New York Press, 1998.

Dean, William D. *Coming To: A Theology of Beauty.* Philadelphia: Westminster, 1972.

Eco, Umberto. *Art and Beauty in the Middle Ages.* New Haven, Conn.: Yale University Press, 1986.

Garcia-Rivera, Alejandro. *The Community of the Beautiful: A Theological Aesthetics.* Collegeville, Minn.: Liturgical Press, 1999.

Langer, Susanne K. *Philosophy in a New Key: A Study in the Symbolism of Reason, Rite, and Art.* Cambridge, Mass.: Harvard University Press, 1960.

Martin, James A., Jr. *Beauty and Holiness: The Dialogue Between Aesthetics and Religion.* Princeton, N.J.: Princeton University Press, 1990.

Ross, Stephen David, ed. *Art and Its Significance: An Anthology of Aesthetic Theory.* 3d ed. Albany, N.Y.: State University of New York Press, 1994.

Rubin, William, ed. *"Primitivis" in 20th Century Art: Affinity of the Tribal and the Modern.* 2 vols. New York: Museum of Modern Art, New York, 1984.

Sherburne, Donald W. *A Whiteheadian Aesthetic: Some Implications of Whitehead's Metaphysical Speculation.* New Haven, Conn.: Yale University Press: 1961.

Sherry, Patrick. *Spirit and Beauty: An Introduction to Theological Aesthetics.* Oxford: Clarendon, 1992.

Taylor, Mark C. *Disfiguring: Art, Architecture, Religion.* Chicago: University of Chicago Press, 1992.

The Spiritual in Art: Abstract Painting 1890-1985. Exhibition catalog. Los Angeles: Los Angeles County Museum of Art, 1986; New York: Abbeville, 1986.

Tillich, Paul. *On Art and Architecture.* Ed. Jane Dillenberger and John Dillenberger. New York: Crossroad, 1989.

Von Balthasar, Hans Urs. *The Glory of the Lord: A Theological Aesthetics.* 7 vols. Trans. Erasmo Leiva-Merikakis. San Francisco: Ignatius, 1982.

Wolterstorff, Nicholas. *Art in Action.* Grand Rapids: Wm. B. Eerdmans Publishing Co., 1980.

Do Race and Gender Matter?
Christina M. Gschwandtner

Do race and gender matter? No.

For almost as long as philosophy, theology, or philosophy of religion have existed, they have mostly been the endeavors of white men. The philosophical and religious problems investigated were the concerns of white, middle-class, male academicians. The God whom they described was, for all intents and purposes, a white, middle- or upper-class male personality, even when everybody "knew" that God does not have a particular gender or color. Race and gender have often not mattered for the concerns of philosophy of religion. Then why this chapter? Does it "matter" that these issues have *not* mattered in the history of philosophy and religion? And if yes, why does it matter and how? This chapter seeks to deal with four questions: (1) How were women and nonwhite races excluded in the history of philosophy and theology? (2) Why is that important? (3) What attempts have been made to remedy this problem, and what issues still remain? (4) What concrete difference does all this make for the subject of philosophy of religion?

I. THE PROBLEM

The issues of race and gender have two aspects to them, a very practical side and a more theoretical one. We will look at both but focus on the second one. The exclusion of women and people who were "different" from almost all important spheres of life in the Western world has been commonplace for several thousand years and is still continuing. Not only were women barred from public life in the political and social sense, but they were often specifically forbidden to preach, to teach, to be active in church, to be educated, to think intelligently about theological matters, or at times even to ask questions. Native Americans were forcibly baptized and then often killed in the name of religion. Africans were hunted like animals, transported to the "new world" under horrible conditions, and there enslaved. Slavery was solidly supported by religious and supposedly "biblical" arguments, as well as by refined philosophical reasoning. Even after the abolition of slavery, segregation and injustices of all kinds continue to be prevalent.

Theologies and philosophies have been complicit in the suppression of women and nonwhite races, and in many ways they remain responsible for such oppression and other injustices. Few churches would call a female or Black pastor, and few religion or philosophy departments would employ either without "political correctness" hanging over their heads. The resistance against women in ministry is still fierce, and this resistance is still supported by all kinds of biblical and theological reasoning. And although few people would dare to advocate openly something like slavery, injustices continue to be perpetrated on the poor, underprivileged, and anybody who apparently does not stem from pure European background. The repercussions of the practices of slavery and colonialism still reverberate throughout the world and impact relationships between countries that often remain characterized by oppression and exploitation.

Yet these injustices in practice often only hide deeper theoretical issues that ground and enable them. How did we come to think of other people as inferior? How did we begin to distinguish people by such categories as "race" and "gender"?

Gender

Early in the history of philosophy, thinkers considered some differences between men and women as fundamental. Philosophers began to describe and define "man" by his ability to think or reason and to produce something by his labor, while they defined "woman" in terms of her biological functions, i.e., her ability to bear children. Quickly, dichotomies emerged: "man" was equated with mind/spirit/reason, while "woman" was equated with body/flesh/passions. To be "male" was to be "active or giving" and "good," while to be "female" meant to be "passive or receiving" and "evil." Many Pythagorean groups associated the "female principle" with evil, "blackness," or night, while the "male principle" stood for goodness, "whiteness," and light. Aristotle described the woman as an incomplete and inferior version of the man. These theoretical definitions were often assimilated by Christian thought that was deeply influenced by Greek philosophy. The dualism of mind and body has characterized Western philosophy and theology for most of history by making sharp divisions between soul and body, spirit and flesh, reason and passion, transcendent and immanent, good and evil. Since at least Augustine, many in the Christian tradition have condemned sex and nature as evil and sinful. Simone de Beauvoir, Luce Irigaray, Hélène Cixous, Julia Kristeva (and other "feminist" philosophers) have highlighted how much of Western philosophy and theology has reduced women to their sexual functions and defined them purely negatively.

More concretely, that Eve ate first of the forbidden fruit and that pain in childbirth is cited by the biblical text as a consequence of that sin were often employed as an argument that women are more sinful and also more responsible for sin as a whole. Simultaneously, they were often thought to be insignificant for or at least marginal to salvation history. Biblical texts against women preaching and admonishing women to obey their husbands are still used to keep them submissive and inferior. Texts arguing otherwise were (and are) usually disregarded.

Jesus' maleness also served as the basis of an argument against women. The official stance of the Roman Catholic Church for why women cannot serve as priests is still based on the assertion that the priest must have a "natural likeness" to Christ and, therefore, must be male. In the Orthodox tradition, women are not permitted to serve in any function that would allow them behind the iconostasis. In the Protestant denominations that ordain women, they are confronted with enormous difficulties and hostility. Women ministers, priests, or theologians are still the exception. Although the philosophical argument that women are naturally inferior to men and lack equal reasoning capacities has been officially abandoned, it is unofficially still firmly lodged in many peoples' heads and emotions.

Finally, God has usually been pictured as a male patriarch. We use male pronouns for God and speak of God as "Father" and "Son." The word for "Spirit" is female in the original Hebrew and neuter in Greek, but we employ a male pronoun in English. Although theologians have usually argued that God is without gender, our language does not reflect that. By speaking and writing in male pronouns, we consciously or unconsciously picture God as male. This is quickly revealed when someone suggests using female pronouns for God or naming the Trinity as "Mother," "Daughter," and Spirit. The outraged reaction this usually provokes goes a long way to prove that many do not really think of God as genderless. We are closely tied to male ways of portraying God. What exacerbates the problem is that the biblical language itself is so *androcentric* [male-centered]. Although one can find some female symbolism for God in Scripture, the male imagery and terminology predominates. Most of the main characters of Scripture are men, the people who are depicted as closely communicating with God are almost all men, and, perhaps even more significantly, the people who wrote down the stories were men, and they generally addressed men with their writings.

Race

The concept of "race" is an Enlightenment construct. People who were different or "strange" were, of course, often suppressed and excluded before that time. Yet, it was not really until the Enlightenment that a philosophical argument was put forth to designate certain peoples as inferior, particularly on the basis of the hue of their skin. The Enlightenment was concerned to find universal definitions of human nature and to organize all knowledge into rational categories. Such human nature was, for example, the basis for their theories of government and for considerations about who could participate in politics. Because "human nature" was for them "universal," however, they had to find ways to exclude certain people from it whom they did not think capable of exercising political functions. This exclusion provided a philosophical argument for slavery: if "Blacks" and "Indians" were not truly human, they could be treated as animals, deprived of all rights, and made to work for the man of culture and reason. The argument that placed nonwhites on the level of the beasts can be found in many Enlightenment philosophers (e.g., David Hume and Immanuel Kant).

Apart from blatant arguments that made a person's color or place of origin responsible for a lack of culture, civilization, and, therefore, human nature, there were also more subtle ones. As the term indicates, the Enlightenment sought to bring matters to light, to expose, dissect, and clarify. Reason was thought to illuminate, to enlighten, to give vision, to reveal. "Whiteness" and human nature were identified with this vision of clarity and light. The language of "blackness" or "color" began to be used as a contrast to "white," the "light," or the "positive." "White" was not really a color—it was the natural or normal way to be. To be "Black" or "of color" meant to be different, wrong, unnatural, abnormal. Analyzing Enlightenment texts now, some scholars argue that "blackness" was necessary to define "whiteness." Unconsciously, the writers and thinkers employed the "nonwhite" *object* as a shadow or negative to outline and highlight the "white" *subject*. Similar to the dichotomies that emerged early in the discourse of gender, the discourse of race displayed the same dualities: "white" was identified with mind, reason, spirit, strength and culture, while "Black" was equated with body, passion, emotion, weakness, and savagery. Often this imagery was further glorified by speaking of the simple but honest savage, a picture maybe even harder to overcome with its deceptively positive connotation.

Contemporary thinkers such as Frantz Fanon, Cornel West, Paul Gilroy, Homi Bhabha, and others have uncovered these inherent ambivalences and ambiguities within the Enlightenment project. They have suggested ways of either enlarging Enlightenment values to include oppressed groups or adopting specifically "black" approaches to deal with the heritage of rationalism in the West. Few philosophers want to dispense with the achievements of the Enlightenment altogether. Yet they seek to elucidate how much of its discourse or its success was possible only through oppression and denial.

II. SIGNIFICANCE OF THE ISSUE

Why should philosophers of religion care? Even if philosophy and/or theology were responsible to some extent for historic suppression, why do the questions of race and gender affect a discussion of philosophy of religion now? We will here briefly consider two aspects of the issue that are of significance.

Who is God?

Much philosophy of religion is deeply concerned with an examination of God's nature and attributes. Yet feminists and liberation theologians have alerted us to the fact that the God whom we have been examining has often been a white and male God (or at least that we have *portrayed* God as white and male). Furthermore, both groups have argued that to define God in terms of adjectives of power (omnipotence, omniscience, omnipresence, and so on) is a male way of arguing about God. The problems that pose themselves for philosophy of religion, such as considering God's omnipotence, are deeply affected when the adjective itself comes under scrutiny. Is God's identity as "Father" and "Son" essential to God's nature, or are they mere terms, mere images, mere modes of revelation that can be easily replaced by others? What does the terminology we employ reveal or presuppose about God's character?

How do we know God?

There is an even more fundamental challenge leveled by the discourses of race and gender. If philosophy and theology have been so deeply complicit in the injustices that have been perpetrated on women and people of other races, how trustworthy and valuable are the disciplines in and of themselves? If biblical language is so heavily androcentric and if theological discourse often portrays God as utterly male, how can this message be trusted? How and on what level does or can the divine be revealed in such flawed language? Of what good is the message of salvation for women, for example, if it is salvation by a *male* God through a *male* agent for a *male* subject reported by *males* to other *males*?

Apart from the merely epistemological question, this is also a question of theodicy: Why has God not intervened and worked against the androcentrism and racism of biblical writers and other theologians? Why did God not hinder the many injustices against women and people of other races throughout the Church's history? Can a God who seems to care only about white, middle-class males be trusted?

III. SUGGESTED SOLUTIONS

There have been various attempts to deal with the situation. In philosophy, feminist philosophy has highlighted the "gender problem," and critical race theory has attempted to deal with the "race issue." In theology, feminists have done important work for both areas, as have liberation theologians. In this section we will explore four attempts to alleviate the problems we have examined, and simultaneously we will point to some places where issues remain unresolved or call for further work.

Rejecting the Tradition

After many attempts to recover female language for God or to find a positive view of women in the biblical and historical traditions, some feminists have concluded that it is impossible to do either successfully. In their opinion, the Christian tradition is so hopelessly androcentric, so biased against women and suppressive of their identities and missions, that it must be rejected. Mary Daly probably represents the most articulate and well-known voice for this position. After first trying to work within the tradition, she has rejected that approach and moved on to formulate a *"thealogy,"* a doctrine of the Goddess and of her priestesses. She wishes to recover early matriarchal traditions and emphasizes the femininity of God. Thus, she and similar scholars hope to balance the negativity toward women and the masculinity of most of religion. We will focus, for the purposes of this chapter, on the approaches of her work that seek to remedy the situation from within.

Exploring Alternative Language

Various suggestions have been put forth for making religious language more inclusive and for recovering the voice of women within the Christian tradition. These include attempts to uncover the female imagery that is used for God, particularly in the Hebrew Scriptures (e.g., descriptions of God as protecting womb, as mother caring for her children) and within the Church's tradition (e.g., female imagery for God in medieval mysticism). Some scholars wish to highlight Jesus' positive attitude toward the women of His time. While certain feminists argue that Jesus should have been asserting himself even more strongly against the androcentrism of his culture, others acknowledge that He was indeed more supportive of women than could have been expected considering his particular historical context. It has been pointed out that if God had been incarnated as a woman and then preached a message of humble submission, love, and servanthood, this would have reinforced precisely the stereotypical expectations of women. Instead, Jesus preached such a message as a male and was therefore more revolutionary to the traditional gender roles than he would have been as a woman with a similar message. Furthermore, women appear to have played an important role in his ministry as his followers, companions, and as the first witnesses of the Resurrection. Some scholars also highlight the significant relationship Jesus seems to have had with Mary Magdalene and her stature in subsequent texts of the first few centuries.

Church historians point to important roles women apparently played in the Early Church when official ecclesial functions were still far more fluent and flexible. Women served as teachers, presbyters, and even official church leaders in many circumstances. Several of the early movements that were later condemned as heretical (for example, Montanism and many gnostic groups) entrusted women with important places in their ministries and even theologies. Some scholars wonder whether these groups were condemned not just for their "heretical" theological views but precisely because they accorded leadership functions to women. Important work is also being done on female medieval mystics (e.g., Julian of Norwich, Catherine of Siena, Teresa of Avila, Hildegard of Bingen) who seem to have exercised considerable power and influence within the medieval Church and to have enjoyed unprecedented freedom. On the other hand, exploring the positive roles of women by examining their particular historical lives also reveals the many injustices to which the Church subjected them. Many more negative than positive examples emerge in such investigation, such as the medieval witch hunt whose victims were almost entirely women and whose theological arguments reveal deeply problematic views of femininity.

Biblical scholars have done careful work on passages that seem to condemn women or forbid them certain functions within the Church. By considering the passages within their original contexts and the particular theological arguments for which they were employed, scholars have found ways of remedying these texts or creatively reappropriating them to be more inclusive and affirmative of women. Of course, not everybody agrees with such exegesis. Furthermore, the very fact that these texts were included in Scripture while others were not continues to be troubling.

Theologians have also begun to work against sexism through various theological arguments and to find ways to be theologically more inclusive of women. Catherine Mowry LaCugna and Anne E. Carr, for example, have spoken of the doctrine of the Trinity as affirming mutuality and loving relationship, thus emphasizing the feminine values it incorporates. They, like many others, believe that a recovery of Christianity's fundamental message can indeed be supportive of women and need not be oppressive.

Finally, some theologians have investigated the significant role that Mariology [doctrine of Mary] has played in Christian theology and hoped to thus recover a positive image of women within biblical and historical Church tradition. Yet because the "virgin mother" acts as a symbol both for maternity and virginity, many feminists have argued that an elevation of Mary further served to reduce women only to their biological functions, not to mention the problematic combination of maternity and virginity. Mariology is intricately connected with many other doctrines that have traditionally contributed to the oppression of women. The doctrines of the fall, original sin, infant baptism, the immaculate conception, the perpetual virginity of Mary, and several others are closely tied to each other theologically. Throughout the Church's tradition, these doctrines have reinforced the view that women are more responsible for the fall, less active in the process of salvation, and somehow more "sinful" than men.

Overall, many of these suggestions toward "solution" struggle with similar ambivalences. While it is indeed important to recover female language for God found within Scripture, some attempts to use inclusive language for God remain unsatisfying and theologically questionable. After all, to speak of God as "Mother" and "Daughter" instead of "Father" and "Son" also ties God to gender. To employ "Creator/Redeemer/Sustainer" instead of "Father/Son/Spirit" is to define the divine persons exclusively by their functions and risks reducing them to particular acts in salvation history. Other terms that have been suggested often result in similar theological problems. To find adequate symbolism for God continues to be an issue for theology and philosophy of religion.

Picturing a God of the Oppressed

The two "solutions" already examined have been concerned mostly with the role of women. For one reason, despite all suppression, women figure far more prominently in the biblical texts than, for example, Blacks. Although there were many supposedly biblical accounts put forth to support slavery, these arguments have been abandoned today. Suppression of nonwhite races within the Church and its theology may be more of a practical nature than a strictly biblical or historical one.

Liberation theology argues against injustice and oppression as a whole. Liberation theologians find many texts in Scripture eminently useful for the fight against oppression. Already before and during the Civil War in the United States, the stories of Yahweh's deliverance of the Hebrew slaves from Egypt became symbols for the struggle for freedom and against white slave-owners. This paradigmatic account of deliverance, paired with the prophets' many sermons against oppression of the poor and disadvantaged and the many scriptural calls to care for orphans, widows, and other underprivileged groups is also heavily used in American struggles for liberation and justice in the South. God, so argue liberation theologians, is pictured as being on the side of the oppressed. The message of Scripture is essentially a message of liberation, a call for justice, a struggle in which God sides with the poor and marginalized.

The theology of James Cone is one particular example of such an argument. Cone identifies the "Black" situation with that of the enslaved Hebrews in Egypt who are freed by Yahweh, the oppressed poor who are defended by the prophets, the captives in Babylon who are led back by Yahweh's promises, the outcast and marginalized to whom Jesus' ministry is addressed, and the early Christians who are persecuted and cruelly killed by the Roman Empire. These oppressed groups are the "people of God" on behalf of whom God is active. All true believers must become part of this people in order to enter into true relationship with God. "Whites" are identified in the role of oppressors: as the Egyptians, the Babylonians, the Pharisees, the Romans. In order to be redeemed, "whites" must renounce their acts of injustice, join God's oppressed people, become like them, and support them in their fight for liberation. God is pictured in Cone's account as militantly at work on behalf of the oppressed. Christ comes to overthrow "whiteness" with all its evils and falseness. Only by erasing this evil completely is new life possible. Not all liberation theologians, however, argue quite as strongly for violence or concur with a complete rejection of "whites." Many think that repentance, forgiveness and reconciliation are necessary steps for renewed and healthy relationships. The fear is always present, however, that talk of reconciliation before fundamental changes for justice have taken place will lead only to token concession. Such partial concessions fail to produce real change and ultimately keep "whites" in power.

Liberation theologians also disagree on their interpretation of the cross of Christ. Some see it as a symbol that God enters into suffering and redeems it from within. Suffering is not necessarily embraced as something positive or valuable in itself, but these theologians recognize that any struggle for justice will entail suffering to some extent in order to remedy systemic evil. Christ's death on the Cross is one example of such redemptive suffering and is an instance of God's willingness to become vulnerable on human behalf. Other liberationists reject the imagery of the Cross because it has been employed to suppress a suffering group further by arguing that they should meekly endure suffering instead of rebelling against it. These thinkers interpret the Cross as a symbol of Christ's victimization by the ruling authorities and as not originally part of God's plan for redemption.

Valuing Experience

Almost all theologians active in the struggle against oppression, whether in the context of gender or that of race, emphasize the value of experience. Both feminists and liberation theologians assert that their experiences have been systematically excluded from the discourses of theology and philosophy. To value such experience, it is suggested, would introduce into the discussion new ways of thinking and speaking of theological matters. In this valuing of experience, it is recognized and emphasized that we are essentially grounded in and strongly influenced by the circumstances and situations of culture, gender, race, class, language, and other differences. These past experiences and backgrounds situate our current experiences and our way of reasoning. It is simplistic to suppose that we could ever fully escape this conditioning. It is neither possible nor particularly coherent to assume an *a priori* and abstract starting point that is not already deeply implicated in experience, education, and other networks of relationships. We are always (often subconsciously) committed to our circumstances, and we can never fully escape the influence of language and other societal frameworks. This situatedness need not necessarily be interpreted negatively. It may constitute a valuable contribution to theology by enriching it and endowing it with relevance. To ignore people's particular experiences and backgrounds is to impoverish and sterilize theology.

On the other hand, some theologians find "experience" a rather fuzzy term that escapes clear definition. This starting point seems rather difficult either to verify or universalize (i.e., make valid or at least compare to that of others). Yet it is also argued that this desire for clarification, verification, abstraction, and universalization is precisely a characteristic of the Enlightenment discourse of established academia. Some liberation theologians assert that this demand to be abstract and theoretical is itself a white and male endeavor that excludes other voices. An abstract theology characterized by a search for theoretical formulae and pure academic language, so they suggest, lacks connection with life.

One particular problem of the "race and gender issue" is what remains unacknowledged in its overlap. White feminist theologians may assume their agenda to include all women without having to give any particular attention to the specific plight of nonwhite women, while liberation theologians (usually male) consider the situation of the nonwhite oppressed but often ignore the particular situations of women. Female theologians from Hispanic backgrounds argue that academic philosophy and theology do not accept their values and ways of being. What they consider meaningful and carriers of truth, such as song, poetry, painting, and more emotive discourse, is not acknowledged as of any "truth value" by "white" academia. This argument is often leveled even against feminist theology. South American or African American women are doubly suppressed and excluded. They argue that their situation is not truly described by either group. Their oppression is not only "double" but qualitatively different and not depicted at all within the discourses of either race or gender. These women often distinguish themselves consciously from what they call "white-feminism," which tends to be a middle-class, academic endeavor, by speaking of their own theology as "womanist." In fact, "white" women have often actually contributed to the oppression and marginalization of Black women in order to further the white woman's cause. Black women writers (for example, Toni Morrison) point out that they have been defined precisely in distinction from and opposition to white women.

This concrete issue reveals a general split between the university and the community. Many feminists have entered the fierce academic struggle and have adopted many male paradigms and tools to survive the academy's often hostile competition or to achieve any measure of academic success. Yet they have been accused subsequently of losing all contact with the everyday plights of women and their right to represent them. A similar argument is often directed against the few Blacks in high academic or political positions. These various groups who have been defined as "other" or nonrational find themselves in an inescapable dilemma. Either they need to appropriate the male/white discourse from which they have been excluded in order to be admitted to the realm of the privileged and powerful, or if they choose to reject that discourse of domination and instead emphasize the values of the repressed group (i.e. stereotypical "feminine" or "black" qualities), they remain precisely within the categories in which the discourse of oppression has placed them. "Feminine" ways of thinking and feeling may be such only because such ways have been imposed upon and expected of women. To emphasize such "female approaches" to subject matters is precisely to submit to this stereotyping of women.

CONCLUSIONS

After outlining the issues and examining some attempts to improve the situation, let us conclude by looking more specifically at how this topic impacts philosophy of religion. What difference do these writings and arguments make for philosophy of religion? We will here suggest two ways in which essential assumptions of philosophy of religion are put in question by the concerns of race and gender.

Truth

First, philosophy and theology influenced by race and gender considerations often challenge the very nature and presupposition of the *discourse* of philosophy of religion. Abstract and purely theoretical language that attempts to prove the term or concept of "God" by logical formulae or abstract reasoning is in many ways a stereotypical white male endeavor. Academia often defines truth and necessity for (or possibility of) belief exclusively in terms of rationality, strict specialization, and abstraction.

The discourses of race and gender suggest that such emphasis on one "master-language" frequently (if not automatically) leads to the exclusion of others and becomes oppressive and intolerant. By suppressing other truths, the "truth" of philosophy of religion becomes complicit with the kinds of injustices of authority and patriarchy that have unfortunately characterized the Church for much of its history. As soon as a monopoly on "truth" is assumed or attempted to be achieved, other truths tend to be eliminated. Metastories or universal discourses that assert knowledge or even possession of the "truth" are apt to become intolerant, suppressive, unjust, and stale.

Feminism and the discourse of race rethink the very foundation of philosophy of religion as an abstract defense of the faith that seeks to convince of God as if one was concerned with a mathematical theorem. To suppose that one can speak of God as he or she talks about things or even other people is to devalue and misconceive the very nature of God. Must not the kind of discourse employed to name God reveal something about the nature of the subject we are attempting to treat? Can we coherently talk about what or who is essentially beyond language?

These reflections on language, however, also open spaces for new possibilities. Feminist and race discourse emphasize the importance of an openness toward "otherness," diversity, and the value of ambiguity. They thus suggest the possibility to think of truth in less static and absolute terms and to get beyond the Enlightenment legacy that has framed (and limited) so many religious questions. Maybe philosophy of religion would be better occupied creating space for a variety of discourses about God instead of attempting to "prove" the existence of God beyond the shadow of a doubt. Philosophy and religion might move closer when they recognize each other's differences and embrace this diversity. Maybe they will meet more easily when they both discover the essential otherness of their subject matters and foster diversity within their own disciplines.

God

Second, race and gender discourse has implications for how we speak about God's nature. If God is without gender, it is blasphemous to employ exclusively male imagery for God. The language one uses to talk about God and how one defines God's nature is always dependent on circumstances and societal conditions. Much of the Western theological and philosophical tradition has pictured God as the Almighty accumulation of "omni-attributes." Yet this specific language is foreign to Scripture and to the experience of most Christians. The discourses of race and gender suggest that God might be, for example, more adequately characterized in terms of loving vulnerability and caring compassion, as concerned with liberty and justice for the oppressed and downtrodden. Many feminist and liberation theologians insist that theology and philosophy would be well-advised to recover some of the emphasis on the importance of imagery, myth, and symbolism of early *apophaticism* [negative theology].

The languages of race and gender raise an awareness of the implications and problems of totalitarian language about God. Whenever God has been defined absolutely and monolithically, whenever there have been strict assertions about the more or less precise and acceptable way(s) of speaking about God, oppression and exclusion of other images and voices have resulted. Feminist and liberation theologies call for diversity in the language and imagery employed for God and matters of faith. They suggest that if philosophy of religion seeks to uncover *the* nature of God or *the* solution to the problem of theodicy or even *the* existence of God, it is on a misguided and dangerous path.

Philosophy of religion, like its fellow disciplines, has suffered from the Western malady of mind/body dualism. The discourses of race and gender alert us to the dangers of this schizophrenic view of the world, humanity, and even divinity. Much philosophy of religion has treated both God and the human as primarily about "mind" or "pure being" with little regard for their embodied existence in the world. Traditional philosophy of religion often does not take account of lived, embodied reality and situated experience. Proofs for God's existence are commonly characterized by these splits of transcendence and immanence, mind, and body. Philosophers and theologians often have not been sufficiently aware of their own presuppositions regarding the nature of God's transcendence. For example, if God's goodness and omnipotence can be rationally argued to be coherent with the abstract idea of evil in the world, the problem of theodicy is thought to be removed without taking account of any actual instances of human suffering. The discourses of race and gender remind us that such approaches and arguments tend to become simplistic, incoherent and irrelevant.

These discourses do not merely demolish, however, but also open new ways to speak of God's transcendence and immanence. By emphasizing the concrete and diverse experiences of human beings and stressing God's solidarity in suffering, God's immanence is highlighted, especially if physical and spiritual are thought as coextensive and not as contradictory. By realizing the ways in which humans have defined each other as essentially "other," we might find new ways of speaking of God's "otherness" and difference. Realizing the ambiguity of so much of our language might aid us in making less absolutist assertions about God (and God's nature) and in developing more sensitivity to the nature of the subject with which we are concerned. The discourses of race and gender, then, call us to rethink both the nature and content of our discourse about God and the corresponding implications for philosophical and theological language about the divine. They alert us to some of the presuppositions underlying our assumption that we are able to define God's attributes and character and can speak intelligently about God's action in the world in a way separate from our own preconceptions and frameworks. They admonish us against any easy solutions to traditional theological problems and cause us to reconsider the very questions we have been posing.

Do race and gender matter? Yes.

Texts for Further Reading

Aquino, Maria Pilar. *Our Cry for Life: Feminist Theology from Latin America.* Trans. Dinah Livingstone. Maryknoll, N.Y.: Orbis, 1994.

Armour, Ellen T. *Deconstruction, Feminist Theology, and the Problem of Difference: Subverting the Race/Gender Divide.* Chicago: University of Chicago Press, 1993.

Beauvoir, Simone. *The Second Sex.* Trans. H. M. Parshleys. New York: Alfred A. Knopf, 1953.

Carr, Anne E. *Transforming Grace: Christian Tradition and Women's Experience.* San Francisco: Harper & Row, 1988.

Chopp, Rebecca S. and Sheila Greeve Davaney, eds. *Horizons in Feminist Theology: Identity, Tradition, and Norms.* Minneapolis: Fortress, 1997.

Christ, Carol, and Judith Plaskow, eds. *Woman-spirit Rising: A Feminist Reader in Religion.* New York: Harper and Row, 1979.

Cone, James. *God of the Oppressed.* New York: Seabury, 1975.

Daly, Mary. *The Church and the Second Sex.* New York: Harper & Row, 1985.

————. *Gyn/Ecology: The Metaphysics of Radical Feminism.* Boston: Beacon, 1978.

DuBois, W. E. B. *The Souls of Black Folk.* Ed. David W. Blight & Robert Gooding-Williams. Boston: Bedford Series in History and Culture, 1997.

Fiorenza, Elisabeth Schüssler. *In Memory of Her: A Feminist Theological Reconstruction of Christian Origins.* New York: Crossroad, 1983.

————, ed. *The Power of Naming: A Concilium Reader in Feminist Liberation Theology.* New York: Orbis, 1996.

Gutierrez, Gustavo. *The God of Life.* Trans. Matthew J. O'Connell. Maryknoll, N.Y.: Orbis, 1996.

Irigaray, Luce. *Sexes and Genealogies.* Trans. Gillian C. Gill. New York: Columbia University Press, 1993.

————. *Speculum of the Other Woman.* Trans. Gillian C. Gill. Ithaca, N.Y.: Cornell University Press, 1985.

Jantzen, Grace. *Becoming Divine: Toward a Feminist Theology of Religion.* Indiana University Press, 1999.

Johnson, Elizabeth A. *She Who Is: The Mystery of God in Feminist Theological Discourse.* New York: Crossroad, 1996.

Keller, Catherine. *From a Broken Web: Separation, Sexism, and Self.* Boston: Beacon, 1988.

King, Ursula, ed. *Feminist Theology from the Third World: A Reader.* New York: Orbis, 1994.

Kristeva, Julia. *Strangers to Ourselves.* Trans. by Leon S. Roudiez. New York: Columbia University Press, 1991.

————. *Tales of Love.* Trans. Leon S. Roudiez. New York: Columbia University Press, 1987.

LaCugna, Catherine Mowry, ed. *Freeing Theology: The Essentials of Theology in Feminist Perspective.* San Francisco: HarperCollins, 1993.

Marks, Elaine and Isabelle de Courtivron, eds. *New French Feminisms.* New York: Schoken, 1981.

McFague, Sallie. *Metaphorical Theology: Models of God in Religious Language.* Philadelphia: Fortress, 1982.

Mollenkott, Virginia Ramey. *The Divine Feminine: The Biblical Language of God as Female*. New York: Crossroad, 1983.

Ruether, Rosemary Radford. *Liberation-Theology: Human Hope Confronts Christian History and American Power*. New York: Paulist, 1972.

———. *Sexism and God-Talk*. New York: Crossroad, 1983.

Tamez, Elsa, ed. *Through Her Eyes: Women's Theology from Latin America*. New York: Orbis, 1989.

Townes, Emilie M. *Embracing the Spirit: Womanist Perspectives on Hope, Salvation, and Transformation*. New York: Orbis, 1997.

West, Cornel. *Keeping Faith: Philosophy and Race in America*. New York: Routledge, 1993.

Young, Pamela Dickey. *Feminist Theology/Christian Theology: In Search of Method*. Minneapolis: Fortress, 1990.

Religious Pluralism

Mark Grear Mann

◆

Religious pluralism is one of the great realities of life today. Economic globalization, the communications revolution, and the urbanization of most societies have combined to create a world become increasingly smaller. Experiences that just decades ago were very rare have now become commonplace. For instance, our neighbors can trace their roots to all parts of the globe. We stand a good chance of growing up and going to school with not just Christians and Jews, but also devout Buddhists, Muslims, and those of other world religions. Even if we were raised or live where such experiences are still infrequent, the Internet makes it probable that we have multiple interactions with people whose backgrounds are religiously diverse and quite different from our own.

The *reality* of religious pluralism has given rise to the *problem* of religious pluralism. Scholars have dealt with religious pluralism in a systematic fashion from two different perspectives: one largely philosophical and the other primarily theological. The more *philosophical* approach to the reality of religious pluralism has been an attempt to define the nature of religion in general, and in a related, more specific fashion, the essence or nature of particular religions, such as Christianity or Buddhism. The more *theological* approach to religious pluralism—often referred to as "theology of religions"—has been the attempt to identify how it is that members of one religious tradition should think of other religions in relation to their own faith. So, for instance, a *Christian* theology of religions seeks to understand how it is that Christians should think of the Christian gospel in light of the varying gospels of Judaism, Buddhism, and so on. Although these two approaches—the philosophical and the theological—seem at first to be quite different, they are actually deeply interrelated. While it is my intention to offer constructive reflection upon the problem of religious pluralism (viz., the Wesleyan theological tradition), we will begin by looking at the issue from the more philosophical perspective of defining the nature of religion.

I. What is Religion?

Defining religion is a lot like attempting to define love. Certainly we all have a notion of what love is, and most of us, if asked to define it, would readily attempt to provide an answer. But defining love is not such an easy matter. We all have very different experiences of love and therefore different views on what defines it. My hunch is that if someone were to ask 50 different persons to define love, our pollster might come up with 50 different definitions. Such is the case with religion. We all *know* what religion is: we have experienced it and see it lived out in our world in many different ways. But what ultimately *is* religion: what is its essence, its defining feature or features? What makes something religious and something else *not* religious?

For nearly two centuries, scholars of religion have attempted to define religion, and there have been almost as many answers to these questions as there have been persons attempting to provide answers. Despite the variety of answers, we can identify some basic approaches to the problem. We will explore these approaches briefly from the three following perspectives: (1) the claim that religion can best be defined by the objective outsider; (2) the claim that religion can best be defined by the religious insider; and (3) the claim that religion cannot and should not be defined.

A. Religion Defined by the Outsider

One of the most important attempts to define religion from an academic and so-called "scientific" perspective was made by pioneering French sociologist Emil Durkheim (1858—1917). In *The Elementary Forms of the Religious Life,* Durkheim defines religion as "a unified system of beliefs and practices relative to sacred things uniting persons into a single, moral community or 'church'" (62). So according to Durkheim, religion is an eminently *social* thing, a reality that both shapes and is shaped by human communities. Indeed, he claimed, the very idea of society is the soul of religion. In other words, that which is most essential to and important about religion is that religion is a byproduct (and projection) of the collective consciousness of human communities. Of course, members of religious communities themselves find it very difficult to see this truth. Those who wish to define religion from the outside say that these members have been so deeply shaped by the beliefs and practices that they are unable to see religion as their own product. It is for this reason that only a scientific and, therefore, objective outside observer can adequately define religion. Only an objective observer, say proponents of this view, can see religion for what it truly is.

Pioneering psychologist Sigmund Freud (1856—1939) shared Durkheim's conviction that religion is best understood as a human product. However, Freud provided his analysis of religion from a more psychological perspective, which we find most succinctly in *The Future of an Illusion.* For Freud, religion is the universal obsessional neurosis of humanity, arising from what he called the "Oedipus complex." According to Freud, the Oedipus complex arises from the complex matrix of relations within the family. The infant (especially the male infant) instinctually desires to possess the mother and thus is resentful of the father's sexual intimacy with the mother. At the same time, this infant fears the father's apparent omnipotence (as one infinitely more powerful than the child) and remains needful of the father's protection. In order to flourish, therefore, the child must repress the natural drive to possess the mother. This repression leads to various forms of psychological neuroses.

In the same way, society demands that individuals repress instinctual desires (in particular, sexual and aggressive drives) as a precondition for successful communal life. According to Freud, religion functions to ease the burden of instinctual renunciation that is necessary for successful social life. Religion helps individuals to become reconciled to socially oblig-atory self-sacrifice as a matter of fate (or God's will) by providing compensation for these concessions in, for instance, the promise of the afterlife.

For this reason, Freud defined the content of religious belief in terms of "illusion" and "wish fulfillment." Religious beliefs are illusions in that they possess no necessary correspondence to reality. Instead, their primary function is to meet our psychic need to have our desires or wishes fulfilled. So, for instance, the Christian belief that God is love and that God has promised a place of eternal blessedness for the righteous has arisen because humans subconsciously need to believe that they will find reward for the sacrifices they make for the sake of communal life. Like Durkheim, therefore, Freud held that only the person who has cast off the naïveté of religious belief—and thus the blinding obsessional neurosis of religious belief—is capable of seeing religion as it truly is. Only a critical outsider can understand the true nature of religion.

It should be noted that in defining religion as a human product, Durkheim and Freud did not deny the existence of a divine reality toward which religious devotion and beliefs are oriented. Both affirmed the theoretical possibility of an existing transcendent reality toward which religious affirmations are directed. Freud, for instance, claimed that calling religious belief an illusion did not necessitate such belief being an error. Freud's central point is that religious beliefs arise as human attempts to fulfill certain subconscious psychic needs. Still, though not necessarily atheistic, Durkheim and Freud's theories were certainly agnostic. Although affirming that, for instance, Christian beliefs about the existence of God or the divinity of Christ may be true, the truth or falsity of such beliefs cannot be known. Ultimately, whether such beliefs are true in this way is secondary to how they function in the formation of human societies (Durkheim) or mediate psychological development within society (Freud). It is easy to see, then, why the claims of Durkheim and Freud (as well as philosophers Ludwig Feuerbach, Karl Marx, and Friedrich Nietzsche, who also argued that religious belief is primarily a human projection) have been offensive to persons of religious faith. When arguing against these so-called objective and scientific observers of religion, religious persons have argued that the perspective of the outsider causes one to miss what is most vital and central in religion: the reality of the "divine" or "transcendent" and a person's relationship to this reality.

B. Religion Defined by the Insider

One of the great scholars of religion to argue for the insider's perspective was Dutch Reformed theologian Gerardus van der Leeuw (1890—1950). In his seminal work *Religion in Essence and Manifestation,* van der Leeuw made the following, oft quoted claim that, in order to understand religion, one must look upon it with "the loving gaze of the lover on the beloved object, for all understanding rests upon self-surrendering love. Were that not the case, then not only discussion of what appears in religion but all discussion of appearance in general would be quite impossible; since to him who does not love, nothing whatever is manifested" (1963, 684).

Van der Leeuw's point is that if one wishes to understand religion, he or she cannot look at it as a distant and somehow objective observer. Rather, to understand religion fully, one must enter into it and participate in the fullness of its life. Religion is not a thing that can be dissected and picked apart on some experiment table. If one wishes to know and understand another person, he or she must develop some form of dynamic and (ideally) loving relationship with that person. Scientific analysis of that person might tell you how his or her organs and cells function, but it will not help you to know that person. Likewise, religion is a living, breathing thing. To attempt to investigate it through dissection is actually to destroy it, to misconstrue it, or to reduce it to something that it is not. For this reason, theologians and persons of faith have a privileged position in defining religion, for they are loving participants in the life of religion. Loving participants are more fully able to know the richness and fullness of its life and its reality.

In a very similar fashion, theologian Paul Tillich (1886—1965) defines religion using language that he also uses to define faith in general. For Tillich, what makes faith unique among all human experiences and activities—and what makes religion unique—is that it involves one's encounter with that which is truly ultimate in life—God. Tillich speaks of God in the language of existentialist philosophy when he defines God as "ultimate concern" or as that which concerns human beings ultimately and, therefore, gives ultimate meaning to life. There are many things that concern people, but only one thing can concern us ultimately, and that is the One (namely, God) who determines whether or not we exist. We sometimes allow *things* (such as fame, fortune, relations with other persons) to become central concerns in our lives. But none of them has the power to determine our ultimate state or provide our lives with ultimate meaning. Therefore, these mere *things* are idols that deter us from having an authentic encounter with the One who is truly ultimate. Thus, Tillich defines both faith *and* religion as the state of being grasped by ultimate concern. In other words, it is the encounter of persons with God as "Ultimate Concern" that defines the true nature and heart of religion. It naturally follows that only those who have been grasped by Ultimate Concern in faith can understand religion, that the best observer of religion is the one whose life is defined by faith, who has been grasped by Ultimate Concern.

Theologian Karl Barth (1886—1968) makes a similar point to that of van der Leeuw and Tillich in an even more radical fashion. He does so by making what seems at first to be a concession to critics of religion such as Durkheim and Freud. In accord with these outsiders, religion for Barth is indeed a human enterprise. But he parts company with them when he argues that religion can truly be understood only in light of God's self-revelation. In light of divine self-revelation, religion turns out to be a human product. Religion is nothing more than human idolatry, self-righteousness, and unbelief. Religion *does* arise out of the human attempt to negotiate some psychic or social need. But divine revelation shows that all such attempts to negotiate these needs—or likewise to bridge the gap between God and humanity—are lies doomed to failure. Even Christianity *as a religion* is called into question and judged harshly by the truth of God's revelation. True religion, as defined by revelation, is solely the work of God and His infinite grace. In this sense, Barth radicalized the perspective of the "insider." God is the only true insider, and therefore God is the only one capable of defining religion. Even Christianity is true only insofar as it is defined and formed by God's creating, electing, justifying, and sanctifying grace. In this way, Barth gives a privileged place to the religious insider in defining religion, because he argues that the so-called objective perspective of the outsider gives no real insight into religion's true nature.

C. The Critique of Defining Religion

In the past few decades, scholars have pointed out that to a certain extent both insiders and outsiders are right. Ultimately, however, both are also wrong. The problem, it is claimed, is that both insiders and outsiders represent particular perspectives on religion that are inherently limited. To a large degree, this claim echoes the concerns of the religious insider who responds to those presuming to offer a scientific and therefore objective understanding of religion. After all, insiders claim that religious faith and devotion enable a person to see something true and essential about religion to which the person who lacks such faith is totally blind. Those who are suspicious of attempts to define religion argue that there is *no* absolute foundation or entirely objective standpoint from which to judge anything in the world, much less something as diverse, complex, and existentially involving as religion. Furthermore, all approaches to investigate the nature of religion come laden with presuppositions that shape how it is ultimately defined and explained.

Anthropologist Clifford Geertz (1926-) has been one of the most influential thinkers refusing to define religion. Geertz has developed a method of studying culture—and thus religion—that focuses on how culture functions as a "web of significance" (i.e., a system of symbols that provide meaning) for persons and societies in their encounter with both the natural and the humanly created world. However, says Geertz, investigators should not aim to provide an "explanation" for religion. Instead, they should aim to understand how it is that cultural symbol systems provide meaning for the members of the religion and how particular symbols function as vehicles or bearers of meaning within the entire web of significance. Geertz refers to such investigation as "thick description," because it seeks to offer an analysis of the entire system of symbols and meaning. This investigation seeks to show how various parts of the system contribute to the functioning of the whole. This is, claims Geertz, all that the scientific study of religion and culture can hope to accomplish. Because no humans can be entirely objective in their approach to the study of religion and culture, the best that cultural analysis can accomplish is a kind of guessing. In this sense, Geertz is much more careful to recognize that all study of religion is perspectival and therefore inherently limited.

Another important voice decrying the defining of religion has been that of Wilfred Cantwell Smith (1916-), one of the preeminent 20th-century scholars of Islam. According to Smith (1981), the whole idea that religion is a distinct and identifiable phenomenon that can be observed and studied by social scientists, and that the essence or true nature of it can be defined is a purely modern and Western idea. He argues in *The Meaning and End of Religion* that a study of any religious tradition shows it to be an incredibly diverse phenomenon. A religious tradition is as diverse as the very number of its practitioners. For instance, if one seeks to study and identify the true essence of Christianity, he or she is immediately confronted by the incredible diversity of faith, practice, organization, and so on throughout the history of Christianity. We should not only cease attempting to identify the essential nature of Christianity but also drop the very idea of Christianity as a religion in the modern sense. Instead, says Smith, it is more accurate to speak of each individual person as having his or her own unique faith. Rather than speaking of particular religions, it is more accurate to speak of the communities and histories of persons of similar faiths as constituting cumulative traditions of religious faith. Only by such a radical shift in our thinking about religion can we account for the perspectival nature of inquiry and the complexity of religious practice and devotion in our world today.

All the scholars that we have investigated thus far have been either Jewish or Christian in terms of their religious background, and all have been distinctly Western in their general outlook and worldview. With the emergence of greater dialogue between members of Western religions (especially Christianity) and members of non-Western religions, and with the entrance of non-Western scholars into the debate about defining the essence and nature of religion, the result has been a deepening of the critique we see emerging in Geertz and Smith. While this critique has emerged from various loci and perspectives, one of the most articulate voices has been contemporary Muslim scholar Talal Asad. In *Genealogies of Religion: Discipline and Reasons of Power in Christianity and Islam* (1993), Asad argues that it is impossible to identify the essence of religion or of any religious tradition. The reason for this is that all observations about religion are historically specific and therefore unable to be made transhistorical. In other words, all attempts to formulate a so-called objective and autonomous definition of religion are actually a product of a historical process involving a constant reorientation of power, knowledge, and truth. Religion is intimately tied to social constructions, and we cannot step outside the constructions that have formed us in order to see religion objectively. Furthermore, the very process of defining religion or the nature of a particular religious tradition is an expression of power in the sense that our definitions affect how it is that we perceive things. And it is those who are most often in positions of power who do the defining and therefore have the most influence in shaping our world through their defining.

Asad presents a powerful critique not only of traditional Western definitions of religion but also of the whole approach to the study of religion that has been popular in the West. One might understand the origin of this critique by looking at the matter from Asad's particular perspective as a Muslim. Most scholars who have studied and written about Islam have been Westerners and Christians (at least by background if not by practice and faith as well). Add this to the fact that for much of the 19th and 20th centuries most of the Islamic world was under the political dominance of Western colonial nations. Western, colonizing Christians imposed not only their political rule but also their definitions of religion. Westerners imposed the definition of Islam itself upon the people of Islamic nations as if Westerners somehow possessed the right to speak for Islam.

Asad's critique is aimed at the outsider who presumes to have found an objective standpoint from which to judge all forms of religion. However, his critique can also be directed at the religious insider. For instance, just because one is a devout and religious Christian insider does not mean that he or she has any understanding of what it means to be a Muslim, Buddhist, or Taoist insider. Therefore, according to Asad, being a member of one religious tradition does not put one in a position to understand religion in any general sense that can be applied to all religions. Furthermore, the devout person of faith needs to be wary of thinking that his or her own particular understanding of his or her faith is valid for all persons who ascribe to that faith. Those who have been privileged and possess a high amount of power—especially intellectual power, as do all scholars— should be especially wary of how they yield that power in the ongoing formation of the world.

While not all scholars share the radically critical views of Smith or Asad, most have come to recognize the thorny problems inherent in attempting to define the essence and nature of religion. The problem is a matter of perspective: no creature is capable of approaching the enterprise from an entirely objective and presuppositionless standpoint. Instead, we *all* bring prejudices and presuppositions to our investigations, and these shape what we see and how we understand. This may not mean that our study of religion and the descriptions and judgments that we have as a result of our study are without value. Instead, it means that we should make our descriptions and judgments with hesitancy and humility. We should describe and judge in ways vulnerable to correction by other perspectives within the public community of inquiry.

II. THEOLOGY OF RELIGIONS

To a certain extent, discussants of the theology of religions inherently recognize the problem that we have highlighted thus far regarding the question of who speaks for religion in general or a particular religious tradition. This is because theology presupposes a particular perspective as a starting point for its inquiry. For Christian theologians the perspective that serves as the starting point for theological reflection is the experience of God as revealed in the person and work of Jesus Christ. This central foundation for Christian reflection has passed from the Early Church to later generations via the medium of the Christian scriptures (both Old and New Testaments), numerous creeds, and both official and unofficial Church theological statements. These, all together, embody the Church's attempt through its history to make sense of Christian revelation in light of its generation-by-generation experience of life in the world. In this sense, both Scripture and tradition serve as a fount for Christian reflection as well as provide norms or standards that guide this reflection. Scripture and tradition are also central for the development of a Christian theology of religions. To a certain extent, then, a Christian theology of religions presumes a particular perspective and outlook as it seeks to come to a coherent view of Christian faith in relationship to the faiths of other religious traditions.

The particular model I wish to use in outlining the key issues for theology of religions is probably the most commonly used. I believe this model is the most helpful because of the way it sets up the problem. According to this model, there are three basic stances toward the religious other: exclusivism, inclusivism, and pluralism. Most importantly, each of these stances makes claims about how it is that the fundamental truth-claims of one's own religious faith and tradition relate to the corresponding truth-claims of other religious faiths and traditions. Each stance also makes claims about how the path to salvation of one's religious faith and tradition relate to the salvation of members of other faiths. Specifically, this typology describes three different ways of thinking about how Christians can understand their own affirmations about God, Christ, salvation, and so on in relation to similar or roughly corresponding affirmations by non-Christians.

A. Exclusivism

Exclusivism is the belief that the truth-claims of one's own religious faith exclude the truth of any conflicting claims within other religious traditions. This way implies the exclusion of members of other traditions from receiving the salvation offered by one's own faith tradition. Christian exclusivists have argued that Christian affirmations about Christ, God, sin, salvation, and so on exclude contradictory beliefs of non-Christians. Non-Christians who do not convert to Christianity are, therefore, necessarily excluded from salvation. There have been two influential forms of exclusivism within Christianity: one largely prevalent among Protestants, the other prominent in Roman Catholic theology. The Protestant version has been especially tied to what George Lindbeck has called a "cognitive-propositional" view of truth, which emphasizes a direct correspondence between divine reality and our affirmations about that reality (Lindbeck 1984). In this view, salvation is tied to affirming orthodox or correct beliefs, especially about the divinity of Christ and the role of Christ as the Savior of humanity. The Roman Catholic version has emphasized the importance of the reception of saving grace through the Christian sacraments, which can be received only by participation in the Christian

Church (i.e., the Roman Catholic Church). As a traditional Roman Catholic saying puts it, "Outside of the church there is no salvation."

Karl Barth provides a third version of exclusivism, and this version is perhaps the most theologically sophisticated exclusivist version of the modern era. For Barth, all religions (including overly humanistic forms of Christianity) are no more than human constructions that are dead ends in the quest for salvation. Religions are therefore found wanting in light of the Christian revelation of the gospel in the person and work of Christ. Despite the diversity of these approaches, their central affirmation remains that the truth of Christianity excludes the so-called truth-claims of, and the possibility finding salvation in, non-Christian religions.

B. Inclusivism

A Christian version of inclusivism involves the belief that Christianity is *the* true religion, that Christ is "the way, the truth, and the life," and that no one comes to salvation except through Christ. Inclusivism follows a different path, however, by affirming that the truths of non-Christians may, in some way, be included within or subsumed by the Christian truth. In fact, non-Christians can still be recipients of the saving grace of God without necessarily affirming the truth of Christianity in any cognitive sense or joining the Christian Church. Probably the most influential Christian inclusivist has been Catholic theologian Karl Rahner (1904-84), who exerted a considerable influence on the Catholic Church's decision at the Second Vatican Council (1962-64) to embrace a more inclusive view of the gospel. According to Rahner, God is graciously present to all persons in an unthematic or noncognitive and, therefore, mysterious fashion as both the ground and horizon of our becoming. In other words, even if we are rationally or intellectually unaware of God, His grace is present and available to us. This grace empowers us in *all* of our choices to be either a "yes" or a "no" to God. As the God-man, Jesus most powerfully exemplifies both this "yes" to God *and* God's infinite love for humanity through His sacrificial willingness to bear the suffering of the world. In accepting this gift of grace upon hearing the gospel, one becomes a Christian in an *explicit* sense; however, one can also be a Christian *implicitly* without ever having heard the story of Christ if one has said "yes" to God's grace with one's life choices. Rahner calls such persons "anonymous Christians," for they are, he claims, true recipients of God's gracious gift of love in Christ *implicitly*. Rahner even goes so far as to suggest that those who have explicitly rejected Christianity may still give an implicit "yes" to God and therefore be anonymous Christians. That such people may be Christians anonymously is especially possible if what these people are really rejecting is a form of Christianity that has in some way distorted or demonically skewed the true gospel.

Those embracing an inclusivism like Rahner's often do so by arguing that the exclusivist view is highly problematic in necessarily damning billions of persons to hell. Many of the damned, they argue, have never even had a chance to hear the name of Christ, much less the opportunity to either accept or reject the gospel. Inclusivists further argue that the idea that God damns the ignorant seems counter to the biblical view of a God who is infinitely loving and merciful and who goes to any length to save "lost sheep." Many inclusivists also find fault with the views of truth assumed by exclusivists. These inclusivists argue that a cognitive-propositional view of truth assumes that the fullness of the infinite God can be reduced to human conceptions, beliefs and affirmations. Furthermore, argue inclusivists, it is problematic to limit the conveyance of God's grace to the medium of the all-too-human Church.

In response, exclusivists argue that an inclusive view of salvation results in a slippery slope that eventually relativizes the gospel and undermines the mission of the Church to preach the gospel and make disciples of all nations. Against this, Rahner responds that preaching the gospel may still have two important results: (1) inspiring those who are merely anonymous Christians to discover the full fruits of the faith already been born in their hearts and (2) converting those who have *not* said "yes" to God implicitly but who may do so upon hearing the gospel with their *heads* as well as their *hearts*.

C. Pluralism

In the past several decades, many Christian thinkers concerned with the challenge of religious pluralism have felt that the inclusivist theory does not go far enough in terms of its openness to the truth of other religions. In fact, these pluralists argue that no religion can be said to be superior to others. All religious traditions should be seen as providing equally valid avenues to ultimate truth and salvation. This is an approach distinct from the kind of humanistic skepticism that claims that all religions are false or a relativism that says that all religions are basically the same. Rather, religious pluralists affirm the importance and validity of religion and the reality of significant differences between various traditions. It is just that these differences are not necessarily antithetical.

Pluralists find no gripe with Christians who affirm the truth of Christianity. Their gripe is that some Christians claim that the truth of Christianity *excludes* non-Christians from truth and salvation and that some Christians claim that their religion is superior to and truer than other religions. This belief in the superiority of one's religion has, they claim, historically been tied to colonialism and imperialism. Believing one's religion is superior is both offensive and disrespectful of the beliefs and traditions of others, contend pluralists. In addition, this claim to superiority is nothing short of scandalous considering the great diversity of religious expression in our world today. Furthermore, they argue, such imperialistic claims about the unique place of Christianity among world religions leads to deep misunderstanding and dissension among peoples of different religions. What is desperately needed today is a religion that leads the way to greater unity among the peoples of the world.

Probably the most prominent Christian pluralist of our time has been the British theologian and philosopher of religion John Hick (1922-). With regard to knowledge of religious matters, Hick sharply distinguishes between religious *noumena* (divinity as it is in itself) and *phenomena* (what we experience divinity to be). This means that we never experience the reality of the divine as it is. All of our experiencing of God is just that— merely *our experience*, the interpretation of which is shaped by our own individual perspective. For this reason, Hick proposes what he calls a "Copernican Revolution" in our thinking about the relationship between Christianity and other religions (1973). Christians have long believed in a Christocentric model of religion in which Christianity is the one true religion, and Christ is the sole path to God. Like the Copernican shift from an earth-centered model to a heliocentric model, Hick proposes that we change our thinking about other religions by moving to a God-centered or "theocentric" model in which Christianity is put in its proper place as one of many valid approaches to God. In later work, Hick recognizes that even to speak of all religions as theocentric presupposes a Western (i.e., Christian, Jewish, or Islamic) view of ultimate reality (1989). It is better to think of the ultimate as "the Real" or "the Transcendent," and this ultimate is *pluriform* or *multifaceted* in its manifestations. All religions, in different but equally valid fashions, affirm and point to such a truth. In fact, argues Hick, the Real is known to us and available to us only through its many manifestations in the belief-systems, practices, and so on of the different religions of the world.

Wilfred Cantwell Smith shares a similar pluralistic outlook to Hick's. Smith argues that we should do away with the term "religion" as an abstraction about the complexity of life and religious experience (1991). He proposes that we instead speak of each individual as having a unique faith and of individuals as forming loose cumulative faith traditions. Additionally, the history of these cumulative traditions is so complex and there has been so much give-and-take between them that it makes much more sense for us to think one worldwide religious history (1981). Despite the fact that Smith's approach is quite different from that which we see in

Hick, the outcome is the same. Smith advocates a view of religion in which no religion should be viewed as the only true religion or even the *most* true religion. All religions provide equally valid paths ultimate truth.

Christian exclusivists and inclusivists have, of course, not been without their response to pluralists. Pluralism, they argue, inevitably leads to relativism, for it does not provide any legitimate basis by which to judge which expressions of religion are appropriate and which are not. In other words, where does one draw the line and say that any particular religious claim or practice (such as human sacrifice, to use an extreme example) is untrue or an invalid means to God and salvation? Additionally, they argue, it is not necessarily a scandal to argue that one view or perspective is true in a way that another view is not. Indeed, this is exactly what the pluralist hypothesis argues: that one perspective (the pluralist) is truer than others (the inclusivist or exclusivist). In this way, it is claimed, the pluralists impose a new and equally insidious kind of imperialism upon those against whom they argue.

We have already seen that all discussions about religion presuppose certain commitments and particular perspectives. Rather than requiring that every religion necessarily surrender claims to uniqueness and superiority, the challenge of a *true* pluralism is to find ways for religions with conflicting claims to proclaim their uniqueness publicly but with mutual respect. This would involve encouraging each to hold true to its own uniqueness while recognizing that other traditions possess the same right to profess publicly their uniqueness and superiority.

III. A WESLEYAN PERSPECTIVE ON THE THEOLOGY OF RELIGIONS

My aim in this concluding section is to explore briefly some of the resources provided by the Wesleyan theological tradition in addressing the challenge of religious pluralism. John Wesley himself did not live in a situation anything like ours today, so we should not be surprised that he or any of his immediate followers did not explicitly argue for one of the particular positions that we have just discussed. Still, there are important aspects of Wesleyan theology that provide a helpful springboard for suggesting how Wesleyans might think about these issues today. I focus briefly on two: the importance of *prevenient grace* in the Wesleyan-Arminian theological tradition and the *centrality of devotion* or love for God (and neighbor) in Wesley's understanding of true religion or religious faith.

A. Prevenient Grace

Building upon the thought of Dutch Reformed theologian Jacob Arminius, Wesley argued that although all persons are born with the sin nature and subject to the conditions of the fall of the first humans, God providentially elects all persons for salvation. In this universal election, God provides all people—no matter how lost or sinful—the opportunity for reconciliation with God. God's grace is at work in our lives through the presence of the Holy Spirit from the day we are born. This grace convicts us of our sin. It encourages and empowers us to be responsive to God's invitation to repent and thereby experience salvation. For Wesleyans, this grace, which reaches out to us before we even repent or are even capable of considering repentance, is *prevenient grace*. It is the fundamental precondition for the salvation of any person, and it is available even to those who have never heard of Christ.

B. True Religion as Devotion or Love

As we saw in W. C. Smith's critique of the scholarly attempts to define religion, the idea of religion as meaning anything but the quality of one's piety or faith is a modern development. This description of the premodern view of religion is an apt one for understanding Wesley's approach to religion in general and Christianity in particular. For Wesley, the true essence of Christianity and therefore religion can be summed up in terms of obedience to the greatest commandment(s): love for God and neighbor. In other words, the mark of true religion is not correct beliefs about God or even correct actions or practices. The mark of true religion is a *heart* fully devoted to loving God and neighbor. This is not to say that beliefs and practice are unimportant for Wesley. The point is that they are secondary. A devoted heart is most important. Correct beliefs and practice are empty opinions and formalism without a heart inflamed with love for God and neighbor.

In light of the importance of prevenient grace and the centrality of religious devotion, it is difficult to imagine Wesley affirming that God's saving grace is necessarily excluded from persons who do not identify themselves as Christians. By affirming prevenient grace, Wesley was affirming that God's grace is universally present and available to *all* persons. By affirming that true religion is primarily a matter of devotion and only secondarily a matter of belief for action, Wesley was also affirming that persons could conceivably receive a heart for God even if they entertained false beliefs about God or Christ.

In *The Last Battle,* the final book in the *Chronicles of Narnia,* C. S. Lewis illustrates Wesley's emphasis upon the heart. In this book, the Narnians (most of whom are talking animals and dwarves) have been enslaved by an evil race of humans called Calormenes, who worship the evil god Tash. Inspired and empowered by the great lion Aslan (the son of the Emperor over the sea and the protector of Narnia), the Narnians have gathered to throw off their oppressors. With the battle lines drawn, the presence of Tash is summoned to instill fear in the Narnians. The god's presence comes to reside in a site near the battlefield. Upon hearing of the god's residence, a young Calormene excitedly goes to meet and offer worship to his god. The young Calormene is not seen again until after the great battle has destroyed the old Narnia, and the Narnians encounter him in the True Narnia (heaven). In the conversation that follows, the young Calormene recounts his surprise at being welcomed into the true Narnia by Aslan, whom he had hated his whole life. Aslan tells him that although the young man had sought after Tash all his days, in truth the young man's desire had been for Aslan. If it had not been for Aslan, the young man would not have "sought so long and so truly . . . for all find what they *truly* seek" (Lewis 1956, 165). Such a view of the truth and availability of God's saving grace to non-Christians fits well with a Wesleyan view of the universality of prevenient grace. And it fits well with the importance that Wesleyans give to knowing God primarily with our hearts and secondarily with our minds.

While it is difficult to imagine Wesley affirming exclusivism, it is equally difficult to imagine him affirming a pluralism in the way that, say, John Hick or W. C. Smith does. For Wesley, it is clearly the work of God in Christ that makes saving grace available to all people. Non-Christians can find salvation, but they do not find salvation through something inherently true or right about their own religious tradition. They find salvation because they possess the graced capacity to respond with their hearts to the presence of the Holy Spirit. For this reason, a Wesleyan theology of religions probably best resembles the inclusivism of the sort that we find in the thought of Karl Rahner. Throughout his life, Wesley maintained a critical openness to the opinions of others, a willingness to have his own ideas shaped by discussion with persons of differing opinions, and a desire to work together in love with those with whom he found himself in even great disagreement. This is an important point for Christians to remember as they seek to proclaim the Christian gospel of love and grace to a non-Christian world. Just as Wesleyan Christians may define other religions from the perspective of their own tradition, so members of other religious traditions possess the same right to define truth and salvation from their perspective. The challenge that religious pluralism brings to all persons of faith is to find ways of affirming the truth of their faith in a way that treats with deep respect those who disagree with them. Doing so engenders the kind of peace and mutual affection between differing cultures and religious communities that will make possible the survival and enhance the flourishing of all peoples in the millennium that we have just begun.

Bibliography and Suggestions for Further Reading

Asad, Talal. *Genealogies of Religion: Discipline and Reasons of Power in Christianity and Islam.* Baltimore: Johns Hopkins University Press, 1993.

Barth, Karl. "The Revelation of God as the Abolition of Religion." *Church Dogmatics.* Vol. 1, Part 2. New York: Charles Scribners' Sons, 1956. 280-361.

Cobb, John B., Jr. *Grace and Responsibility: A Wesleyan Theology for Today.* Nashville: Abingdon, 1995.

Durkheim, Emile. *The Elementary Forms of the Religious Life.* New York: George Allen and Unwin, 1915.

Flemming, Dean. "Foundations for Responding to Religious Pluralism." *Wesleyan Theological Journal* 31.1 (Spring 1996): 51–76.

Freud, Sigmund. *The Future of an Illusion.* New York: W. W. Norton and Co., 1951.

Geertz, Clifford. *The Interpretation of Cultures.* New York: BasicBooks, 1973.

Hick, John. *God and the Universe of Faiths: Essays in the Philosophy of Religion.* Oxford: Oneworld, 1993.

———. *An Interpretation of Religion: Human Responses to the Transcendent.* New Haven, Conn.: Yale University Press, 1992.

Lindbeck, George. *The Nature of Doctrine: Religion and Theology in a Postliberal Age.* Philadelphia: Westminster, 1984

Maddox, Randy. "Wesley and the Questions of Truth or Salvation Through Other Religions." *Wesleyan Theological Journal* 27.1/2 (Spring/Fall 1992): 7–29.

Meadows, Philip R. "'Candidates for Heaven': Wesleyan Resources for a Theology of Religions." *Wesleyan Theological Journal* 35.1 (Spring 2000): 99–129.

Rahner, Karl. "Anonymous Christians and the Missionary Task of the Church." *Theological Investigations.* Vol. 11/12. Trans. David Bourke. New York: Seabury, 1974.

———. "On the Importance of the Non-Christian Religions for Salvation." *Theological Investigations.* Vol. 18. Trans. Edward Quinn. New York: Crossroad, 1983.

———. "The One Christ and the Universality of Salvation." *Theological Investigations.* Vol. 16. Trans. David Morland. New York: Crossroad, 1979.

Smart, Ninian. *Dimensions of the Sacred: An Anatomy of the World's Beliefs.* Berkeley, Calif.: University of California Press, 1996.

———. *The World's Religions.* Englewood Cliffs, N. J.: Prentice Hall, 1989.

Smith, Huston. *The World's Religions: Our Great Wisdom Traditions.* San Francisco: HarperSanFrancisco, 1991.

Smith, Wilfred Cantwell. *The Meaning and End of Religion.* Minneapolis: Fortress, 1991.

———. *Towards a World Theology: Faith and a Comparative History of Religion.* Maryknoll, N.Y.: Orbis, 1981.

Tillich, Paul. *Christianity and the Encounter of World Religions.* New York: Columbia University Press, 1963.

———. *Systematic Theology.* Vol. 1. Chicago: University of Chicago Press, 1951.

Van der Leeuw, Gerardus. *Religion in Essence and Manifestation: A Study in Phenomenology.* 2 vols. New York: Harper and Row, 1963.

Weber, Max. *The Sociology of Religion.* 4th ed. Trans. Ephraim Fischoff. Boston: Beacon, 1956.

Wesley, John. *The Works of John Wesley.* London: Wesleyan Methodist Book Room, 1872.

IMMORTALITY AND THE AFTERLIFE
Eric Manchester

◆

". . . that whoever believes in him shall not perish but have eternal life" (John 3:16). These words at the end of perhaps the most famous verse in the Bible, is known by most people who have gone to Sunday School even a few times or who have seen its scriptural citation scrawled on a fan's sign or shirt at a sporting event. It is only one of many verses that have been interpreted as referring to heaven (and hell).

While many religions, particularly Christianity, are typically thought to entail belief in life after death on the basis of faith, a philosophical person must ask what *evidence* there is for existence beyond this life. Without rational evidence, even a person of faith may give up his or her beliefs. For this reason, many philosophers have devoted time to finding rational evidence for life after death. A responsible philosopher must also consider the arguments against his or her point of view. This chapter will both explore arguments supporting the possibility of life after death and examine common objections to this possibility.

Before examining arguments concerning immortality, a few words should be said about the connection between the question of an afterlife and that of the reality of a divine being. Theists typically think of the afterlife in terms of God issuing eternal punishment or reward. Strictly speaking, however, belief in the afterlife requires neither belief in God nor belief in reward and/or punishment. Plato (428/7—348/7 B.C.), for instance, does not necessarily believe in a personal deity, although he seems to believe that human souls continue to exist after death. Similarly, belief in God does not require belief in life after death. Aristotle (384-322 B.C.), a student of Plato, clearly believes in an eternal divine being, but Aristotle does not appear to accept the possibility of ongoing personal existence after death.

Some philosophies and religions (like certain forms of Hinduism and Buddhism) include the belief that personal identity ends at death. Human souls live on in some sense, however, by being "absorbed" into a divine mind into which each of us "tap" in this life. This view is sometimes referred to as *pantheism,* or the belief that everything in the universe (or, in this case, all souls) is part of God.

This chapter contains two main parts. The first examines some basic questions as to whether it is even possible to form an intelligent position on the possibility of an afterlife. (1) If there is life after death, how could we know it? (2) Can this question be resolved scientifically, or if not, can it be answered apart from faith some other way? (3) Can we make sense of asking what it is like for a soul to exist without the body, or is such a scenario totally beyond our comprehension? In addressing these preliminary questions, we will also consider arguments made against immortality on the basis of negative answers to these inquiries. After this, we will look at arguments that reject belief in the afterlife as being nothing more than a psychological defense mechanism created to cope with death.

The second part will examine arguments supporting the afterlife, along with prerequisite accounts of the soul's nature. Three main philosophers will be covered: (1) Plato, who views the afterlife as a state of disembodied existence while also considering the possibility of reincarnation (i.e., the belief that our soul after we physically die comes back to exist in another animal or human body), (2) Aristotle, who does not believe personal identity continues after death, although he develops an explanation of the mind-body relationship that paves the way for others to argue for immortality, and (3) 13th-century Catholic philosopher Thomas Aquinas, who adapted Aristotle's view and proposed a Christian concept of heaven, hell, and the resurrection of the body.

PART I: PRELIMINARY ISSUES AND ARGUMENTS AGAINST THE AFTERLIFE

Can Science Comment on Life After Death?

Philosophically speaking, the burden of proof in discussions about the afterlife typically rests with those who believe in the afterlife. Few would argue that they have directly experienced someone continuing to exist after bodily death.

One could respond that just because we have no direct experience of existence after bodily death, this does not prove that there is no afterlife. After all, it could be that those in the afterlife are simply unable to communicate with the living. This rebuttal, however, commits the fallacy of *unfalsifiability*. One commits the fallacy of unfalsifiability when he or she tries to "prove" that something might be true by refusing to acknowledge any possible circumstances in which the theory could be proven false. A person who defends belief in the afterlife on the grounds that it is impossible to *disprove* life after death would be making an unfalsifiable argument. We seem not to be rationally justified in believing something that is theoretically impossible for anyone else to verify or falsify.

Because it is reasonable to refuse to believe in something for which there is no evidence, the burden of proof is on the person who asserts something to be true that is not yet evident to others. Without such proof, the skeptic is justified in denying the possibility of the afterlife. At most, one could perhaps argue that if we cannot determine if there is life after death, we should not reject the possibility completely. Instead, we should remain undecided. What is clear, however, is that one is not philosophically justified to believe in an afterlife without some kind of evidence.

Antony Flew (1923-) is an example of someone who rejects immortality on the grounds that there is not and could not be evidence for an afterlife. According to Flew, the only way we could verify that life after death was possible is if we could name an experience that would offer evidence of this. Presumably, however, the only way I could know that I had survived my own death is if I were able to observe my dead body (say, for example, if I could observe my own funeral). In this case, I would be "looking at" myself without the use of my body (Flew 1993, 100). It is impossible for Flew to make sense of the claim that we can "see" our dead body with our soul alone. "Seeing" is a physical activity, and we cannot perform any physical activities without a body.

One might attack Flew's position by insisting that our inability to understand what disembodied "seeing" is like does not mean that it cannot happen. On his thinking, however, such insistence would commit the fallacy of unfalsifiability. This amounts to saying, "We are justified in believing that it is possible to see without the body, because one cannot prove that it is impossible." But, of course, one cannot "prove" that seeing without the body is impossible if we already assume (as Flew thinks we must) that "proof" involves verifying or falsifying a theory through physical sensory observation. Flew's position, consequently, can be summarized as follows: (1) anything that cannot be empirically proven through observation should not be assumed to be possible, (2) the possibility of seeing without use of the body cannot be empirically proven, because such proof involves *nonphysical* activity, (3) therefore, we cannot assume that seeing without the body is possible.

Flew's argument relies on the acceptance of the first premise—that is, one should not believe in anything that is not observable by the senses. Indeed, people who report so-called near-death experiences will claim that they, contrary to Flew's assumptions, *have* had experiences during the time in which their bodies were considered "dead." In fact, these people may claim that the one who has had such experiences *is* able to comprehend what it is like to perceive without the use of the body. What should we make of such claims?

There is a great deal of documentation concerning so-called "near-death," "after-death," or "out-of-body"-experiences. For example, Elisabeth Kubler-Ross, a famous researcher on the psychology of terminal illness, is persuaded that life can continue after bodily death (1991; 1997). Even so, other scholars suspect that these experiences can be accounted for scientifically. For example, Hans Kung, a contemporary Roman Catholic theologian, cites studies from the psychologist Ronald Siegel and others that indicate that the "experiences" of those who have been clinically dead and revived are strikingly similar to the effects of certain hallucinogenic drugs, certain biologically-linked mental disorders, and even dreams (Kung 1991, 15-17). To him, this indicates a possible physical cause.

The authenticity of many near-death experiences is also questioned by the American-born Russian Orthodox monk Seraphim Rose (1934-82). In his book *The Soul after Death* Rose details a number of differences between contemporary "after death" experiences and those reported in early Christian writings on the lives of the saints. He maintains that vague experiences of "seeing lights," "tranquil feelings," and seeing living persons can often be explained medically (Rose 1980, 12-13). Rose believes that definite experiences, such as apparent meetings with deceased persons, "out-of-body" experiences (especially when achieved through intentional effort), and encounters with "angels" or "lights," should be regarded as demonic deceptions within the spiritual realm of *this* world rather than a glimpse into what eternal life is like (114-21).

Unlike most of the contemporary research that depicts these out-of-body experiences to be primarily peaceful and religiously indifferent, historical accounts of saints involve, much like Paul's record in 2 Cor. 12:1-10, a terrifying awareness of God's power. Furthermore, many holy men and women have neither sought such experiences (as occultists often do) nor do they seek them as replacements for ordinary prayer and devotion (Metropolitan of Nefpaktos Hierotheos 1995, 125-30). Unfortunately, the experiences of ancient Christians lend themselves no more to scientific verification than modern accounts, because these experiences occurred long ago and involved a "spiritual realm" that is presumably beyond scientific investigation. Stories of people who have allegedly communicated with the dead are supported by even less scientific evidence. The verdict appears to still be out, then, on whether there can be reliable evidence of disembodied experience.

Some who, like Flew, maintain that only empirical evidence is acceptable for resolving philosophical disputes (a position known as empiricism) ascribe to a basic philosophy known as materialism. Materialism is the belief that physical reality (matter and physical laws affecting matter) are the only things that are real. Thus, materialists generally deny the existence of disembodied souls, angels and demons, and even God. Empiricist materialists often hold (as Flew does) that statements about things that cannot be observed in the physical world make no sense. They are called *nonsense* statements. On this view, one cannot know what someone means when he or she speaks of "disembodied seeing" and the like.

On the other hand, even materialism may allow for some kind of "immortality." Friedrich Nietzsche alludes to immortality in his idea of "eternal recurrence" in his work *Thus Spake Zarathustra* (e.g. III, 2 and 3 and IV, 19). Though written in literary form, the idea is also scientific: if time constitutes a circle rather than a line (or, given an infinite amount of time with a finite amount of energy), every event will be relived infinite times, or every combination of atoms will recur infinite times. While Nietzsche is making a literary point for the ultimate value of this life against a (he believes) fictitious heavenly life, and not a philosophical argument for immortality, the possibility of recurrence is still worth considering scientifically. Current physics undermines this possibility, however, because the principle of entropy suggests that the universe is in a state of increasing disorder, so that no two events could ever be exactly replicated. On the other hand, physicists like Stephen Hawking have speculated that, once the universe "entropizes" into a state of completely unusable energy where no physical events can take place, this energy may collapse into a cosmic "Big Crunch." A "Big Bang" explosion would follow this Crunch, and the cycle of the universe would start all over again (1988). Even so, because we have no awareness of having lived our lives before, such a recurrence would not involve an awareness of ongoing existence.

Given the perceived lack of reliable empirical evidence for the afterlife, philosophical arguments for immortality are often defended by demonstrating that empirical verification is not the only justified basis for forming beliefs. This view points to issues far beyond the topic of this chapter, such as the legitimacy of what philosophers call "metaphysical" explanations of reality. Metaphysical explanations are those that are not scientifically provable but which can be derived from scientific observation and applied as a conceptual foundation for science itself. For instance, just as some philosophers conclude that physical causation cannot be understood without supposing there to be an eternal cause they call "God," those who believe in an afterlife may argue that thoughts derived from sensory experience cannot be adequately explained purely on the basis of empirical observation. From this, they may infer that human consciousness must at least be partly attributable to a nonphysical reality.

In the next section, we will show how various philosophers defend immortality by offering *metaphysical* arguments for the nonphysical nature of the soul or "mind." (Traditionally, philosophers equate the term "soul" with "mind" or at least take the mind to be the intellectual function of the soul.) Before a discussion of these metaphysical proofs, one more issue must be touched upon briefly in light of a materialist rejection of the afterlife. To the point: if we have no empirical evidence of life after death and cannot even comprehend what such an existence would be like, where do people get this idea that humans survive death?

The "Wishful Thinking" Objection

Some who deny the possibility of the afterlife explain the fact that others believe in it by proclaiming that such people are psychologically weak and unable to deal emotionally with the fact that they will one day die. According to this line of thinking, people who are unable to face death simply talk themselves into believing that there is an afterlife so that they can go on living without falling into despair. This is the view of the German philosopher Ludwig Feuerbach (1804-72). In *Thoughts on Death and Immortality* (1830), Feuerbach declares that a belief in both God and the afterlife is linked to the fact that most people feel insecure in their existence. As a result, they allegedly "project" a father-image into a belief in a God who takes care of them in this life and the next.

Kung notes three limitations with Feuerbach's argument (1991, 30-33). To begin, the fact that the prospect of death frightens us neither proves nor disproves that this fear is the only basis of our idea of God or the afterlife. Imagine that a man is convinced that a woman is in love with him because he cannot handle the thought of rejection. The fact that his conviction can be attributed to a psychological fear of rejection does not rule out the possibility that the woman actually is in love with him.

Second, one could argue that a psychological disposition toward believing in an afterlife could be regarded as evidence that there really is an afterlife and that we have inborn tendencies to believe this. Kung asks, "Does recognition of the fact that psychological factors play a significant factor in my belief in eternal life . . . exclude the possibility that these factors may be oriented toward a real object, to a reality [that exists] independent of our consciousness?" (1991, 30) In fact, as we will explore later, one must ponder why it is that we fear death in the first place. Could we fear death because we are intuitively aware that we are divinely ordained to live and enjoy life or because we instinctively realize that death indicates that something is "out of whack" with this world?

Third, the psychological projection theory can be used on Feuerbach himself to explain away *his* tendency to *disbelieve* in an afterlife. For example, one could turn the tables on Feuerbach and suggest that some people do not believe in an afterlife because they cannot deal psychologically with possible eternal consequences of their wrongdoing!

II. PROOFS FOR IMMORTALITY

Having looked at arguments against immortality, it is now time to look at arguments that defend immortality by countering the assumptions of materialism. Our discussion will focus upon Plato, Aristotle, and Thomas Aquinas.

Plato and Dualism

In Plato's *Phaedo,* the character Socrates (Plato's actual teacher) spends the last day of his life trying to convince his distraught friends that his soul is likely to go to a better place after he dies. He assures his friends that he is hopeful his soul is going to be with the souls of other good people, and he is as sure as he can be that his soul will go to live with "the gods." There is reason to question what Socrates is up to here, because he clearly casts doubt on the existence of the gods in other works. And he seems less certain of his existence with individual souls than with "the gods." In addition, the actual arguments for immortality offered in the *Phaedo* contain what Plato himself must have realized was dubious reasoning. Still, here and in other works, Plato does seem convinced at least that the soul is a separate reality from the body and that the soul is connected to eternal realities.

The view that the mind and body exist together as fundamentally distinct realities, much like a "ghost inside a machine," is known as *dualism.* Plato demonstrates the essential difference between body and soul by appealing to his theory of the "Forms" or perfect "Ideas." As he sees it, our minds are capable of grasping intellectual concepts—like mathematical equality, perfect justice, beauty, and goodness—that we never experience in the physical world. For example, I can never find two objects that are *exactly* equal in length. Likewise, no object or action seems to capture beauty, justice, or goodness to the highest degree imaginable. Our ideal expectations based on these values always exceed what actually occurs in this world as we know it. From this, he reasons that there must be a nonphysical realm of perfect "Forms" or "Ideas." Furthermore, because these ideal Forms never change (the concept of a circle, for example, will always be the same), the realm of Forms and the mind that comprehends them must be eternal.

Plato's conception is coupled with another insight. If the soul did not gain knowledge of these Forms from the senses that we have been using since before birth, it appears that not only may our souls live on *after* our body dies, but they may also have existed with these Ideas *before* we had a body. Given this, Plato asserts that souls follow a pattern: they exist without a body, then exist with a body, then exist again without a body, and so on. This view ultimately supports *reincarnation.* Plato speculates that, after a series of incarnations, some people will become so obsessed with bodily pleasures that their souls will come to live forever in a disembodied state of eternal torment, in which they crave things they cannot enjoy without a body. Those dedicated to the love of eternal truth, on the other hand, will blissfully ponder perfect Beauty, Justice, Goodness, and other Ideas eternally, because they are freed from the imperfections and distractions of the body and the physical world. It is important to note that Plato's view actually has much less in common with Christian views of the afterlife than one might at first think. Unlike Plato, many Christians do not regard the body as a "hindrance" to the soul, because God created all things good. And Antony Flew would insist that Plato's reference to disembodied souls amounts to incomprehensible nonsense.

Aristotle and Hylomorphism

Many prefer a view of the mind-body relationship that is not purely dualistic. As it turns out, Plato's own student Aristotle provides an account of the soul that is neither dualistic nor materialistic. Unlike Plato, Aristotle did not believe that the soul is strictly separate from the body. For one thing, given the popular Greek idea of *logos* that regards the universe as having an eternal *logical* (*logos*) structure, Aristotle presumes that nature has a rational purpose in giving us bodies in the first place. The idea that the soul would be better off without the body, as if the body is somehow a negative reality, fails to explain why an orderly universe would give us bodies if bodies were detrimental. Consequently, Aristotle believes that it must be good for the soul to have a body, and the purpose of the soul cannot be to "escape" the body. But how can we understand the body-soul relationship in a way that is neither materialistic, like Flew, nor dualistic, like Plato?

In response to this issue, Aristotle developed a concept of *hylomorphism* (*hyle*, meaning "matter," and *morph*, meaning "form"). Hylomorphism entails the claim that the soul is a metaphysical principle that gives both biological and intellectual functioning to the body. Insofar as it "forms" the body so that it is able to perform these functions, Aristotle also refers to the soul as "the form" or "formal cause" of the body (*On the Soul* 2.1). On this view, one can no more separate the soul from the body than one can, to use his example, separate the structure of a piece of wax from the wax itself. For Aristotle, matter is merely passive with the potential to be structured in an indefinite number of ways. The soul, on the other hand, acts on bodily matter to structure it in a definite way and give it certain functions. The soul "actualizes" the matter; it makes matter *actually* one thing when it was *potentially* many things.

Just as one can imagine a bit of wax having a different structure than it currently does, one can imagine bodily matter having been organized by a different formal principle that may have given us different functions than the ones we now have. In this way, Aristotle's view is not strictly materialistic, because the principle that structures matter to act in specific ways is not itself something material or physical. A *metaphysical* reality acts on matter. At the same time, there can be no actualization of matter where there is no matter. Therefore, one can abstractly distinguish between the matter itself and its structural functions. In short, the soul is conceptually *distinct* from the bodily matter without being actually *separate* from it. Aristotle's view, then, is neither materialistic nor dualistic.

Unlike Plato, Aristotle did not regard the body as a hindrance to the soul. Instead, the body is intended by nature to receive its structure and operations from it. Bodily matter enables the soul to perform its intended function. In addition, Aristotle claims that human thinking requires the use of mental images, or *phantasms,* derived from sense experiences (3.7). Although his view is more positive toward the body, he concedes that it involves the unfortunate consequence that individual personal identity, which is generally associated with particular memories and experiences, is lost at death when the brain ceases to function (3.5).

While Aristotle's view is generally interpreted as ruling out personal immortality, it actually does not rule it out completely. In the same passage in which he discusses the destruction of memory and imagination in the brain, Aristotle goes on to say, in a famously obscure statement, that "that in us which thinks" survives death (3.5). The meaning of this remark was debated furiously for centuries, and it leads to the development of all kinds of theories regarding the nature of the soul. A few words of clarification are appropriate.

Aristotle maintains that, while we always refer to mental images in forming thoughts, the abstract concepts we form from these images—like the abstract concept of an animal species derived from our multiple experiences of creatures of that species—transcend these particular images. Therefore, these abstract concepts cannot be directly equated with brain functions, such as sensation and memory (3.4). Furthermore, Aristotle's belief that the universe is rationally ordered suggests that these abstract concepts correspond to the natures of real-life species (principles) that actually form the individual creatures we classify under a common species (1941, 1.19). This means that our abstract universal concepts correspond to a real, permanent structure of nature, inasmuch as nature is designed to maintain the existence of these species-principles through procreation. Consequently, our abstract ideas are of principles that are *eternal* and *universal,* while experiences of individual creatures are *temporal* and *particular.* Aristotle's position, in any case, indicates that the part of our mind that understands abstract concepts is linked to the eternal structure of the universe. It therefore has a reality beyond particular brain-based memories and experiences. This has numerous possible implications concerning the afterlife. Some philosophers after Aristotle speculated that because we are able to communicate about these abstract concepts (such as when we discuss the traits of a particular species), we must all share the same concept. To them, this idea suggests that the part of the mind that understands eternal and unchanging concepts does not belong to us individually. It belongs to a Being with higher intelligence who we somehow "tap into" through our individual sense experiences.

Thomas Aquinas on the Immaterial Soul and the Vision of God

Although Aristotle's thought was adopted by other religions (e.g., Islam), Thomas Aquinas embarked on a mission to use Aristotle in defense of Christianity. Aquinas employs three main lines of reasoning to defend personal immortality. The first approach is to develop a view combining hylomorphism with dualism to show that while the soul is designed to work together with the body, it is nonetheless immaterial in nature and thus able to survive bodily death. Second, Aquinas argues that our ability to reason abstractly reveals that we not only desire to stay alive at any given moment but that we have a general desire for survival that abstractly encompasses all particular moments in time. Based on Aristotle's idea of an orderly universe, he reasons that this general desire only makes sense if we were, in fact, designed to never die. Last, he declares that we possess a natural desire for a level of happiness that goes beyond what is possible to attain in this life, a desire an orderly universe (or God) would not have given us if such happiness was impossible to achieve.

The argument concerning the immateriality of the soul is developed from Aristotle's view articulated earlier. Aquinas notices that when we have a particular thought, our minds are momentarily "shaped" by that thought. However, because the mind is able to move from being shaped by one thought to being shaped by another, the mind itself must transcend any of these particular thoughts and never be strictly equated with any of them. He illustrates this by comparing the mind to the tongue: just like the tongue's ability to go from tasting bitter to tasting sweet shows that it is not intrinsically bitter or sweet in its own nature but "transcends" all flavors, it is in the nature of the mind to possess temporarily the quality of various thoughts while maintaining its own distinct nature (*Summa Theologica*, Part I, Question 75, article 2). Moreover, because human minds, unlike animal minds, are able to be "shaped" by abstract concepts and not just particular sense-based thoughts, their distinct nature must be immaterial.

Although the mind derives its abstract concepts from sense experience, thereby showing that it is naturally intended to work hand-in-hand with the body, it has a distinct nature from the body. The mind is capable of existing without the body (I, 75.6). To show that the *individual* human soul is immortal and it is not just some higher Intelligence into which we temporarily "tap," Aquinas offers reasons why human souls must be immaterial. Only two will be mentioned here. First, we know that abstraction takes place *by* us and not just *in* us. If abstraction takes place only in us, every time one person was conscious of an abstract concept, all people possessing mental images corresponding to that concept would become conscious of it. They would all be joined to the higher Intelligence in which the abstract concept was actually being thought (I, 76.2). Second, even those who "tap into" the understanding of an immaterial intellect need an immaterial mental function that enabled them to "connect" with anything outside the physical world (I, 79.4).

Aquinas contends that, although the separation of the soul from the body at death hinders its natural way of knowing, the separation also allows the soul to have better awareness of beings that are by nature distinct from bodies (i.e. "separate substances"). These include demons, angels, God, and the souls of other deceased persons (*Questions on the Soul,* Q.17). At the same time, the human soul is designed to use mental images even when thinking of abstract concepts. This means that, without the body, the soul no longer understands abstractions through its own function. Rather, the soul understands abstractions through its interaction with higher intelligent Beings that are capable of such knowledge without use of bodily senses (Q.18, 20).

Abstract knowledge by itself is insufficient for enabling the disembodied soul to realize its own individuality, because abstract concepts are the same for all people who understand them. Disembodied individual self-awareness can be preserved, Aquinas declares, only by the fact that we retain spiritual effects of past sense experiences (Q.20). This makes it possible to remain aware of the love, anger, fear, and so on we have experienced, even if we cannot recall sense-memories of them. The souls of the dead, therefore, are not aware of what happens in the physical realm. Without recourse to this concept of spirit-interaction, Aquinas's hylomorphism would lend itself much more plausibly to the view that the soul, prior to the body's resurrection, continues to exist almost unconsciously. Such a notion has much in common, for instance, with the notion of "soul sleep" held by Martin Luther and others (e.g. Moltmann 1996, 101). In any case, even for Aquinas the resurrection has the benefit of restoring proper bodily enjoyments.

Aquinas's argument that we have a desire to never die that must be capable of being fulfilled is also related to his claim that the immateriality of the soul enables us to grasp abstract concepts. On his view, our desire to avoid death is not limited to a simple reaction against immediate danger, as it seems to be for animals. Our awareness that we want to stay alive in *this* moment leads us to an awareness through abstract reasoning that we desire to stay alive for *all possible* moments (Q.14). In fact, the awareness of death hinders our satisfaction of life. Contrary to Ludwig Feuerbach, Aquinas believes that the fear of death is not the basis of an afterlife *fantasy*. It is evidence of an afterlife *reality*.

Finally, according to Aquinas, human beings have a natural intellectual desire to understand the causes and relationships between the things they observe in this world. This curiosity, however, is never satisfied. No matter how much we learn, we are always curious to know more. Because God is the cause of all things, Aquinas concludes that only a direct knowledge of God could ever satisfy fully our desire for knowledge. However, no finite amount of time is enough to comprehend something infinite that transcends time. Hence, this desire to know all makes sense only if we are designed to live eternally.

Those who seek this knowledge come to experience what Aquinas's calls the *Beatific Vision* of God's divine Essence, which fulfills us in every way for all eternity (I-II, 3.8, Supplement to Part III, 89). Those who concentrate on the pleasures of this world without due respect for God, however, will be left to experience eternally only the painful aspects of these activities. This latter group cuts itself off from God, who is the true source of all genuine enjoyment and pleasure.

Aquinas's view, it should be noted, differs somewhat from Eastern Orthodox conceptions of the afterlife, which typically deny that we can understand the *essence* of God at all. The Eastern Orthodox insist that God's essence remains totally incomprehensible in this life and the next. On their view, however, we *can* come to "partake of the divine nature" (2 Pet. 1:4) by becoming fully Christlike (what they call "deified") through uncreated "divine energies" (grace), which eternally "flow" from God's essence. Still, we as remain less than Christ in that He is uncreated and is God. "Energies" and "deification" are mentioned, for example, in the fourth-century writings of Athanasius, Gregory of Nazianzus, Basil, and others, and they are developed especially by Maximus the Confessor (580—662) and Gregory Palamas (1296—1359).

Apart from the question of "knowing" the "essence of God," Aquinas suggests that while heaven is fulfilling and hell agonizing, individuals will experience varying degrees of eternal fulfillment and torment based on the extent to which they have expanded, in this life, their capacity to desire good and evil (Suppl. Part III,69.1). In this world, all creatures are ordained to desire God's goodness to some limited extent. Christ alone possesses the capacity to experience joy equal to that of God (*Questions on the Soul*, Q.16). To the extent that one strives to be like Christ (with the aid of the Holy Spirit), he or she expands his or her own capacity to experience goodness. This seems similar to the idea of "deification" noted previously. To the extent that one willfully resists being like Christ, he or she increases his or her capacity for eternal suffering. In purgatory the souls of the saved must be "purged" of the effects of sinful acts not committed out of malicious rebellion against God (which would result in damnation) but from human weakness and ignorance. Individuals who maximize their capacity for understanding and serving God in this life avoid purgatory.

Before concluding this chapter, two alternative views about the condition of the unsaved should be mentioned. These views are known as *annihilationism* and *universalism*. These theories proclaim that a just and merciful God would not punish people eternally for sins committed during a finite lifetime. An early Christian universalist, Origen, went as far as to say that Satan himself would eventually be saved! Both views, however, realize that God cannot allow sin to enter heaven. Annihilationists therefore conclude that God does not eternally condemn the unsaved but instead destroys them. Universalists often stipulate that because God's will is all-powerful, His desire "that none should perish" must be fulfilled. Unrepentant souls will eventually all be cleansed through a process similar to purgatory (which Catholics reserve only for the perfection of those already saved). Those rejecting these two views typically argue, much like 17th-century theologian Arminius, that while God desires by God's "antecedent will" that all people desire to be with Him, He desires by His "consequent will" that people who do not want to be saved will be allowed to reject His love. Rejecting divine love amounts to choosing freely the darkness of hell.

CONCLUSION

We have seen that arguments against immortality typically rely on materialistic assumptions about the nature of the mind, which are generally based on the conviction that we should not believe in things that cannot be observed by the senses. Psychological dismissals of the afterlife are less effective; just because someone wants something to be true, this desire is hardly proof that this something is not true. In fact, *disbelief* in an afterlife can be written off as a form of psychological denial just as easily as belief. Those defending immortality, on the other hand, must provide metaphysical, rather than purely empirical, explanations of the mind. As metaphysical theories, dualism is suited to defend an afterlife apart from the body, while hylomorphism is one explanation for how the mind and body are meant to work together. For both views, hell is the result of being unable to experience reality as we are intended to, due to a choice to ignore the ultimate source of goodness behind all other pleasures. Heaven, on the other hand, awaits those who value all other things only in respect to this highest good.

Bibliography

Aquinas, Thomas. *Questions on the Soul.* Trans. James H. Robb. Milwaukee: Marquette University Press, 1984.

——. *Summa Theologica.* Westminster, Md.: Christian Classics, 1981.

Aristotle. *On the Soul.* Trans. J. A. Smith. In *The Complete Works of Aristotle.* Ed. Richard McKeon. New York: Random, 1941.

Arminius, James. *The Writings of James Arminius.* 3 vols. Grand Rapids: Baker, 1956.

Athanasius. *On the Incarnation of the Word.* In *Nicene and Post-Nicene Fathers.* Vol. 4. Second series. Ed. Philip Schaff and Henry Wace. Peabody, Mass.: Hendrickson Publishers, 1994.

Basil the Great. *On the Holy Spirit.* Trans. David Anderson. Crestwood, N.Y.: St. Vladimir's Seminary Press, 1980.

Brown, Warren, Nancy Murphy, and H. Newton Maloney. *Whatever Happened to the Soul? Scientific and Theological Portraits of Human Nature.* Philadelphia: Fortress, 1998.

Cooper, John W. *Body, Soul, and Life Everlasting.* Grand Rapids: Wm. B. Eerdmans Publishing Co., 1989.

Feuerbach, Ludwig. *Thoughts on Immortality and Death. From the Papers of a Thinker Along with an Appendix of Theological-Satirical Epigrams.* Trans. James A. Massey. Berkeley, Calif.: University of California Press, 1980.

Flew, Antony. *Atheistic Humanism.* Buffalo, N.Y.: Prometheus Books, 1993.

——. *The Logic of Mortality.* Oxford: Basil Blackwell, 1987.

Gregory of Nazianzus. *On God and Christ: The 5 Theological Orations and Two Letters to Cledonius.* Crestwood, N.Y.: St. Vladimir's Seminary Press, 2002.

Hawking, Stephen. *A Brief History of Time: From the Big Bang to Black Holes.* New York: Bantam, 1988.

Hick, John. *Death and Eternal Life.* San Francisco: Harper and Row, 1976; and London: Macmillan, 1976. Reissued 1987.

Hierotheos. Metropolitan of Nafpaktos. *Life After Death.* Trans. Esther Williams. Levadia, Greece: Birth of the Theotokos Monastery, 1995.

Kant, Immanuel. *Critique of Practical Reason.* Book II, ch. 2. Trans. L. W. Beck. New York: Macmillan, 1993.

Kübler-Ross, Elisabeth. *Death Is of Vital Importance: On Life, Death, and Life After Death.* Ed. Goran Grip. Barrytown, N.Y.: Station Hill, 1995.

——. *On Death and Dying.* New York: Macmillan, 1969.

Kung, Hans. *Eternal Life? Life After Death as a Medical, Philosophical, and Theological Problem.* Trans. Edward Quinn. Garden City, N.Y.: Doubleday, 1984.

Meyendorff, John. *Byzantine Theology: Historical Trends and Doctrinal Themes.* New York: Fordham University Press, 1979.

Moltmann, Jurgen. Trans. Margaret Kohl. *The Coming of God: Christian Eschatology.* Minneapolis: Fordham, 1996.

Nietzsche, Frederick. *Thus Spake Zarathustra.* Vol. 12 of *Frederick Nietzsche: First Complete and Authorized English Version.* 18 vols. Ed. Oscar Levy. New York: Garden Press, 1974.

Pannenberg, Wolfhart. *Theology and the Kingdom of God.* Ed. Richard John Neuhaus. Philadelphia: Westminster, 1969.

Penelhum, Terence. *Survival and Disembodied Existence.* London: Routledge and Kegan Paul, 1970.

Plato. *Phaedo,* in *Five Dialogues.* Trans. G. M. A. Grube. Indianapolis: Hackett, 1981.

Rose, Fr. Seraphim. *The Soul After Death: Contemporary "After-Death" Experiences in Light of Orthodox Teaching on the Afterlife.* Platina, Calif.: St. Herman of Alaska Brotherhood, 1980.

Suchocki, Marjorie Hewitt. *The End of Evil: Process Eschatology in Historical Context.* Albany, N.Y.: State University of New York Press, 1988.

Swinburne, Richard. *The Evolution of the Soul.* Oxford: Clarendon Press, 1986.